'A worthy successor to Roberts' earlier editions. This third edition
brings the account up to the immediate present and continues to have
the strength of integrating the insights of very recent scholarship
on all periods of Chinese history.' – **Anthony DeBlasi, Associate
Professor and Chair of the Department of East Asian Studies,
University at Albany**

It has been said that the twenty-first century will be China's century.
Such a remark highlights the importance of being informed about
China's long and tumultuous history.

J. A. G. Roberts traces the main course of that history, from the
earliest times, through the centuries of imperial government, to the
present day. Chapters on China's imperial history identify the main
political and economic changes, whilst introducing key social themes.
Turning to the modern period, Roberts then traces the dramatic events
of the Opium Wars, the 1911 Revolution and the Republican era. The
book ends with a detailed discussion of China under Communist rule
and a wide-ranging review of new developments, including China's
economic achievement and its costs.

Thoroughly revised and expanded in the light of the latest research,
and now featuring a helpful chronology, this up-to-date, authoritative
overview of China's past is ideal for students and general readers
alike.

J. A. G. Roberts is Visiting Research Fellow in History at the
University of Huddersfield. He has taught and written extensively on
the histories of China and Japan.

PALGRAVE ESSENTIAL HISTORIES
General Editor: Jeremy Black

This series of compact, readable and informative national histories is designed to appeal to anyone wishing to gain a broad understanding of a country's history.

Published

A History of the Low Countries   *Paul Arblaster*
A History of Italy   *Claudia Baldoli*
A History of Russia   *Roger Bartlett*
A History of Spain (2nd edn)   *Simon Barton*
A History of the British Isles (2nd edn)   *Jeremy Black*
A History of Israel   *Ahron Bregman*
A History of Ireland   *Mike Cronin*
A History of Greece   *Nicholas Doumanis*
A History of the Pacific Islands   *Steven Roger Fischer*
A History of Korea   *Kyung Moon Hwang*
A History of the United States (3rd edn)   *Philip Jenkins*
A History of Denmark (2nd edn)   *Knud J.V. Jespersen*
A History of the Baltic States   *Andres Kasekamp*
A History of Poland (2nd edn)   *Anita J. Prazmowska*
A History of India (2nd edn)   *Peter Robb*
A History of China (3rd edn)   *J.A.G. Roberts*
A History of Germany   *Peter Wende*

Series Standing Order
ISBN 1–4039–3811–3 HB
ISBN 1–4039–3812–1 PB

If you would like to receive future titles in this series as they are published, you can make use of our standing order facility. To place a standing order please contact your bookseller or, in case of difficulty, write to us at the address below with your name and address and the name of the series. Please state with which title you wish to begin your standing order. (If you live outside the United Kingdom we may not have the rights for your area, in which case we will forward your order to the publisher concerned.)

Customer Services Department, Macmillan Distribution Ltd
Houndmills, Basingstoke, Hampshire RG21 6XS, England

A History of China

Third Edition

J. A. G. Roberts

palgrave
macmillan

First edition published 1999
Second edition published 2006
Third edition published 2011 by
PALGRAVE MACMILLAN

Palgrave Macmillan in the UK is an imprint of Macmillan Publishers Limited, registered in England, company number 785998, of Houndmills, Basingstoke, Hampshire RG21 6XS.

Palgrave Macmillan in the US is a division of St Martin's Press LLC, 175 Fifth Avenue, New York, NY 10010.

Palgrave Macmillan is the global academic imprint of the above companies and has companies and representatives throughout the world.

Palgrave® and Macmillan® are registered trademarks in the United States, the United Kingdom, Europe and other countries

ISBN 978–0–230–24983–7   hardback
ISBN 978–0–230–24984–4   paperback

This book is printed on paper suitable for recycling and made from fully managed and sustained forest sources. Logging, pulping and manufacturing processes are expected to conform to the environmental regulations of the country of origin.

A catalogue record for this book is available from the British Library.

A catalog record for this book is available from the Library of Congress.

10   9   8   7   6   5   4   3   2   1
20   19   18   17   16   15   14   13   12   11

Printed and bound in China

Contents

List of Maps

Preface

When in 2008 China hosted the Beijing Olympics, Chinese leaders used the Games as an opportunity to show the world how the country had transformed itself into a superpower. After watching the opening ceremony on her mobile phone, a young woman said: 'This shows the greatness of our 5000-year history. I'm so proud I was born Chinese.' These contrasting responses – a claim to prominence and a pride in tradition – indicate how important it is today to appreciate China's history and culture.

This one-volume account of the entire span of Chinese history assumes no prior knowledge of China's past and is intended for a wide readership. It sets out to provide a clear account of the major events in Chinese history and at the same time to introduce some of the main interpretations of key events.

Chinese personal and geographical names have been transliterated into pinyin, the official system of romanization, rather than the traditional Wade-Giles system. Pinyin is now used in newspapers and is being adopted generally in scholarly works, although Wade-Giles is still used in the *Cambridge History of China*. All Chinese personal and place names have been transliterated into pinyin. Thus Mao Tse-tung is rendered as Mao Zedong and, rather less familiarly, Chiang Kai-shek is referred to as Jiang Jieshi. Likewise, Peking is transliterated as Beijing, Canton as Guangzhou and Hong Kong as Xianggang. Direct quotations which contain spellings in the Wade-Giles system have been amended to pinyin. When familiar names first appear in unfamiliar forms, the familiar form is also quoted; this practice is also followed in the index.

For the most part, pinyin spelling approximates to the phonetic values of English, with the following notable exceptions:

c	is pronounced 'ts' as in Tsar
i	is pronounced 'ee', except when it follows c, ch, r, s, sh, z or zh, in which case it is pronounced approximately 'er'
ian	is pronounced 'ien'
q	is pronounced 'ch' as in cheap

r   is similar to the English 'r' but is pronounced with the
      tongue behind the front teeth
x   is pronounced 'sh' as in sham
z   is pronounced 'ds' as in hands
zh   is pronounced 'j' as in jasmine

When citing Chinese names, the family name is given first, followed by the given name. However, in the notes, to maintain consistency with the citation of other names, the Western practice of putting the surname last is observed.

Following the usual practice, Chinese emperors before the Ming dynasty are designated by their posthumous titles, for example 'the Emperor Huizong'. Under the Ming and Qing dynasties they are designated by their reign name (*nianhao*), for example 'the Kangxi Emperor'. Non-Chinese names, for example Mongol or Manchu names, are cited in the form in which they are best known in the West.

Acknowledgements

This book is a direct descendant of Juan Gonzalez de Mendoza's *History of the Great and Mighty Kingdom of China*, which was published in Rome in 1585 and was both the first, and the first one-volume, Western history of China. Like all writers who have followed in Mendoza's footsteps, I owe a tremendous debt to my predecessors, to the many scholars who have written about China. What I have written is a synthesis of the labours of others, particularly those whose efforts in recent years have deepened our understanding of Chinese society and transformed our concept of Chinese history.

I must thank my colleagues and students, past and present, at the University of Huddersfield, who have given me their time and ideas. I owe a debt of gratitude to the staff of the University of Huddersfield Library Services and to Mr Steve Pratt, the University's cartographer. My most substantial debt is to my wife Jan, who has endured my prolonged commitment to the task of writing and subsequently revising this history.

Every effort has been made to trace all the copyright holders, but if any have been inadvertently overlooked the publishers will be pleased to make the necessary arrangements at the first opportunity.

Introduction

The People's Republic of China, excluding Taiwan, has a surface area of 9,560,900 square kilometres, slightly larger than that of the United States. Only the Russian Federation and Canada are larger than China. Its population, which in June 2010 was estimated as 1.34 billion, is greater than that of any other country in the world. Modern China is divided into twenty-two provinces, four municipalities (Beijing, Shanghai, Tianjin and Chongqing) and five autonomous regions. In terms of both area and population, the single province of Sichuan is much larger than Germany.

These statistics illustrate one of the problems of writing a history of China. Modern China is a continental country, which contains within its borders a very wide range of ethnic, linguistic and regional variations. As it is not possible to encompass all aspects of this complex society in a one-volume history, the approach adopted has been to concentrate on the national picture and to make only sporadic reference to developments at regional or provincial levels. In the past this decision might have been excused on the grounds that there were few good regional studies, but this is no longer true. For example, James Millward has recently published a history of Xinjiang, which follows the history of this key region from the earliest times to the present day.

An important feature of this book is the emphasis which is placed on historical interpretation rather than on historical narrative. On a number of topics the variety of views which have been expressed is summarized. However, Chinese history has also provoked wider debates which have had a profound effect on historical interpretation. The influence of some of these debates may be discerned in the presentation of events, but they are not referred to explicitly. It is convenient to identify and discuss four of them briefly at this point.

THE 'DIFFERENTNESS' OF CHINA

In the eighteenth century some French *philosophes* regarded China as a model for Europe and suggested that features of Chinese society should be adopted in Western states. By the nineteenth century this admiration had been replaced with condescension. Western travellers delighted in identifying Chinese 'contrarieties', pointing out the ways in which Chinese custom was the direct opposite of Western practice.

The idea that Chinese society was in some fundamental way different from the societies of the West was given fresh impetus by Karl Marx. He posited that all human societies would pass through four stages – communal, slave, feudal and bourgeois society – before advancing to communism. However, he had also referred to an 'Asiatic mode of production', characterized by isolated village communities, large-scale public works projects, particularly for education and defence, the absence of private ownership of land and the lack of a meaningful class struggle. By identifying an 'Asiatic mode' he implied that Asian societies had not evolved on the lines followed by those of Europe, an apparent contradiction of his general thesis. A variation on this theme was developed by Karl Wittfogel in *Oriental Despotism* (1957). Wittfogel argued that in a 'hydraulic society' such as China, where the farm economy depended on the control of water resources, the government had to be able to mobilize vast numbers of peasants for irrigation and flood-control works. This situation ensured that government remained autocratic, and that commercial and industrial development was inhibited. References to an Asiatic mode of production continue to appear in Marxist studies of Chinese history. For example, Li Xiaojun has argued that the Asiatic mode of production remains a valid concept, but it was the dominant mode of production only in the Western Zhou period (*c.* 1122–771 BCE).

References to an Asiatic mode of production, even in its attenuated form, distance China's historical experience from that of other societies. Of course, Chinese society, like any other society, is *sui generis*; that is to say, it has its own unique characteristics. The richness of Chinese culture, the complexity of China's political experience, the drama of China's recent past might seem to justify treating China as a special case. Nevertheless, in these pages the history of China is presented as being in no fundamental way different from the history of any other nation or society.

THE PERIODIZATION OF CHINESE HISTORY

Traditional Chinese historiography divided the country's history into dynastic periods and explained the divisions by reference to a dynastic cycle. According to that view, dynasties were founded by able and virtuous rulers, but their successors failed to maintain the standards that their forefathers had set. If later rulers did not respond to repeated warnings, which took the form of portents, the mandate of heaven was transferred to the founder of a new dynasty. Some modern historians, while accepting that the personal qualities of its rulers had some influence on a dynasty's fortunes, have argued that the dynastic cycle was essentially the product of economic and administrative factors. When a new dynasty was founded, the ruler eliminated his rivals, established an effective government, levied moderate taxes and secured the frontiers. Under later rulers the costs of government rose, powerful families began to evade taxation and the frontiers became over-extended. In time, officials became corrupt, public works were neglected and the burden of tax borne by the peasants increased. Finally, the peasants rose in rebellion and overthrew the dynasty.

Even if the concept of the dynastic cycle has some validity, a repetitive cycle is not a consistent feature in imperial history. For prolonged periods, for example between 220 and 589, no one dynasty ruled over the whole of China. At other times the dynasty changed but there was no evidence of a cyclical pattern; the continuity between the Sui and the Tang, for example, was very marked. Some of the most important historical turning points in China's history have come in the middle of a dynastic period. Although the rebellion of An Lushan had a devastating effect on the Tang dynasty, the Tang emperors remained on the throne for another 150 years. On the other hand, the change from one dynasty to another might coincide with a major social transition. The Japanese historian Naito Torajiro put forward what became known as the 'Naito hypothesis'. He argued that modern Chinese history began not with the arrival of Westerners in China, but at the end of the Tang and the beginning of the Song periods. That point, he claimed, marked the end of aristocratic government and the beginning of the period of autocratic rule.

From the above, it will be apparent that the division of Chinese history into dynastic periods is often questioned. Nevertheless, periodization by dynasties remains the most commonly used chronological framework. As it is the organizational principle which is most accessible to the reader, it has been used in a modified form in this book.

HAN NATIONALISM

The Chinese call themselves Han Chinese, a reference to the Han dynasty (206 BCE–CE 220), when Chinese culture first spread across the territory which is now called China. Inevitably, a history of China is a history of the Han Chinese. It will make only passing reference to China's minority nationalities, who comprise 8 per cent of China's population, and it will adopt a Chinese perspective on the long periods in Chinese history when part or all of China was ruled by non-Chinese peoples.

In 1967 Ho Ping-ti, then President of the Association for Asian Studies, gave an address entitled 'The Significance of the Qing Period in Chinese History'. He began by asserting that the Manchus, the founders of the Qing dynasty, had established the most successful dynasty of conquest in Chinese history. He then argued that the key to Qing success was the adoption by the early Manchu rulers of a policy of systematic sinicization. Thirty years later Evelyn S. Rawski, also giving the presidential address, responded to her predecessor. She began by drawing attention to the wealth of Manchu-language materials which until recently Western and Chinese scholars had spurned as being mainly translations of Chinese documents. She suggested that the picture which was now emerging from close study of these materials contradicted Ho's assertion that Manchu success was based on sinicization.

> The new scholarship suggests just the opposite: the key to Qing success, at least in terms of empire-building, lay in its ability to use its cultural links with the non-Han peoples of Inner Asia and to differentiate the administration of the non-Han regions from the administration of the former Ming provinces.

Such a view acts as a corrective to the imbalance created by unreflective Han nationalism, which has denigrated the periods in Chinese history, for example the Yuan or Mongol dynasty, when China was under foreign rule.

CHINA'S RESPONSE TO THE WEST

Much of China's modern history, particularly since the Opium wars, has been presented in Western historical literature as a 'response to the West'. The most important dynamic in China's modern development is assumed to be the reaction to the West's 'challenge' and the question is then posed: Why did China not respond more rapidly and more effectively to that challenge? Such an approach defines the dynamic in nineteenth-century history as Sino-Western contact – which means a concentration of interest on the treaty ports, Western economic imperialism and so on, while ignoring the broader context of cultural and social changes already taking place in Chinese society. The 'response to the West' approach also assumes that the Western impact on China, whether beneficial or oppressive, was the catalyst which enabled China to escape from the confines of 'traditional' society. This view has been challenged in a number of recent works which take as their starting point the perception that Chinese society was not unchanging, nor were Chinese intellectuals unthinking. In these books there has been a conscious effort to present a more 'China-centred' history of China. It is hoped that something of the same emphasis may be found in this volume.

RECENT SCHOLARSHIP

Since the first edition of this book was published in 1999, many new books have appeared which offer fresh interpretations of Chinese history and explore different aspects of that record. This new edition aims to incorporate at least some of this new material. The main areas of new interpretation are:

- China's prehistory in the light of recent archaeological discoveries.
- The property rights of women in the Song period, leading to a broader review of the condition of women through Chinese history.
- The role of the Manchus in Chinese history, as revealed in what R. Kent Guy referred to as '*the* Four Books of Manchu studies'.
- A re-evaluation of the use of the term 'sinicization' to describe the response of neighbouring peoples to the Han Chinese.
- China's relationship with Central Asia, a topic developed by James Millward and Peter Perdue.

- The debate, revived by Kenneth Pomeranz, on why China did not industrialize at the end of the eighteenth century.
- The application of the concept of 'civil society' to recent Chinese history.
- Reinterpretations of aspects of the Republican period (1911–49), including the 'Nanjing Decade' (1928–37) and the War of Resistance (1937–45).
- A reconsideration of the place in history of the Communist victory in 1949.
- A more critical view of Communist China in the era of Mao.
- A summary of the extraordinary economic, social, political and cultural changes which have occurred since the death of Deng Xiaoping.

Map I Prehistoric and early historic sites in north China

Map 2 China at the time of Confucius, c. 551–479 BCE

Map 3　China Proper on the eve of the rebellion of An Lushan

Map 4 China under the Southern Song and the Jin, c. 1140

Map 5 The Manchu invasion

Map 6 China Proper, c. 1800

Map 7 The rise of rebellion, 1796–1873

Map 8 Foreign encroachment on China, c. 1900

Map 9 The Long March, 1934–5

Map 10 The People's Republic of China

I

The Prehistory and Early History of China

PREHISTORIC AND PROTOHISTORIC CHINA

The earliest evidence found in China of habitation by hominins, that is to say of creatures regarded as ancestral to human beings, was discovered in excavations which began in 2001 at Majuangou III, a site in the Nihewan Basin in Hebei province. Stone flaked tools were uncovered which have been dated at 1.6 million years old.[1]

In 1927 remains of Beijing man, *Sinanthropus pekinensis*, now classified as *homo erectus*, were discovered at Zhoukoudian, 30 miles south-west of Beijing. Beijing man, who occupied the cave intermittently between 780,000 and 200,000 BCE, was a hunter-gatherer who made stone tools and may have used fire. Most of the Zhoukoudian finds were lost in transit in 1941, an event described as 'the greatest palaeontological tragedy of the twentieth century'.[2] Fortunately good-quality casts had been made, and these were supplemented by other finds in post-war excavations. Further remains of *homo erectus* have been discovered at other sites, including Yuanmou in Yunnan.[3]

The archaeological evidence relating to the appearance of *homo sapiens* in China is still being interpreted. A skull found at Dali in 1978, which was dated *c.* 200,000 BCE, appears to display a mixture of *homo erectus* and *homo sapiens* features. In 2008 an almost complete skull dating back to between 100,000 and 80,000 years BCE was found in Hunan province and named Xuchang man. Chinese archaeologists have cited these finds as evidence of an evolutionary sequence from *homo erectus* to modern man, with early *homo sapiens* inhabiting sites between 200,000 and 50,000 BCE. Many

Western archaeologists, however, accept the evidence of recent genetic studies of mitochondrial DNA which indicate that all modern human beings derive from a small population of *homo sapiens* which evolved in eastern and southern Africa. One branch of this group, it is claimed, reached China between 67,000 and 42,000 years ago and was ancestral to the Chinese people.[4]

The best-documented find of early *homo sapiens* remains in China was made at the Middle Cave at Zhoukoudian. This find, which included three restorable skulls, was given an unconfirmed radiocarbon date of 16,922 BCE. Other sites, dating from this period and yielding large quantities of stone implements, have been found throughout the Ordos region in northern Shaanxi.

At the start of the Neolithic period, which in China dates approximately from 8000 to 2000 BCE, the climate of East Asia was warm and moist. North China was covered by dense forests and the fauna included crocodiles and elephants. At one time it was supposed that Chinese neolithic culture, marked by the cultivation of crops and the domestication of animals, had originated in one area of the North China Plain, but recent archaeological discoveries have revealed a more complex picture, and several regional cultures are now considered to have achieved the transition from food gathering to food production. These include the Yangshao culture of the middle Yellow river, the Dawenkou culture in Shandong, the Majiabang culture of the lower Yangzi river, and the Dapenkeng culture along the south coast and on Taiwan. The Majiabang culture, which emerged in the sixth millennium BCE, was characterized by the cultivation of rice and the use of pottery with incised motifs. In 1973 an early Neolithic settlement was found at Hemudu in south-east China. Finds included terracotta pottery, the remains of pigs and buffaloes, and articles made of wood and bone.

The Yangshao culture was named after a village in northern Henan, where in 1921 the Swedish archaeologist J. Gunnar Andersson had found a fragment of painted pottery. Its most famous site is at Banpo, near Xi'an, which was occupied from about 4500 BCE. Banpo was a village of some 45 houses. Its inhabitants cultivated millet and kept pigs and dogs. They produced pottery which was not only decorated but also occasionally bore incised markings. As similar markings have been found on pottery excavated at other sites within the region, it has been suggested that these are not simple potters' marks but an early stage in the development of Chinese characters, a suggestion which has been challenged.[5]

In 1928, not long after Andersson's discoveries at Yangshao, specimens of a different type of pottery, which became known as Longshan ware, were found at Chengziyai in north-west Shandong. Whereas Yangshao pottery was red and was sometimes painted with stylized renditions of birds and flowers, Longshan ware was unpainted, more finely made and usually elevated on a circular foot or on tripod legs. Because the first examples of Longshan ware had been found in Shandong, it was assumed to be the culture of eastern China, whereas Yangshao was regarded as the culture of the Central Plain, an interpretation which became known as the 'Neolithic hypothesis'. When the site at Miaodigou in Henan was excavated, Yangshao ware was found *below* Longshan finds, and this gave rise to a second theory, that Longshan culture was later than, and derived from, Yangshao culture. However, the evidence to support a developmental theory has not been forthcoming; it now seems probable that the two cultures developed separately and that Longshan culture, which was widely distributed in eastern China, gradually spread to the Central Plain, where the painted pottery tradition was already dying out.

THE XIA DYNASTY

According to Chinese legend, human beings had their origin in the parasites on the body of the creator, Pangu. After his death a succession of sage rulers introduced the key inventions and institutions of human society. The first sage ruler was Fuxi, who domesticated animals and instituted marriage. He was followed by Shennong, who introduced agriculture, medicine and trade. Then came Huangdi, the Yellow Emperor, to whom was credited the invention of writing, ceramics and the calendar. Some centuries later came the Emperor Yao, who ruled wisely and introduced flood controls, but whose particular claim to fame was that he decided his son was unworthy to be his successor and chose instead a humble sage named Shun. The reigns of Yao and Shun were later regarded as a golden age in Chinese history. Shun in turn awarded the succession to his faithful minister Yu. It is at this point that China's prehistory merged with history. Yu, whose reign according to tradition began in 2205 BCE, supposedly founded the Xia dynasty, the first of the three dynasties of ancient China, the Xia, the Shang and the Zhou.

When archaeological investigations began in the 1920s, the traditional view of the Xia dynasty was questioned and Yu was reduced to
a mythical figure. More recently the place of the Xia dynasty in early
Chinese history has been reasserted; not as the first of a sequence of
dynasties, but as perhaps the most powerful of the very many small
states to be found along the Yellow river valley, co-existing with the
early Shang and Zhou states. The Xia dynasty state, which is thought
to have existed between approximately 2070 and 1600 BCE, has
been identified with Erlitou in Henan, where palace-like buildings
and tombs have been excavated and the earliest known bronze vessels
have been found. The genealogy of Xia rulers was preserved in the
Shiji or *Historical Records* compiled by Sima Qian, and later corrob-
orated by oracle-bone inscriptions. However, it should be added that
there is still no archaeological evidence which links Erlitou culture
with the existence of the Xia state.[6]

THE SHANG DYNASTY

The second of the ancient dynasties was the Shang, the traditional
dates for which were 1766 to 1122 BCE. The modern consensus dates
are 1600 to 1046 BCE. As mentioned above, it was once supposed that
the three ancient dynasties were successive, but it is now understood
that the Shang was already a powerful entity before it overthrew the
Xia, and that the Xia, Shang and Zhou dynasties overlapped both
in time and in territory. The early Shang period, 1600 to 1300 BCE,
was characterized by the Erligang culture, which had its capital
at Zhengzhou. The capital in the later period of the dynasty was
Anyang, which was occupied *c*. 1300–1046 BCE.

Erligang sites, which were often walled settlements, have been
found over much of north China. The largest of these was Zhengzhou,
where a city wall some four miles long enclosed a large settlement.
The wall and the buildings within were constructed using the 'stamped
earth' technique. The houses and workshops which have been found
there indicate that Erligang society was highly organized and socially
stratified. This evidence confirms the impression of Shang society
which was obtained from the finds made at the late Shang capital at
Anyang, first excavated in the 1930s. Outside Anyang, at Xiaotun,
the remains have been uncovered of what perhaps was the ceremonial and administrative centre of the late Shang state. At Xibeigang,

two miles north of Xiaotun, 11 very large cruciform graves have been found, which may belong to the 11 Shang monarchs who were recorded as having reigned at Anyang.

Much has been written about the Shang, but here the discussion will be limited to three themes: the character of the Shang state, the significance of the oracle bones, and the implications of the Shang bronzes. The Shang rulers performed an important ritual role, but they were also involved in the administration of the state and were served by officials who had specialized functions. They were supported by aristocratic clans with whom they had either kinship or marriage connections. Aristocratic society practised military skills and fought using horse chariots. The relationship between the Shang kings and the clan leaders was a personal one, but it was formalized through ceremonies of investiture which gave the king the right to demand services from the clans, which included labour services and military duties. The Shang kings, or their aristocratic support-ers, waged aggressive campaigns against their neighbours, thereby obtaining prisoners and loot. The extension of Shang authority was also achieved by commissioning the establishment of new towns and the opening of new land for farming. Through these means the late Shang state extended from its core along the Yellow river to the Wei valley and to the north of present-day Shanxi.

However, the assumption that the Shang dynasty was the only significant early bronze age culture has been contradicted by recent archaeological finds. The Shang established relations with a state named Shu, which may refer to the culture that had developed inde-pendently in Sichuan. In 1986, at Sanxingdui, a settlement just north of Chengdu, two underground caches of bronzes were found which were quite different in character from those of the Shang. Among the bronze items unearthed were a life-sized statue on a pedestal and very large trees carrying peach-like fruits and inhabited by birds and a dragon. Three years after this discovery, a tomb was found at Xin'gan in Jiangxi which proved to be the second richest early bronze age burial find yet made; the richest being that of Fu Hao, described below. The bronzes it contained were of 'undeniable local character', and the remains were indicative of 'a local power, a city and the cemetery of its rulers'.[7]

The economic basis of the Shang state was agriculture, the most important cultivated crop being millet. The climate of the North China Plain was warmer and moister than it is at present, and the area was well forested, thus requiring considerable amounts of labour to clear for planting. It has often been asserted, particularly by Marxist historians such as Guo Moruo, that the labour to perform this and many other tasks was slave labour, and that Shang society should be defined as the slave-society stage in China's social evolution. This view has been supported by the evidence of the human sacrifices which accompanied royal burials and by references in oracle inscriptions. Recently Li Xiaojun has suggested that the bulk of the population were not slaves, in that they were not bought or sold, nor were they deprived of their personal freedom. Nevertheless, they were subject to coercive work, building city walls and performing agricultural tasks, and they were conscripted for military duties.

Much of the information available on Shang society comes from inscriptions made on the shoulder-blades of oxen (scapulimancy), or less commonly on the shells of turtles (plastromancy). At one time such items were described as 'dragon bones' and were ground up for medicine. In the late nineteenth century the bones and their inscriptions were recognized for what they were. Oracle bone inscriptions appear first in the reign of Wu Ding, c. 1250–1192 BCE. Over 200,000 fragments of oracle bones have been found at Xiaotun and these provide a major source of evidence about the Shang state. Many of the inscriptions refer to future events and they have been translated as questions addressed to an oracle. Recently it has been argued that the inscriptions are not questions but statements or predictions, and that the divination process formed part of a sacrificial rite. Once the bones had been inscribed, a heated bronze tool was applied to them and the cracks which appeared were interpreted as a response to the question or prediction. Some of the inscriptions relate to the actions of the king and his allies and from these information may be gleaned about the organization of the Shang state. Others refer to the weather, to the planting and harvesting of crops, and to the siting of buildings. The inscriptions use a vocabulary of more than 3000 different graphs and they include a dating system based on a 10-day week and a 60-day cycle.

The most prized archaeological finds from the Shang period are the bronze vessels and implements, many of which were made for ceremonial purposes. Because the vessels are very sophisticated, and because evidence had not been found of an earlier and more primitive stage in bronze work, it was long assumed that the technology for their production had been imported into China. However, the evidence accumulated in recent years supports the hypothesis of the independent discovery of metallurgy in China and the rapid transfer of skills from pottery to the manufacture of bronzes. The production and use of bronze were controlled by the king, and the quantity of bronze objects found indicates that the extraction of metal ore and the manufacture of bronze objects was a major industry, employing large numbers of skilled craftsmen. Early bronze technology in the West used the lost-wax technique, but early Shang vessels were cast in several moulds and the parts assembled later. The lost-wax technique was used later, in the Zhou period, and may have been introduced from the West. Small-scale industry producing bronze implements and ornaments appeared in Gansu *c.* 2000 BCE. This technology was the basis on which a large-scale bronze industry was developed.

The earliest bronze vessels have been found at Erlitou and important finds of bronze vessels were made at Zhengzhou and Anyang, the two Shang capitals. These vessels had a ritual function. An early bronze vessel found at Zhengzhou, which has a lobed body and a tripod of legs, a shape derived from a Longshan pottery prototype, was used for the preparation of sacrificial meats. Other ritual vessels were intended for the heating of wine. Many of these vessels are decorated with stylized surface decorations, the most famous motif being the *taotie,* a monster mask intended to avert evil. Jade was also used for ritual purposes, as it had been in the Longshan culture. Two jade forms were common: a pierced disc known as a *bi* and a tube of square cross-section known as a *cong.*

The Shang kings were buried in vast pits, which would have required the labour of many hundreds of men to excavate. Their corpses were placed in wooden coffins and these were surrounded by grave goods. On the ramps leading to the bottom of the pit lay human bodies and those of horses. The human victims, who may have been prisoners of war, had sometimes been beheaded. More than 10,000 human sacrifices have been found in these pits. The main royal tombs at Anyang were robbed long ago, but the tomb of Fu Hao, the consort of a Shang king who died *c.* 1250 BCE, was discovered intact in 1976. It contained over 200 bronze vessels, some in the shape of animals. The bronzes in Fu Hao's tomb are much larger than those found in other aristocratic graves, and the remains of 16 human sacrifices were also found in it. Her name appeared frequently in oracle-bone inscriptions, where she is referred to as raising forces to go into battle, and even going on campaigns herself.[8]

From the evidence of the oracle bones and bronze vessels, and from the burial practices that were followed, some understanding may be obtained of Shang religion. The Shang people worshipped many deities, most of whom were royal ancestors, although some were nature spirits and others perhaps derived from popular myths or local cults. This veneration of ancestors was practised by much of the population, and it has remained an essential part of Chinese religious practice until modern times. It has long been assumed that Shang religion also had a single supreme deity, referred to as Di, who was part ancestral figure, part natural force, and who presided at the apex of a complex Shang pantheon. A recent study has rejected the idea of Di as a high god, claiming that in Shang religion *di* was the term used to refer collectively to 'the gods' and that it was only under the Zhou that the idea of a supreme god emerged. From the evidence of the tombs it is clear that the Shang believed in an afterlife, and that divination may have been addressed to departed ancestors. The Shang court may have been attended by shamans, and the king himself was perhaps a shaman. If these suggestions are correct, then the character of Shang religion was very different from the rational approach of the philosophical schools which were to gain influence during the Zhou period.

In a recent book, David N. Keightley has returned to the question of the relationship between the Shang and the Zhou, and more generally to the cultural legacy of the Shang. He accepts that the Shang cosmology was not the only cosmology of the time, but claims that knowledge of it survived because the diviners left extensive written records. He points out that little is known of the belief systems of individuals and of all those who did not belong to the elite. Nevertheless, he concludes that the cultural legacy of the worldview of the late Shang elite was profound. This legacy included a writing system which recorded divinatory contacts as well as the increasingly complex operations of the late Shang state; the development of religious and ancestral hierarchies; a protobureaucracy and systems of labour control by a central elite; and a pervasive concern with divination, timeliness and good or bad fortune.[9]

THE WESTERN ZHOU PERIOD

The Zhou dynasty is traditionally dated from 1122 to 256 BCE, and this immensely long period is divided into the Western Zhou, from 1122 to 771 BCE, and the Eastern Zhou, the latter age being further subdivided into the Spring and Autumn period, from 771 to 481 BCE, and the Warring States period, from 481 to 221 BCE.

Long before the fall of the Shang, the Zhou had emerged as a powerful state somewhat to the west of the main centre of Shang activities. The origin of the Zhou people is not clear. According to Mencius, a disciple of Confucius, 'King Wen was a Western barbarian',[10] and some support in the past has been given to the theory that the Zhou were of proto-Turkish origin. However, there is no linguistic evidence to indicate that they came from far afield. A more plausible theory suggests that they originated in the Fen valley in Shanxi, and later migrated to the Wei valley in Shaanxi, to the west of Xi'an. There, in proximity to the Shang state, the Zhou people came to adopt many features of Shang culture, a process which enabled them to acquire administrative techniques and facilitated their seizure of power.

The establishment of the Zhou dynasty provides the first example of the right of a dynasty to rule being based on an ethical justification. According to the *Shujing* or *Book of Documents*, one of the earliest surviving Chinese historical sources, the fall of the Shang came about because of the shortcomings of the last Shang ruler. As a result, the protection or mandate of heaven was taken from him and awarded to the rulers of Zhou. Of these, King Wen was a paragon of virtue, and his son King Wu, who overthrew the Shang after a great battle at a place called Muye, was an outstanding warrior. It was recorded that the Zhou headed a coalition of eight nations which included Shu, and that the Zhou and their allies gained the victory because the Shang troops were driven to mutiny by the cruelty of their ruler. These events probably took place *c*. 1045 BCE; that is, nearly 80 years later than the traditional date for the overthrow of the Shang.

Shortly after the conquest, perhaps in 1043 BCE, King Wu died and was succeeded by his son. This arrangement was a break with the past, for under the Shang the succession had passed to surviving brothers. It established the important principle observed by later Chinese dynasties that the heir should come from the succeeding generation. However, the new King Zheng was a minor, and in the first part of his reign authority was wielded by the Duke of Zhou, one of the most famous figures in early Chinese history. The duke consolidated Zhou control over Shang territory and defeated a rebellion in the east led by survivors of the Shang royal family. Nevertheless, even after the rebellion had been defeated, the Zhou continued to appoint members of the deposed Shang lineage to be in charge of territories in the east. The Duke of Zhou also waged campaigns against the Huai Yi, a people who lived in the Huai valley, who remained undefeated throughout the Western Zhou period. Expansion also took place by more peaceful means, through the transfer of groups of people to newly opened territory, where they intermarried with non-Zhou people, thus extending the influence of what may now be called Chinese culture.

Western Zhou society has been described as feudal. The use of the term was first proposed by the Marxist historian Guo Moruo in the 1930s, and its application to China is based on two assumptions. The first is that feudalism is a form of social organization which arises under certain conditions, namely the decline of a powerful centralized state and its replacement by a congeries of small states owing only nominal loyalty to a central ruler. This situation may have prevailed in China after the fall of the Shang (which Guo Moruo regarded as a slave society) and the occupation of the Shang territories by the Zhou. The transition also came about, it is claimed, because of technological improvement – the introduction of iron – and the general economic advance which that implied.

The second ground for describing the Western Zhou as feudal concerns the essential element of the feudal relationship, the granting of fiefs to vassals, who in return promise to provide their feudal lord with military support. Under the Zhou, according to the famous early Zhou text the *Shijing* or *Book of Songs*:

> Everywhere under vast Heaven
> There is no land that is not the king's.
> To the borders of those lands
> There are none who are not the king's servants.[11]

Under the Western Zhou, grants of territory were formalized at ceremonies at which the king gave presents that had a symbolic meaning, and which became increasingly lavish. The ceremonies and the gifts which had been presented were commemorated in inscriptions on bronze vessels. The wide distribution of these vessels, many of which date from early in the dynasty and in particular from the years following the Duke of Zhou's suppression of rebellion, indicate that this form of appointment played an important part in the establishment of the Western Zhou's political structure over its newly acquired eastern territories. Appointees were given graded titles of rank, which have sometimes been equated with the aristocratic titles used in the West. Some of the bronzes recorded military activities, which confirm that the relationship involved military assistance, although they give the lie to the idealized picture of the Western Zhou period as a golden age of peace, a time when Chinese did not fight Chinese, although they might fight against the surrounding 'barbarians'.

Notwithstanding this evidence, the appropriateness of the term 'feudal' to describe the Western Zhou has been queried. The argument that the China of 3000 years ago was a very different society from mediaeval Europe needs no elaboration, and any close comparison between the two societies is difficult to sustain. Whereas in Europe the feudal relationship was typically impersonal and prescribed in detail, under the Zhou the dominant relationship was one of kinship and the contractual element in the relationship was not specified. In Europe feudal lordships were hereditary, and enfeoffments, providing that the vassal remained loyal, were irrevocable. However, under the Western Zhou appointments required reconfirmation and could be revoked. Appointments, which might be defined in terms of particular duties, have been described as 'protobureaucratic', the implication being that whereas in Europe bureaucracies emerged as a counter to feudal society, in China the beginnings of a bureaucracy existed alongside the supposed feudal order. In Europe the term feudalism has been used to describe a particular mode of economic organization, namely the binding of the peasant to the land and the compulsory provision of labour for the feudal lord, but such a system did not exist under the Western Zhou. In short, if the term feudalism implies merely a 'system of government in which a ruler personally delegates limited sovereignty over portions of his territory to vassals',[12] it may fit the Western Zhou, but the contemporary evidence does not justify the use of the term with its more precise definition.

THE SPRING AND AUTUMN PERIOD

The Western Zhou period was characterized by rapid but unstable expansion, which saw Zhou influence extend over much of north China and as far south as the Huai valley. At first the appointment of members of the ruling dynasty and its allies to semi-independent fiefs created a viable political structure, and the power of the Western

Zhou kings over them was considerable. During the reign of King Mu (*r.* 956–918 BCE), signs of 'incipient bureaucracy' emerged. Bronze inscriptions recorded the appointment of individuals, often without apparent relationship to the king, to positions of responsibility at court.[13] King Yi, who reigned *c.* 865–858 BCE, wielded sufficient authority to have Duke Ai of Qi boiled to death for supposedly criticizing him, though this insubordinacy may indicate the diminishing authority of the Zhou king. By the end of the ninth century BCE the kings' authority had declined, their appointees and their successors had become increasingly integrated into their local society, and the fiefs were assuming the character of independent states. The early Zhou rulers had mounted expeditions to the north west and west of their main centre in Shaanxi, but they now came under pressure from the Rong and the Di, non-Chinese peoples who inhabited the steppe regions and who may have used horses in warfare. In 771 BCE a Rong invasion forced the Zhou to move their capital eastwards to Luoyang, hence the use of the term Eastern Zhou to refer to the subsequent period.

The years 771–481 BCE are known as the Spring and Autumn period, after the annals which describe the events of those years in the small state of Lu. The key political development of the time was the rise of states which professed only symbolic allegiance to the Zhou kings, who in the end only ruled a small area around Luoyang. Up to 170 states are recorded as having existed in those years, of which about 15 were of significant size and importance. By the end of this period warfare and succession disputes had reduced the number of states to seven, of which four deserve particular mention. One was Qi, which occupied the area of modern Shandong. In the early seventh century BCE, Guan Zhong, the chief minister of the state, introduced a reform which transformed military service from the prerogative of the nobility into an obligation on the common people. The state of Jin, which was located in present-day Shanxi, also introduced reforms after a military disaster. Jin fought campaigns against the Di people and, finding that the mountainous terrain was unsuitable for chariots, developed infantry armies. Its leaders also intermarried with the Di people. To the south lay the expanding state of Chu, which occupied the middle Yangzi region, and which was regarded by the other states as semi-barbarous. Finally, to the west lay the state of Qin, which had emerged at the time of the fall of the Western Zhou, and which was considered by the other major states to be non-Chinese. These states acted as sovereign bodies and have been described as 'seven different cultural spheres'.[14]

The Spring and Autumn period saw frequent wars between states and with the surrounding peoples. One calculation suggests that in the entire period only 38 years were peaceful. When Guan Zhong was first minister of Qi, an attempt was made to reduce conflict by claiming for the state of Qi the status of *ba*, the 'senior one'; that is, the state privileged to make war on behalf of the Zhou court. In 651 BCE, the *ba* system was institutionalized. To achieve stability and to counter a threat from the north, Duke Huan of Qi invited representatives of the central states to a conference and obtained their agreement to a set of principles concerning good government. He was chosen as hegemon of the 'five leaders of the feudal lords'. However, this system did not last and conflicts continued through the period.

These wars reflected the rapid political, social and economic changes which were occurring at the time. At the beginning of the Spring and Autumn period, the political elite was composed of the king, the feudal lords and their hereditary ministers, each of whom had a defined status, a prescribed role in ritual performances, and an obligation to fight to defend the honor of the lineage. Under the impact of constant war, this elite began to fragment. State governments became more centralized, administrative units were established, and junior members of the aristocracy were appointed to supervise them. A class of men known as *shi,* meaning knights or warriors, emerged in the seventh century BCE and by the fifth century BCE the *shi* had eclipsed the former elite in government.

At the same time, major technological and economic changes were taking place. The use of bronze became much more widespread, and recent discoveries have shown that by this time bronze agricultural tools were in common use in the lower Yangzi valley. By the middle and late Spring and Autumn period cast iron and steel were being produced. However, iron was not generally adopted for making weapons, implements and vessels until the Warring States period, considerably later than the same development in the West.

Up to this time Chinese farmers had probably practised a form of communal agriculture, which was later to be described in idealistic terms as the 'well-field' system. Under this arrangement plots of land were divided into nine holdings, eight of which were farmed by individual families, with the ninth farmed communally and the produce delivered to the lord. Communal agriculture began to decline during the Spring and Autumn period, perhaps because of the spread of the iron plough, which increased productivity. In 594 BCE the state of Lu instituted a system of land taxation which required peasants to pay taxes rather than to provide labour service. Some evidence suggests that individual ownership and a free market in land began to appear at this time. Accompanying this change was a growth in commerce and the appearance of coinage. In the Shang period, cowrie shells had been used in transactions and cloth was also used as a medium of exchange. By the late Spring and Autumn period metallic currencies had been introduced, early coins being in the form of spades or knives.

THE WARRING STATES PERIOD

The transition from the Spring and Autumn period to the Warring States period was once represented as a change from an age of relative peace to one in which war was the dominant theme. It has been demonstrated, however, that wars were equally frequent in both periods, though the character of war did change, ceasing to be an aristocratic monopoly and becoming an activity which involved authoritarian leadership, standing armies and peasants performing military service. In this period military specialists appeared, the most famous being Sunzi, supposed author of the *Art of War,* which dates back to the fifth century BCE. In it he declared:

> All war is based on deception. Hence, when able to attack, we must seem unable; when using our forces, we must seem inactive; when we are near, we must make the enemy believe we are far away; when far away, we must make him believe we are near.[15]

New weapons were adopted, notably the crossbow and the improved iron sword, and armour was developed. From the middle of the sixth century, armies composed solely of infantry began to appear and the number of combatants rose sharply, with armies of 600,000 men being recorded.

In the Warring States period the economic and social changes which had begun in the Spring and Autumn period accelerated. In agriculture, the availability of iron tools, the application of fertilizer and the use of irrigation all became more common. The number of walled towns increased and some of these developed commercial quarters. Occupational specialization and the development of trade were accompanied by the spread of the use of money. There is evidence for the existence of markets and of extensive interregional trade. The names of a few merchants have been preserved, including that of Lü Buwei, whose career in the state of Qin will be noted shortly. However, the implication of this evidence is disputed. Marxist historians have suggested that the most significant development was the disappearance of communal land ownership and the emergence of a private landlord class. Other writers have argued that the rise of trade indicated a change to a more individualistic society. The evidence for either interpretation is fragmentary, and the most that can be said with confidence is that this was a period of rapid development, which was reflected in the intellectual activity of the period.

*   *   *

Kong Fuzi, Master Kong, known in the West as Confucius, a latinized form of his name, lived approximately 551–479 BCE. He was born in the small north-eastern state of Lu. His parents probably belonged to the minor aristocracy and his search for an official position was perhaps typical of *shi* or common gentlemen of his day (the term was being redefined in the evolving social context). He became an expert on ceremony, genealogy and ancient lore and was appointed to a junior post in his own state until he was forced to go into exile. He visited a number of states and held office in Wei before returning to Lu for his last years. He acquired a number of followers, who recorded his sayings in a compilation made long after his death, known as the *Lunyu* or *Analects*.

Confucius's teachings were influenced by his perception that he lived in troubled times, and by his belief that in the early Zhou period China had experienced a golden age. He frequently cited the actions of Kings Wen and Wu, and those of the Duke of Zhou, as examples of appropriate behaviour. He believed that they had followed the *dao* or Way, which in this context meant 'the Way of running a state so that good order and harmony can prevail among men'.[16]

For centuries the written record was the sole basis for the analysis of Confucius's teaching and the reference to the early Zhou period remained unquestioned. However, new archaeological evidence indicates that twice in the Zhou period, in *c.* 850 BCE and *c.* 600 BCE,

ritual practices, for example those governing funerals, were transformed, which suggests that when Confucius and his contemporar-
ies were talking about appropriate behaviour, they were reacting to
recent changes in ritual.[17]

Confucius's concern for the promotion of good government led
him to seek a position as minister to a king who would heed his advice
and practise ethical government. In order to achieve this the ruler
should select good officials, set a moral example and treat his people
with benevolence.

A number of other themes were prominent in Confucius's teaching.
He made frequent reference to standards of conduct and to the ideal
of the *junzi* or princely man, a term often translated as 'gentleman'.
Two quotations from the *Analects* illustrate this concept. In the first,
Zi Lu, one of Confucius's disciples, asked about the gentleman.
Confucius replied:

'He cultivates himself and thereby achieves reverence.'
'Is that all?'
'He cultivates himself and thereby brings peace and security to
his fellow men.'
'Is that all?'
'He cultivates himself and thereby brings peace and security to
the people.'

In another passage Confucius distinguished between the gentleman,
who is superior not because of breeding but because of superior
moral accomplishments, and the small man. 'The gentleman', he said,
'understands what is moral. The small man understands what is
profitable.'[18] Confucius constantly emphasized the importance of
education and of self-cultivation, and thus established a respect for
book learning which was to last throughout the imperial period.
Self-cultivation was not only a matter of scholarship, it was also a
commitment to learning how to behave. The essential quality was
jen, a term often translated as benevolence, but which also connoted
dealing with other human beings as a man ideally should. One aspect
of *jen* was reciprocity: 'Do not impose on others what you yourself
do not desire.'

Confucius believed strongly in the importance of ritual and ceremony and in the value of politeness and good manners. The correct
performance of ritual was an essential part of the government of a

state. Within the family it was important to observe the niceties of behaviour towards others and to apply restraint with regard to eating, drinking and dress. Confucius placed particular stress on the importance of filial piety, which implied obedience to one's parents during their lifetime and care for them as they grew old. After their death it was essential to provide them with a proper funeral and to observe mourning over a period of three years. There was also an obligation to make the correct sacrifices to the dead, in particular to male ancestors. Though referred to as 'ancestor worship', these ceremonies did not imply the deification of forebears. Confucius had little to say about religion, but he did define wisdom as keeping one's distance from gods and spirits while showing them reverence. In all his teaching Confucius was not announcing a new doctrine but expounding what he believed to be the principles which had been observed by rulers and families in the past.

Confucius's most famous opponent was Mozi, who lived approximately 470–391 BCE. Tradition has it that Mozi was initially a disciple of the Confucian school, but he later rejected its teachings. His family may have come from a class of prisoners or slaves, which may explain a degree of rancour in his attack on Confucianists as aristocrats. Whereas Confucius had stressed what was described as 'graded love', implying the reservation of a greater concern for one's family and ancestors than for other people, Mozi urged men to practise universal love. By this he meant in particular the satisfaction of the ordinary people's material needs, and he condemned elaborate funerals and prolonged mourning as inappropriate expenses. He regarded ritual as superfluous and had no time for music, which played an important part in Confucius's concept of how harmony could be achieved in human affairs. But like Confucius he condemned war, and his passionate denunciation of its effects was characteristic of his teaching.

> Now among all the current calamities, which are the worst? I say that the attacking of small states by large states, the making of inroads on small houses by large houses, the plundering of the weak by the strong, the oppression of the few by the many, the deception of the simple by the cunning, the disdain of the noble towards the humble – these are some of the calamities in the world.[19]

Quite distinct from Confucius's and Mozi's concern with morality was the preoccupation with nature, which was the keynote of the philosophical ideas known in the West as Daoism. The *dao* in this context was a metaphysical concept, sometimes referred to as the absolute. The impossibility of defining it was asserted in the opening lines of the oldest Daoist text, the *Laozi*:

> The way that can be spoken of
> Is not the constant way;
> The name that can be named
> Is not the constant name.
> The nameless was the beginning of heaven and earth;
> The named was the mother of the myriad creatures.[20]

This text, otherwise known as the *Daodejing* or *The Way and Power Classic*, was supposedly written by Laozi, a contemporary of Confucius. It is now generally accepted that there was no such person and that the text is a compilation dating from the fourth century BCE. Inevitably it reflected the troubled times in which it was composed. The ideal ruler was the sage, who had acquired enlightenment and who then applied it to the art of government. The most important principle was *wuwei*, which meant that the ruler should avoid interfering in people's lives:

> Not to honour men of worth will keep the people from contention; not to value goods which are hard to come by will keep them from theft; not to display what is desirable will keep them from being unsettled of mind.

> Therefore in governing the people, the sage empties their minds but fills their bellies, weakens their wills but strengthens their bones. He always keeps them innocent of knowledge and free from desire, and ensures that the clever never dare to act.

> Do that which consists in taking no action, and order will prevail.[21]

The other main Daoist text, the *Zhuangzi*, is more reliably associated with a man of that name whose supposed dates are 369–286 BCE. A constant theme in the book was how man might free himself from his earthly constraints. Its most famous anecdote told how Zhuangzi once dreamed that he was a butterfly fluttering about, enjoying itself. It did not know that it was Zhuangzi. Suddenly he awoke with a start and he was Zhuangzi again. But he did not know whether he was Zhuangzi who had dreamed that he was a butterfly, or whether he was a butterfly dreaming that he was Zhuangzi. Between Zhuangzi and the butterfly there must be some distinction. That is what is called the transformation of things.[22]

In all this philosophical activity Confucius's teaching was not forgotten and its main themes were to be restated by Mengzi, known in the West as Mencius, who lived between 372 and 289 BCE. Mencius, like Confucius, gathered a group of disciples around him and their collection of his sayings is the basis of the text known as *Mencius*. Mencius made three important additions to Confucius's thought. The first concerned human nature, on which Confucius had merely observed: 'Men are close to one another by nature. They diverge as a result of repeated practice.'[23] Mencius believed that what set man apart from animals was the heart, by which he meant the essential moral nature of man. Gao Zi, a critic of Mencius, likened human nature to whirling water, and said that if you gave it an outlet to the east it would flow east, and if you gave it an outlet to the west it would flow west. Mencius responded by asking whether water showed the same indifference to high and low: 'Human nature is good, just as water seeks low ground. There is no man who is not good; there is no water that does not flow downwards.'[24]

Like Confucius, Mencius had much to say on the subject of good government. He stressed that the economic welfare of the people was the basis of political stability, and advocated a return to the well-field system, the system of equal land-holding which he believed had existed early in the Zhou period. He added that if a ruler failed to rule benevolently then his people had the right to rebel.

Xunzi, who lived between 298 and 238 BCE, took exception to Mencius's view of the inherent goodness of human nature. He famously argued, 'The nature of man is evil; his goodness is acquired.' Man, he insisted, is born with desires and passions, which if not curbed will lead to disorder.

Crooked wood needs to undergo steaming and bending by the carpenter's tools; then only is it straight. Blunt metal needs to undergo grinding and whetting; then only is it sharp. Now the original nature of man is evil, so he must submit himself to teachers and laws before he can be just; he must submit himself to the rules of decorum and righteousness before he can be orderly.[25]

Xunzi therefore emphasized education and the study of those books which he regarded as classics. Although it is not clear to which books he referred, it was at about this time that the canon of Confucian literature began to be defined. Five books were designated as classics: the *Yijing* or *Book of Changes,* a book of divination; the *Shujing* or *Book of Documents,* a collection of writings and speeches ascribed to the Shang and early Zhou periods; the *Shijing* or *Book of Songs,* an anthology of poetry and folksongs; the *Spring and Autumn Annals*; and the *Liji* or *Book of Rites,* a collection of ritual manuals and philosophical works to which Confucius was believed to have contributed. Many centuries later, in the Southern Song period (1127–1279), four works, to be known as the Four Books, became the basic texts for primary education. These were the *Analects* of Confucius and *Mencius*, which have already been mentioned, and two sections from the *Book of Rites*, the *Great Learning*, an essay on self-cultivation and the ordering of the family and society, and the *Doctrine of the Mean*, which is concerned with how man and his actions may be brought into harmony with the universe.

While these philosophical issues were being debated, theories relating to the order of nature were formulated into two concepts, *yin* and *yang* dualism and the 'five elements'. According to dualist theory, all matter may be classified as either *yin* – which is the negative, female and yielding principle of the universe – or *yang* – which is the positive, male and active principle. These two principles are regarded as complementary and their relationship is necessary for cosmic harmony. The theory of the 'five elements', which are wood, fire, earth, metal and water, asserts that these are the five permanently active principles of nature. The five elements are related to the five directions, the five seasons, the five metals, the five atmospheric influences and so on. They are also incorporated into the divination techniques of the *Book of Changes*.

THE RISE OF QIN

During the Warring States period the most dynamic of the seven principal states was Qin, situated on the Wei river. The other states accused the inhabitants of Qin of having the same customs as the Rong and Di, non-Chinese groups living to the west and north of their territory. Qin expansion was at first achieved at the expense of the Rong, who were finally subdued in the fourth century BCE. Meanwhile Qin had modernized its government and had adopted practices from other parts of China, notably the introduction in 408 BCE of a land tax payable in kind rather than in labour. In its dealings with other states, Qin had often clashed with the state of Jin, its neighbour to the north east. However, in 403 BCE Jin was partitioned between its three most influential ministerial families. The successor states of Han, Zhao and Wei, although still powerful entities, became involved in interstate rivalry which was exploited by Qin.

Qin was reputedly willing to employ able men from other states. The ruler of Wei had been warned about a young man from his state named Yang Gongsun: '[he] has marvellous talents – if he is not employed in an official post, it would be better to put him to death, lest another kingdom obtain his services!' For a time Yang served as a minister in Wei, but in about 361 BCE he was attracted to Qin, where he was created Shang Yang and placed in control of a reform programme. Though unprecedented in its scope, the programme was not entirely novel, for it consolidated changes which were already under way in Qin and in other states.

Shang Yang was the first exponent of the ideas and practices later to be known as Legalism. Whereas the Confucianists had urged that rulers should rule through benevolence for the benefit of their people, and that ethical and moral issues should have primacy, Legalists argued that the interests of the state came first and that the state should be organized rationally to maximize its power against that of its rivals. To achieve this, Shang Yang supported the use of war and he himself led a campaign against his own state. He also implemented a wide range of reforms. One of his objectives was to abolish feudalism, implying ending the devolution of power to hereditary landowners in favour of direct state administration. It was at this time that the *xian,* or district, became the standard administrative subdivision. An agrarian reform abolished the 'well-field' system, in so far as it still existed, and replaced it with a free market in land. Farmers were honoured for increasing their productivity, whereas traders, whose activities were regarded as against the interests of the state, were liable to punishment.

Strict laws and punishments were instituted and fixed administrative procedures were introduced. The population was divided into groups of five or ten families and individuals were held responsible for the wrongdoing of any member of the group. All adult males were registered and were liable to a capitation tax. A comprehensive law code was introduced which prescribed severe punishments for offences. A collection of bamboo slips, found in 1976 in the grave of a Qin official buried in Yunmeng *xian,* Hubei province, contains details of a legal code in existence before Qin united China, which may be the code established by Shang Yang. For his part in promoting these reforms Shang Yang has traditionally been condemned, although more recently he has been praised. To Confucianists he was a destroyer of tradition who coerced the people into submission. In the 1970s, at the time of the anti-Confucius campaign, he was cited as an example of how revolutionary violence might be used to suppress the aristocracy and to introduce radical reforms.

In 338 BCE, after the death of his patron, Shang Yang was accused of plotting rebellion and put to death. Nevertheless, the direction that he had given to Qin policy remained influential. In 316 BCE Qin began to dismember the state of Chu, first seizing the territory of Shu, centred on present-day Chengdu, and subsequently subjugating the neighbouring territory of Ba. There followed a series of campaigns against the other states, all marked by victories for Qin and reports of very heavy casualties. In 256 BCE the remaining territory of the Zhou was annexed and the dynasty extinguished. Qin was successful in each of these campaigns because of its location in the west which gave it a secure base, because of its strict social discipline which enabled it to mobilize its manpower, and because of its strong economy which provided ample resources. The theory that Qin won because it had better weapons, in particular iron swords, has not been supported by archaeological evidence.

By the middle of the third century BCE Qin appeared to be on the verge of becoming the dominant state, but its triumph was to be delayed for a generation. In those years a number of individuals emerged who were to play key roles in the final victory. The first was Han Fei, who had been born in the state of Han in about 280 BCE and had been a student of the philosopher Xunzi, who had taught that 'the original nature of man is evil'. Although a Confucianist by training, Han Fei turned against Confucianism. The *Hanfeizi,* which contains a number of his essays, is the most coherent expression of the ideas of Legalism. Han Fei rejected the Confucian idealization of the past, and accepted something of Mozi's utilitarian view of the function of the state. He also agreed with the idea of *wuwei* as expressed in the *Laozi,* arguing that if a state has effective laws, laws which reward the people for good behaviour and punish them severely for transgressions, then there is no need for the ruler to play an active role in government.

The second individual was a wealthy merchant named Lü Buwei who, when trading in the state of Zhao, had befriended Zichu, a son of the ruler of Qin, who had been sent there as a hostage. As a mark of his friendship he gave the prince his favourite concubine. According to the account of Sima Qian, the Grand Historian, she was already pregnant by Lü Buwei. The latter then went to Qin and persuaded the heir to the Qin throne, who was childless, to accept Zichu as his heir. In quick succession the Qin ruler and his heir died, to be succeeded by Zichu, who himself died in 247 BCE after a reign of only three years. Zichu had appointed Lü Buwei as his chancellor and Lü continued in that post until 237 BCE, during the minority of King Zheng, who was supposedly his son. In that time Lü Buwei further strengthened Qin by encouraging the construction of canals and by sowing dissension between the other states. He was also a patron of the arts, commissioning a major literary compilation known as the *Lü shi chun jiu* or *Spring and Autumn Annals of Mr Lü*, which summarized existing knowledge on a wide variety of matters. Ill advisedly, he continued his liaison with the concubine who was allegedly the king's mother. The scandal which this caused led to him being forced to commit suicide in 235 BCE.

By now a third important character had appeared on the scene. This was Li Si, who had studied under Xunzi and alongside Han Fei. Whereas Han Fei was a theoretician, Li Si was a practical politician, who had come to Qin because he considered that the career prospects in his native state of Chu were poor. He attached himself to Lü Buwei, and would probably have fallen with him, had he not presented to King Zheng a document entitled *Memorial on Annexation of Feudal States*, in which he argued the value to Qin of employing advisers from other states. He did not extend this tolerance to others, for he is reported to have engineered the death of Han Fei after the latter had been sent as envoy to Qin by the state of Han.

THE QIN DYNASTY, 221–206 BCE

In 230 BCE Qin started the series of campaigns which led to the unification of China. The other states tried to form alliances to oppose the advance of Qin and in 227 BCE Yan sent an assassin to murder

King Zheng. But this attempt failed, as did all other efforts at resistance, and in quick succession the surviving states were defeated. In 221 BCE the king of Qin assumed the title of Qin Shi Huangdi, the First Emperor of Qin. It was suggested to him that the newly acquired territories should be distributed to a feudal nobility, but in an outspoken memorial Li Si opposed the idea. Instead, the empire was divided into 36 commanderies and prefectures under officials appointed by central government. The emperor's and Li Si's distrust of those who served them was apparent in the arrangement in which military and civil authority was separated and a third supervisory official was appointed to each commandery, thus initiating a pattern of control through division of authority which survived through the imperial period. Many aristocratic families were required to move to the capital at Xianyang, near present-day Xi'an. Vast quantities of weapons belonging to these families were confiscated and melted down to make statues, and city fortifications were destroyed.

After the conquest Li Si embarked on a series of measures which applied Legalist principles to the new state. A major effort was made to standardize measurements, and examples have survived of inscribed weights and vessels. Other reforms provided for a network of roads radiating from the capital and fixed the axle width of carts using them. Standard gold and copper coins were circulated, and the form of the latter – a round coin pierced by a square hole – established the shape of future coinage. These measures encouraged commerce, although the emperor shared the prejudice of Legalists in favour of agriculture and against merchants, who on occasions were rounded up and settled in distant regions.

The *Shiji* or *Historical Records,* compiled by Sima Qian a century later, state that Li Si carried out a reform of the written language, that he 'equalized the written characters, and made these universal throughout the empire'. The probability is that a group of scholars under Li Si's direction developed a standard script known as the Small Seal, which was used in official communications. It was also used on seven stone stelae erected in various parts of the empire to commemorate the inauguration of a new age and to record the journeys made by the emperor. The emperor's relationship with scholars was a difficult one. In 213 BCE a scholar cited the historical record to criticize the emperor for having accepted Li Si's recommendation with regard to feudal fiefs. In response, Li Si presented a memorial to the emperor suggesting that scholars, other than those attached to the court, should surrender all historical records other than those of Qin and that these should be burned. Copies of works such as the *Book of Songs* and the *Book of Documents* were collected and destroyed, but the destruction was by no means complete and many books, in particular treatises on technical and literary subjects, survived the holocaust. If that incident were not enough to earn Qin Shi Huangdi the enduring disapproval of Confucian scholars, the action he allegedly took in the following year certainly was. Having heard that certain scholars were criticizing him, he ordered that more than 460 of them should be buried alive. Descriptions of both these events are given in the account written by Sima Qian a century later. The truth of the allegations is uncertain and the latter incident may never have happened.

After the unification, Qin Shi Huangdi continued the drive for territorial expansion. Expeditions were sent south to modern Guangdong and Guangxi and Chinese were sent or deported to colonize those regions. To support the military expeditions a canal, known as the 'magic transport canal', was dug to link the Yangzi and Xi (West) rivers. Meng Tian, the most famous general of the day, led a large force against the Xiongnu, the name now given to the northern nomads, and forced them to retreat beyond the Ordos region, thereby abandoning their pasture lands. Chinese settlers were sent to populate the area. This incident has been described as 'the first deep and massive conquest of nomadic territory by a Chinese state'. Meng Tian then used a vast army of convicts to construct a 'great wall' extending for more than ten thousand *li* (a *li* is approximately one third of a mile; the phrase 'ten thousand *li*' means 'extremely long') to protect the recently conquered nomadic territories.[26] This has long been taken as a reference to the building of *the* Great Wall. However, the Great Wall of today dates mainly from the Ming period, and Meng Tian's wall was a more modest construction, joining together earth walls which had been built in the Warring States period. Meng Tian also built the Straight Road, which ran northwards for some 500 miles from Xianyang to the Ordos desert, and which was intended to facilitate the supply of troops operating on the new frontier.

During his reign Qin Shi Huangdi had become increasingly preoccupied with the theory of the five elements and the secret of immortality. As the Zhou dynasty had been associated with the element of fire, the Qin dynasty was identified with the element which fire does not overcome, namely water, and also with the colour black and the number six. In all garments black became the dominant colour and in measurements six was taken as the basis of calculation. On his tours the emperor despatched people to collect herbs believed to grant immortality and he sent an expedition to the island of Penglai, where immortals were believed to reside. In 210 BCE he travelled to the coast of modern Shandong, where in response to a dream he hunted and shot a large fish. Shortly afterwards he fell ill and died. In an attempt to manipulate the succession, Li Si and Zhao Gao, the eunuch chief minister of Qin, concealed the emperor's death by keeping his body in the sleeping-carriage and disguising the smell by surrounding it with carts loaded with salted fish. By this means they bought time to procure the succession of a younger son, who became the Second Emperor.

Even before he became emperor, Qin Shi Huangdi had started to plan his tomb. Construction began in 212 BCE or earlier at a site 30 miles east of Xianyang. The position of the tomb has long been known, but it was not excavated, as records showed that it had been rifled twice. However, in 1974 a chance discovery led to the uncovering of three vast pits to the east of the burial mound. In these pits were over 7000 life-size terracotta figures of soldiers. The mausoleum itself has yet to be excavated. According to the description left by Sima Qian, it contained a model of the empire which had rivers of quicksilver and a mechanism for operating the tides. The model was lit by candles made of whale fat. The tomb incorporated boobytraps which would shoot any intruders and to guard its secrets the workers who had constructed it were also entombed.

The Second Emperor set out to rule as his father had done. In a famous memorial Li Si advised him about 'supervising and holding responsible', a method of control advocated by the Legalists. However, very quickly things began to go wrong. Discontent had arisen over the heavy taxes levied to complete the Epang palace, which had been started by Qin Shi Huangdi. Before the new emperor had been on the throne a year a rebellion headed by Chen Sheng and Wu Guang, two poor farmers, had broken out in the former state of Chu. Less than a year later other uprisings had occurred and Chen Sheng's forces were within 30 miles of the capital. At court Zhao Gao intrigued against Li Si, who was executed by being cut in two at the marketplace at Xianyang. Zhao Gao's political ascendancy increased to such an extent that in 207 BCE he forced the Second Emperor to go into retirement and then to commit suicide. Two months later the new emperor had Zhao Gao killed, but by then the empire was lost and he was forced to submit to Liu Bang, one of the rebel leaders, who became the first emperor of the Former Han dynasty.

Early in the following century, a poet and statesman named Jia Yi wrote an essay entitled 'The Faults of Qin', an analysis of the reasons for the precipitous fall of the Qin dynasty. Jia Yi criticized Qin Shi Huangdi for his overweening ambition, his disregard for the ways of former kings, and in particular for his burning of the books. Having pacified and fortified the empire, he had supposed that it would last ten thousand generations. But the Qin empire had a fatal flaw: it was not ruled with humanity and righteousness and it was this which enabled Chen Sheng and others to overthrow it. Marxist historians have emphasized the role of poor peasants in the fall of the dynasty, describing their rebellion as the first great popular revolt in Chinese history. Western historians have suggested that the dynasty fell because of a combination of factors, including the moral short-comings of its rulers, the discontent brought about by their policies and the magnitude of the task they attempted.

THE FORMER OR WESTERN HAN DYNASTY, 206 BCE–CE 9

The first of the rebellions against the Qin, that headed by Chen Sheng and Wu Guang in the north, collapsed in the face of Qin resistance and internal disputes, and both leaders were killed. In the meantime a second rebellion had broken out headed by Xiang Yu, whose family had previously been generals in the state of Chu. Xiang Yu resented the Qin centralization of power and, after gaining an important victory at Julu, he put himself forward as the supreme general of the feudal states. Among his supporters was Liu Bang, a peasant from the district of Pei in modern Jiangsu, of which he had proclaimed himself the feudal lord. In 206 BCE Liu Bang captured the Wu Pass, which left the Qin capital at Xianyang at his mercy, and he then negotiated the surrender of the third and last emperor of the Qin. He was said to have spared the inhabitants of the capital, to have prevented looting, and even to have rescinded the most severe of the Qin laws. However, when Xiang Yu arrived the city was looted and the last emperor was put to death. Xiang Yu then revived the feudal states, appointing 19 rulers with himself as hegemon. At this point he and Liu Bang fell out and over the next four years they fought a series of campaigns, in which Liu Bang was often defeated, but nevertheless his reputation for moderation earned him the support of a number of the feudal lords. In 202 BCE, after Liu Bang had gained a decisive victory at Gaixia in modern Anhui, Xiang Yu was captured and killed.

Liu Bang, who had adopted the title of King of Han, now assumed the style of *huangdi* or sovereign emperor, and used the name of his state as the title of the new dynasty. From now on he will be referred to as Gaozu, his posthumous title. During his reign, which lasted until 195 BCE, and the reigns of his two sons and his grandson, that is until 141 BCE, a remarkable consolidation of political power took place and many of the features of the imperial system, which was to last initially for two centuries and subsequently for two millennia, took shape. Gaozu himself represented for all time the possibility that a man of peasant origins but of outstanding virtue might rise to become emperor. His supporters, three of whom became known as the Three Heroes of the Han dynasty, were all said to have known poverty and to have performed acts of charity on behalf of the poor and dispossessed.

Gaozu began his reign by announcing an amnesty and measures to restore the country to peace. Being aware of the limitations of his authority, he moved cautiously to assert central control. In the west of the country, and in the area around the new capital, which was established at Chang'an, he continued Qin practice and applied direct rule in the form of commanderies. But in the east and the south he accepted the existence of ten kingdoms, whose rulers professed allegiance to him. Later, in a piecemeal fashion, he and his successors replaced the rulers of these kingdoms with members of the imperial family. In the commanderies he rewarded senior officials, military leaders and leaders of non-Chinese groups who had submitted to the Han, by conferring on them the rank of *hou*, or marquis. These titles gave them the right to raise taxes, part of which they remitted to the state and part of which they were allowed to retain.

Gaozu introduced two other important measures to ensure the stability of the dynasty. The first was to formalize the system of bureaucratic government which had been introduced under the Qin. The emperor was assisted by three senior officials, known as the Three Excellencies, and they in turn were supported by nine ministers, each of whom had a defined area of responsibility. To restrict the power of the senior officials, the terms of their appointment made them mutually dependent. Likewise, ministers and military officials were often appointed in pairs with overlapping responsibilities. The other measure was less specific, but nevertheless of great significance. Gaozu was notorious for his contempt for scholars, declaring that he had won the empire on horseback and had no time for the Confucian classics. However, a Confucian scholar named Lu Jia, who had been an early supporter of the emperor, compiled for him the *New Analects,* a collection of essays which identified the shortcomings of the Qin dynasty and recommended that the new emperor's government should observe ethical standards. This may have marked the beginning of the adoption of Confucian values as the basis of imperial government, a process which was advanced further in 196 BCE when an edict was issued regulating the recruitment of able persons – that is, men of merit – to the administration.

During Gaozu's reign steps were taken to stabilize the frontiers of the empire. To the north the main threat came the Xiongnu, who were once identified with the Huns, but are now described as a confederacy of steppe people originating in Mongolia. This confederacy had been established in 209 BCE by a charismatic leader named Maodun in response to the crisis caused by the Qin occupation of nomadic pasture lands. He defeated the main rivals of the Xiongnu on the steppe and established his capital at Longcheng in Outer Mongolia. He then began to raid into the Ordos region. Gaozu could not tolerate this challenge and in 200 BCE he led a large army against the Xiongnu, but was defeated at Pingcheng in modern Shanxi and he himself narrowly escaped capture. He then switched to diplomacy, initiating a policy known as 'harmonious kinship', which involved the marriage of a Chinese princess to the Xiongnu leader, the exchange of gifts tantamount to a yearly tribute, and the recognition of a frontier demarcating Xiongnu and Chinese territory.

When Gaozu died in 195 BCE the throne passed to his son, then a minor, and subsequently to two other descendants, both minors. During those years real power lay in the hands of Gaozu's widow, the Empress Lü. The empress herself, and the Lü family which came from the province of Shandong, later came to epitomize the danger to the imperial succession of usurpation by the family of the empress dowager. While Gaozu was still alive he was supposed to have required her to swear an oath not to elevate members of the Lü clan to the rank of king. But she manipulated the succession and killed off rivals, and from 188 BCE until her death eight years later she ruled as regent. She had hoped to assure the position of her family after her death, but after the succession of another of Gaozu's sons, who became the Emperor Wendi, the Lü family was eliminated.

Under Wendi and his son, who reigned as Jingdi – that is, between 180 and 141 BCE – the Chinese Empire achieved new levels of stability and prosperity. It was during this period that the agricultural economy of China Proper first exhibited its characteristic features: intensive cultivation involving sophisticated techniques of irrigation and seed selection; an economic interdependence in which a free peasantry produced a marketable surplus of primary goods, and supplemented its income through domestic handicrafts; and an economic vulnerability to natural disasters and the encroachment of landlordism and state exactions. It was this last feature which encouraged migration, and in particular the drift of population to the southern provinces.

This period also saw a refinement of religious beliefs and practices concerning the dead. A vivid illustration of this was provided by the tomb of the Countess of Dai at Mawangdui in Hunan, which was discovered in 1972. The tomb, which dates from about 168 BCE, contained the mummified body of the countess and various talismans which would enable her to make the journey to paradise. These included a painting on silk which depicted the route her soul would take, first to the magical island of Penglai and then to the gates of paradise. An indication of the increased complexity of the belief in an afterlife can be found in the appearance, in tombs dating from the first century, of bronze TLV mirrors. These mirrors, which have markings like the letters T, L and V, may have been used for divination. They are ornamented with a design incorporating the twelve symbols which represent the divisions of time, and the five elements. These mirrors served to reassure the bearer, whether alive or dead, that he or she stood in the correct relationship with the cosmos.

The most glorious period of the Former Han dynasty was the reign of the Emperor Wudi between 141 and 87 BCE. During those years the frontiers of the empire were extended, important political reforms were instituted and major achievements were recorded in the fields of thought and culture. However, before the end of his exceptionally long reign a challenge on the frontier had appeared, financial problems had arisen and tensions had developed at court. These were a forewarning of the crisis that was to overwhelm the dynasty.

When Wudi came to the throne the gravest frontier threat was posed by the Xiongnu, who, despite the agreement made with

Gaozu, had continued to raid Chinese territory and in 166 BCE had penetrated to within 100 miles of the capital at Chang'an. Under Wudi the policy of appeasement on the frontier was replaced by one of divide and rule. The first step was for the Han to seek allies among the opponents of the Xiongnu. In 138 BCE Wudi sent Zhang Qian to contact the Yuezhi, known enemies of the Xiongnu. Zhang Qian failed to obtain their assistance, but his epic journey extended Chinese influence for the first time into the Western Regions; that is, modern Xinjiang. From 129 BCE Wudi launched a series of attacks against the Xiongnu. Although the Han forces won a number of victories, they were unable to campaign on the steppe for more than 100 days at a time, and so could not subjugate their opponents.

Meanwhile expansion had taken place in other directions. In 128 BCE an expedition was sent to Korea and 20 years later a longer campaign led to the establishment of four commanderies in the north of the peninsula. Nor was the south neglected, for in 111 BCE an expedition reached Guangzhou and subsequently commanderies were established to administer the territory of the modern provinces of Guangdong and Guangxi as well as the northern part of Vietnam.

Wudi had received a good education from Confucian teachers, and during his reign he appeared to observe the teachings of the famous Confucian scholar Dong Zhongshu (c. 179–104 BCE), who had defined the 'threefold obligations of the ruler'. These were to serve the basis of heaven by making the appropriate sacrifices and setting the correct moral example; to serve the basis of earth by performing symbolic acts such as ploughing a furrow and feeding silkworms; and to serve the basis of man by establishing schools and enlightening the people by education.

The most significant of the reforms which fulfilled those obligations was to start recruiting to the bureaucracy men of talent who had been educated through the medium of the Confucian texts. In 141 BCE, and in subsequent years, senior officials were called on to nominate candidates for the civil service who exhibited the right qualities for appointment. Five years later official posts were established for academics who intended to specialize in the interpretation of the Confucian texts. This arrangement was formalized in 124 BCE with the establishment of an imperial academy where a quota of 50 students studied the classics in preparation for an examination. If they passed they became eligible for an official appointment. This reform did not immediately replace the qualification for office through birth. The kingdoms which had been established at the start of the dynasty still remained in existence, as did the marquisates, held by the second rank of nobility, which were likewise hereditary positions. In the early years of his reign Wudi had conferred a large number of new marquisates on meritorious officials, military leaders and tribal leaders. However, by 112 BCE the civil service had become such an effective arm of imperial government that dependence on marquisates was no longer necessary and the great majority of them were extinguished. In Wudi's reign the most celebrated example in Chinese history of social mobility occurred. This was the case of the Confucian scholar Gongsun Hong, who rose from the condition of swineherd to become chancellor in 124 BCE.

In Wudi's empire scholarly activity thrived. The ruler of Huainan, a kingdom in modern Anhui, commissioned a compilation known as the *Huainanzi*, which brought together a variety of explanations of the working of the universe as understood by Daoist scholars. This project indicated the popularity of Daoist thought at the time, and illustrated the tendency to adopt an eclectic approach which was to recur in the future. The Confucian scholar Dong Zhongshu, author of the treatise on the obligations of the ruler which has already been mentioned, also wrote an influential work on portents, which he claimed were 'heaven's threats', a warning to the emperor of heaven's displeasure. This doctrine was to provide officials with a pretext for making indirect criticisms of the throne. Dong Zhongshu also synthesized the concepts of the five elements, the *yin* and *yang* forces and the principle of the *dao,* to form one cosmic system. At the same time Sima Qian, the Grand Historian, was working on the *Shiji*, the *Historical Records*, a comprehensive survey of the history of China, which had been begun by his father.

From what has been said it might be supposed that by Wudi's reign Confucian ideas dominated the practice of government. In reality, a complex struggle was taking place between two attitudes which Michael Loewe has termed 'modernist' and 'reformist'.[27] The modernist attitude looked back to the achievements of the Qin dynasty and the principles of Legalism for its inspiration. It conceived the task of the state to be the enrichment and strengthening of China, which implied intervention in the economy and the expansion of frontiers. The reformist attitude looked to the teachings of Confucius for guidance, and like him harked back to the traditional values of the kings of Zhou as the epitome of ethical rule. It emphasized the interests of the people, which it believed were best served by allowing individual freedom and only intervening in the running of the economy to protect the poorest in society. It therefore advocated frugal government and a cautious foreign policy. According to Loewe, modernist policies dominated in the first century of the Former Han, whereas reformist policies gained the ascendancy in the latter half of the dynasty's span, the point of change occurring during the reign of Wudi.

The event which provides the best evidence of this conflict of attitudes, as expressed in economic terms, is the conference which was held shortly after Wudi's death to discuss the cause of the hardship suffered by the people. The record of the conference is known as the *Discourses on Salt and Iron*, a reference to the government monopolies which were at the heart of the debate. The modernist viewpoint was represented by government spokesmen, who argued that a state-planned economy was of benefit to the population as a whole. Their critics, the reformists, responded by saying that government should be based on principles rather than on material considerations. The debate ranged widely and included criticism of the over-ambitious foreign policy which had prompted the government to try to tap new sources of revenue. It is generally agreed that the reformists had the better of the argument and that thereafter Confucian principles played a larger role in determining government policy.

The contest between reformism and modernism also appears in a debate about how children should be raised. A key figure on the reformist side was Liu Xiang (*c.* 80–7 BCE), whose *Biographies of Exemplary Women* contains the earliest extant extended discussion on fostering the development of children. Mothers should play an important role in their moral development. They should begin with 'foetal instruction', by their behaviour influencing the development of the child in the womb. After the birth they should provide the child with gradual and persistent moral guidance. This emphasis on the acquisition of moral virtue, as opposed to claiming authority on the grounds of birth – an emphasis which was to apply to the ruler as much as to the subject – was to cast a long shadow over Chinese history.[28]

Liu Xiang also emphasized the role of women in establishing, or re-establishing, patrilineal values; that is, values that strengthen the kinship group. A key issue was the remarriage of widows, with Liu Xiang extolling examples of women who had committed suicide rather than remarry. Tributes to such women were to become a mainstay of female education. This theme and that of female obedience to the kinship hierarchy were to be the subject of *Admonitions for Women* by the Later Han writer Ban Zhao (*c*. 45–51 to *c*. 114–20 CE), who has been praised by Confucianists as China's greatest female scholar, and excoriated by feminist writers as a tool of reactionary misogynists. A recent view is that she tried to reconcile 'a "conservative" advocacy of chastity and submission to kinship hierarchies with a "progressive" advocacy of female literacy and cultivation'.[29]

After Wudi's death the dynasty experienced a series of damaging succession disputes. Wudi's successor was a minor and power was held by a triumvirate headed by Huo Guang, the most famous kingmaker in Chinese history, who retained power throughout that reign and then played a key role in the selection of a grandson of Wudi to become the Emperor Xuandi in 74 BCE. The occurrence of a minority did not necessarily weaken the dynasty, for emperors rarely played an active part in the administration of the state. However, the excessive influence of a great family undoubtedly was a threat. Huo Guang was praised for his support of the interests of the common people, but his wife was reviled for having murdered the empress and then having her daughter nominated empress in her place. After Huo Guang's death in 68 BCE, the emperor ordered the elimination of the leading members of the Huo family.

During Xuandi's long reign, from 74 to 49 BCE, the dynasty recovered a measure of stability. The danger on the frontiers had declined, for in 60 BCE rivalry between the Xiongnu leaders fragmented their power and nullified their threat. In the meantime trade had developed along the Silk Road, which passed through the Western Regions.

However, after Xuandi's death the characteristic features of dynastic decline multiplied. His successors either suffered from ill health or came to the throne as minors. The court was criticized for its extravagance and for the excessive influence of the eunuchs. Economic problems emerged which were traced to government expenditure and some dramatic, if short-term, reforms were initiated, including the temporary abolition of the government monopolies. Ineffectual measures were taken to try to reverse the growing problem of the concentration of land-holding and the evasion of taxation by landlords. River defences were neglected and in 30–29 BCE the Yellow river burst its banks.

THE USURPATION OF WANG MANG, CE 9–23

It was in this atmosphere of dynastic decline that the famous usurpation of Wang Mang occurred. Few characters in Chinese history have been the subject of such contrasting assessments. He was at pains to present himself as a devout Confucian and friend of the people, and he fabricated evidence of portents to enable him to claim to have heaven's mandate. Nevertheless, Confucianists denounced him as a tyrant and a hypocrite. He was a reformer, and in 1928 the famous scholar Hu Shi described him as a pioneer of state socialism. More recently he has been described as one who tried to reconcile the conflicting attitudes of the modernists and reformists.

Wang Mang was born in 45 BCE. He was the nephew of the Empress Wang, who was the consort of Yuandi and the mother of Chengdi, the emperor who reigned from 33 to 7 BCE. The Wang family, and Wang Mang in particular, had at various times held positions of authority, including that of regent. Under Aidi, who was on the throne from 7 to 1 BCE, the Wang family lost influence, but under his successor, another minor, Wang again became regent. Wang had gained a reputation as an able administrator and as a paragon of Confucian virtues. This reputation enabled him in CE 9 to usurp the throne and declare himself emperor of the Xin; that is, the New dynasty.

After seizing power Wang Mang carried through a series of reforms, which he presented as an attempt to end abuses. He first attacked the increasing concentration of land-holding. In an edict dated CE 9 he 'nationalized' the land; that is to say he abolished private land ownership, prohibited the sale of land and slaves, and called for a return to the 'well-field' system of equal land-holding. The second reform reintroduced the monopolies in salt and iron which since Wudi's reign had fallen into disuse, and applied controls to the market in grain, cloth and silk. Through other measures the coinage was devalued, the nobility was required to surrender its holdings of gold in exchange for coin, and new taxes were imposed on merchants and craftsmen. During his reign Wang Mang suppressed a rebellion in the south-west province of Guizhou and negotiated a successful agreement with the Xiongnu. He was a patron of Confucian scholarship. He also encouraged scientific research and conducted an experiment to test the claims of a man who asserted that when coated in feathers he could fly thousands of *li* and spy out the movements of the Xiongnu.

Notwithstanding these achievements, in CE 23 Wang Mang was driven from the throne and then killed by rebels. Why did the Xin dynasty last for so short a time? According to Ban Gu, the compiler of the history of the Former Han, the reason was obvious. Wang Mang was an usurper whose radical and ill-judged reforms brought disaster on the people. This negative view has been echoed by modern writers, for example Nishijima Sadao has decried his anti-mercantile policies as both ineffective and a cause of his downfall.[30] Hans Bielenstein, however, has argued that Wang Mang was no innovator, but a pragmatist who governed much as his Former Han predecessors had done. The true cause of his downfall was a series of disasters which began in CE 11 with the shifting of the Yellow river to its southern course.[31]

This natural disaster, which had been preceded by prolonged neglect of the river defences, brought about a tremendous loss of life and precipitated a long-term migration from the north to the south. It also gave rise to a massive peasant rebellion in Shandong province. The rebels, who became known as the Red Eyebrows because they painted their foreheads red, professed no political objective other than a vague demand for a restoration of the Former Han. However, their activities created such disorder that gentry families became apprehensive. One of the migrant routes passed through Nanyang in southern Henan, which was the home of the Liu, a clan which claimed imperial descent. The Liu raised a rebellion against Wang Mang, and after three years of confused fighting, in which the imperial troops were defeated and the Red Eyebrows driven back, a member of the clan, Liu Xiu, proclaimed himself emperor of a restored Han dynasty. He is better known by his posthumous name, Guang Wudi.

THE LATER OR EASTERN HAN DYNASTY, CE 25–220

The restoration of the Han dynasty may be explained in the first instance by referring to the military skill and political sagacity of Guang Wudi. Despite his claim to the title of emperor, it took him ten years to defeat all opposition. His most dangerous opponent, Gongsun Shu, who had likewise declared himself emperor, came from a prominent Sichuan family. However, although the territory over which Gongsun Shu claimed to reign was very extensive, it was sparsely populated. Guang Wudi had greater resources at his disposal and this enabled him to invade Sichuan and in CE 36 to capture Gongsun Shu's capital at Chengdu.

Marxist historians have defined the fall of the Xin dynasty and Guang Wudi's victory in class terms. Wudi has been described as a representative of the landlord class which had seized the fruits of the struggles of the peasant Red Eyebrows. Such a view was firmly rejected by Hans Bielenstein, who argued that the struggle between the Nanyang gentry and the Red Eyebrows was not a class struggle, for both sides accepted the existing social and political order. It was essentially a regional struggle, which was eventually won by the Nanyang faction supported by some other factions. Nevertheless, according to Bielenstein, an important social change did occur at this time. Under the Former Han, great clans had dominated the high offices of state. At first these clans had been the followers of Gaozu, the first Former Han emperor. Later other great families had risen to national prominence, the last example being the rise of the Wang clan, which was followed by the usurpation of Wang Mang. However, most of Guang Wudi's 35 chief supporters were not from the great clans but from the lesser gentry. The regional factionalism, which was apparent in the early years of Guang Wudi's reign, reflected the basis of his support and was to prove an underlying weakness of the dynasty.

The Later Han dynasty fixed its capital at Luoyang, 200 miles east of the Former Han capital at Chang'an, hence the dynasty's alternate title of the Eastern Han. Within the city walls were situated the royal palaces, government offices and the residences of nobles and officials. Outside were extensive suburbs which housed half a million people, making it the most populous city in the world at that time. Luoyang was an important centre of commerce, which the evidence suggests was as flourishing as under the Former Han. Money was widely used and part of the labour-service obligation was commuted into a monetary tax. Another sign of commercial activity was the construction of roads and bridges. This was a period of important agricultural improvements, with the widespread adoption of iron ploughshares, a greater use of draught animals and the extension of irrigation. It was also a bad time for poorer peasants, who may have been unable to afford these technological improvements.

During the reigns of Guang Wudi and his successors Mingdi (r. CE 57–75) and Zhangdi (r. CE 75–88), many of the administrative practices of the Former Han were continued. At central government level the most senior official was the grand tutor, whose task was to give moral advice to the emperor. The three officials known as the Three Excellencies were placed in charge of finance, the military and public works. Nine ministers supervised other aspects of the administration. Of growing importance was the secretariat, which was responsible for the receipt and drafting of documents. A more sinister development, which can be traced back to the reign of Mingdi, was the increasing influence of the eunuchs, castrated males who had been placed in charge of the imperial harem and who also maintained the imperial palace. The country as a whole was divided into about 100 commanderies and kingdoms and these in turn were divided into counties. In CE 2 there had been 1577 counties, but by CE 140 this number had fallen to 1179, an indication of the extent to which the north had become depopulated. Each commandery and each county had appointed officials, while the kingdoms were headed by the sons of emperors.

Ever since the First Emperor had ordered the confiscation and melting down of weapons, a policy of gradual demilitarization of the peasant and urban populations had been pursued. Military service on the frontier was delegated to marginal elements of society, often to exiled convicts. Nomads were recruited to the Former Han army, and a policy of divide and rule was applied to the tribal groupings. Then, in CE 31, it was accepted that peasant conscripts were useless as frontier soldiers and universal military service was formally abolished.[32]

Nevertheless, the first three Later Han emperors attempted to reassert Chinese influence on the periphery of the empire. The outcome was short-term success and longer-term problems. One of Guang Wudi's principal allies, Ma Yuan, led an expedition to Vietnam, where he suppressed a rising led by two sisters. In the north and west the main threat continued to come from the Xiongnu, who had taken advantage of the change of dynasty to regain control of the Western Regions. However, they now suffered an internal split. The southern Xiongnu were allowed to settle in the Ordos region. The northern Xiongnu remained hostile, but after a series of defeats their influence dwindled. This allowed the dispatch of the famous general Ban Chao to the Western Regions and led to contact with states as distant as Sogdiana. To the north east, relations had been established with the Wuhuan and Xianbei. The former had been allies of the Xiongnu, but now accepted a tributary relationship with China and were encouraged to settle beyond the Great Wall. The Xianbei had been used by the Chinese as allies against the Xiongnu, but after the decline of the Xiongnu, they in turn became the main threat on China's northeastern frontier.

The middle period of the Later Han dynasty – that is to say, from CE 88 to 168 – was marked by increased factionalism at court and the alienation of scholars. A succession of minors occupied the throne, and power often fell into the hands of the family of the empress. A notorious example of this was the case of Liang Ji, brother of Emperor Shundi's consort. Between CE 141 and 159 he held a series of important positions and gained an unenviable reputation for rapacity. The court eunuchs continued to grow in numbers and in influence. In CE 135 they gained the right to hand down noble titles to their adopted heirs. The eunuchs entered into the struggles at court, for example a group of eunuchs procured the murder of Liang Ji. While these intrigues dominated palace affairs the literati class felt excluded from influence and some of them became concerned about the changes which they believed were taking place in society. Foremost among the critics was the scholar Wang Fu, who raised the alarm about the growing unevenness of the distribution of wealth. He deplored the excessive luxury of the upper classes and the poverty of the peasants, the producers of the essentials.

From CE 168 the Later Han dynasty suffered a series of disasters from which it was never to recover fully. The crisis began with a succession dispute, which was eventually resolved by a coup which placed a eunuch faction in control of the court. The new emperor, Lingdi, could not stem the rapid deterioration in the authority of the dynasty. The selection of officials on the criterion of merit was replaced by the widespread sale of offices. On the north-east frontier the Xianbei, under Tanshihuai, formed a great steppe confederation which inflicted a series of defeats on Chinese forces until Tanshihuai's death in CE 180. In CE 184 the Yellow Turban and Five Pecks of Grain rebellions broke out. These movements were the work of impoverished peasants inspired by the prophecies of Daoist priests who predicted the coming of the Great Peace, a golden age marked by complete equality and common ownership of goods. The Yellow Turban movement was centred on the lower Yangzi; that of the Five Pecks began in Sichuan. Both rebellions spread extremely rapidly and the rebels attacked officials whom they blamed for their misery. Both rebellions were repressed with a tremendous loss of life, but other popular movements arose in their place.

After the Emperor Lingdi died in CE 189 the dynasty subsided quickly. His death led to another succession crisis, this one notable for a massacre of the eunuchs. Thereafter, although Han emperors remained on the throne, the empire was divided between three contestants, all generals of the Later Han. The most famous of these was Cao Cao, later immortalized as the hero of the *Romance of the Three Kingdoms*. Until CE 220 the fiction of the survival of the dynasty was preserved, but after Cao Cao's death, which was followed shortly by the abdication of the emperor, it was clear that the dynasty had come to its end.

The record of the Han dynasty has sometimes been compared with that of the Roman Empire. The two empires were remarkably similar in area and population. Both extended to the limits of the known world; both recorded remarkable technological achievements; both developed sophisticated administrative and legal systems; and both enjoyed a similar span of power until their collapse. Similarities have also been found in the explanations for their fall: the rise of privileged families owning vast estates; the degeneracy of the imperial line and factionalism at court; and an ideological failure, precipitated in the Roman case by the rise of Christianity, in China by the attraction of popular Daoism. Both empires were threatened by 'barbarian' tribes on their frontiers and both made the fatal error of allowing these 'barbarians' to settle within their boundaries. Yet the collapse of the two civilizations led to very different outcomes, for the Chinese Empire rose again but the Roman Empire was never to be reconstituted.

This has prompted reflection on why the Chinese Empire had the resilience to survive. Maybe it was because it was a land empire, whereas the Roman Empire was both united and divided by the Mediterranean. Maybe it was the cultural homogeneity derived from a common Chinese written language and the persistent strength of Confucianism. Maybe it was the durability of the notion of ethical rule through the imperial institution. And maybe it was the strength of its institutions, which, according to Hans Bielenstein, 'formed the most impressive system of government in the world at the time, and for centuries to come'.[33]

2

From the Period of Division to the Tang Dynasty

Between CE 220 and 589, apart from a brief interlude between 280 and 316, no one dynasty ruled the whole of China. Between 220 and 280 the empire was divided into three kingdoms. The Western Jin then briefly and ineffectually reunited the country, but from 316 there was a prolonged division between the north and the south. In the south, six dynasties established their capital at Jiankang; that is, modern Nanjing. In the north, until 384, there was a period of extreme fragmentation known as the time of the Sixteen Kingdoms. Then the Tuoba, a branch of the Xianbei, established the Northern Wei dynasty with its capital at Luoyang. In 534 the dynasty split and a further period of political fragmentation ensued until Yang Jian not only conquered the north but also subdued the south and in 589, having established the Sui dynasty, reunified China. In 618 this dynasty was replaced by the Tang, and one of the most glorious periods in Chinese history commenced.

THE PERIOD OF DIVISION, 220–589

Between 220 and 280 China was divided into three states. In the north, with its capital at Luoyang, was the kingdom of Wei, ruled by Cao Pei, the son of Cao Cao, the famous poet and general of the closing years of the Later Han. To the south west, in the region of present-day Sichuan, was the kingdom of Shu Han, ruled by a descendant of the Han royal family. Finally in the south was the extensive, and only partly sinicized, kingdom of Wu. In 263 Wei absorbed Shu Han and then, following an usurpation by a general named Sima Yan, subdued Wu. Sima Yan established the Western Jin dynasty and briefly ruled over a unified China. However, after his death in 290 the country lapsed into civil war and in 311 the Xiongnu sacked the capital Luoyang.

The exploits of Cao Cao, the arch-villain and popular bogeyman, and others are entertainingly described in *The Romance of the Three Kingdoms*. However, a detailed account of political developments of the time would make dull reading. Of greater interest is an important social change which began under the Later Han and continued through to the Tang. This was the emergence of a new aristocratic society dominated by great families. After the collapse of the social and political structure of the Later Han, families which in the past had achieved national importance by obtaining office at court began to concentrate on perpetuating that influence in their locality. In 220, under the Wei dynasty, a 'nine-rank system' was introduced. A local arbiter, a member of the local upper class, classified candidates for office into nine ranks, according to character and ability. The higher the rank a man received, the higher the level at which he could enter the bureaucracy. As a result of this reform, and as a consequence of the changing political situation, within three generations '[b]irth, status, and office-holding became inseparably bound'.[1]

Early in the fourth century, the danger of allowing the Xiongnu to settle within China's boundaries was made manifest. Liu Yuan, a sinicized Xiongnu king, captured Luoyang and declared the restoration of the Han dynasty, thereby founding the first alien dynasty in Chinese history. Although his dynasty did not last long, it set a precedent for the political division which was to persist for several centuries, with the north of China being ruled by non-Chinese dynasties and the south remaining under Chinese control.

The first of the southern dynasties, the Eastern Jin, which had its capital at Jiankang on the Yangzi, was founded by a survivor of the Western Jin. Other great families moved south to the Yangzi valley and were joined by large numbers of refugees, many of whom became servants of the great families, which caused tension between the old and new settlers and the rise of popular movements. The political situation was very unstable and in 420 one of the dynasty's generals usurped the throne and established the Liu-Song dynasty, which survived until 479. This dynasty, and those which followed it, made sporadic attempts to limit the power of the aristocracy.

However, a more effective counter to that power came through the rapid increase in commercial traffic on the Yangzi and the growth of a merchant class, a development which was particularly apparent in the reign of Emperor Wu of the Liang dynasty (r. 502–49).

In the meantime the north had been subject to a series of invasions by non-Chinese peoples. The first incursion was by the Xiongnu who, as noted above, seized Luoyang in 311. They established the short-lived Earlier Zhao dynasty (304–20), which was to founder on the issue which was to perplex all non-Chinese invaders: Should they adopt Chinese culture and risk losing their own identity? The second major incursion came from the Di and Qiang, proto-Tibetan tribes from the west. In 351 the Di established the Earlier Qin dynasty centred on Chang'an. Fu Jian, their most famous leader, conquered much of north China and in 382 invaded the south, but his army, which was unused to campaigning in the damp conditions of the Yangzi valley, was defeated decisively by the Western Jin at the battle of Fei river.

The third and most enduring incursion was that of the Tuoba, a tribe of which the leadership group may have been Turkish in origin, but which came to incorporate many Xianbei who had been allowed to settle in northern Shanxi. In 386 the Tuoba established the Northern Wei dynasty, based at Pingcheng (near modern Datong), which they laid out according to the Chinese conventions for a capital city. This was the first example of the adoption of Chinese practices, which in time led the Tuoba to employ Chinese as officials and to abandon the tribal system in favour of a bureaucratic state. Before this transformation could be completed, the Tuoba had to assert themselves as the paramount power in north China. Taking advantage of the effects of the campaigns fought by the Earlier Qin, they overcame the neighbouring kingdoms, drove back the Ruanruan, a new confederation of Mongol tribes, and extended their influence into Central Asia. They achieved these victories because they could put massive cavalry forces into the field. By 440 the Tuoba had created the most powerful state in East Asia.

The sinicization of the Tuoba empire proceeded apace under the Emperor Xiaowen, who reigned from 471 to 499. He issued a series of decrees which amounted to 'a conscious and deliberate attempt to bring the country closer to the ... ideal of a Han-Chinese, Confucianized bureaucratic monarchy ruling an ordered, aristocratic state'.[2] These reforms included the adoption of Chinese surnames, the encouragement of intermarriage with Chinese, and the use of the Chinese language at court and for official business. At the same time restrictions were placed on Tuoba religious and social customs. In 486 an important land reform was introduced but probably never fully implemented. It decreed that all land belonged to the state and that every free man and woman would receive a share which they could enjoy as long as they paid taxes, but which would then revert to the state. The reform echoed Wang Mang's attempt at land equalization. It may have been intended to check the increasing impoverishment of the Tuoba who, after having settled in China, could no longer plunder or graze their horses, and whose increasing poverty contrasted with the growing prosperity of the Chinese settled in the region. An alternative explanation of the reform is that it was intended to increase grain production and curb the influence of Chinese landowners.

In the 490s the Tuoba court abandoned Pingcheng and established a new capital at Luoyang, 500 miles further south, a place redolent with historical associations and at the heart of the most populous and prosperous region of north China. Luoyang quickly acquired a population of half a million people and became one of the great cities of the world. The city was set out on a grid system and graced with many elegant buildings, including over 1300 Buddhist monasteries. It was also an important commercial centre and housed a large community of foreign traders.

These developments alienated the more conservative aristocratic elements in Tuoba society. The sinicization policy marginalized them politically. A change in frontier policy, away from aggressive intervention and towards static defence, deprived them of their military role. Tension within Tuoba ranks grew acute after the move to Luoyang, and when in 524 the Ruanruan crossed the frontier in force, the Tuoba border garrisons mutinied. This 'revolt of the six garrisons' was followed by ten years of conflict, which culminated in the abandonment and sack of Luoyang. The Northern Wei empire split into the sinicized Western Wei state with its capital at Chang'an and the more traditional Eastern Wei in the north east.

INTELLECTUAL, RELIGIOUS AND ECONOMIC DEVELOPMENTS DURING THE PERIOD OF DIVISION

In the centuries which followed the collapse of the Han empire, important new intellectual and religious movements gained a following.

These included the transformation of Daoism and the introduction and rise of Buddhism.

Even before the end of the Han period it seemed that Confucianism neither served the state well, because it endorsed filial piety which underwrote the excessive influence of the great families, nor helped the individual, who could find little comfort in its moral exhortations. This apparent failure provided the opportunity for the emergence of neo-Daoism. A precocious exponent of these ideas was Wang Bi, who, having written commentaries on the *Laozi* and the *Daodejing,* died of the plague in 249 when only 23 years old. Wang Bi, like many other neo-Daoists, remained an admirer of Confucius and did not argue that Daoism and Confucianism were incompatible.

Other writers and philosophers were more hedonistic and anarchic in their views and behaviour. A group which called itself the Seven Immortals of the Bamboo Grove met near Luoyang and engaged in *qingtan* or 'pure conversation', which took the form of metaphysical discussions and recitals of poetry. The term *qingtan* also implied 'criticism by the pure', a theme followed up by Bao Jingyan, who has been described as China's first political anarchist. Other Daoists investigated medicine, alchemy and personal hygiene. It was at this time that an important connection was established between the Daoists' predilection for communing with nature and landscape painting, a theme explored in *Introduction to Landscape Painting* by Zong Bing (375–443). Meanwhile, Daoism had developed as an organized church with priests and places of worship.

By now Buddhism had gained its first foothold in China. Buddhism had its origins in India and it was through commercial contacts along the Silk Road that Buddhism reached China. The Emperor Mingdi, who reigned between 57 and 75, is said to have dreamt of a golden deity who was later identified as Buddha, and this prompted him to send to India for copies of the Buddhist scriptures. Evidence that Buddhism reached China during his reign has been found in an edict dated 65 which used the Sanskrit term for a Buddhist monk. By the end of the second century Buddhist communities had formed at Luoyang and in several other places, notably Pengcheng in the Huai river valley. Buddhist temples had been constructed and a start had been made on the translation of Buddhist scriptures.

It is usually suggested that Buddhism spread slowly in China because a variety of obstacles stood in the way of its acceptance. These included the resistance of the Chinese educated classes to a religion which elsewhere had appealed to an illiterate community;

the incompatibility of the Buddhist emphasis on the renunciation of worldly concerns with the Confucian emphasis on the importance of the family; and the difficulty of translating Buddhist religious concepts into Chinese, partly because of Chinese ignorance of Sanskrit, and partly because the translators subsumed Buddhist ideas into the vocabulary used for Daoist concepts.

In south China Buddhism gained its first adherents among those educated Chinese who had been attracted to neo-Daoism and who now found Buddhism intellectually attractive. An example of such a person was Zhi Dun (314–66), who engaged in 'pure conversation', using Buddhism to illuminate Daoism and vice versa. Huiyuan (c. 334–417), a Confucian scholar who became a student of the Daoist texts, converted to Buddhism and later established a religious community at Lushan in northern Jiangxi. His followers sought salvation through the worship of Amida, the infinite Buddha. Huiyuan successfully asserted the principle that on grounds of conscience Buddhist monks should not be required to pay homage to the ruler. In 399 a monk named Faxian travelled from Chang'an to India to collect Buddhist scriptures, which he brought to Jiankang, and translated them there. He also wrote an account of his travels, the *Record of the Buddhist Countries*. The most famous Buddhist convert in south China was Emperor Wu of the Liang dynasty. In 504 he ordered his family to change their adherence from Daoism to Buddhism and he then called for the destruction of Daoist temples.

Because the northern dynasties did not have the same reservations against foreign religions as did the Chinese, Buddhism made more rapid progress in the north. A monk from Central Asia named Fotudeng reached Luoyang in 310. A legend relates that he conjured a display of blue lotus flowers in a bowl of water and this enabled him to obtain the patronage of the Later Zhao dynasty. Buddhism was welcomed not only for its magical powers, but also as a counterbalance to the Confucian influence of Chinese officials retained by non-Chinese dynasties. The first Northern Wei ruler, conscious of the growing influence of Buddhism, appointed a monk named Faguo to administer the Buddhist communities. This appointment made him a government official and liable to pay homage to the ruler, a relationship which Huiyuan had previously declared unacceptable. Faguo's ingenious response was to declare that the ruler's virtue made him the embodiment of the Buddha, so he had no scruples about subjecting himself. Nevertheless, the foreign origin of Buddhism made it an object of suspicion and the Emperor Wu of the Northern Wei, who reigned 424–51, was persuaded by his Confucian advisers to carry out a pogrom against Buddhist monks. The persecution did not last long, for in 460 work began on the Buddhist cave temples at Yungang, ten miles west of the capital at Pingcheng. In the 490s, after the Northern Wei had transferred their capital to Luoyang, another complex of cave temples was commenced at Longmen. In these temples the representation of the Buddha shows a transition from Indian to Chinese artistic conventions. The inscriptions in the caves, which refer to the cult of ancestors, also demonstrate how Buddhism was becoming sinicized.[3]

During the long period of division significant changes occurred in agricultural technology. The *Qi min yao shu*, the *Essential Methods of the Common People*, compiled by Jia Sixie between 533 and 544, contains the first written description of the technique of harrowing and advice on the selection of seeds and how to promote germination of rice. Jia Sixie described the method of transplanting wet rice and the use of fertilizer and green manures. He also explained a system of crop rotation, which would allow multiple cropping. By this time sophisticated water mills were in use to grind grain and to press plants to extract oil. In the south tea was being grown commercially, its use being assisted by the association between drinking tea and Buddhism.[4]

THE UNIFICATION OF CHINA UNDER THE SUI DYNASTY, 589–618

In the middle of the sixth century China was composed of four main political units. After the collapse of the Northern Wei, the north was divided between the Northern Zhou, to the north west, and the more sinicized Northern Qi, to the north east. On the middle Yangzi was the small state of Liang. South of the Yangzi valley the Chen empire, ruled by the last of the Six Dynasties, spread extensively, although its control was ineffectual.

The Northern Zhou and Northern Qi competed for control of north China, but their actions were limited by the threat from a new steppe confederation headed by the Tujue, a Turkish people whose influence had spread from Manchuria across Central Asia to the borders of Persia. Nevertheless, in 577 the Northern Zhou, with the assistance of the state of Chen, attacked and defeated the Northern Qi. Events then came to their aid, for in 582 the Turkish Empire split into an eastern and a western part and the threat from the north was reduced. This gave the Northern Zhou the opportunity to go on the offensive. In 587 they overran Liang and two years later overwhelmed Chen.

Northern Zhou society was dominated by a small group of non-Chinese aristocratic families. One such family, the Yuwen, occupied the throne. Yang Jian, the prime mover behind the events which were to follow, came from another of these aristocratic families, one which was probably of Xianbei extraction. He had been born and brought up in a Buddhist temple. His wife, also a Buddhist, came from a prominent Xiongnu clan and his daughter was married to the heir apparent. Yang Jian rose to prominence as a military commander during the invasion of the Northern Qi. In the following year the Northern Zhou emperor died and Yang Jian's son-in-law succeeded to the throne. Within a year, Yang Jian deposed him and then attempted to wipe out the Yuwen family. This provoked a civil war, which Yang Jian might well have lost if he had not received support from Gao Jiong, a wily military leader who later became his long-serving minister. In 581 he defeated his opponents and established a new dynasty, to be known as the Sui. Thereafter Yang Jian is better known by his posthumous title, Wendi.

It soon became apparent that Wendi's ambitions extended beyond achieving a military coup. He claimed to be the legitimate heir to the Han dynasty and went through the appropriate rituals to confirm this. This claim provided him with a moral justification for the conquest of the south, which he achieved with great efficiency in 589. The city of Jiankang was sacked, but the Chen aristocracy and its officials were treated leniently to win their allegiance. Wendi's determination to broaden the basis of his support was also apparent in the manner in which he placated the Confucianists by endorsing the virtue of filial piety, while at the same time ending the persecution of Buddhism, which had been practised under the Northern Zhou.

During his reign, which lasted until 604, Wendi introduced many other measures to ensure the stability of the dynasty which he had founded. He commenced construction of a great new capital at Chang'an. Aware that the aristocratic and non-Chinese tradition of the Northern Zhou government was unsuited to ruling a newly unified China, he set out to reconstitute a central government which echoed the practices of the Han dynasty, but which also served the autocratic tendencies of the emperor. More Chinese were now employed in the service of the state, but the most important offices were monopolized by close relatives of Wendi and those who had previously held office in the Northern Zhou. Wendi himself served as his own chancellor. Provincial and local government was rationalized and all appointments were made by the ministry of Civil Office. After appointment, officials were subject to regular supervision, and censors were sent on tour to report on their conduct. The emperor himself when travelling investigated the work of his officials. It was at this time that two enduring techniques of control were adopted, the 'law of avoidance', whereby an official was not permitted to serve in his district of origin, and that of rotation, which limited the length of time an official could hold a post.

Although Wendi himself had scant regard for scholars, it was during his reign that the essential characteristics of the examination system took shape. Examinations were conducted by the ministry of Civil Office; they were held triennially and degrees were awarded at three levels. To obtain a lower degree a candidate had to demonstrate literary ability and knowledge of a classical work. The most prestigious degree, the *xiucai* or 'cultivated talent', assessed the candidate's broader learning. Successful candidates were appointed to official positions, although the proportion of Wendi's officials holding degrees is unknown.

Wendi also initiated important reforms relating to law and taxation. He promulgated the Kaihuang Code, which synthesized northern and southern legal traditions and abolished some cruel punishments. It defined crimes and their punishments in plain terms and allowed guilty officials to commute their punishment by payment of a fine or by accepting demotion. The Kaihuang Code was to provide a model for all future imperial legal codes. Wendi also overhauled the land and taxation systems, revived the 'equal field' arrangement and the periodic distribution of land to the common people, and revised the tax registers. The common people were required to pay three taxes: a land tax payable in grain, a textile tax payable in silk or linen, and a labour tax requiring 20 days' labour per year from adult males.

As might be expected, Wendi also reviewed the military situation and reorganized the armed forces under central control. In 590, having completed the conquest of the south, he took the bold step of demilitarizing the population of the North China Plain, and later he ordered the confiscation of all weapons. This did not imply that Wendi had abandoned all military activity. He sent an expedition south to recover control of Champa, known in modern times as Annam. In the north he contained the Turks by establishing military colonies and by building walls.

In many of his actions Wendi received the advice and encouragement of his consort, the Wenxian empress. That a woman should play this role was accepted in northern aristocratic families, but such a relationship was unique in China's dynastic annals.

It was on the empress's advice that the emperor's second son was nominated heir. The Emperor Yangdi succeeded his father in 604. His name was to be execrated by Chinese historians, for he was suspected of parricide. Because of this crime, and as a consequence of his megalomania, extravagance and licentiousness, he was said to have forfeited the mandate of heaven and thereby to have brought the Sui dynasty to a premature end. Arthur Wright, however, has noted that in many respects Yangdi continued the policies inaugurated by his father, and has added that he was also a faithful husband, a devout Buddhist and a connoisseur of the arts.

Two aspects of Yangdi's reign are always held up for criticism: his programme of canal building and his fixation with the conquest of Korea. The purpose of the canal-building programme was to enable the resources of the productive land in the south to be brought to the north, by connecting the drainage of the Yellow, Huai and Yangzi rivers. The programme had been started by Wendi and in places it merely consisted of restoring or improving existing waterways. Yangdi carried it much further, creating a network of canals extending for about 1200 miles, which has been described as 'probably an engineering feat without parallel in the world of its time'.[5] This national system of communications was to provide the basis for the prosperity of the Tang period. However, it was achieved by large-scale state intervention in the economy and by drafting many thousands of men and women labourers, features which earned it the condemnation of Confucian historians.

Yangdi's foreign policy was shaped by his awareness of the threat still posed by the eastern Turks in what is now Mongolia. His response was to continue his father's strategies of building walls, using marriage diplomacy and seeking alliances with the eastern Turks' potential enemies. To achieve the last objective he sent his frontier expert Pei Ju on a fact-finding tour to the western Turks and in 607 the emperor himself travelled to Yulin, where he was infuriated to hear that an embassy from Koguryo, the state occupying eastern Manchuria and the northern part of the Korean peninsula, was present. It was the threat of an alliance between the Turks and the Koreans which prompted Yangdi's disastrous expeditions against Korea. The first attack was launched in 612, but poor planning and Koguryo resistance forced the Chinese to withdraw. Further campaigns were launched in 613 and 614, with similar results, but in the meantime widespread rebellion had broken out in China. The emperor was not informed of the true extent of the disaffection until it was too late to take effective action. After many of his former supporters had abandoned him, in 618 he was murdered by a descendant of the Yuwen family, whom his father had deprived of the throne.

The collapse of the Sui dynasty has often been attributed to Yangdi's personal failings and his overweening ambition. Sometimes it is conceded that fortune turned against him, in that the disastrous flooding in the Yellow river valley in 611 was the prelude to the rise of rebellion. However, Yangdi is held responsible for the rebellions, which are ascribed to the harsh conscription of peasants for canal building and to the military disasters in Koguryo. On the other hand, the collapse of the dynasty may be explained by reference to the continued rivalries within the northern aristocratic clans, to the survival of separatist sentiment in the territory of the former Northern Qi, and to the willingness of Li Yuan, who was to seize the throne and found the Tang dynasty, to reach a demeaning accommodation with the Turks.

THE ESTABLISHMENT OF THE TANG DYNASTY

Li Yuan, the founder of the Tang dynasty, was a member of a northern aristocratic family which later claimed descent from the Han nobility, but which probably derived from a Hebei family which had intermarried with the Xianbei tribal aristocracy. Under the Northern Zhou his grandfather had been created Duke of Tang. Li Yuan, like his forefathers, pursued a military career, and under the Sui his success in suppressing rebellion led to his promotion to command the important garrison at Taiyuan.

It was from there that in 617 Li Yuan decided to raise a rebellion. His motives for so doing have been the subject of debate. As the situation of the Sui dynasty had deteriorated, Yangdi had grown apprehensive of the danger of an attempt on the throne, and hearing of a prophecy that the next ruler would have the surname Li, he had ordered the execution of prominent holders of that name. Fear for his own safety may therefore have prompted Li Yuan to action. According to traditional historiography, however, the real reason for his decision was the ambition of his son Li Shimin, who tricked his father into an act of disloyalty and then laid plans for a success-ful rebellion by negotiating secretly with the eastern Turks. This explanation, which minimizes the role played by Li Yuan, has been found to be largely the concoction of Li Shimin himself, the man who later became the famous second emperor of the Tang dynasty. According to the evidence of a contemporary account, Li Yuan had nourished plans to rebel before his appointment to Taiyuan. He had taken part in planning the revolt, and in the negotiations with the Turks in which they were promised all the booty seized by the rebels and were encouraged to believe that Li Yuan was willing to become their vassal.

Within a year of the outbreak of the rebellion, Li Yuan had captured Chang'an and had declared the establishment of the Tang dynasty. He was later given the posthumous title of Gaozu, by which he will now be known. It took Gaozu another six years to complete the conquest of the country. One reason for the slowness of the conquest was the multiplicity of rebellions and claims to the throne, which required extensive military campaigns to extinguish. Another reason was the restraint exercised by Gaozu, who preferred whenever possible to win over rebel leaders and to confirm Sui officials in their posts.

The transfer of sovereignty from Sui to Tang did not imply any major shift in the locus of power. Gaozu's background, and the support he mustered, came from the same northern aristocratic clans as did that of the Sui. At first he largely continued Sui practices in central and local government and maintained their legal and taxa-tion systems. However, it would be unfair to Gaozu to imply that he did nothing new. During his reign mints were established and a new currency was issued. A revised code of law was produced which went further than that of the Sui in incorporating features of southern practice. He revived the examination system, although he continued to appoint aristocrats to senior posts. He reduced the throne's reliance on Buddhism as a unifying force. Early in his reign he appointed Fu

Yi, a Daoist priest known as a fierce critic of Buddhism, as his chief astrologer. Gaozu made his own preferences clear in an edict in which he declared that Daoism and Confucianism were key pillars of the state, whereas Buddhism was a foreign religion, whose monks' involvement in worldly affairs sharply contradicted the tenets of their faith. Gaozu's manner of dealing with the eastern Turks showed that his position remained fragile, for he was forced to retain their good-will through bribery. However, he gained a breathing space which allowed him to consolidate his position in China.

Gaozu's reign came to a sudden end. Li Shimin, to whom had been credited his father's rise to power, was a bitter rival of his elder brother, the heir to the throne. Li Shimin had played a major part in the campaigns to consolidate Tang control in the east, and this had enabled him to build up a strong personal following. The heir apparent's strength lay at court and in the capital, Chang'an. In an atmosphere of intrigue and plots, Li Shimin chose to break the deadlock by carrying out a coup. The event, known as the Xuanwu Gate incident, resulted in the death of the heir apparent, the abdication of Gaozu and the succession of Li Shimin, henceforth to be known as Taizong.

THE REIGN OF TAIZONG, 626–49

Taizong's reign, which lasted until 649, has long been regarded as a golden age in Chinese imperial history. Taizong himself, though he had obtained the throne through the murder of his brother and the enforced abdication of his father, has been regarded by Confucianists as a model ruler, a view echoed in the West where he has been described as 'probably the greatest monarch in China's history'.[6]

In the first part of his reign, that is until 636, he presented himself as a humble student of the art of civil government. He employed a succession of capable ministers who came to epitomize the ideal relationship between an emperor and his advisers. Among them was Wei Zheng, an 'unbending moralist and fearless remonstrator',[7] who even criticized Taizong himself. He preserved many features of the government of his father's reign, which were later to be regarded as ideal institutions. The central government comprised the secretariat which drafted edicts, the chancellery which reviewed them, and the department of state affairs which put them into effect. It also included the censorate, the body which investigated abuses, and the supreme court, which reviewed sentences for crimes. The country at large was divided into circuits, which were divided into prefectures which in turn were subdivided into districts. Circuits were administered by commissioners, prefectures by prefects and districts district magistrates. Hitherto, service in the provincial bureaucracy had been disparaged. Now Taizong took a personal interest in the careers of those appointed to provincial posts and despatched commissioners to check the quality of their work. Further revisions were made to the law codes and the severity of punishments was reduced. His father had adopted the 'equal field' land system of the Sui, which included provisions for the registration of households and the periodic redistribution of land. Taizong continued to support the system, although it was already apparent that it was far too rigid and idealistic to suit the changing economic situation in many parts of China.

Taizong was a member of a northern elite which had sprung from intermarriage with non-Chinese peoples. Their enjoyments were outdoors; one of his brothers once remarked that he would rather forgo three days' eating than one day's hunting. Although Taizong never lost these preferences, it was during his reign that the distance between the emperor and his social equals and between the emperor and the common man began to increase. An example of this tendency was Taizong's concern to establish the superiority of the imperial line above that of the 'four categories of clans', the leading Chinese families of the north east. In 638 a revised national genealogy was published, which showed the Li clan in a pre-eminent position. His actions relating to education and scholarship suggest a similar motive. A system of state schools and colleges was instituted, one of which was reserved for children of the imperial family and those of the highest officials. Many students came to Chang'an to study and a variety of scholarly projects were sponsored, notably the writing of the dynastic histories which served to legitimize the succession of the Tang. The examinations were held regularly. The great majority of officials continued to come from the great clans, but the highest positions now tended to go to those who had passed one of the literary examinations.

Whereas the Sui had used Buddhism as an integrating force, Gaozu had relegated it to an inferior position. Taizong, having gained the throne by a coup, was at first careful to avoid alienating the Buddhist community. In 629 he ordered the building of seven monasteries where prayers would be offered for the souls of those who had died in the battles which had led to the victory of the Tang.

Later in his reign he adopted a harsher line, passing measures to control corruption in the Buddhist church. In 637 he promulgated an edict criticizing the prominent position which Buddhism had come to occupy in China, and decreed that Daoist clergy would take precedence over Buddhist monks and nuns. In the same year he issued a legal code which contained a section regulating the Buddhist clergy, and restricting their participation in secular life.

Although Taizong remained critical of Buddhism, in the year before he died he gave audiences to the famous Buddhist pilgrim Xuanzang. In 629 Xuanzang had left China secretly and had travelled overland to India to collect Buddhist texts. This journey provided the inspiration for the sixteenth-century novel by Wu Cheng'en, *Record of a Journey to the West*, which is better known in the West as *Monkey*. When Xuanzang returned to Chang'an in 645 he was received by Taizong. Perhaps the emperor hoped to gain new insights into Buddhism, but more probably his curiosity had been aroused by Xuanzang's knowledge of foreign countries. The most Taizong ever offered Buddhism was a 'measured patronage'.[8]

In 637 Taizong's mentor Wei Zheng had the temerity to memorialize that he had observed that whereas in the early years of his reign the emperor had always made righteousness and virtue his central concern, now, thinking that the empire was without troubles, he had become increasingly arrogant, wasteful and self-satisfied. This change in the behaviour of the emperor had followed the death of his father, the retired emperor, in 635, and that of the empress, who had been his close confidante, the following year. Thereafter Taizong engaged in extravagant building projects and, more significantly, pursued an expansive foreign policy.

Soon after Taizong had seized the throne, the eastern Turks under their khaghan Xieli had invaded China and had come within 75 miles of Chang'an. Taizong was forced to bribe them to withdraw. However, in 628 the eastern Turks were split by an internal feud. Taizong gained the support of Xieli's enemies and two years later a large Chinese force inflicted an overwhelming defeat on Xieli's men. Xieli himself was taken prisoner and the eastern Turks were forcibly resettled on Chinese territory. Such was Taizong's domination of the situation that he himself became the 'heavenly khaghan'. Thus began a remarkable expansion of Chinese power in Central Asia. With the eastern Turks now his allies, Taizong was able to split the western Turks and to recover the influence which the Han had once exerted in the Western Regions. In 657 Su Dingfang fought a memorable engagement near Issyk Kul which reduced the western Turks to vassals of China and advanced the Chinese Empire to the borders of Persia. In the meantime, China had been sending punitive expeditions against the Tuyuhun, a Xianbei people who lived around Lake Kokonor, not realizing that the reason the Tuyuhun were raiding Chinese territory was that they were coming under increasing pressure from a newly unified Tibet.

Taizong's final campaign was directed against Koguryo, which also had once been part of the Han empire, but which more recently had been the graveyard of Yangdi's ambitions. Gaozu had pursued a more cautious policy and Koguryo had resumed tributary relations, but in the 640s the Koguryo throne was usurped and the new ruler began to menace the south Korean state of Silla, China's faithful tributary. The threat of a unified Korea was sufficient to prompt Taizong to act, and in 645 he led an invasion of Koguryo. The expedition made slow progress and had to be withdrawn before the onset of the Korean winter. A similar fate frustrated an attack in the following year. Plans were made for an even larger campaign in 649, but Taizong died before it could be launched.

Taizong's foreign wars had been conducted against a background of difficulties at court. Early in his reign he had named Li Chengqian, his eldest son, as his heir apparent. However, complaints were made that Li Chengqian was homosexual and that he behaved eccentrically, and a faction formed to support the claim of Li Tai, a younger son. Both sons attempted plots against each other and against the emperor, and in 643 Taizong settled the succession on Li Zhi, his ninth son, who was to reign as the Emperor Gaozong.

GAOZONG AND THE EMPRESS WU

Gaozong, who was only 20 years old when he came to the throne, reigned until 683. He suffered from ill health and from 660 his consort, the Empress Wu, was the effective ruler. Gaozong was succeeded by two of his sons, but the empress continued to control affairs, and in 690 she herself usurped the throne and established the Zhou dynasty, thus becoming the one example in Chinese history of a female monarch.

Gaozong began his reign cautiously. He relied on advice from his father's ministers, among them his uncle Zhangsun Wuji, a notable historian. The machinery of government operated smoothly and reforms continued to be introduced; for instance a commentary on the penal code was promulgated, which was to remain authoritative for centuries.

However, Gaozong's court was riven by a continuance of the factional fighting which had emerged late in his father's reign. Although modern historians have attempted to link these factions to regional bases and policy issues, it seems more likely that their source was vendettas which had their origin in the succession dispute. After Gaozong came to the throne, Zhangsun Wuji continued to pursue those who had supported Li Tai, and this situation was exploited by Wu Zhao, who later became the Empress Wu.

Wu Zhao was born in 627 into a 'merchant' family, and her supposed background has been used to identify her as a member of a newly emerging mercantile class. It has been suggested that the preference she showed when in power for officials who had succeeded in the examination system confirmed her support for social mobility. She came from the north east, and this fact has been interpreted as proof of the ascendancy of the leading families of that region over the north-western aristocracy, which had played a major role in the rise of the Sui and Tang. Her decision to transfer the capital from Chang' an to Luoyang may support this view. However, there is little evidence to show that either class or regional affiliation played a significant role in her rise or in the policies that she pursued as a ruler, which largely continued those of her predecessors on the throne.

Wu Zhao had been a concubine in Taizong's harem. In defiance of convention, Gaozong started an affair with her and in 652 she bore him a son. She then began to intrigue against Gaozong's consort, the Empress Wang, and incriminated the empress in the death of her newborn daughter. In 655, having secured her position by having her son declared heir apparent, she disposed of her enemies, first the former empress and then Zhangsun Wuji, who had resolutely opposed her rise. In 660, when Gaozong suffered a stroke, the empress made herself *de facto* ruler.

The Empress Wu proved to be a shrewd ruler and over the next twenty years she continued many of the policies and practices of her predecessors. Some of her actions, however, have been taken as examples of her selfish and irrational behaviour. The first concerned her decision, taken in 657, to designate Luoyang as a second capital, and then to transfer the court periodically between the two capitals, at great disruption and heavy expense, until finally relocating it at Luoyang in 683. Her motive has been identified as political, favoring her power base in the north east, but there was also a sound economic reason for the transfer. The area around Chang'an could not produce enough grain to feed the court and garrison, and the transportation of grain up the Yellow river, traversing the Sanmen rapids, was extremely expensive. Luoyang, however, was favourably situated at the terminus of the water route from the south. Another claimed example of her irrationality occurred in 666, when the empress decided to hold, and then in defiance of precedent to participate in, the *feng* and *shan* sacrifices on Taishan, the holy mountain in Shandong province. These costly ceremonies, which announced to heaven the glory of the dynasty, had not been performed since the Han period. Her selfishness has been detected in her patronage of Buddhism and in particular her commissioning of work on the cave temples at Longmen. On her orders a large number of statues were carved, including one of the Vairocana Buddha, the features of which were said to be those of the empress herself.

Under Gaozong and the Empress Wu attempts to extend and consolidate the empire continued. Koguryo was defeated and a short-lived Chinese protectorate was established at Pyongyang. However, by 676 a resistance movement, which had started in the southern state of Silla, forced China to withdraw. Although Silla went on to unify the Korean peninsula, Chinese influence in the area remained strong and Silla became China's most dependable tributary state.

The more pressing threat to China's interests at this time was the rise of Tibet. At the beginning of the seventh century Tibet had emerged as a unified state. Buddhism had been introduced and, in the form of Lamaism, had made rapid progress. Under Song-tsen Gampo, who ruled from 620 to 649, Tibet started to send tribute to China. At the same time the Tibetan state began to expand, pressing on the territory of the Tuyuhun pastoralists, and moving into parts of Sichuan and the Tarim basin. Chinese influence in the Tarim basin was later restored, but the expansion of Tibetan power into modern Qinghai and Sichuan proved irresistible.

THE REIGN OF EMPRESS WU, 690–705

Gaozong died in 683 and was succeeded by his third son Zhongzong. Within months the Empress Wu, now the empress dowager, compelled his abdication in favour of his brother, who remained on the throne for six years. In 684 Li Jingye headed a revolt of those families which had been disgraced and exiled to the Yangzi valley. He was quickly defeated and the empress dowager used the revolt as a pretext to purge her opponents at court. She formed a secret police and conducted a reign of terror, for which hostile critics have condemned her as a mass murderer, whereas her apologists have argued that the powerful prejudice against a woman's open exercise of power forced her to use terror to safeguard her position.

In 690 she usurped the throne and established a new dynasty, the Zhou. She may have taken this unprecedented step because of the threat of rebellion, but as that had been averted it was more probably a calculated move justified by the urgings of her supporters. Much was made of the discovery of a white stone bearing an inscription prophesying her elevation. She was encouraged to act by Buddhist clergy, whom she had patronized and who now hailed her as the incarnation of the Maitreya Buddha. She was presented with three petitions, one said to have contained 60,000 names and each urging her to ascend the throne, which have been taken as evidence that she had some popular support.

Two views have been expressed on the character of the Zhou dynasty. The traditional one has subsumed it within the Tang tradition and has perceived little difference between the policies that the empress pursued and those of the preceding Tang emperors. The other is that her usurpation marked a significant social revolution, the rise of a new class, which the empress tried to use in her struggle against the traditionalist aristocracy. The truth perhaps lies somewhere in between. Court intrigues and an attempt by the empress's family to establish its dominance were familiar elements in the political process. However, there is some evidence to show that the empress did try to free herself from the influence of her chief ministers and the control of the big families by favouring officials who had advanced through the examination system. Unlike her predecessors she favoured the Buddhist community, and elevated the status of Buddhism above that of Daoism. She also approved the construction, at great expense, of a Mingtang, or Hall of Light, described in the classics as the supreme shrine to heaven. Allegedly it was used for wild religious rites supervised by the abbot, Xue Huaiyi, said to be the empress's lover. When he fell out of favour he took his revenge by burning the building down. Thereafter the empress began to show more concern for Confucianism.

The most serious crisis of the reign arose on the north-eastern frontier, where a new tribal confederation was taking shape. It was headed by the Qidan, from whose name the word Cathay was to be derived. The Qidan, who spoke a language ancestral to Mongolian, were pastoral nomads who lived in Manchuria, in the marginal zone between the open steppe and the settled areas. It has often been noted that it was from this zone that most of the dynasties of conquest originated. In 605 the Qidan had been severely chastised after a raid into Chinese territory and they had subsequently become vassals of China. In 695 they rebelled against Chinese maladministration and gained a dramatic victory near the site of modern Beijing. This encouraged trouble at other points along the frontier, with the Turks invading Gansu and the Tibetans threatening the Chinese hold on Central Asia. The empress responded with a mixture of diplomacy and force, concluding a marriage alliance with the Turks and defeating the Qidan in battle.

The closing years of the empress's reign saw a decline in her influence. Her extravagant building programme and expensive frontier campaigns had emptied the treasury and attempts to raise new taxes exposed the seriousness of the fiscal problem facing the dynasty. The empress's behaviour also continued to cause scandal. From 697 she became enamoured of the brothers Zhang, who paraded around in fancy costume and overrode the authority of senior ministers. When the Turks again invaded China in 698, she found it so difficult to raise support that she was obliged to decide an issue that she had always sidestepped, that of the succession. She agreed that in due course the throne would revert to her son Zhongzong, whom she had set aside in 684. It was not until 705, however, that a plot hatched by her senior officials accomplished the death of the Zhang brothers and forced the empress to abdicate. She died later that year. Her usurpation, her extravagance, her scandalous behaviour, the very fact that she was a woman, all ensured her unanimous condemnation by Confucianist historians. More recently her record of achievement in all but the closing years of her reign has been rehabilitated, nevertheless. She has been credited with providing strong leadership and having presided over an age of relative peace and prosperity, for which she earned the gratitude of the people.

The Empress Wu's career has been used to support the description of the Tang as an age of unprecedented female prominence. The Sui Emperor Wendi's consort had been his most trusted adviser, and this northern tradition of the active participation of women in politics continued throughout the Tang period. Shangguan Wan'er (c. 661–710) was the Empress Wu's secretary and then became an imperial concubine as well as an accomplished poet. Royal princesses were ordained as Daoist nuns and women pursued education and a literary career in Daoist convents. A courtesan culture developed and several courtesans gained a reputation as poets. Among them was Yu Xuanji (844–68), who expressed her frustration with the limitations placed on her sex thus: 'these gauze-like robes of mine which hide my lines of verse'.[9]

THE REIGN OF XUANZONG, 712–56

The Tang restoration of 705 was followed by another period of court intrigues and weak leadership. However, in 712 the succession fell to a talented man of 27, who was to be known as the Emperor Xuanzong and whose reign was to be remembered as a high point in China's history. During the early years of his reign the fortunes of the dynasty were revived and achievements were recorded in literature and the visual arts.

Xuanzong's reign has traditionally been divided into three parts: an initial period of consolidation and reform, a central period during which constructive policies were still being applied but serious problems had begun to emerge, and a final period during which the emperor withdrew from direct involvement in government and the crisis developed which led to the rebellion of An Lushan.

During the first period, which lasted until 720, Xuanzong was assisted by several outstanding ministers, notably Yao Chong, who had risen through the examination system and who had been chief minister under the Empress Wu. Yao Chong had proposed a ten-point programme to address problems of administration and several of his suggestions were now implemented. The number of chief ministers was reduced and their authority was strengthened. Those who had passed the examinations were promoted and an attempt was made to compel able officials to serve in neglected locations in the provinces. The administrative and penal codes were revised to ensure uniformity of treatment throughout the empire. Measures relating to supply and taxation were introduced. These included some improvement to the supply of grain to Chang'an and an extension of the system of 'price-regulating granaries' whereby grain was stockpiled for sale when prices were high. However, the most serious problem of the time – how to revise the tax registers so that they recorded all households, including migrant households – remained unsolved.

The most significant reforms concerned the military. Early in the dynasty troops had been recruited through the *fubing* militia system, under which men of good families served on the frontier and at the capital. This system had proved inadequate to deal with the more formidable threats of the eastern Turks, the Qidan and the Tibetans, and by Xuanzong's reign it demanded change. The frontier of the empire was now divided into nine sectors, each headed by a military governor. He commanded a force of professional soldiers capable of responding rapidly to incursions, an arrangement which allowed him considerable freedom of action. The professional forces were supported by military colonies, which supplied them with food and military reserves.

In the middle period of the reign many of these policies were continued under new ministers, but at the same time a change of emphasis occurred. Whereas under the Empress Wu, and in the early part of Xuanzong's reign, many of the chief ministers had passed an examination and might be termed literati, from 721 men of aristocratic background, whose principal qualification was hereditary privilege, increasingly obtained appointments. The political history of the period to 736 has been interpreted as a struggle between these two groupings. The first member of the aristocratic group to achieve prominence was Yuwen Rong, who in 721 had proposed a solution to the problem of unregistered households. His suggestion was that 'runaway households' – that is, the numerous households which had migrated to escape taxation – should be offered an amnesty from arrears of tax. This measure proved remarkably successful and Yuwen Rong was promoted to a number of key positions. Pei Yaoqing, also an aristocrat although he had passed the *mingqing* examination, tackled another chronic problem, the supply of grain to Chang'an. By reducing the distance that grain had to be carried overland, he cut the costs of transportation and greatly increased the quantity of grain available. This enabled Xuanzong to fix his capital permanently at Chang'an, rather than making periodic, expensive and disruptive moves to Luoyang.

In 736 another aristocrat, Li Linfu, rose to power and until his death in 752 was virtually a dictator. Because he was regarded as the enemy of the literati (scholar-officials) and as the author of the misfortunes which accumulated in the closing years of the reign, his name has been execrated. His elevation came after a prolonged struggle with Zhang Jiuling, who had become chief minister in 734. Zhang, who came from the south, was the epitome of the austere scholar-official. Li Linfu, who came from the north west, had risen through intrigue, although the allegations of his lack of scholarship were probably exaggerated. Li Linfu's triumph has been seen as the victory of guile over honesty, but alternatively it has been interpreted as being a result of Xuanzong's desire to establish a strong, centralized and financially sound government, and of his conclusion that he would achieve this better through the ruthlessness of Li Linfu than through the moral injunctions of Zhang Jiuling.

When in sole power Li Linfu acted to improve the efficiency of the administration. Legal reforms were instituted, changes were made to the deployment of military forces and currency reforms were introduced. But from the 740s the emperor, who was 60 in 745, ceased to play an active role in government and became increasingly infatuated with Yang Guifei, the most famous beauty in Chinese history. At court the relations between aristocratic factions became embittered. These circumstances provided the context for the rebellion of An Lushan, which broke out in 755.

LITERATURE AND THE VISUAL ARTS UNDER XUANZONG

The Tang period is often referred to as a golden age in Chinese culture, and the reign of Xuanzong is accounted its high point. The poetry written during that reign was later regarded as a model which all Chinese poets might try to emulate, but could never hope to surpass. An eighteenth-century anthology, the *Three Hundred Tang Poems*, has become a treasury of poems familiar to all educated Chinese.

The composition of poetry goes back a long way in China's literary history. Mention has already been made of the *Book of Songs*, the collection of poems dating back to the Zhou period which became a classic text. Cao Cao, the military leader at the fall of the Later Han, had been a renowned poet. The most famous poet of the period of division was Tao Qian (376–427), whose poems celebrated the pleasures of a simple life in the country. In the early Tang period many poets were closely associated with the court and their poems were written to commemorate events there. However, during Xuanzong's reign a new generation of poets, both men and women, wrote to express their feelings, which had often been aroused by absence or exile. Wang Wei (699–759), who was also a famous painter, was master of a form of brief verse which left it to the reader to complete the sentiment implied. The following poem alludes to the custom of giving a departing traveller a piece of willow.

Willow Waves

The two rows of perfect trees
Fall reflected in the clear ripples
And do not copy those by the palace moat
Where the spring wind sharpens the goodbye.[10]

Li Bo (701–62), sometimes described as China's best-loved poet, was a close contemporary of Wang Wei. He cultivated a reputation for eccentricity and in his poems made use of Daoist metaphysics. In 'My trip in a dream to the Lady of Heaven mountain', he conjured up vivid images of height and depth, of light and darkness:

A thousand cliffs, ten thousand turns, a road I cannot define;
Dazzled by flowers, I rest on a stone and darkness suddenly falls.[11]

Many of his poems refer to the moon and to his love of wine, preoccupations which have been associated with some Turkish influence, perhaps from his father. The legend of his death, that when trying to embrace the reflection of the moon in water he fell from a boat and was drowned, neatly and tragically brought those two preoccupations to a conclusion.

Whereas Li Bo's commitment was to Daoism, Du Fu (712–70), the poet with whom Li Bo's name is forever linked, was a Confucian. Du Fu's failure in the examinations had left him with a lasting disappointment and with a hard struggle for subsistence. The An Lushan rebellion separated him from his wife and children for over a year. In a poem he recalled the moment that they were reunited, by which time his hair had gone white:

And then my son, pride of all my days,
With his face, too, whiter than the snows,

Sees his father, turns his back to weep –
His sooty feet without socks or shoes;
Next by my couch two small daughters stand
In patched dresses scarcely to their knees.[12]

Xuanzong's reign also saw important advances in the visual arts. Wu Daozi (*c.* 700–60), who has been described as the Michelangelo of China, painted Buddhist subjects and transformed 'the essentially sculptured ideals of India into the linear, painterly terms of the Chinese tradition'. Though none of his work survives, the style which he established can be traced in the frescoes at Dunhuang, the Buddhist centre on the Silk Road.[13] Another important advance was in the field of landscape painting. According to the Ming art critic Dong Qichang (1555–1636), it was at this time that the division of landscape painting into 'southern' and 'northern' schools occurred. Artists of the southern school were amateurs and scholars, the best-known early exponent being the poet Wang Wei, who was known for his evocative monochrome paintings of winter scenes. Those of the northern school were professionals and court painters, the most famous of whom were Li Sixun and his son Li Zhaodao (died *c.* 735). A painting entitled *Minghuang's Journey to Shu*, said to depict the flight of the emperor from An Lushan's rebels, preserves the characteristics of their style, which was marked by dramatic mountain peaks and blue-green colouring. From Xuanzong's reign dates perhaps the most famous of all Chinese paintings, *Shining White of the Night*, a depiction of the emperor's favourite horse by Han Gan (*c.* 715–81).

THE TANG WORLD AT THE TIME OF XUANZONG

During the Tang period China's relations with the outside world were transformed. At the beginning of the period only one neighbouring state, Koguryo, could claim to be a stable political unit. By the reign of Xuanzong, China was surrounded by states which, having borrowed culture and institutions from China, now aspired to a separate political identity.

During the Sui dynasty China had recovered control of Annam and in the early Tang period, despite a number of rebellions, Chinese dominance of the region remained secure. North of Annam was the state of Nanzhao, centred on present-day Yunnan, which was ruled by people of Tai origin who had adopted the Chinese language and features of Chinese government. In the eighth century China encouraged the emergence of a unified Nanzhao state, with its capital at Dali, to act as a buffer against the rising power of Tibet.

Tibet itself had become a centralized monarchy and had adopted Buddhism. Song-tsen Gampo (r. 620–49) had initiated a period of sinicization. Thereafter the country began a phase of rapid expansion, challenging China's influence in Central Asia and advancing into modern Qinghai. In 696, during the Empress Wu's reign, a Tibetan army had defeated a large Chinese force less than 200 miles from Chang'an. During Xuanzong's reign Tibetan raiding began again, but now it was China which emerged victorious and in the ensuing peace treaty, Tibet acknowledged Chinese suzerainty and the border between the two countries was defined.

On China's northern borders, political entities were less clearly established. At the beginning of the eighth century the eastern Turks were China's most threatening neighbours. They dominated the steppe region from Manchuria to Ferghana, and their raiding had forced the Chinese to maintain an expensive defence system along the Yellow river. However, the death of the eastern Turk leader in 716, and a subsequent succession dispute, provided the opportunity for the rise of the Uighur empire in Mongolia. The Uighur, who are an important minority in modern China, speak a Turkic-related language. They had formerly been vassals of the eastern Turks, and they now became clients of the Chinese. Up to this time they had been nomadic tribespeople, but with Chinese encouragement they established a capital at Karabalghasun. For the next hundred years, until 840, the Uighur provided China with a reliable ally on the steppe, receiving in exchange enormous benefits in terms of trade and subsidies.

To the north east Koguryo had been absorbed by Silla, and in 676 Korea for the first time became a unified state. Over the next century Silla borrowed heavily from Chinese culture, encouraging Confucian scholarship and introducing competitive examinations. When Koguryo was defeated, refugees had fled to near Jilin in northern Manchuria. In 713 they founded a state known to the Chinese as Bohai, which like Silla was organized on the Chinese model. By this time Japan too had emerged as a unified state. After the reunification of China under the Sui, Japan had begun to adopt many aspects of Chinese culture. In 604 the regent, Prince Shotoku, promulgated the Seventeen-Article Constitution, which set out the principles of government based on Confucian doctrines. The Taiho Code of 702 was based on Chinese legal and administrative practices.

With the emergence of these states on China's periphery, states which had borrowed heavily from Chinese institutions and practices, the 'Chinese dominated east Asian cultural sphere' had taken shape.[14] States which had adopted Chinese culture, and which accepted the superiority of China even though they were independent countries, were treated by China as tributaries. At fixed intervals these states sent tributary missions to China bearing gifts and in return they were rewarded with trading privileges. However, the essential significance of these missions was not economic, but political, as the ceremonial to be performed on these occasions was an acknowledgement of Chinese superiority.

The relationship which developed with the nomadic peoples of the steppe was different in character. The economies of the nomadic and settled populations were in some respect complementary. The relationship evolved over a period of time and varied according to the relative strength of the steppe peoples and of the Chinese state. It took a variety of forms: marriage arrangements, usually with a Chinese princess becoming the bride of a steppe leader; trade agreements; and the payment of subsidies to tribal leaders. If these arrangements broke down, the nomadic peoples might employ what has been described as the 'outer frontier strategy', in which they raided Chinese territory to seize or extort what they required.[15]

While China's frontiers were becoming more clearly defined, the process of Han Chinese expansion within Chinese territory continued apace and the sinicization of the non-Chinese population made stealthy progress. The main movement of Chinese settlers was to the south. The area known as Nan Yue, or southern Yue – that is present-day Guangdong and Guangxi – had been conquered during the Han dynasty, but thereafter the Yue people had recovered their independence. The region was now placed firmly under Chinese control as the Lingnan circuit. To administer the indigenous population the *tusi* system, a form of indirect rule through the appointment of tribal chiefs as officials, was adopted. At the same time the establishment of military colonies in the south encouraged Chinese migration. The region was also used by the Empress Wu as a place of exile for her opponents. As the Chinese community grew, a few southern Chinese achieved distinction in the Tang administration, the most notable example being Zhang Jiuling, Xuanzong's austere first minister.

A similar advance was occurring in what is now Fujian province. Chinese migration to this area dates back to the Han period, but the settlement of the marshy coastal region was impeded by the prevalence of malaria and schistosomiasis. By the eighth century the draining of the marshes and acquired immunity against infection had allowed Chinese settlers to start cultivating wet rice on the coastal plains and to open up the excellent harbour of Quanzhou bay, which by the ninth century had become the main centre of trade with the South Seas.

The Tang empire of the eighth century was the most advanced civilization of its time and its capital, Chang'an, was probably the world's greatest city. The city had a population of about one million living within its walls and another million living in the suburbs. Chang'an was the hub of the empire, served by a network of roads and canals which linked it to the Silk Road to the west and the expanding population of the Yangzi valley to the south. To Chang'an's two great markets came traders bearing exotic goods from Central Asia. Each market was divided into nine sections, and these in turn were divided into lanes, each devoted to a single commodity, such as apothecary supplies, ready-made clothes or gold and silver. Gold and silver merchants also offered a safe deposit service and served as proto-banks. The city's cosmopolitan population practised their religion in numerous religious buildings. In the early eighth century, Chang'an had ninety-one Buddhist monasteries, some of which were very large and extremely wealthy, sixteen Daoist temples, two Nestorian Christian churches and four Zoroastrian shrines. Far to the south, the country's greatest port was Guangzhou, and here too a cosmopolitan mercantile community had assembled, which included traders from India and Persia.[16]

THE REBELLION OF AN LUSHAN, 755–63

Between 755 and 763 the Tang empire was shaken to its foundations by the rebellion of An Lushan. Although the rebellion was eventually defeated and the dynasty survived for another century and a half, it never recovered its former authority or glory. So sweeping were the changes which followed the rebellion that it has been identified as a major turning point in Chinese history.

The immediate causes of the rebellion related to the situation at court and the military arrangements on the frontier. As noted earlier, from the 740s Xuanzong had increasingly left the conduct of government to Li Linfu, while he first immersed himself in a search for personal enlightenment and then became infatuated with Yang Guifei. Although she had some powerful personal connections, she came from a family of modest standing, her father having been a local official in Sichuan. After gaining the emperor's favour, Yang Guifei obtained various court posts for her relatives, including her second cousin, Yang Guozhong, who became a law officer working for Li Linfu. In 746 Li Linfu began a series of bloody purges directed against his critics, and Yang Guozhong used the opportunity to advance the interests of the Yang family. From 749 Yang Guozhong began to intrigue against Li Linfu himself. When the latter died in 752, Yang Guozhong took his place as the most powerful figure at court.

The military situation derived from the division of the frontier into nine sectors, each headed by a military governor. Initially this system worked well, as many of the military governors came from aristocratic backgrounds and were closely connected with the bureaucracy. Some governors made their reputation by waging successful frontier campaigns, which enhanced their reputation and that of the dynasty, albeit at a heavy financial cost. However, in the 740s Li Linfu began to appoint non-Chinese governors, on the grounds that they were better soldiers and had no political ambitions. This gave An Lushan, a professional soldier who was half-Sogdian and half-Turkish, the opportunity to rise to prominence. In 742 he was given the key military governorship of Pinglu in the extreme north east, an area where the leading families nurtured some antipathy towards the aristocracy of the region around Chang'an. His military success in this post ingratiated him with the emperor, and despite his being grossly fat he also became the favourite – and, scandal said, the lover – of Yang Guifei, who adopted him as her son. After Li Linfu's death, rivalry developed between An Lushan and Yang Guozhong. The latter held the military governorship of Sichuan, but otherwise his power base was at the court, and it was there that he tried to drive a wedge between the emperor and An Lushan.

Realizing that he was in danger, in late 755 An Lushan marched south, seized Luoyang and declared the establishment of a new dynasty. For the next eight years the country was plunged into a civil war. After Yang Guozhong had made an ill-judged attempt to recapture Luoyang, the emperor was forced to abandon Chang'an and flee north. During his flight one of the most poignant scenes in Chinese history took place, one commemorated in the famous poem by Bo Juyi (772–846), the *Song of Unending Sorrow*. The commander of the emperor's escort held Yang Guozhong responsible for the disaster and had him killed. He then demanded the death of Yang Guifei and, with immense sadness, the emperor ordered her execution. The emperor fled to Chengdu in the south west and later that year abdicated in favour of his son, who had gone to the north west to rally support. An Lushan was assassinated in 757, but it was only after Xuanzong's grandson, the Emperor Daizong, succeeded to the throne in 762 that the remaining rebels were defeated with Uighur assistance.

The rebellion had a number of immediate and longer-term consequences. Some parts of the country became depopulated, others suffered severe economic and social dislocation and the state's financial machinery collapsed. The north east of the empire became virtually independent and elsewhere provinces fell under the control of military governors. The fall of the capital deeply shocked the Tang aristocracy, some of whom moved to the south. The violence of the rebellion had a lasting impact on the minds of some writers, who thereafter concentrated their intellectual inquiries on the lessons of history. The involvement of the frontier armies in a civil war encouraged the Tibetans to advance and in 763 they briefly captured Chang'an. Although they withdrew quickly, their attacks continued, a sign that the Tang empire was no longer an expanding power, but one which had difficulty defending its frontiers.

The rebellion has been seen as a turning point in Chinese history, although, according to Edwin G. Pulleyblank, it acted more as a catalyst than as a cause of the most profound transformation. In his study of the background of the uprising, he referred to the economic revolution which had taken place in the early Tang period, noting in particular the great agricultural expansion in the south and the movement of population to the Yangzi valley. These changes had undermined the fiscal position of the government and had weakened the authority of the north-western aristocracy. The importance of these changes was revealed by the dynasty's rapid collapse in the face of rebellion. Their longer-term significance was made manifest by the inability of the later Tang rulers to emulate the achievements of their predecessors.

THE POST-REBELLION RESTORATION

From the above it might be supposed that the post-rebellion period was characterized by unremitting dynastic decline. Undoubtedly the central government lost power to provincial regimes, to the extent that the 'Tang regime survived only at the cost of becoming highly decentralized'.[17] However, after the rebellion many of the processes of government continued to operate, significant reforms to the taxation and administrative systems were introduced and a new frontier policy was applied. Only in the ninth century did unequivocal evidence of decline appear.

Some of the most important innovations concerned fiscal reform. During the Emperor Daizong's reign (762–79), an official named Liu Yan tackled the twin problems of supplying Chang'an with grain and improving the dynasty's finances. His solution was to use the profits of the salt monopoly to pay for the maintenance of the canal and the barge fleets. As the centre for salt production was the Yangzi delta and the hub of the transport system was at Yangzhou where the canal joined the Yangzi, this was a neat and practical solution. Some of Liu Yan's reforms were undone by his great rival and successor Yang Yan, who was chief minister under the reforming Emperor Dezong, who reigned 779–805. However, it was Yang Yan who put into general application the most significant tax reform of the age, the 'two-tax system'. This tax consolidated various taxes into one single tax, which was to be paid, in two instalments a year, not only by the peasantry but by all the productive classes. A second purpose of this reform was to restore imperial control over taxation, which had fallen into the hands of the financial specialists of the salt administration and the eunuchs who controlled the treasuries. This system of taxation was to remain in force for the next seven centuries.

As an example of an administrative reform, one might refer to the so-called restoration under the Emperor Xianzong (r. 805–20). Xianzong aspired to regain control of those provinces which had become autonomous, and he was prepared to use force to achieve this. In 806 he sent a punitive expedition to Sichuan which defeated the general who had usurped the command there and replaced him with a governor willing to accept central government direction. He followed this with other military interventions, which secured control of the central provinces but were less successful in the north east. At the same time, he instituted reforms to reduce provincial autonomy in the matter of taxation and to increase the contribution which the wealthy Yangzi provinces made to the exchequer.

The rebellion had completely undermined the Tang frontier strategy. The system of military colonies had been abandoned. China had lost to Tibet the pasture lands from where it had obtained its supply of war horses, and these now had to be purchased at vast expense from the Uighur. They demanded a large annual subsidy for refraining from attacking China. Between 780 and 787 the Emperor Dezong attempted to negotiate a settlement with Tibet, which involved signing away large tracts of territory and agreeing a frontier between the two countries, but the Tibetans would not abandon their long-term ambitions. This situation led Dezong to conclude a formal alliance with the Uighur, which involved the marriage of Dezong's daughter to the Uighur leader and a costly commitment to an annual exchange of Uighur horses for Chinese silk. In return, he obtained Uighur support against Tibet. This alliance was to be the cornerstone of China's frontier policy until the Uighur empire disintegrated in 840.

THE RISE AND SUPPRESSION OF BUDDHISM

Wendi, the first emperor of the Sui dynasty, had used Buddhism to legitimize his right to rule and to provide a common faith for all people of all classes, thus providing a unifying force after a long period of disunion. The early Tang rulers had given their preference to Daoism, but at the same time they had recognized the strength of the Buddhist church, which by now had achieved very wide acceptance and had become a powerful presence within Chinese society.

> By the eighth century, Buddhism was fully and triumphantly established throughout China. Its canons were revered, its spiritual truth unquestioned. It marked and influenced the lives of the humble and the great and affected every community, large and small, in the empire of Tang.[18]

In achieving this level of acceptance, Buddhist doctrine had become sinicized and Chinese Buddhist sects had emerged. The four most influential Buddhist schools in China are the Tientai and Huayan schools, which are best known for their doctrine, and the Meditation and Pure Land schools, which are more significant for their practice.

The Tientai school is entirely Chinese, being based on the teaching of Zhiyi, who established a school at Tientai, the sacred mountain in Zhejiang, late in the sixth century. His teaching centred on a minute examination of the *Lotus Sutra*, and his school offered a doctrine of universal salvation through intellectual inquiry and meditative practice. The Huayan or Flower Garden school had in effect been founded by Fazang, a man of Sogdian descent born in Chang'an in 643. This school categorized the various Buddhist sects into vehicles and claimed that Huayan doctrine combined all that was valuable in each of these vehicles, a syncretic approach typical of Chinese thought.

The Meditation school, known in China as Chan and more familiar to the West as Zen, the Japanese pronunciation of its name, traces its origin to the Indian master Bodhidharma, who arrived at the court of the Northern Wei in about 520. He emphasized the importance of contemplation and his teaching later subsumed elements of Daoism. In the eighth century Chan Buddhism split into a northern and a southern school, the former believing in gradual enlightenment, the latter in sudden enlightenment. The latter school, which stressed intuition rather than intellect, has remained popular to this day. Bodhidharma's influence was also apparent in another field, for when he was abbot of the Shaolin monastery, some 20 miles south east of Luoyang, he was so perturbed by the poor physical condition of the monks that he introduced the Shaolin style of boxing. Another very popular school was the Jingtu or Pure Land School, which claimed that salvation came through faith rather than through good works. It took its name from the Pure Land, or Western Paradise, presided over by Amituofo, and claimed that the believer could reach that land by the frequent repetition of Buddha's name. It popularized the cult of the boddhisattva ('one who is to become enlightened') Avolokitesvara, who became Guanyin, the Chinese goddess of mercy.

Most descriptions of Chinese Buddhism, while readily admitting that the religion has become sinicized, nevertheless convey the impression that it has 'a clear-cut independent tradition different from that of other types of religion'. Erik Zürcher has challenged this and has produced evidence to show that this was the view of Buddhism promoted by its intellectual leaders. In fact, the vast majority of Buddhist monks were barely literate, and at the popular level Buddhism fused with Chinese indigenous religion, readily accepting beliefs and practices such as spirit possession and spirit writing.[19]

Whereas the Sui emperors had found an ally in Buddhism, the early Tang rulers gave their support to Daoism, although at times they found it expedient to conciliate the Buddhist community. Xuanzong took a harder line, failing to grant any of the typical signs of imperial favour, for example the building of monasteries, the mass ordination of monks or imperial participation in Buddhist rites. However, he did attempt to strengthen the link between Buddhist monasteries and the imperial institution by requiring them to commemorate the emperor's birthday and to install images of the Buddha in the likeness of the emperor.

The An Lushan rebellion had a disastrous impact on the Buddhist church. Forced to raise revenue quickly, the government permitted unrestricted ordination for all willing to pay the official fee. As monks were exempt from taxation, this lost the state future revenue, but for the church the more important consequence was the debasement of the quality of the clergy. The rebellion itself brought about the destruction of many monasteries and the loss of many important collections of manuscripts, which caused particular damage to the philosophical schools. On the other hand, Pure Land Buddhism gained in popularity and for the first time achieved recognition at court.

After the rebellion, Buddhism at first received increased imperial patronage. Daizong, convinced that the dynasty owed its survival to Buddhism, supported the construction of many monasteries and authorized the ordination of thousands of monks. He demonstrated his personal piety by venerating Buddhist relics and by sponsoring vegetarian banquets for the clergy. His successor, Dezong, was more cautious in his support, looking with favour on schemes which would reduce the economic burden the Buddhist church imposed on the state. However, he too became a great patron of monastic building and of Buddhist scholarship.

The growth of the Buddhist church had long been the subject of criticism by its opponents, the recurrent theme being the foreignness of its origins and its doctrine.[20] In 621 the Daoist priest Fu Yi had argued that monastic communities were a burden on the state. He urged the emperor to disband the Buddhist clergy and put the monasteries to a better use. Under Dezong, a Confucian official in the Bureau of Records named Peng Yan told the emperor that he should eliminate the abuses within the Buddhist church, citing the ignorance of the clergy, and the loss of tax revenue. He estimated that the annual cost of supplying a monk with food and clothing equalled the taxes paid by five adult males.

When in 819 the Emperor Xianzong had the supposed finger-bone of Buddha brought to Chang'an so that he could worship it, Han Yu, a famous Confucian scholar, presented a memorial in which he stated that he was surprised that the emperor should see fit to encourage Buddhism by greeting the relic, which he described as 'this loathsome thing'. He declared:

> Now Buddha was a man of the barbarians who did not speak the language of China and wore clothes of a different fashion. His sayings did not concern the ways of our ancient kings, nor did his manner of dress conform to their laws. He understood neither the duties that bind sovereign and subject, nor the affections of father and son.[21]

The emperor's reply was first to threaten Han Yu with death, and later to order that he go into exile in the far south.

Although these criticisms had been voiced, it was not until the reign of Wuzong (840–46) that decisive action was taken against Buddhism. Wuzong was strongly committed to Daoism and was said to hate the sight of Buddhist monks. However, there is no evidence to support the allegation that a Daoist pressure group was responsible for his decision. Buddhist historians have often blamed Li Deyu, the authoritarian chief minister, for the suppression. Li Deyu was a committed Confucianist, who shared the scholars' disdain for the excesses of popular Buddhism, although he did not express the outrage voiced by Han Yu. If he was involved in the decision it may have been for political reasons, to curb the power of the eunuch Qiu Shiliang, who was responsible for Buddhist affairs. However, the most compelling reason for the emperor's action, and Li Deyu's support for it, was financial. Since An Lushan's rebellion there had been a severe shortage of copper for the minting of coins. Part of this shortage was attributed to the use of copper in the casting of images and bells and chimes for Buddhist temples. More generally, the Buddhist church was regarded as too wealthy and because of its tax exemption it was considered to be too great an economic burden for the state to support.

The great suppression began with the seizure of the private property of Buddhist monks and restrictions on pilgrimages. It reached its climax in 845, when Wuzong ordered all monasteries to surrender their land and wealth and all monks and nuns under the age of 40 to be laicized. As a result of these measures, some 4600 monasteries and a further 40,000 temples and shrines were destroyed, a quarter of a million monks and nuns were laicized, several million acres of land were confiscated, and sufficient copper was recovered to allow the temporary resumption of the payment of salaries in cash.

THE FALL OF THE TANG DYNASTY

Signs of dynastic decline appeared after 820, when a series of young emperors proved unable to assert their authority over courts which were riven by factional infighting. This often involved the eunuchs, who controlled the imperial palace and were in a position to manipulate the emperor and determine the succession. Their influence even extended to the military, as the emperor relied on eunuch army supervisors to spy on his generals and keep them in line. Through the efforts of Li Deyu, who became Wuzong's chief minister in 840, the fortunes of the dynasty temporarily revived. His decisive action against Buddhism has already been noted. He also took steps to control the eunuchs and to restore the bureaucracy. However, he was dismissed by the Emperor Xuanzong,[22] who came to the throne in 846. The new emperor, or his ministers, did attempt a reform of the grain transport system and the salt monopoly, but the more serious problems went unaddressed. The most important of these were the growth of large landed estates, chronic fiscal problems which the government had attempted to resolve by loading the tax burden on the lower Yangzi provinces, and a deteriorating situation on the frontiers.

The fall of the dynasty came about because of a rising tide of disorder. The first wave of mutinies and rebellions had occurred in the lower Yangzi area during Xuanzong's reign, but these were suppressed. In the 860s the state of Nanzhao attacked Annam and only retreated after a campaign which exhausted the Chinese treasury and prompted another wave of mutinies. One mutinous band was headed by Pang Xun, who led his soldiers back to their homes in the lower Yangzi region, pillaging as they went.

In 874 a disastrous rebellion broke out between the Yellow and Huai rivers, in an area which had been overtaxed and which had suffered from a succession of floods and droughts. Its two leaders, Wang Xianzhi and Huang Chao, were heads of bandit gangs. They have been represented by Marxist historians as fighting for the interests of the peasantry, but this claim is rejected in Western accounts, which argue that they were motivated by self-interest and only became rebels when government forces attempted to suppress them. Wang Xianzhi was killed in 878. Huang Chao then made a dramatic sweep south, during which he captured and sacked Guangzhou. He returned to the lower Yangzi, where he should have been cornered and defeated, but he was allowed to escape and in 880 he captured Chang'an, forcing the emperor to flee to Chengdu. Huang Chao founded a new dynasty, but failed to establish an effective government. The imperial forces rallied, and with the help of the Shatuo, a Turkish tribe, they defeated the rebels and Huang Chao was killed in 884.

Although the emperor returned to Chang'an, the dynasty had collapsed. The imperial writ only ran in the area around Chang'an and even the traditional Tang support in that region had crumbled. To the north, large parts of the country were occupied by non-Chinese forces; in the east, military governors had seized power; much of central and south China had seceded and formed independent states. The final demise of the dynasty occurred in 907 when Zhu Wen, a former lieutenant of Huang Chao and now a military governor, who had already extended his control over a large part of north China, established the Liang dynasty.

3

The Song and Yuan Dynasties

After the fall of the Tang in 907, China experienced another period of disunity. However, whereas after the Han it had taken over three centuries to reconstitute a centralized empire, on this occasion the period of division lasted only half a century. This has been taken as proof of the strength of the political institutions created by the Tang. Despite the frequent changes of regime, the ruling elite remained the same and the personnel of the civil service which maintained the functions of government continued in office. Since that time the expectation that China should be a unitary state has been accepted as the norm and periods of disunity have been viewed as aberrations from that standard.

From 907 to the establishment of the Song in 960, the extreme north east of China was ruled by the Qidan Liao dynasty. The rest of the country was divided into two, the northern section being ruled by a succession of five dynasties and the southern section being fragmented into ten kingdoms. In 960 Zhao Kuangyin, a general from the last of the five dynasties, usurped the throne and established the Song dynasty (also known as the Northern Song). At its height, in the middle of the eleventh century, the Song dynasty ruled over much of China Proper. Part of north-eastern China and Manchuria was the territory of the Qidan Liao dynasty, and from about 1038 the north west, the area of modern Gansu, was controlled by the Tangut Xi Xia kingdom. Early in the twelfth century the Qidan Liao dynasty became involved in a disastrous war with the Jurchen from eastern Manchuria. In 1125 its last ruler was captured by the Jurchen, who had established the Jin dynasty. Qidan survivors fled west and established the Western Liao kingdom in Central Asia, which lasted from 1131 to 1213. In the meantime the Jin dynasty had continued to expand into northern China and by 1127 had confined the Song to the southern half of the country. Now known as the Southern Song, they remained in power there until 1279.

THE FIVE DYNASTIES AND THE TEN KINGDOMS

This complex period in Chinese history was marked by three main developments. The first was the emergence of a new structure of power based on military strength. This development had begun in the late Tang, with the appearance of military governors of provinces, and it was to be carried further after the collapse of the dynasty. As an example of the process one could refer to the career of Zhu Wen, who had first come to prominence as a supporter of the rebel Huang Chao. After capturing Chang'an, Huang Chao appointed Zhu Wen to control a key prefecture to the east of the capital. When the rebellion faltered, Zhu Wen defected to the Tang side and was made military governor of Xuanwu, in the area of modern Henan. During the closing years of the dynasty he concentrated on building up his power base, mainly by creating a professional army which was personally loyal to him. It comprised infantry and an elite cavalry force, the latter provided by the wealthy families who supported him. By 903 Zhu Wen was in a position to dominate the court and in 907 he deposed the last Tang emperor and founded the Liang, the first of the five northern dynasties.

The second important development concerned the situation along China's northern borders. It will be recalled that from the 720s the Tang had relied on the Uighur to stabilize the frontier region. However, the Uighur empire collapsed in 840, and this led to a general disintegration of political authority throughout northern Asia. It was this situation which allowed the rise of the Shatuo Turks. They had formerly been subject to the Uighur, but early in the ninth century some Shatuo tribes switched their allegiance to China and were permitted to settle in Shanxi. Shatuo forces, commanded by Li Keyong, assisted the Tang in the recovery of Chang'an from Huang Chao's rebels. In the closing years of the Tang dynasty the Shatuo allied with the Qidan of Manchuria. Their influence in north China increased and in 923 they defeated the Liang dynasty and established their own dynastic state, to be known as the Later Tang. Although this state only lasted until 937, it expanded to cover a large part of north China, anticipating the future reunification of China. The Later Tang state also set a precedent for the rule by non-Chinese people of Chinese territory inhabited by a majority population of Han Chinese.

The third significant development was occurring in the south. There the fragmentation of political authority was extreme, the region becoming divided into some ten independent states, the Ten Kingdoms. Political weakness may have encouraged development, as regional economies grew rapidly and interstate trade flourished. Because of the persistent shortage of copper, the southern states permitted the use of lead, iron and even pottery for coinage. These have been described as forerunners of a paper currency, and it was at this time that promissory notes or 'flying cash', the immediate ancestors of paper money, began to be used. The kingdoms of the Southern Han and Min (modern Guangdong and Fujian) both expanded their overseas trade. The state of Wu on the lower Yangzi was not only prosperous, but also encouraged a lively literary culture; some of the earliest printed books were produced in this region. The Later Shu state in the area of modern Sichuan became a refuge for former Tang officials, artists and poets, and consciously attempted to preserve the best features of the Tang empire. In these ways the Ten Kingdoms may be said to have contributed to the future success of the Song dynasty.

THE QIDAN LIAO DYNASTY

The ethnic identity of the Qidan is uncertain, as little is known of their language. The most that can be said is that they probably shared a common ancestry with the people called the Xianbei. In the seventh century they had invaded Hebei but had been defeated heavily and forced to submit to Chinese authority. As Tang authority declined, the tributary relationship, which the Qidan had accepted, was replaced by the more aggressive stance of the military governors of the frontier provinces, and this may have been the catalyst for the unification of the Qidan tribes. An ambitious leader named Abaoji emerged who encouraged changes in the Qidan nomadic lifestyle. Chinese captives and refugees were placed in urban centres where trade and manufacturing developed. The Qidan began to farm and to produce cloth, iron and salt.

Abaoji was also a formidable warrior and under his leadership the Qidan made raids deep into Chinese territory. In 905 he reached an agreement with Li Keyong, the Shatuo leader, offering him support against Zhu Wen, and over the next few years the Qidan became embroiled in the struggle between the successor states to the Tang dynasty in north-east China. Abaoji forced the Qidan to accept him not simply as a tribal leader, but as an emperor in the Chinese style. In 907, according to subsequent chronology, he founded the dynasty to be known as the Liao. In 916, having adopted a Chinese reign title, he laid out a capital on the Chinese pattern in the north west of present-day Liaoning. At the same time he built up his personal power base by recruiting a bodyguard composed of warriors from different tribes.

The Qidan now began to expand their territory. In 924 a major expedition was launched to the west and obtained the subjection of the Uighur. Two years later a campaign to the east overthrew the sinicized kingdom of Bohai. Before his death in 926, Abaoji had made it clear that his next objective was north China. In 937, the Qidan intervened in a succession dispute in the Shatuo Later Tang kingdom. The price for intervention was the cession to the Qidan of the strip of Chinese territory known as the Sixteen Prefectures and the recognition by the Later Tang (now known as the Jin) of the suzerainty of the Qidan. In 947 the Qidan invaded Jin territory, and for a few months attempted to rule a vast tract of China, but, realizing their mistake, they withdrew to the north.

The Qidan Liao dynasty ruled part of north China and the territories beyond until 1125. The Qidan method of ruling, which owed something to the precedent set by the Tuoba in the Northern Wei dynasty, has been described as 'dualism'. In the northern territories they preserved many features of traditional Qidan society, and Qidan filled the important military and civil posts. The southern region, which had its capital in the Sixteen Prefectures on the site of modern Beijing, was modelled on the governmental institutions of the Tang. Many of the middle-ranking officials were Chinese who had qualified for office through success in the examinations. Whereas in the north Qidan customary law applied, the Chinese population of the south was subject to Tang codified law. This dualistic arrangement inevitably caused tension between the two halves of the state, which hinged on the extent to which sinicization should be allowed to threaten the separate identity of the Qidan. The Qidan rulers' skill in relieving this tension provided a model for the later empires of the Jurchen Jin and the Manchu Qing dynasties.

THE ESTABLISHMENT OF THE SONG DYNASTY

The Song dynasty was founded by Zhao Kuangyin, later to be known as the Emperor Taizu. He had been a military leader under the Later Zhou, which in its brief existence from 951 to 960 had already made considerable progress towards reunifying north China. Having usurped the throne, he then used a combination of guile and persuasion to obtain the submission of the provincial commanders. Instead of attempting to defeat them on the battlefield, he won them over by offering them honours and pensions. At the same time he created a professional army loyal to the dynasty. Once he had achieved the unification of the north, he proceeded with similar caution to win over the states south of the Yangzi. When he died in 976, all of China Proper, apart from two independent kingdoms in Zhejiang and Shanxi and those parts of China ruled by Nanzhao and the Qidan, had come under Song control.

This process was continued by his brother, the Emperor Taizong (r. 976–97). He obtained the submission of the Zhejiang and Shanxi kingdoms. He also received tribute from the Xi Xia state, which had been founded by the Tangut in the Ordos region, and present-day Gansu. Only in its contacts with the Qidan was the Song dynasty forced to compromise. In 979 Taizong invaded the Sixteen Prefectures, but was defeated near Beijing. After two further unsuccessful campaigns an uneasy truce was agreed. In 1004, after another series of campaigns had led to yet another stalemate, an agreement known as the Treaty of Shanyuan was reached. It confirmed the Qidan claim to the Sixteen Prefectures and carefully regulated the protocol for relations between the two states. The Song agreed to pay not tribute, but an annual 'contribution to military expenses' amounting to 200,000 lengths of silk and 100,000 ounces of silver. This payment has been represented as a heavy burden on the Song state, but it has been argued that the Song more than recouped the cost through increased trade. The subsidy also stabilized the Qidan economy. In short, it was 'a good bargain for both parties'.[1] It has been pointed out that the Song relations with the Qidan Liao 'were the nearest thing to equality in Chinese history until modern times'.[2]

In the meantime, the first Song emperors had been laying the foundations of one of the most famous dynasties in Chinese history. Its capital was situated at Kaifeng on the Grand Canal, a city more readily supplied from the south than Chang'an or Luoyang. Many features of Tang administration were revived in a modified form. Central government comprised a secretariat and a chancellery, which respectively formulated and reviewed policies before presenting them to the emperor for approval. If accepted, the policies were passed to the department of state affairs, which was composed of six ministries, for implementation. The officials at the head of the chancellery and secretariat were recognized as the chief ministers. Military affairs were kept separate from civil affairs and the military affairs bureau reported directly to the emperor. The same was true of the censorate, which oversaw the bureaucracy on behalf of the emperor and which had the power to impeach officials.

The same continuity was evident in Song provincial government. The basic administrative unit was the prefecture, formerly known as the commandery, of which there were about 300. Prefectures were responsible for many of the functions of central government, for example each prefecture had a revenue quota defining the amount of revenue it had to remit to the treasury. However, whereas in Tang times the prefecture had enjoyed a high degree of autonomy, under the Song this was reduced. Military matters became the prerogative of the state and the powers of the prefecture to make appointments or to deal with capital offences were circumscribed. A new level of administration, the circuit, was introduced to oversee the operation of groups of prefectures, an arrangement which anticipated the provincial administration of the late imperial period.

This complex and sophisticated governmental structure was manned by a civil service. A bureaucracy had been in existence since Han times, and in the early Tang period its operations had been rationalized, its chain of command clarified and its importance vis-à-vis the aristocracy and local interests confirmed. It was then that the examination system began to assume the importance it was to bear in the later imperial period. However, in the late Tang and Five Dynasties period the collapse of central authority had allowed wide variations in bureaucratic practice to develop, and the authority of civil officials had become overshadowed by that of military commanders.

Under the Song, recruiting the right type of personnel to the bureaucracy was regarded as an important issue, and three responses to it may be noted. The first was the improvement and expansion of the examination system. Under Taizu, the Tang system of annual examinations, which led to the award of a variety of degrees to a small number of successful candidates, was continued. Under Taizong the number of candidates awarded the *jinshi*, the highest degree, rose from 10 a year to over 140. In response, the number of candidates rose sharply. In 1002, 14,500 men who had been selected as candidates by their prefectures converged on the capital Kaifeng for the *jinshi* examinations. To deal with this rapid growth in numbers several reforms were instituted, which included the incorporation of prefectural examinations into the examination system, the definition of quotas determining how many candidates should pass at the prefectural level, and provisions for impartiality, including the anonymity of the candidates. A second response was to improve educational facilities. Officially sponsored schools had existed under the Tang, both in the capital and in the prefectures, but the provision was very limited. Under the Song, local officials began to establish new schools and to provide them with a set of the Confucian classics, which were now available in print. At Kaifeng the Imperial University, which had originally been reserved for children of officials, was opened to prefectural candidates.

The most striking response to the need to find suitable candidates for public service appeared to run counter to the principle of competitive examinations. This was the revival of the Tang dynasty's use of the *yin* privilege, a system of sponsorship which allowed certain senior officials to nominate members of their family for official appointments. This method of recruitment was justified by a saying of Confucius, 'Raise to office those of virtue and talent whom you know.' Whereas the examination system might produce clever candidates, the sponsorship system emphasized character and the candidate's suitability had to be guaranteed by the official making the nomination.

In the early Song period the bureaucracy was quite small, numbering fewer than 10,000 officials. By the end of the twelfth century that figure had quadrupled. Nevertheless, the examinations and the sponsorship system still produced far more qualified men than there were offices. To deal with this situation there was often a protracted delay between qualification and appointment, and officials might take lengthy career breaks. Two other conventions, which had already been applied in the Tang period, affected appointments: a 'law of avoidance' debarred an official from serving in his own locality, and a system of tenure regulated the length of time an official might occupy a particular post.

Did the bureaucracy of the Song period offer a 'career open to talent'? According to E. A. Kracke, an analysis of the examination lists for 1148 and 1256 shows that nearly 60 per cent of the successful *jinshi* candidates came from families with no history of civil service appointment in the previous three generations. Nevertheless, a candidate needed a wealthy or literate family background to be successful. Certain groups, possibly including merchants and artisans, were excluded from the examinations.[3] According to John W. Chaffee, the early Song emperors, remembering how the Tang rulers had been challenged by the great families, aimed to create a meritocratic state in which the emperor rewarded achievement with office. However, the meritocratic principle was subverted by the spread of learning, which increased the competition and encouraged the imperial clan and bureaucratic families to find ways of bypassing the examination system and so maintain their privileged position.[4] Winston W. Lo has argued that the system of recruitment strengthened the dynasty by creating a body of graduates who came from both the north and the conquered south and who were ideologically committed to the service of the emperor.[5]

One might suppose that a bureaucratic state would be committed to the preservation of the status quo. However, the administration of early Song China was more concerned to rectify what were considered to be the deficiencies of the state, particularly if its record was compared with that of the Tang. The Song empire was much smaller, for it did not control large parts of Inner Asia; even within the Great Wall the territory known as the Sixteen Prefectures was ruled by a Qidan dynasty which the Song had been forced to recognize as its equal. The urge to recover these territories caused the Song to break with the practice of the early Tang period of basing military strength on the recruitment of militia. Instead, the dynasty depended on a professional army of over a million men. It has been estimated that military expenditure consumed 70 per cent of government revenue. This level of expenditure would undoubtedly have caused an early financial crisis but for the efficient revenue-collecting systems in operation and the fact that the emperor also had access to substantial private funds.

The raising of so much revenue was only possible because the economy was expanding. Between the eighth and twelfth centuries China experienced what has been described as a 'medieval economic revolution'. Mark Elvin identified five aspects of the economy which were transformed. The first was agriculture, which supplied the driving force for the other changes. During this period migration south, in particular to the Yangzi valley, and improvements to the techniques of wet-rice cultivation led to a large increase in food output and allowed a doubling of the population. The second important development was a revolution in water transport, with the completion of an integrated system of internal waterways. At the same time, the introduction of technical improvements to ships, including watertight bulkheads and the magnetic compass, facilitated coastal and oceanic voyages. Important changes occurred in the use of money and the availability of credit. Whereas under the Tang a shortage of copper had limited monetary transactions, under the Song copper became readily available and the annual output of copper cash rose by twenty times. At the same time, the use of credit instruments and promissory notes increased. The fourth change was a vast increase in commerce, a result of the linking of the rural economy to the market mechanism. Trade was now carried out not only in luxuries but also in necessities, and a national market developed for some commodities. One consequence of this was an urban revolution, with at least 10 per cent of the population now living in market towns and cities. Kaifeng, the capital, carried out a trade which was valued at nearly 50 per cent more than that of London in the year 1711. Finally, the period saw systematic experimentation, rapid technological advances and the appearance of large-scale industry, for example for the production of iron.[6] These developments led Charles O. Hucker to observe:

> In most respects, eleventh-century China was at a level of economic development not achieved by any European state until the eighteenth century at the earliest.[7]

These developments have been interpreted as the beginnings of capitalism, and such an interpretation immediately poses the question of why this process did not continue and lead to an industrial revolution. Responses to this question often conclude that development was inhibited by particular obstacles. Etienne Balazs pointed out that the key economic and social changes had occurred in the Tang–Song period, when national sovereignty was divided and the power of the state and the scholar-official class was weak. Once the Song had become established, limitations on individual freedom, the lack of laws protecting property, above all the overwhelming prestige of the state bureaucracy, prevented the emergence of a capitalist bourgeoisie.[8] Charles O. Hucker suggested that the complexity of the economy outgrew China's managerial competence. Other writers referred to a shortage of capital, an overabundance of cheap labour, a failure to develop a scientific outlook and the effects of the Mongol invasions.

Albert Feuerwerker has observed that the question which should be addressed is not why China failed to proceed to an industrial revolution at this stage, but why Europe achieved this later. He pointed out that despite the economic achievements of the Song period, the Chinese economy remained at the 'premodern economic growth stage'. The economy was highly productive and the state had developed sophisticated social, political and economic institutions. Europe was to face a different situation. The rise of population which began in the sixteenth century threatened a decline in living standards and this forced an early technological and organizational response. In China the potential of the technology which had been developed by the Song period was not exhausted until modern times, and a response was consequently delayed.[9]

THE REFORMS OF WANG ANSHI

From early in the Song period, scholars and officials proposed schemes of reform to deal with the perceived problems of the day. During the reign of the Emperor Renzong (1023–63), Fan Zhongyan advanced a ten-point programme of reform, which included measures to improve the efficiency of the bureaucracy, to raise the standard of the examinations, to increase agricultural production and to reduce the demands for labour service. Of these proposals only some educational reforms were implemented. Fan Zhongyan is also credited with pioneering the creation of a national school system and introducing anonymity for examination candidates. Another proponent of reform was the famous writer Ouyang Xiu (1007–72), who urged a renovation of Chinese society to bring it closer to the ideal Confucian society of the past. He called on able men to form a 'party' committed to reform. He was, of course, aware that the organization of an opposition was unacceptable in Chinese politics, but he justified his proposal on the grounds that his supporters would be men of principle, whereas their opponents would be men motivated solely by profit.

It was against this backdrop that Wang Anshi (1021–86), China's most famous reformer, took the stage. Wang Anshi, a protégé of Fan Zhongyan, had held a number of official positions in the provinces, and in 1058 had presented to the Emperor Renzong a document known as the *Ten Thousand Word Memorial*. In it he expressed anxiety about the current state of the empire and advocated a series of conventional Confucian measures to remedy the situation, in particular by increasing the number of capable officials available for the service of the state. However, he also made two novel suggestions: that men should be placed in positions for which they had special qualifications, an idea which ran counter to the Confucian ideal that an official should be a man of wide general learning; and that the emperor himself should do more than merely oversee the government, and should actually sponsor a programme of reform. The Emperor Renzong ignored these suggestions, but when Emperor Shenzong (*r.* 1068–85) came to the throne he appointed Wang Anshi his chief minister, a post he occupied until 1076 and reoccupied from 1078 to 1085.

During his first period in office, Wang Anshi embarked on a reform programme to be known as the New Laws. These reforms affected the economy and taxation, security and military affairs, and the administration. He had identified a shortage of revenue as one of the main weaknesses of the state. He therefore proposed a number of novel ways in which revenue might be increased, including the purchasing of surplus products in one area and selling them in another, thereby stabilizing prices and realizing a profit for the state. Another project concerned Sichuan, which up to this date was only loosely incorporated into the empire and only lightly taxed. In 1074 Wang Anshi created the Tea and Horse agency, which established a monopoly over the Sichuan tea industry, and used the tea to purchase war horses from Tibet. The agency was to operate successfully until 1126, when the north of China was lost to the Jin and the supply of horses ceased. Thereafter the monopoly ruined the Sichuan tea industry.

Other measures took account of the interests of the common people. Farmers were offered low-interest loans to enable them to escape from the clutches of moneylenders. As the moneylenders were usually landlords, the intention behind the measure was to reduce the concentration of land-holding and the evasion of taxation which accompanied it. Wang Anshi inveighed against the extravagance of the rich and threatened to take measures to restrict the manufacture and sale of luxury articles. The military reforms aimed to reduce the crippling cost of the army. To achieve this he revived the *baojia*, the age-old system of collective security. Groups of ten households (the *bao*) were to take responsibility for local security and were also to supply men to be trained as a militia. With reference to the administration, his main reform was intended to encourage the promotion of candidates of good character. The exposition of the Confucian classics, rather than the exercise of literary skills, was now the main emphasis of the examinations. To encourage this, Wang Anshi himself composed commentaries on the classics.

Although much of his reform programme fell within the Song tradition of pragmatic reform, Wang Anshi was immediately criticized. Lü Hui, a member of the censorate, attempted to impeach him, alleging that 'Wang Anshi is overbearing in his relations with his associates, and brooks no opposition'. He claimed that he was scheming to get all military and financial authority into his own hands, and that he had commissioned members of his faction to tour the country, ostensibly to devise measures of financial economy but in fact to stir up trouble. Lü Hui's criticism may have been motivated by personal feelings, but other critics challenged the practicality of Wang Anshi's reforms. Su Dongpo, an official who was also well known as a poet and calligrapher, suggested that the offer of low-interest loans to peasants might in future be used to oppress poor households. The outstanding scholar Sima Guang resigned in protest against the reforms and later wrote that the New Laws derived from Wang Anshi's desire to satisfy his own ambitions and that their effect was to oppress the poor.

Sima Guang's attack on Wang Anshi's reputation permanently blackened the reformer's reputation among Confucian scholars. Since his day more sympathetic assessments have been offered. The famous nationalist scholar Liang Qichao noted the resemblance between the New Laws and modern ideals. Marxist historians identified a class struggle behind the political criticism, claiming that Wang Anshi was a member of the bureaucrat-landlord class and came from the south (he was a native of Jiangxi province), whereas Sima Guang came from the big landlord class (whose strength lay in the north). His reforms were supported by the dynasty as a means of containing peasant discontent, but were opposed by the big landlords because they threatened their interests. The Japanese sinologist Miyazaki

Ichisada related Wang Anshi's reform programme to the impetus to reform which had marked the early Song period, and more generally to the transition from an aristocratic to an autocratic society. Miyazaki argued that the reforms, rather than causing the downfall of the Northern Song, had prolonged the life of the dynasty. James T. C. Liu stressed not only the importance of the reforms, but also the significance of their rejection. Wang Anshi had tried to introduce state economic planning and the development of economic resources, while at the same time attempting to curb administrative and fiscal abuses. Although he was suspected of being 'a Legalist in disguise' he was in fact a Confucianist, albeit an unorthodox one. The rejection of his utilitarian policies left the field to an orthodox Confucianism which stressed the moral qualities of the bureaucracy.[10]

Wang Anshi's reforms, and the conservative reaction to them, were to divide the bureaucracy and weaken the dynasty. In 1086, after the death of the Emperor Shenzong, Sima Guang became chief minister and repealed several of the New Laws. However, the Emperor Zhezong, who reigned from 1086 to 1101, appointed Cai Jing, Wang Anshi's son-in-law, to office, and he revived the New Laws, though perhaps without Wang Anshi's high motives. Political opponents were labelled as disloyal and hounded out of government. Cai Jing remained in power under the Emperor Huizong (*r.* 1101–26), who is better remembered as an artist and patron of the arts than as an effective head of state. During his reign court extravagance weakened the state's finances, the bureaucracy continued to grow, corruption increased and other signs of dynastic decline appeared. In 1120 the Fang La rebellion broke out in Fujian and Zhejiang. Fang La, the owner of a plantation of lacquer trees, was incensed by the amount of tax he was expected to pay. The rebellion had secret society links and also had a connection with Manichaeism, a religion which had been brought to China in the eighth century by Uighur merchants. This rebellion, and others which broke out at this time, were the inspiration for the famous novel *Water Margin*.

However, the most serious threat to the dynasty was the rise of the Jurchen in the north. Until the beginning of the twelfth century the Qidan Liao empire had appeared to be relatively stable. The dualistic system of government was cumbersome and poorly organized, and it had not resolved the conflict of interest between the traditionalists of the Qidan aristocracy and sinicized Qidan officials, who aimed to create a centralized, pro-Chinese state. Nevertheless, when Tianzuo came to the throne in 1101 the succession was uncontested and relations with China, with the Xi Xia empire to the west and with Koryo to the east were amicable.

In 1112 Tianzuo visited the eastern part of his empire. Near Harbin he entertained the chiefs of the north-eastern tribes, including the Jurchen, a semi-nomadic Tungusic people who had been subjugated by the Qidan in the tenth century. At the feast, Aguda, the chief of the 'wild' Jurchen – that is, the Jurchen who lived furthest from the Qidan empire – refused to perform the dance which signified the submission of his tribe. His refusal caused a breakdown in relations between the Qidan and the Jurchen. In 1114 Aguda proclaimed the establishment of the Jin dynasty, with himself as its first emperor. Tianzuo seriously underestimated the threat that this implied. Qidan forces were defeated in the field and the Qidan Liao dynasty was shaken by an internal rebellion. Moreover, the Song court had rashly involved itself in the situation by forming an alliance with Jurchen in the hope of dismembering the Liao empire and recovering the Sixteen Prefectures. In 1122 Song troops attacked, but failed to capture, the Qidan southern capital. This gave the Jurchen the opportunity to invade and occupy the entire Qidan territory, and in 1125 Tianzuo was captured and forced to relinquish the title of emperor. Qidan survivors moved west and between 1131 and 1213 they ruled the Western Liao empire in Central Asia.

In the meantime, the situation of the Song dynasty had become critical. Weakened by internal rebellion, it was in no condition to withstand the aggression of the Jurchen Jin empire. In 1125 Jurchen forces invaded China and besieged Kaifeng. Before retiring, they forced the Song to promise them an enormous indemnity. In 1127 they returned, captured and pillaged Kaifeng, and carried the emperor off as a prisoner. Over the next few years the Jurchen tightened their grip on north China and forced the Song court to retreat south of the Yangzi. However, the Jurchen did not have the capacity to conquer the south and in 1141 a peace was agreed between the Jin and Song dynasties, which left the former ruling much of north China and the latter controlling the south of the country. The Song also agreed to pay to the Jin an annual tribute of 200,000 taels of silver (a tael was about 1.3 ounces) and 200,000 bolts of silk.

THE JURCHEN JIN DYNASTY, 1115–1234

The Jin empire at its height encompassed north China, Manchuria and Inner Mongolia. Its history may be divided into three stages: a period of dualism, which lasted until about 1150; a period of increasing sinicization; and from 1215 a period of decline.

Through its conquest of north China the Jin had come to rule about 40 million Chinese, a task for which it had made no preparation. Not surprisingly, the dynasty chose to emulate the Qidan Liao and adopted a policy of dualism. In Jurchen territory north of the Great Wall, the tribal structure was retained and a separate system of taxation was applied. In north China, until a peace was agreed with the Southern Song in 1142, a series of regimes headed by Chinese puppet rulers exercised ineffectual control. Large numbers of Jurchen 'farmer-soldiers' moved south, where they acted like an occupying power, quelling Chinese rebellions harshly and forcibly resettling many thousands of Chinese in Manchuria. Their treatment of the Qidan was even more severe.

In 1150, after a disputed succession, Hailing became emperor and pressed ahead with a policy of sinicization. He established the central capital at Yanjing, present-day Beijing. Having ruthlessly curbed the power of the Jurchen aristocracy, he used the examination system to admit Chinese and Qidan into his service. He himself studied Chinese and adopted Chinese customs such as drinking tea. Nevertheless, he distanced himself from Chinese tradition by sanctioning the public flogging of senior officials at court. His successor Shizong (r. 1161–89) attempted to reverse the process of sinicization by promoting the study of the Jurchen language, which was already falling into disuse, and by prohibiting Jurchen from adopting Chinese dress. However, he too pursued centralizing policies, in particular the adoption of a Chinese form of central government, which employed thousands of Chinese officials and which ran counter to the traditional tribal organization of the Jurchen people. After his death, token Jurchenization was abandoned and sinicization proceeded apace, the ban on intermarriage between Jurchen and Chinese being abandoned in 1191. By then the Jin rulers regarded their dynasty as a legitimate Chinese dynasty which preserved the traditions of the Tang and Northern Song, and this view was shared by at least a proportion of their Chinese subjects. Within the Jin empire, Chinese intellectual activity continued, but it was a conservative intellectualism which rejected the reform ideas of Wang Anshi and his followers.

The collapse of the Jin dynasty was brought about by a combination of internal and external events. In 1194 the Yellow river shifted to its southern course, causing immense damage and seriously affecting the economy. The aftermath of this disaster may have encouraged the Southern Song minister Han Tuozhou to declare war on the Jin in 1206. The Southern Song attack was easily repelled, but it was a distraction at a time when a graver danger had appeared, the rise of Genghis Khan and the threat of a Mongol invasion from the north east. The first wave of Mongol attacks occurred between 1211 and 1213, at a time when the Jin court had been paralysed by a coup. The Mongols also attacked the Xi Xia state to the north west. In response to the disruption caused, the Xi Xia supported a rebellion against the Jin which lost the latter much of north-west China. In 1215, the Jin abandoned Yanjing and transferred their capital to Kaifeng.

Over the next few years the principal threat was a popular rebellion, that of the Red Coats in Shandong. Genghis Khan died in 1227 and there was a brief respite from Mongol raids. However, in 1230 the new khan Ögödei renewed the attack and in 1232 he besieged Kaifeng. The siege, which lasted for over a year, was notable for the endurance of the Jurchen and Chinese defenders, and also because both sides used firearms. The last Jin emperor fled the capital and appealed to the Southern Song for assistance, warning them that if the Mongols were victorious, they would be their next victims. Instead, the Southern Song allied themselves with the Mongols against their Jurchen enemies. The outcome was inevitable; in 1234 the Jin emperor committed suicide and the dynasty came to an end.

THE SOUTHERN SONG, 1127–1279

After the loss of Kaifeng and the capture of the emperor in 1127, resistance to the Jurchen was led by Gaozong, a younger son of the Emperor Huizong, who reigned until 1162. He established his capital at Hangzhou, and gradually reasserted Song control over southern China. Lacking the military power to suppress the separatist movements which had sprung up, he adopted a policy described as 'summoning to pacification', whereby outlaw bands were given the choice of either surrendering and being incorporated into the imperial army, or being attacked and eliminated. Behind this policy was an acknowledgement of the deep shame felt over the loss of northern China to the Jurchen, and the potential strength of loyalist feeling.

Among those who responded to the loyalist cause was a young man named Yue Fei. He played a key role in subduing rebel bands around the Dongting lake in Hunan and then campaigned against the Jurchen, in 1140 raiding as far north as Kaifeng. But then the Southern Song, in the person of the emperor's chief minister Qin Gui, negotiated a settlement with the Jurchen, accepting terms which acknowledged the Song to be vassals of the Jin. These terms gave the Southern Song security and enabled the dynasty to free itself from an unacceptable dependence on its generals. However, many on the Song side regarded the terms as a disgrace. To protect the emperor's reputation, the negotiations were conducted by Qin Gui. He was also to take the blame for the execution of Yue Fei on a trumped-up charge. Yue Fei's true fault was his determination to continue the war of resistance, and for his patriotism he became one of the great heroes of Chinese history.

The desire for revenge against the Jurchen Jin remained a key issue for the Southern Song dynasty. In 1161, the last year of Gaozong's reign, the Jurchen Jin emperor Hailing made an unprovoked attack on Song territory south of the Huai river, but was halted on the Fei river, a battle which became a byword for heroic resistance. Soon after this defeat Hailing was assassinated and in 1165 his successor Shizong concluded a treaty with the Southern Song, which retracted the assertion of vassal status and the use of the term 'tribute', although the Song's annual payments to the Jin continued. For the next 40 years there was an uneasy peace.

Early in the thirteenth century Han Tuozhou, the Song Emperor Ningzong's chief minister, used the issue of revenge to assert his authority. Having heard reports of the damage caused by the Yellow river floods, and believing that the Chinese living under the Jin yoke would rebel if encouraged, in 1206 he invaded Jin territory. The invasion was badly planned, the Jin's Chinese population did not rebel, and the Jurchen replied with a raid deep into Song territory. This disaster led to the dismissal and murder of Han Tuozhou. When peace was agreed in 1208, the annual payments were increased and the Jin demanded and were given Han Tuozhou's head in expiation of his crimes. By now the Mongol threat to the Jin was apparent, yet the Southern Song leaders, oblivious to the danger to their own country, continued to oppose the Jin until that dynasty was extinguished.

Northern Song dynasty emperors had presided over but had not directed the administration, for that was the task of the bureaucracy. The bureaucracy was composed of scholar-officials who in theory governed according to moral principles. The administration was divided into distinct areas, with military and financial affairs kept separate from general administration. If officials failed in their duties they were liable to be impeached by the *yanguan* or 'opinion officials'. Such a system of government was centralized, but not necessarily autocratic, although this was to change in the Southern Song period. Gaozong, the first Southern Song emperor, was diligent if not officious in the performance of his role. Early in his reign he delegated power to a team of ministers who, because of the crisis situation, exercised both civil and military authority. However, in 1139 the ministerial team was dispensed with and Qin Gui became the 'sole surrogate', a chief minister who exercised power on behalf of the emperor. The immediate reason for this shift towards absolutism was the emperor's decision to make peace with the Jin, a decision which stemmed 'not from Confucian principles, but from power calculations'.[11]

This political arrangement was to continue to the end of the dynasty. In 1162 Gaozong abdicated in favour of his son, but until his death in 1187 he remained the power behind the throne. After his death his son, the Emperor Xiaozong, fell into a deep depression and eventually he too abdicated. Recurrent illness was to affect all subsequent Southern Song emperors. Throughout the long reign of the Emperor Ningzong (1194–1224), two chief ministers were successively in control. Han Tuozhou, the nephew of Gaozong's empress, gained office through intrigue and in particular through cultivating close ties with the eunuchs. He conducted a vendetta against moralistic scholar-officials of the neo-Confucian school, who were critical of his lack of formal education. His rash decision for war in 1206 may have been prompted by the domestic political struggle in which he was engaged. His murder in 1207 – he was bludgeoned to death by palace guardsmen – was perhaps tacitly agreed by the emperor. His end was welcomed by the neo-Confucianists, but the circumstances indicated another serious departure from the principles of Confucian government, for whereas an emperor might well dismiss a minister in whom he no longer had confidence, to procure his death by violence was a very different matter.

Ningzong's second 'sole surrogate' chief minister was Shi Miyuan, who gained office after the death of Han Tuozhou. The Shi family, a well-established provincial family from Ningbo in the south east, produced a succession of men who gained office through the examination system. On appointment, Shi Miyuan reversed Han Tuozhou's policies, making peace with the Jin and rescinding the ban on neo-Confucian teaching; all acceptable, if authoritarian, actions. However, when Ningzong died in 1224 he interfered with the succession, setting aside the heir to the throne in favour of his own nominee. The controversy which this caused preoccupied the court at the very time that the Mongols were destroying the Jin empire. Nevertheless, Shi Miyuan remained in office until his death in 1233.[12]

The most notorious of the Southern Song long-serving chief ministers was Jia Sidao, who became chief minister in 1259 and remained in office until shortly before the dynasty collapsed. His posthumous reputation was that of a licentious dilettante who had gained high office through intrigue. In fact, when he was appointed chief minister he had twenty years of experience in a variety of official posts. His notoriety derived from two particular incidents, the first occurring in 1259 when he was accused of treachery for his dealings with the Mongols, who in that year had crossed the Yangzi and were investing the town of Ezhou on the middle Yangzi. According to his accusers, Jia Sidao, having falsely claimed to have gained victories over the Mongol forces, agreed with the Mongols that they should withdraw in return for the Song defining the Yangzi as the frontier and agreeing to pay an annual tribute. However, no agreement was reached on that occasion, and the reason for the Mongol withdrawal was the succession crisis caused by the death of the Great Khan Möngke.

The second incident concerned Jia Sidao's pursuit of radical agrarian and economic policies, reminiscent of the reforms of Wang Anshi. His aim was to counter the increasing concentration of landholding and the evasion of taxation which large landowners could procure. In 1263 he introduced laws which fixed the maximum size for a landed property and provided for the compulsory purchase of excess land-holdings. The revenue from the land acquired by the state was to be used to support the army. These measures remained in force until 1275; some land was confiscated and some revenue was raised for defence. However, the measures also alienated large landowners and others who might have been expected to support the dynasty. By now the Mongols were across the Yangzi and Jia Sidao himself took command of the Song forces. The defeat which followed ensured his fall and the immediate revocation of his laws. Nevertheless, as the Mongols approached, many Song gentry decided to go over to the invaders' side, an ironic confirmation that Jia Sidao was responsible in some degree for the fall of the dynasty.

INTELLECTUAL AND CULTURAL TRENDS UNDER THE SOUTHERN SONG

Whereas the political record of the Southern Song has often been criticized, the intellectual and cultural achievements of the period have long been held in high esteem. Two particular aspects of this achievement will be considered: the emergence of neo-Confucianism, and the development of landscape painting and ceramics.

Neo-Confucianism in its broader sense refers to the Confucian revival, which had begun under the Tang through the activities of Han Yu and others. Under the Northern Song the revival was continued by intellectuals such as Ouyang Xiu, whose call for a renovation of Chinese society has already been noted. This Confucian revival then acquired a political connotation, for its exponents ranged themselves in opposition to Wang Anshi and the reformers, who were likened to the Legalists.

During the Northern Song period, Confucianism extended its range and borrowed ideas from Daoism and Buddhism. Zhou Tunyi (1017–73) used the *Book of Changes*, the five agents and the concepts of *yin* and *yang* to identify the 'Great Ultimate', the principle from which all being derives. Zhang Zai (1020–77) suggested that the entire universe was composed of a single primal substance, referred to as *qi*. These ideas were developed by Cheng Hao (1032–85) and his brother Cheng Yi (1033–1107). The former emphasized the unity of the human mind with the mind of the universe. His writings later engendered the neo-Confucian school of the Mind. The latter adopted Zhang Zai's ideas on the *qi*, but added a second concept, that of *li* or principle, the original nature of all things. His ideas led to the school of Principle. These ideas were later synthesized by Zhu Xi (1130–1200) into a single doctrine, and it was his ideas which later became enshrined in what, according to the narrow definition, is neo-Confucianism. To the metaphysical ideas of the Northern Song philosophers, he added a revived emphasis on the *dao*, the Way that all individuals should strive to follow, and this required a greater emphasis on self-cultivation and a deeper understanding of the Confucian classics. Because of Zhu Xi's emphasis on the Way, his teaching became known as the True Way school. This attracted many devout followers, who adopted archaic rites, old-fashioned styles of dress and strict deportment to emphasize their separateness from conventional career-minded Confucian bureaucrats.

In 1195, soon after Han Tuozhou had become chief minister, the True Way school was condemned as false learning and Zhu Xi, who was briefly in office, was dismissed. However, the ban was soon lifted and after Han Tuozhou's death the True Way school gradually became the orthodox state doctrine. As the Mongol threat increased, and as the Mongols themselves in north China began to adopt features of Confucianism, the Southern Song turned to the True Way (now known as the school of Principle) as true Confucianism. Although neo-Confucianism provided a sense of identity and an integrative ideology which enabled Chinese intellectuals to survive the Mongol occupation, its effects have been described as 'China turning inward'. As a defence mechanism this reinforced belief in Chinese cultural superiority; as a state orthodoxy it threatened to deprive scholars of the right to criticize the growth of autocracy; and as a personal philosophy it elevated self-cultivation above political reform or practical improvement.

This view, that a great transformation of Chinese culture took place under the Song, was criticized by Edward L. Davis in a recent study. He questioned whether the Song elite rejected Buddhism and Daoism as intellectually moribund, and therefore embraced neo-Confucianism, which was henceforth to become the dominant ideology and even synonymous with Chinese culture. In his view this interpretation entirely neglects 'the enormous evidence preserved in the Daoist and Buddhist canons and the miscellaneous writings of Song literati'. He supported his argument with reference to some of the scores of Daoist lineages, such as the Rites of the Celestial Heart, which were active in South China in the twelfth and thirteenth centuries and which became popular among the Song bureaucratic elite.[13]

It has been said of Song painting, particularly of bird-and-flower and bamboo painting, that it reflects the profound and subtle examination of the visible world which is characteristic of neo-Confucianism. Su Dongpo (1036–1101), already referred to as a critic of Wang Anshi, said that when a scholar paints a landscape, he seldom depicts a real place. Instead, he borrows the forms of mountains and trees as a vehicle to express his feelings and his ideas. The value placed on the art of painting is indicated by the attention paid to it by Huizong, the last emperor of the Northern Song, who was both a practitioner of the bird-and-flower style and the patron of an academy of painting. Under the Southern Song, the restrained style of the earlier period was replaced by the more expressive style of painters such as

Xia Gui (*fl.* 1180–1224). Chan Buddhist painting also flourished at this time. It was characterized by a concentration on certain details of the subject, with all else left undefined. The most famous exponent of this style was Mu Qi (*c.* 1200–70), whose painting *Six Persimmons* is well known in the West.

The Tang period had seen important technical advances in the manufacture of ceramics, including the development of porcelain. Under the Song, technical improvement continued and it was accompanied by a very high aesthetic standard. Under the Northern Song, state kilns near Kaifeng produced a variety of high-quality wares, including Ding ware, a white porcelain which was very thin and translucent and which was often incised with delicate patterns. When Kaifeng fell to the Jin some of the potters fled south, for Ding ware was later made in Jiangxi. The best-known Southern Song porcelain is that known in the West as celadon. The very best celadon, which had a greyish-green glaze, came from Longquan in southern Zhejiang. This ware became a major export item, much of it going to Japan.

ECONOMIC AND SOCIAL CHANGES

During the Southern Song period, economic growth continued apace. Agricultural output was increased by the adoption of new seeds, a notable example being the introduction of fast-ripening Champa rice from Vietnam. Irrigation was extended and multiple cropping was used more widely, and as a result in some areas seasonal unemployment almost disappeared.

By the Song period the *juntian* or 'equal field' system had long been abandoned and had been replaced by a free market in land. All modern writers agree that this produced a new pattern of land-holding, but the characteristics of that pattern are disputed. Mark Elvin referred to it as 'manorialism', implying that this was a period of large private estates or manors, worked by tenant-serfs who were bound to the land. Evelyn Rawski, however, claimed that agriculture was dominated by free, small-scale farmers, working under a system of private ownership. More recently, Peter Golas has calculated that at the end of the eleventh century, official and first- to third-rank households, which constituted a mere 14 per cent of the population, owned 77.5 per cent of the land under cultivation, and he concluded from this that large land-holdings made up a very important part of Song agriculture.[14]

Under the Song there was a marked trend towards urbanization. Under the Northern Song, Kaifeng had been the world's largest city. That position was now taken by Hangzhou, the 'temporary residence' of the Southern Song, the city known to Marco Polo as Quinsai. In the thirteenth century Hangzhou, which was both the residence of the court and a great commercial centre, had a population of perhaps two million. It was the hub of China's most important silk-producing region, and its lively commerce encouraged the adoption of increasingly sophisticated commercial methods, for example the use of paper currency. Hangzhou was also a port handling foreign trade. For the first time in China's history, maritime trade became an important part of the economy and tariffs became a significant contributor to the imperial revenue.

Under the Song, and particularly under the Southern Song, a new elite emerged which entirely displaced the aristocratic clans of the Tang period. A key element in the formation of this elite was the expansion of the examination system. What is less clear is whether the examination system had created that new elite and was continually renewing it through the introduction of new blood, or whether the elite had a different origin and was largely self-perpetuating through various means, of which the examination system was only one. According to Richard L. Davis, who studied the Shi family of Ningbo which produced the chief minister Shi Miyuan, the rise of the Shi was the product of examination success. In that system it was difficult for any family to maintain a position of power for long, and for its extended prominence the Shi clan owed much to the longevity of its leading members. However, Robert P. Hymes, who investigated the elite of Fuzhou in Jiangxi during the same period, has argued that the formation of the elite largely occurred independently of the examination system. The elite of the Song period was heavily southern in its origins, and was far more durable than reliance on examination success would imply. This durability was based on the role that elite families had established for themselves in their locality. This finding led Hymes to suggest that during the Southern Song period there was a marked tendency for the elite to shift its attention from the pursuit of office to the consolidation of its home base, and thereby to separate itself from the state.[15]

The spread of printing, and the intellectual ferment which that inspired, has ensured that more is known about Song society, and in particular about the lives of women, than about the society of any previous period in Chinese history. It used to be supposed that under the Tang, women participated in society with considerable freedom, but that under the Song, women's situation took a turn for the worst. This deterioration was exemplified by the spread of foot-binding and the condemnation of the remarriage of widows. To explain this decline, reference is made to neo-Confucianism, alleging that Cheng Yi and Zhu Xi promoted the idea that women must value chastity. This view has been challenged by Patricia Buckley Ebrey, who has pointed to the contradictory evidence that women had particularly strong property rights during the Song period. She noted the spread of foot-binding, but warned that to assume that it implied the subjection of women was anachronistic, for the evidence suggests that it was adopted by women to promote their attractiveness. Southern Song culture encouraged men to bookishness, to reinforce the contrast with the martial virtues of the Jurchen and Mongols. In turn this favoured a stereotype of women as beautiful and deferential. Foot-binding was originally associated with dancers, and then more generally with courtesans and concubines. It was to allow other women to match this claim to beauty that foot-binding came into general use. As for the remarriage of widows, there was certainly a strong popular prejudice against this, although the law allowed a woman to remarry. However, Ebrey argues that this prejudice has been misunderstood in modern times. During the Song period a marriage was about how families perpetuated themselves through the incorporation of new members. A man was incorporated at birth, a woman at marriage. If a husband died and the woman remarried, she renounced her loyalty to the family into which she had been incorporated.[16]

Ebrey's interpretation in part derived from the appearance, in 1987, of a new edition of a collection of Southern Song legal documents known as *The Collection of Lucid Decisions by Celebrated Judges*. Several cases in this collection suggested that a daughter had a legal right to a share of property half the size of a son's share. If this were the case, the property rights of daughters in the Southern Song were stronger than at any time in Chinese history before the twentieth century. However, Kathryn Bernhardt has argued that either the half share did not exist in law, or it was highly anomalous and had no impact. Therefore, the change after the Song was much less dramatic than Ebrey would have us believe. Another view was expressed by Bettine Birge, who noted the contrast between women's property rights and Confucian patrilineal ideals (that is, a man had to be succeeded by a son for ritual as well as for property purposes). This contrast, she argued, was at its most extreme under the Song dynasty, with daughters receiving a half share of property – an arrangement which made widow remarriage extremely attractive. These developments were deplored by neo-Confucianists such as Zhu Xi, and were also in conflict with traditional Mongol law, which attached property to the male line even more firmly than did Chinese law. The combined effect of these two influences caused a sharp curtailment of women's property rights after the fall of the Southern Song dynasty.[17]

Neo-Confucian philosophy also redefined Chinese child-rearing culture. Now acquiescence and quietness were emphasized and pets and outdoor games were forbidden. Indoctrinating literature was produced, such as *Words for Little Children* and *Words for Little Girls*, and teaching materials reinforcing these virtues were produced.[18]

THE MONGOL CONQUEST

The traditional view of Mongol rule over China was that it was an unmitigated disaster. Hongwu, the founder of the Ming dynasty, claimed that one of his aims was to restore the integrity of Han Chinese civilization, which had been partially despoiled during the Yuan period. Three particular charges have been levelled against the Mongols: that they discriminated against the Chinese both racially and economically; that they failed to build on the technological and economic achievements of the Song period and so contributed to the introverted and non-competitive position adopted under the Ming; and that they instituted practices – the example given is the public flogging of ministers – which contributed to the development of despotism. However, some modern historians have suggested that whereas the Mongol invasion of China caused extensive damage, the period of Mongol rule did have some positive features. The Mongols reunified China, and their adoption of the dynastic title 'Yuan' and other practices of a Chinese dynasty entitled them to a place in the Chinese dynastic record as legitimate holders of the mandate of heaven. Chinese civilization was not fundamentally altered by the episode of Mongol rule and in several ways scholarship and the arts benefited. Moreover, in some respects Mongol rule was more humane and less ideologically restrictive than that of the Song. The *pax mongolica,* the 'Mongol peace', which spread across Asia, exposed China to a wide variety of external influences. At a personal level, the hostility of Chinese for Mongol was not so intense as to prevent many Mongols remaining in China after the flight of the Mongol court.

The Mongols were pastoral nomads who, by the late eleventh century, were living as a tribal society in present-day Mongolia. Already accomplished warriors on horseback who were in frequent conflict with the Tatars, their neighbours to the west, the Mongols now began to develop an ethnic consciousness. This political situation was exploited by Temujin, the son of a tribal leader, who was born in about 1167. According to *The Secret History of the Mongols,* his father had been poisoned by the Tatars and this grievance motivated him to claim the leadership of his tribe. He raised a disciplined army divided into groups of 1000 men and devised new military tactics. This enabled him to unite the Mongol tribes and in 1206 he was acclaimed Genghis Khan, the universal sovereign of the steppe peoples. He claimed to be heaven's chosen instrument and declared that all who stood in his way did so in defiance of heaven's will.

Genghis Khan then embarked on a remarkable sequence of conquests. In 1210 he invaded the Xi Xia kingdom and forced it to pay him tribute, thereby cutting China's trade routes to the north west. In 1215 he captured the Jin capital at Yanjing, but instead of destroying the Jurchen dynasty he turned west and seized Bokhara and Samarkand. In the meantime he began to recruit Chinese and Qidan officials and appointed Mukhali, one of his most reliable generals, to administer the Chinese territory which he had occupied. In 1226 he turned to destroy the Xi Xia kingdom, but died during the campaign. He was succeeded as khaghan, or khan of khans, by his third son Ögödei, and the Mongol Empire was divided between his sons and grandson. Ögödei continued the conquests, invading Korea and in 1234 completing the destruction of the Jin dynasty. In the west, Mongol forces overcame Russia and inflicted devastating defeats on the states of eastern Europe. Only Ögödei's death in 1241 halted this extraordinary expansion.

After the conquest of north China, the Mongols looked for ways to exploit their gains. A famous anecdote tells how a Mongol nobleman suggested that the entire population should be annihilated and the region turned over to pasture. This led Yelüchucai, a sinicized Qidan in Mongol employ, to propose as a more effective means of exploitation the granting of an amnesty to those Chinese who had unwittingly broken Mongol law, the establishment of a new administrative system and the creation of bureaux to organize regular tax payments. Ögödei rejected the entire reliance on sinicized officials and granted licences to Central Asian Muslims to farm taxes, thereby undermining Yelüchucai's fiscal strategy. Later in Ögödei's reign, Yelüchucai's hope of restoring a form of Confucian rule to north China was further undermined when the khaghan awarded large landed estates to the Mongol princes and princesses. Ögödei drank himself to death in 1241 and his widow became regent. It was not until 1251, when Möngke became khaghan, that Mongol expansion resumed. Rather than make a direct attack on the Southern Song, Möngke decided to outflank them and in 1252 he ordered his brother Khubilai to attack and destroy the south-western kingdom of Nanzhao, which the latter had achieved by 1254. Möngke's next objective was the province of Sichuan, but he died in 1259 while pursuing that campaign. Once again, a succession dispute delayed a decisive Mongol assault on China.

Möngke had entrusted the administration of north China to his younger brother Khubilai, who had shown a willingness to accept advice from Confucian advisers and to promote the prosperity of the region. In May 1260 he was elected khaghan and shortly afterwards adopted a Chinese reign title. His chief Chinese adviser, a former Buddhist monk named Liu Bingzhong, supposedly repeated the old observation: 'Although the empire had been conquered on horseback, it could not be administered on horseback.' It was with his encouragement that Khubilai laid out a Chinese-style capital at Kaiping in Inner Mongolia. Later renamed Shangdu or 'upper capital', it became known in the West as Xanadu.

As emperor of China, it was inevitable that Khubilai would at some point resume the assault on the Southern Song, who continued to assert their claim to the entire country. By 1268 he was ready to attack, his first objective being the key city of Xiangyang on the Han river. For this campaign Khubilai had to obtain ships and engineers proficient in siege warfare. After a five-year siege, in which the Mongols used a large mangonel to batter down the walls, the city surrendered and the route to the Yangzi valley was clear. In 1275 Bayan, the leading Mongol general, met and defeated a large army led by Jia Sidao, the last chief councillor of the Southern Song. Jia's land policies had already alienated wealthy landowners and this defeat ensured his dismissal. Song resistance now collapsed and the Song court surrendered. However, it was only in 1279 that the last Song loyalists were defeated at sea and the last Song emperor drowned.

CHINA UNDER MONGOL RULE

Although Khubilai had triumphed in China, his other military ventures were less successful. Twice, in 1274 and 1281, he attempted to invade Japan, but on both occasions was driven back by fierce Japanese resistance and bad weather. On the second occasion a typhoon, referred to by the Japanese as *kamikaze,* a 'divine wind', caused the destruction of half the Mongol force. Campaigns in South-east Asia took the Mongols into terrain in which their military skills were of little value and they suffered disastrous reverses. These failures, ill health and the death of his favourite wife cast a shadow over Khubilai's final years. He suffered further from difficulties over the succession, which was to prove a chronic problem for Mongol emperors. Whereas the Chinese practice was for the emperor to nominate one of his sons to succeed him, Mongol custom prescribed that the political succession should go to whichever of the khaghan's male relatives was acclaimed at a council of notables. Khubilai, as emperor of China, attempted to follow Chinese custom and nominated Zhenjin, his eldest son by his principal wife, as his successor, but Zhenjin died in 1285. When Khubilai himself died in 1294, it seemed that he had bestowed the succession on his second son Temür, but this was contested by his eldest surviving son. The rivalries engendered by this dispute were reawakened every time a Mongol emperor died, and were a significant factor in the decline of the dynasty.

Temür, who reigned from 1294 to 1307, continued many aspects of Khubilai's rule. His successor Khaishan, who came to the throne after a violent conflict, spent lavishly and acted arbitrarily. He in turn was succeeded by his brother Ayurbarwada, perhaps the most sinicized and cultured of the Mongol rulers, who ruled as the Emperor Renzong from 1311 to 1320. After his death the court split into factions, divided partly by the struggle for the succession between the two lines of descent from Khubilai and partly by the stand taken towards sinicization. In 1323 Yesun Temür, a man hostile to the influence of Chinese scholar-officials, seized the throne and held it until his death five years later. After an even more savage succession dispute, Tugh Temür, a man regarded as committed to China rather than to the steppe, held the throne for another five years. The last Mongol ruler, Toghon Temür, came to the throne as a minor in 1333, and survived until the Mongol court fled from China in 1368.

Khubilai established the pattern of Mongol rule over China. In 1272 he adopted *Da Yuan*, or 'Great Origin', as the title of his dynasty and established its claim to be a universal empire. He retained many superficial features of Song government, for example the secretariat and the six ministries, and the traditional division between the civil, military and censorial branches of government. He adopted Chinese court ceremonial and Confucian rites and even set up an office to collect materials for a history of the preceding dynasties. However, Khubilai declined to restore the examination system, on the grounds that it might restrict his choice of officials to those who had a knowledge of the Confucian classics. Officials were selected with reference to birth and the *yin* privilege. Although Yuan government appeared to be highly centralized, even under Khubilai the direct authority of the central government did not run much beyond the metropolitan province (known crudely as 'the guts'), which comprised north-east China and Inner Mongolia. As Mongol armies pacified the rest of the country, 'branch central secretariats' were created in eleven other provinces. The authority of the emperor was paramount in these provinces and he appointed all the senior officials. This tendency towards regionalism was to become even more marked under Khubilai's successors.[19]

One of the most notorious of Khubilai's actions, in Chinese eyes, was his division of the population into four groups: the Mongols at the top of the social pyramid; below them the *semu ren,* that is miscellaneous aliens, a reference to Western and Central Asians; then the *Han ren*, the inhabitants of north China; and finally the *nan ren*, the Chinese of the newly conquered south. Although the division between these groups was not as rigid as may have been intended, it clearly discriminated against the Chinese. Despite this discrimination, some Chinese scholars were prepared to accept office. Before the conquest of the south, Khubilai had employed a number of Chinese advisers, including Xu Heng, a notable neo-Confucian scholar, who thought that the duty of a scholar was not to shun the Mongols but to civilize them. Khubilai had been persuaded to establish a history office by the historian Wang E, on the grounds that the history of previous dynasties provided models for the present which all great emperors had found it prudent to observe. The bureaucracy was ethnically very mixed, and because no metropolitan examinations were held for 40 years, the opportunity existed for educated men to work their way up to a salaried official position. When in 1315 the Emperor Renzong permitted the reintroduction of examinations, it was in a form which was heavily weighted in favour of Mongol candidates.

To counterbalance Chinese influence in government, Khubilai and later Mongol emperors employed many foreigners in key positions. The largest and most influential group were the Turks, a group which included the Uighur, a significant number of whom were employed as top-ranking officials. They provided an infrastructure between the Mongols and their Chinese subjects. An important religious role was performed by Tibetan Buddhists. A Tibetan monk, 'Phags-pa, was placed in charge of all Buddhist clergy and advised on relations with Tibet. In return, he identified Khubilai as the universal emperor of the Buddhist tradition. Throughout the Yuan period, Tibetan Buddhism or Lamaism was granted a privileged status, and this became a source of complaint among Chinese, particularly in the south. In 1285 a Tibetan or Tangut lama named Yang, who had been made responsible for Buddhist teaching south of the Yangzi, caused particular offence by breaking open the tombs of the Song royal family and using the treasures obtained to restore Buddhist temples.

The early Mongol emperors employed a significant number of Muslims, many of whom came from Central Asia, in key positions in China. Islam was not new to China, for it had been introduced in the Tang period and Muslim traders had settled in Guangzhou and other southern ports. Islam had also made converts among the Chinese in Central Asia. However, the engagement of foreign Muslims rather than sinicized Turks and Tibetans was a distinct departure from dual government as practised by previous dynasties of conquest. Muslims in China were classified as *semu* and were granted special privileges. They performed a wide variety of specialized tasks, particularly in matters of finance, but also in the fields of medicine, astronomy and architecture, although they were excluded from the higher ranks of the armed forces. While Muslims did not play a major role in the administration of China, there was one notable exception in the case of Saiyid Ajall, a Central Asian Muslim who was appointed governor of the newly conquered territory of Yunnan.

The most notorious Muslim was Ahmad who, from 1262 until his death in 1282, directed Khubilai's state financial administration. His principal task was to boost state revenue and he did this by increasing the number of households liable to pay tax and instituting profitable state monopolies on tea, liquor, vinegar, gold and silver. Ahmad also encouraged the overland trade between China and Central Asia. Much of this was financed by merchant associations known as *ortogh*. This trade was profitable to the government, for all merchants on reaching China were required to exchange precious metals for paper currency. The *ortogh* were also a source of loans for the Mongol nobility. In return for their services, *ortogh* merchants were given a preferential position when raising capital to finance trade caravans.

Although Khubilai used Muslims in high office, he was aware of Chinese hostility towards them and he grew concerned about their increasing influence. Ahmad's Chinese critics accused him of nepotism, exploitation and profiteering. From 1279 Khubilai adopted a harsher policy towards Muslims and in 1282 he may have been implicated in the murder of Ahmad by Chinese conspirators.

The *pax mongolica* and the increase in trade along the Silk Road enabled the establishment of the first direct contacts between China and the West. For most early travellers the motive was trade, but some had a political objective, to seek allies at a time when Islam was seen as a threat by both Mongols and Christians. For some, proselytism was the prime purpose of their journey. The first European to place his journey to China on record was a Franciscan monk, John of Plano Carpini. He had been sent by Pope Innocent IV and the Holy Roman Emperor to seek an agreement with the Mongols and to convert them to Christianity. He failed on both counts, but he left a record of his travels which included a description of the enthronement of Güyüg Khan in 1246. Guillaume Boucher was one of several European artisans who were employed by Möngke Khan in the 1250s.

In about 1265, soon after he had become emperor of China, Khubilai received two Venetian merchants, the brothers Maffeo and Niccolo Polo. They returned to the West in 1269, having been commissioned by Khubilai to ask the Pope to send 100 Christian scholars to China. In 1271 they set out for China again, without the scholars but with Niccolo's son Marco. Marco Polo's *Travels*, written or dictated by him after his return to Europe twenty years later, contained a detailed description of Khubilai's court, of north China or Cathay as it was then known to Europeans, and of the great city of Hangzhou, which he called Quinsai. Some features of Marco Polo's book, for example his failure to describe the Chinese mode of writing or to mention the Chinese habit of drinking tea, have aroused suspicion about the authenticity of the text and the question has been raised whether he actually reached China. The book certainly contains some false claims, for example the statement that Marco Polo advised the Mongols on the capture of Xiangyang, whereas the city had fallen to the Mongols two years before he reached China. However, Marco Polo's detailed reference to the naval expedition which conveyed the Mongol princess Kokecin from China to Persia has been cited as clear evidence of his participation in that event.[20]

In 1287 Rabban Sauma, a Turk born in China, reached Naples and subsequently had audiences with Philip IV of France and Edward I of England. In 1295 another Franciscan monk, John of Montecorvino, reached Khanbalik, the Mongol capital, and was allowed to establish a Christian mission which survived for fifty years. Another Franciscan, Odoric of Pordenone, wrote a narrative of his travels which became the source of many of the Western stereotypes about life in China.

In Chinese eyes the period of Mongol rule was one of damage to the economy and a decline in Chinese living standards. A puzzling piece of evidence to support this view concerns the demographic record. According to taxation figures, the combined population of Song and Jin China amounted to well over 100 million, but according to the census carried out in 1290, which excluded Yunnan and other areas and did not enumerate several categories of people, it was less than 60 million. So large a discrepancy led Frederick W. Mote to assume that there was a catastrophic reduction in China's population between 1200 and 1400, the most extreme in the history of China'.[21] This population decline has been attributed in the first instance to the Mongol invasion of the north, to the confiscation of land for distribution to the invaders and the application of heavy taxation to those Chinese who retained their land. This precipitated a wave of southward migration, although the depopulation of the north was not balanced by a population increase in the south. The Yuan dynasty also stands accused of sins of omission and commission in its subsequent management of the economy. The consequence of its failure to maintain river defences finally became evident with the massive flooding of the Yellow river in 1344.

Mongol extravagance had first been demonstrated by the building of the summer residence at Shangdu, which contained a magnificent marble palace. In 1266 Khubilai ordered the construction of a new capital at Dadu (otherwise Khanbalik, the city of the khan) near modern Beijing, and the cost of this project placed a heavy burden on the treasury. Financial problems were exacerbated by instances of official corruption. Paper money had been introduced under the Song and Khubilai extended its use to promote trade. At first this currency, backed by a silver reserve, proved a success, but in 1276 the number of paper notes in circulation was greatly increased to finance the conquest of the south. This was the beginning of a loss of confidence in paper currency, and by the beginning of the Ming period it had become entirely discredited.

Such a presentation of Mongol handling of economic affairs is certainly one-sided. Khubilai quickly recognized the need to restore the devastated economy of north China. Impoverished areas were granted tax concessions and villages affected by natural disasters were given assistance. In 1261 he established an 'Office for the Stimulation of Agriculture', which helped peasants to make the best use of their land. Khubilai also endorsed the existence of peasant self-help organizations which promoted irrigation and land reclamation. He encouraged internal trade and greatly improved the postal relay system. After the conquest of the south, measures were introduced to relieve areas affected by the war. Large landowners were allowed to retain their land and the land-tax burden was relatively light. The encouragement of maritime commerce was also beneficial to the region. Later in Khubilai's reign the Japanese campaigns and ambitious attempts to improve the canal network to facilitate the supply of grain to Dadu imposed further heavy burdens on the treasury, but it was still possible to conclude that Khubilai left his successors 'a stable and generally prosperous state'.[22] Later Yuan emperors were less proactive in economic matters, and Ayurbarwada in particular has been cited as reverting to the Confucian ideal of cutting government expenditure and lightening taxation, while doing little to encourage economic activity. As a consequence, and perhaps advantageously to them, the large landowners of the south were largely left to their own devices.

Another aspect of Mongol rule, which in Chinese eyes amounted to discrimination, related to legal matters. Whereas the Mongols had brought with them the *jasagh*, the collection of rules promulgated by Genghis Khan for the regulation of a nomadic society, the Chinese were accustomed to statutory law as codified under the Tang. Under the Yuan, Mongols and *semu ren* were tried according to Mongol law, while Chinese were tried according to Chinese law. Critics of this arrangement pointed to differences in punishment for the same offence, and in particular to the provision that a Chinese offender should be tattooed as well as receiving the prescribed punishment for his crime. However, tattooing (to identify a criminal) was not a Mongol innovation, for the provision already existed under Song law. Legal cases involving both Mongols and Chinese were dealt with in special courts, and in these actions Mongols did have some advantages; for example, marital disputes involving a mixed marriage were normally adjudicated according to the law of the husband unless the wife was a Mongol, in which case Mongolian law applied. A further example of discrimination which has been quoted concerns the prohibition of a Chinese retaliating if assaulted by a Mongol. However, this example is misleading, as the law elsewhere provided the Chinese with a legal remedy for the injury.

The Mongol emperors, beginning with Khubilai, sought to preserve their Mongol inheritance. Mongol religion, a form of shamanism, was retained and Khubilai performed its traditional rituals, for example scattering mare's milk. No attempt was made to impose Mongol religious beliefs on the Chinese and the Yuan period was notable for its religious freedom. Möngke and later Khubilai encouraged open debate between Buddhists and Daoists, who were currently involved in bitter rivalry. In 1281, after having invited eminent Buddhist and Daoist scholars to court to debate their religious claims, Khubilai decided that the Buddhists had won the contest and that Daoist excesses should be curbed.

The Mongol attitude towards Confucianism was more circumspect. Khubilai's ignorance of written Chinese debarred him from a proper understanding of the Confucian texts; not until Ayurbarwada came to the throne did a Mongol emperor have a working knowledge of written Chinese. Nevertheless, Khubilai recognized the importance of Confucianism and he employed Confucian officials and promoted the translation of the Confucian classics into the Mongol language. Ayurbarwada went further in modifying the Mongolian character of the state, but the Confucian elements which were now incorporated remained superficial features. Early in Toghon Temür's reign effective power was held by his chancellor Bayan,[23] who, to the dismay of Confucian scholars, attempted to turn the tide of sinicization by abolishing the examinations as a route of entry into the civil service. Bayan was overthrown in 1340 and thereafter, until the fall of the Yuan, Confucianism recovered some of its ideological preeminence and the restoration of the examination system offered not only to Chinese, but also to Mongols and *semu*, a common objective and a commitment to a unified state.

In the Yuan period Confucian scholars were therefore placed in a dilemma. Some, such as Xu Heng, whose name has already been mentioned, reasoned that their Confucian duty required them to serve the Mongols. Wang Yun (1227–1304), author of a book which offered advice on the actions to be expected from a model ruler and was translated into Mongolian, achieved the same effect by different means. But other scholars refused to condone the Mongol presence and would not accept office. A notable example was Liu Yin (1249–93), who in 1291 refused an invitation to become an academician at the Imperial College. His feelings were revealed in a poem, part of which read:

> The streams and hills now shelter thieves and bandits;
> The fields are now abandoned to brambles and thorns.
> Our heritage is a burden of moral obligations,
> But we lack a ruler who grieves at committing murder.[24]

Liu Yin's refusal to commit himself to public service has been seen as an example of 'Confucian eremitism', a withdrawal of Confucian scholars from worldly affairs as a protest against Mongol rule.

Another form of protest has been identified in drama. Drama as a form of popular entertainment had emerged in the Tang period, and plays and sketches were commonly performed under the Song, but it was not until the Yuan period that plays as a distinct literary form appeared. These plays, known collectively as the 'Yuan northern drama', were mainly written for performance in Dadu, but the theatre also became popular in the south. Their popularity may be linked to the development of a sophisticated urban culture. It has also been suggested that their appearance was connected with the exclusion of Chinese scholars from government employment and with the consequent diversion of their energies into other fields. Some left the world of public affairs to become 'Confucian eremites', others earned a living and found a spiritual outlet in the world of popular entertainment. Allegedly the plays they wrote contained protests against the Mongol presence and the popular response to their productions contributed to the collapse of the Yuan dynasty. This interpretation has not stood up well to critical evaluation, however. The Yuan northern drama evolved from earlier dramatic forms to which both Chinese scholars and professional writers contributed. The popularity of the theatre in the Yuan period owed a lot to Mongol patronage. Few plays contained overt political criticism and the fact that plays were written in the vernacular, and hence comprehensible to Mongols, made the claim of a subversive intent implausible.

THE FALL OF THE YUAN DYNASTY

Traditional Chinese explanations of the fall of the Yuan emphasized the persistent Chinese hatred of the invaders and the Mongols' failure to modify their rule to meet Chinese expectations. It was therefore only a matter of time until a combination of dynastic decline and righteous rebellion would bring about the collapse of the dynasty.

In the early Ming period and in more recent years, a rather different interpretation has been proposed. This suggests that under Khubilai and his immediate successors the Mongols devised an effective, and to an extent acceptable, means of ruling China, and that Mongol rule might have persisted for much longer but for a sequence of disastrous events occurring in the 1350s and 1360s which undermined the dynasty.

For two reasons the long-term survival of the Yuan dynasty was doubtful. The first concerned the military superiority of the Mongols, which at the time of the conquest of the south had been a decisive factor, but which did not last the span of the dynasty. Whereas the Chinese military tradition was one of conscripted forces, the Mongols were accustomed to military status being hereditary. Soon after the conquest of the south, they divided all the military forces in China into four: the Mongol army, the Mongol and associated nomadic forces used to garrison conquered areas, the Chinese and Qidan forces from north China, and the 'newly adhered' Chinese forces from the south. The first three categories were provided with plots of land and slaves (often war captives), were given tax concessions and were expected to be self-sustaining. Each Chinese military household was required to provide one soldier, but in the Mongol households virtually all adult males performed military service. This system soon proved to be impracticable, for many of the slaves ran away and Mongol households could not subsist on their own by farming. As early as the 1290s there were reports of impoverishment and a decline in military standards. By the 1340s many Mongol military households were no better off than poor Chinese peasants and the garrison system, created to repress internal disturbances, had almost ceased to function.

The second reason concerned the extent to which the Mongols were prepared to become sinicized. Khubilai had presented himself as a Chinese emperor and none of his successors entirely rejected that role, though some of them were more willing to accept it than others. At first the Mongols had ruled China as a subordinate part of a Mongolian empire, but from 1307 that situation was reversed and the Mongolian steppe was being incorporated into China. From 1328 there began a process of thorough Confucianization of the government and increasing patronage of Chinese culture. Nevertheless, in other respects all the Mongol emperors refused to allow themselves to be absorbed into Chinese culture. They treated their empire as a feudal patrimony and rewarded their relatives and retainers with hereditary privileges, a form of advancement incompatible with the Chinese bureaucratic system. As a consequence by the time of Toghon Temür, the last Yuan emperor, the Yuan state was 'a state whose roots in Chinese society, though deep, were still not deep enough'.[25]

The crisis which was to overwhelm the Yuan dynasty began in the 1340s with the outbreak of local rebellions, with the rise of piracy which threatened the shipment of grain to the capital by sea and with the flooding of the Yellow river. In 1351 the emperor called on Toghto, a young and able man who had previously served as chancellor, to return to office and deal with the situation. Toghto took steps to increase revenue, control the floods and suppress the rebels, at first with some success. He embarked on an ambitious project to reopen the Grand Canal, which had silted up, drafting in thousands of peasants as labourers, but this in turn aroused a new and greater rebellion. In 1355 Toghto's opponents persuaded the emperor to dismiss him and this act has been seen as marking the end of the Yuan government as an integrated political system. The dynasty now controlled only the capital and the surrounding regions, while other parts of the country were held by independent commanders. As the rebellion grew and acquired a moral dimension, a civil war broke out among the Yuan supporters. In 1368 the court fled to Manchuria and the Yuan dynasty came to its end.

4

. . . .

The Early Modern Period: The Ming and the Early Qing

In January 1368, nine months before the departure of the Mongol court from China, Zhu Yuanzhang ascended the throne. He adopted the reign name of Hongwu and called his dynasty Ming, meaning brightness. His reign was to last until 1398, by which time he had established the most durable dynasty in Chinese history. He was succeeded by his grandson, but in 1403 the throne was usurped by Hongwu's fourth son, known as the Yongle emperor. The reigns of Hongwu and Yongle provide examples of effective rule in the early stages of the dynastic cycle. After Yongle's death the dynasty began a long decline, briefly interrupted by a period of reform in the late sixteenth century. From the 1620s onwards the dynasty was weakened by factional disputes and it collapsed in 1644 in the face of peasant rebellions and a Manchu invasion.

The Manchu invaders adopted the dynastic title of the Qing and, building on the experience of previous dynasties of conquest, created a highly successful form of Sino-Manchu rule. Under a sequence of three able emperors, Kangxi (*r.* 1662–1722), Yongzheng (*r.* 1723–35) and Qianlong (*r.* 1736–95), the Chinese Empire reached its greatest extent and Chinese culture achieved its highest level of sophistication. However, in the late Ming period, and increasingly under the Qing, foreign contacts proliferated. By the end of the eighteenth century the dynasty was showing evidence of decline. The implications of relations with the Western world, and the consequences of population growth, had raised questions about the capacity of the imperial system to meet the challenge of changing circumstances.

THE ESTABLISHMENT OF THE MING DYNASTY

In the preceding chapter only brief reference was made to the rise of the rebellion which led to the expulsion of the Mongols. More should be said on the subject, because the character of the movement, and the temperament of its leader, determined the style of early Ming government.

Zhu Yuanzhang was born in 1328 near Fengyang in modern Anhui, an area soon to be affected by the change of course of the Yellow river, by the silting up of the Grand Canal and by the depredations of pirates. The area was under the influence of the Maitreya cult of the White Lotus sect, which anticipated the coming of the future Buddha and the establishment of a 'pure land'. From about 1340 White Lotus sect adherents turned to collective violence and became known as the Red Turbans. Zhu Yuanzhang was caught up in this disorder. After the death of his parents in the famine of 1344, he became destitute. In 1351 Toghto, the Yuan chancellor, conscripted thousands of men to work on rerouting the Yellow river and dredging the Grand Canal. His coercive measures provoked the outbreak of the Red Turban rebellion, which within a year had swept through the Yangzi valley and had confined the government forces to Nanjing and the other major cities of the region. In 1352 Zhu Yuanzhang joined a Red Turban band led by Guo Zixing, which was active near Fengyang. Within a year he had recruited 24 men from his native area and had married Guo Zixing's adopted daughter. Over the next two years the forces commanded by Toghto suppressed much of the rebel activity, but in January 1355 Toghto was dismissed and rebel movements revived. Han Liner, the leader of the northern Red Turbans, who claimed descent from the Song, declared himself emperor. By the end of the decade the Yuan dynasty had lost control of the Yangzi valley, which was being contested by several regional leaders.

From this struggle Zhu Yuanzhang emerged the victor. His success may be attributed in part to his military ability and his skill in making tactical alliances. As his influence grew, he gained a reputation for willingness to take advice from Confucian scholars and for benevolence towards the common people. By 1355 he had established a base camp and had built up a personal army. In the following year he captured Nanjing, and began the transformation 'from leader of a populist sectarian revolt to leader of a political movement aspiring to traditional legitimacy'.[1] Whenever his forces captured a town he appointed a new civil administration staffed by scholar-officials, some of whom had previously served the Yuan. He engaged officials to supervise the repair of river defences and to promote the revival of agriculture. He gradually severed his links with the Red Turban ideology and with the northern Red Turban dynasty, which came to an end in 1367 when Han Liner was drowned. In these ways he demonstrated his eagerness to acquire the qualities associated with a Chinese emperor. In January 1368, having defeated his main rivals and feeling confident that the Mongol court could offer no significant resistance, he declared the founding of the Ming dynasty and assumed the reign title of Hongwu.

Hongwu's first task was to gain control of the rest of China. A military expedition was sent north, where it forced the flight of the Mongol court and captured Dadu, which was renamed Beiping, meaning 'the north is pacified'. The most serious threat was posed by Kökö Temür, who in the 1360s had established himself as an independent military leader in Taiyuan. In 1372 a large force pursued Kökö Temür into Mongolia and inflicted a heavy defeat on him, but he later recovered and only after his death in 1375 did the Mongol threat decline. In the meantime an expedition had been sent to recover Sichuan, which had been seized by the southern branch of the Red Turbans. In 1377 the Korean state of Koryo was persuaded to abandon its loyalty to the Yuan rulers and to recognize the Ming, and in 1379 Tibet, which had also failed to acknowledge the legitimacy of Ming rule, was brought into obedience by force.

Although Hongwu claimed to be restoring the practices of the Tang and Song periods, from necessity in the early years of his reign he continued nearly all the features of government employed by, and in some cases introduced by, the Mongols. He retained their military structure, in that the army continued to be treated as an occupational caste commanded by an hereditary officer class. The Ming armed forces derived from Hongwu's early followers and the bands which had surrendered to him. The latter had been promised that their units would be kept intact and that their leaders' commands would be made hereditary. From 1364 these forces were organized according to the *weiso* system; that is, into guards, numbering 5000 men, and battalions, numbering 1000 men. This force could not be demobilized without a risk of serious disorder, but it was too costly to maintain as a charge to the state, so Hongwu continued the Yuan practice of making the armies self-sufficient through the extension of the military colony system. The commanders of these forces, in particular those who were the survivors of Hongwu's original band of 24 men or of those who had joined him early in his campaign, were rewarded with noble titles and ranked higher than military and civil officials.

The same principles were applied to the early Ming system of government. The Yuan central government had consisted of a Secretariat-Chancellery headed by two chancellors, who conducted all routine administrative business, a powerful and independent Bureau of Military Affairs and a Censorate, which was more concerned with the surveillance of the operation of government than with receiving remonstrations from officials. At the intermediate level a variety of administrative bodies had been created, the most important being the branch secretariats, which administered areas which were the forerunners of the modern provinces of China. This structure had been adopted by Hongwu during his rise to power and it was retained through the first decade of his reign. The most significant, albeit symbolic, change was the reversal of the precedence the Mongols gave to the official designated as 'of the right', in favour of the Chinese custom of giving precedence to the left. These arrangements led Edward L. Dreyer to remark, 'As originally conceived, the Ming empire was thus Mongol in form and structure; it was Chinese only in rhetoric and personnel.'[2]

The moderation and caution which had marked the early years of Hongwu's reign came to an abrupt end in 1380 when Hu Weiyong, the chancellor of the left, was accused of conspiracy and executed. The charges levelled against him included having dealings with the Mongols, but his real fault was to have challenged the authority of the emperor by building up a power base in the civil bureaucracy. Hu Weiyong's death was followed by a ferocious purge, which was said to have cost the lives of 30,000 of his supporters. It also led to important changes in government. The office of chancellor was abolished and the emperor demanded that it should never be restored by his successors, the Secretariat-Chancellery was dismantled and the authority of the military commission was fragmented. Hongwu in effect became his own chief minister.

During the remaining years of his reign, Hongwu ruled as a conscientious autocrat. He followed a punishing schedule of audiences and concerned himself with many details of government, for example the promulgation of a Ming legal code, which was eventually completed in 1397. He was particularly concerned with education. In 1382 he revived the examinations, which now became the main avenue for entry into the civil service. In 1397, having discovered that not a single northerner had passed the *jinshi* examination, he amended the pass lists and so initiated a quota system which reserved a proportion of examination passes to certain groups. *Jinshi*, or 'presented scholars', so described because the successful candidates were presented to the emperor, numbered 871 for the entire Hongwu reign, only a small proportion of the civil bureaucracy which comprised about 15,000 officials. However, many *jinshi* attained positions of influence and provided an important counterbalance to those who owed their appointment to heredity.

Hongwu also ordered the establishment of schools in every prefecture, subprefecture and district, with staff and students supported with public funds. In a move described as 'nothing short of extraordinary in the fourteenth-century world', he instituted a system of 'community schools' in every village to educate every boy.[3]

Hongwu's most enduring legacy related to taxation. As the first emperor of a dynasty, unencumbered by heavy financial commitments, he was in a strong position to reform the tax system. He took steps to equalize the land-tax burden, while maintaining a punitive level of taxation on ten prefectures south of the Yangzi, where opposition to his rise had been strongest. His ambition was to apply a new level of detailed control over the entire land and tax system. In 1370 he ordered that each household in the country should be issued with a certificate which recorded details of the family, including its status and occupation, with the implication that these could not be changed. In 1381 these records were consolidated in the 'Yellow Books' or registers. Hongwu also commissioned a monumental cadastral survey, the returns being edited into land registers called 'fish-scale books' because the topographical charts they contained resembled fishes' scales. The emperor's priority in tax matters was control and this was demonstrated by two other measures. Rural communities were organized into the *lijia* system, under which groups of 110 households were grouped as *li* and made responsible for the payment of taxes and the discharging of labour services. Overlapping this arrangement was the tax-captain system, under which wealthy families were made responsible for the collection of grain taxes in their area.

Although Hongwu laboured hard to create an efficient centralized tax structure, his projects have been heavily criticized for being too ambitious for the technological means of the Ming state. The tax reforms were based on a serious misunderstanding: the country was not over-taxed but under-taxed, and as a consequence state revenues were not sufficient to provide effective public services. Moreover, the tax system was not progressive, it did not encourage enterprise and it had become so complex that it defied reform.

Hongwu died in 1398 and was buried on Zijinshan on the outskirts of Nanjing. His reputation has oscillated between praise for having expelled the Mongols and having founded the Ming dynasty, and condemnation for having been a tyrant whose policies established a trend towards despotism. The Marxist historian Wu Han, who became notorious at the time of the Cultural Revolution, depicted Hongwu as a man of the people who betrayed the popular cause and sided with the landlord-gentry class to obtain power. Wu Han's critics have argued that Hongwu was motivated solely by his own ambition and was never a sincere supporter of the poor. F. W. Mote traced Hongwu's abolition of the post of chancellor to a trend towards despotism already evident under the Song, but suggested that his harshness and unreasonableness had its precedent in the brutal world of the Yuan.[4] Other historians have described traits of Hongwu's personality, noting his ugliness, his suspicion of rivals and his extreme sensitivity to supposed insults, which caused him to execute almost all his longest-standing supporters and thousands of others. The one redeeming feature of his personality was his attachment to the Empress Ma, who, until her death in 1382, may have exercised a moderating influence on her husband.[5]

THE REIGNS OF JIANWEN, 1399–1402, AND YONGLE, 1403–24

Hongwu was succeeded briefly by his grandson, who reigned as the Jianwen emperor until he was deposed by his uncle, Hongwu's fourth son the Prince of Yan, known as the Yongle emperor. It is difficult to assess Jianwen's abilities, as it was in the interests of his uncle's supporters to denounce him as ineffectual and depraved. He certainly was better educated than his grandfather and he accepted the advice of his Confucian tutors to rescind some of the despotic measures of Hongwu's reign. He also attempted to reduce the autonomy of the hereditary princedoms founded to accommodate Hongwu's sons. This prompted the rebellion of the Prince of Yan, the commander of the northern frontier army, which concluded with the reported death of Jianwen in a fire in the imperial palace.

Yongle was vulnerable to the charge of being a usurper, and so he moved quickly to consolidate his position by restoring features of government as practised under Hongwu. He did make some changes, the most important of which was the creation of a new grand secretariat to replace the Secretariat-Chancellery, which his father had abolished in 1380. To it he appointed seven officials, four of whom were holders of the *jinshi* degree. They enjoyed security of tenure throughout the reign and this allowed the creation of an efficient bureaucracy.

Yongle also took the momentous decision to transfer the capital from Nanjing to Beijing. The main reason for the move was to permit closer control over the military forces in the north. To secure the food supply to Beijing required the restoration and extension of the Grand Canal, a major task which was completed in 1415. The construction of the new capital began in 1406 and involved the accumulation of vast quantities of timber and bricks and the deployment of thousands of labourers and artisans. By 1417 the walls and the major palace buildings had been completed, and thereafter Yongle was resident there unless absent on campaigns.

Yongle's reign was notable also for his pursuit of an ambitious foreign policy, which in some respects echoed the aspirations of Khubilai's reign. Before he became emperor he had commanded troops on the northern frontier, and so it was not surprising that his first concern was for the security of that region. At first the most significant threat came from the Mongol ruler known in the West as Tamerlane. Having conquered a vast Central Asian empire, in 1404 Tamerlane set out to invade China, but died en route. On China's north-eastern frontier the Urianghad and Jurchen tribes were disunited and Yongle persuaded them to accept Chinese overlordship. Further to the west, in what is now Mongolia, the Tatar and Oirat still presented a danger. Between 1410 and 1424 Yongle led five expeditions against them, on the last of which he died. Although these expeditions were recorded in Chinese annals as successful, they were extremely expensive and failed to eliminate the Mongol threat. These facts indicate that even during Yongle's reign, 'sclerosis had begun developing in the Ming military establishment'.[6]

In the south, Yongle's forces eliminated surviving pockets of Yuan and tribal resistance and then moved against Annam, which since the Tang period had been an independent state sending tribute to China. In 1406 the Annamese throne was usurped and this provided the pretext for sending a Chinese army, which conquered the territory and organized it as a province. However, the Chinese administration was corrupt and the military forces were too small to maintain control. Within a decade a powerful patriotic resistance movement had emerged, which shortly after Yongle's death forced a Chinese withdrawal.

The most spectacular aspect of Yongle's foreign ventures was the despatch, between 1405 and 1421, of six grand maritime expeditions. Yongle's motive for launching these expensive voyages has been debated. The suggestion that their purpose was to find the Jianwen emperor, who, according to rumour, had escaped overseas disguised as a monk, is not supported by any evidence. Nor is it likely that the expeditions went in search of treasure, or that the primary purpose was exploration. The most probable reason for their despatch was to aggrandize Yongle, who was a usurper, by adding to the number of foreign rulers who recognized him as emperor. The ships built for these voyages were perhaps the largest wooden ships ever built, estimates of their length varying from 385 to 440 feet and their beam between 150 and 180 feet. The first expedition, commanded by the grand eunuch Zheng He and comprising 317 ships and 27,870 men, put in at several Indian ports, including Calicut. On subsequent voyages Zheng He sailed to Hormuz on the Gulf of Oman, and ships from his expeditions reached Jidda and explored the African coast as far south as Malindi. After Yongle's death one further fleet was sent out, but then the voyages ended, perhaps because their political purpose no longer applied, and very probably because of their very high cost. As a consequence, China's lead in oceanographic knowledge and command of the seas were soon overhauled by the Portuguese.[7]

THE MIDDLE YEARS OF THE MING DYNASTY: POLITICAL ASPECTS

The death of Yongle in 1424 ended the expansionist stage of the Ming dynasty, and later Ming emperors pursued defensive policies. An incident which occurred in the reign of the Zhengtong emperor, who came to the throne as a minor in 1436, may be the reason for this change. In the 1440s the Oirat tribes were united by a leader named Esen and began to encroach on Chinese territory. In 1448 a very large Oirat tribute mission to the Chinese court was treated contemptuously by Wang Zhen, the chief eunuch. In the following year, Esen responded by invading and defeating a Chinese force near Datong. The 22-year-old emperor, with the encouragement of Wang Zhen but against the advice of his officials, decided to lead a counter-attack. His forces, said to number half a million men, were ambushed at Tumu, 70 miles north west of Beijing. The emperor was captured and Wang Zhen was killed.

The disastrous Tumu incident had a variety of consequences. Some officials, anticipating that Esen would now press home his advantage, suggested that the court should abandon the capital. This idea was opposed by Yu Qian, the vice-minister of war, whose resolution led to his being enshrined in Chinese folklore as a symbol of patriotic resistance. The hereditary military elite, which had been established by Hongwu and revived by Yongle, was blamed for the defeat, and Yu Qian's rise to power represented a long-lasting victory of the civil bureaucracy over the military.

To reduce the leverage the Oirat exerted over the Chinese court by holding the emperor hostage, it was decided to enthrone his half-brother in his place and the latter took the era name of Jingtai. The deposed Zhengtong was referred to as the 'retired emperor' and after his release was excluded from power. Inevitably he became the focus of opposition to Jingtai and after he had been restored by a coup in 1457, the subsequent settling of scores, which included the judicial murder of Yu Qian, left a legacy of factionalism at court. Finally, the Tumu incident forced the dynasty to review its strategy towards the Mongols. Recognizing that it did not have the resources to control the steppe transition zone – that is, the intermediate zone between the steppe and the settled areas, where threats to China from nomadic peoples usually originated – the dynasty adopted a defensive strategy. The Mongol threat was most apparent in the Ordos region and it was there that in 1474 the construction of the Great Wall, as it is known today, began.

*   *   *

The political character of the Ming period is often referred to as 'Ming absolutism', a reference to the growth of imperial power from the late fourteenth century. This tendency was already apparent under the Song and it advanced further under the Mongols. Under Hongwu it assumed its highest form. His decision in 1380 to abolish the post of chancellor or chief minister had placed him in direct control of central government. The branch secretariats, which administered the proto-provinces, comprised three separate agencies: a civil administration, a military commission and a surveillance office. As each agency was under the supervision of the central government, the branch secretariat itself enjoyed no element of autonomy. China was a country which had large cities and numerous towns, but its citizens had failed to secure the privileges which civic communities had obtained in the West. Hongwu had overseen the production of a revised Ming legal code, but although this was enforced by a sophisticated judicial system, imperial power could not be challenged in the courts.

This absolutist framework was supported by systems of surveillance and by harsh punishments. Hongwu believed that the laxity of the Yuan administration had contributed to the dynasty's fall and he consequently took a very severe line on official corruption. For example, an official found guilty of receiving a bribe of over 60 taels[8] of silver was decapitated, his head was spiked on a pole, and his corpse was skinned and stuffed with straw. Hongwu maintained an elaborate surveillance operation through the use of spies, secret agents and the Embroidered Guards, who carried out the major purges of his reign. These autocratic but effective policies were continued under Yongle, but were neglected by the later Ming emperors.

The agency which existed to control abuses of power was the censorate. The censorate as a separate branch of government, entrusted with the task of surveilling the work of officials through the empire, had emerged under the Han. In addition to censors, 'speaking officials' were appointed to perform the task of remonstrance; that is, offering advice and warning to the emperor. Under the Yuan censors acquired the power to punish junior officials for wrongdoing, and took over the duty of remonstrance. During the Ming period the censorate played an active role in government. Overmighty officials, and the eunuch dictators of the latter part of the reign, were frequently impeached. Censorial officials submitted numerous memorials to the emperor offering advice on various matters, and occasionally criticized decisions taken by the emperor himself. However, the censors' role was marginal; they were neither agents of popular nor of bureaucratic resistance to imperial domination. Under strong emperors they were effective defenders of tradition, but under weak rulers, when corruption and inefficiency proliferated, they did not challenge absolutism, although their criticisms could immobilize the actions of government.

Another aspect of Ming government associated with absolutism was the assumption of a political role by court eunuchs. As no uncastrated male, apart from the emperor himself, was permitted to enter the imperial harem, eunuchs had exceptional access to the emperor and could exert considerable influence on him. The eunuchs' role was of particular importance if the emperor was enthroned when still a minor, as were eight of the eleven emperors who succeeded to the throne between 1435 and 1644. In 1384 Hongwu had ordered the erection of an iron tablet bearing the inscription: 'Eunuchs are forbidden to interfere with government affairs. Those who attempt to do so will be subjected to capital punishment.' Notwithstanding this injunction, he sent eunuchs as his personal envoys to tributary states and to the provinces as tax auditors. Yongle went further, entrusting eunuchs such as Zheng He with the command of major ventures. He also removed the eunuchs from bureaucratic control and appointed them to head the Eastern Depot, the headquarters of the secret police. The Xuande emperor (r. 1426–35) rescinded the ban on eunuchs being educated and established a palace eunuch school. Thereafter, eunuchs gained key positions as the emperor's personal secretaries, controlling the flow of information and so bypassing the secretariat.

Emperors trusted eunuchs because they were dependent on imperial favour, and in return eunuchs exploited their privileged position at the expense of the bureaucracy. The consequence was the emergence of eunuch dictators, the first being Wang Zhen, whose role in the Tumu incident has already been mentioned. The next notorious example of a eunuch's misuse of power was the case of Liu Jin, the chief of imperial staff for the Zhengde emperor, who had come to the throne as a minor in 1506. Liu Jin was flagrantly corrupt and oppressive, and his excesses led to his enemies accusing him of plotting to kill the emperor, for which crime he was executed. The last and most infamous of the eunuch dictators was Wei Zhongxian, who achieved a total ascendancy over the Tianqi emperor (r. 1621–7), who showered him and his relatives with gifts and titles.

Before concluding the discussion of Ming absolutism, one should return to the earlier reference to educational policies and to the community schools which were part of Hongwu's ambitious plan to extend imperial authority through the process of *jiaohua*, or transformation through education. At first these were centrally mandated local institutions, but in time the initiative shifted downwards towards the local community, and this shift has been cited to show that the relationship between central government and local community was not as autocratic as has been alleged.

The Ming state was built from below as well as from above; as people colonized government institutions and documents for their own aims, they lengthened the reach of the state.[9]

ECONOMIC AND SOCIAL ASPECTS OF THE MING PERIOD

Hongwu's compilation of the Yellow Books and the 'fish-scale' registers ensured that a large amount of data relating to population and the acreage of land under cultivation was amassed during the Ming period. However, much of this information was plainly inaccurate; for example, in 1582 one county reported that it had 3700 households with residents over 100 years old. As a consequence, only the roughest estimates can be made of the correct land and population figures. It is estimated that during the Ming period the population rose from about 65 million to about 150 million persons and that the acreage of land under cultivation increased from under 400 million *mou* to approximately 500 million *mou*.[10] The increase in cultivated land was partly due to internal migration, most notably to Yunnan and Guizhou. There were no major advances in agricultural technology, but the slow diffusion of improved planting materials – including early ripening rice introduced from Vietnam in the eleventh century and plants originating in the New World, the most important of which were maize, sweet potato, peanuts and tobacco, which reached China in the late Ming period – enabled food supply to match population growth. This growth might have been greater but for constraints. The decades of the 1430s and 1440s were marked by a devastating succession of droughts, floods, pestilences and epidemics, which caused severe loss of life. It is also apparent that female infanticide was widely practised, for example it was said that 'Jiangxi people are fond of drowning girls'.[11]

The great majority of the population lived in the countryside and depended on agriculture for a living. However, in the Ming period, particularly in the sixteenth century, cities and towns grew and some industries flourished. Jingdezhen, the porcelain centre in Jiangxi, claimed to have a population in excess of one million. The local magistrate complained that the fires of its kilns were so bright and the sound of its pestles so noisy that he could not sleep. Hangzhou, the great centre of silk production, was a city of similar size. In Songjiang prefecture in the Yangzi delta, numerous towns specialized in the production of cotton textiles. From the fifteenth century a division of labour had been established, with cotton spinning remaining a cottage industry, but weaving being transferred to the urban environment. Alvara Semedo, a Jesuit missionary, estimated that in 1621, 200,000 looms were being operated in and around Shanghai. It was said that 'Songjiang cotton cloth clothes the empire'. Goods produced by these industrial centres were distributed widely. At the beginning of the seventeenth century, Linqing on the Grand Canal, a major distribution centre for north China, claimed to handle more than 1.6 million shiploads of freight every year.

This urbanization was accompanied by the development of a thriving city culture. Beijing was the great bureaucratic and military centre and also was a major venue for Daoist and Buddhist ceremonies. The southern cities of Hangzhou, Suzhou and Nanjing were famous for their conspicuous consumption, their sophisticated social life and their lavish festivals. Urban life prompted the appearance of new literary forms, colloquial fiction in the shape of short stories and novels. One of the most famous writers of the late Ming period was Feng Menglong (1574–1646), a failed examination candidate who lived in Suzhou. Many of his stories depicted women, whom he portrayed engaged in a variety of roles, as entertainer, virago, predator or recluse. Of the four famous novels which appeared in the Ming period, three of them, *The Romance of the Three Kingdoms*, *Water Margin* and *Journey to the West*, otherwise known as *Monkey*, had all circulated previously in oral or handwritten form. Now they came out in print, part of a surge of publication which produced books of a wide variety of genres. The fourth famous novel, the notorious *Jin Ping Mei*, a scandalous story about women and sexual intrigue, first appeared in print in Suzhou in 1610.[12]

In the late Ming the cost of publishing fell, which allowed the production of compendia for a popular audience on subjects such as agriculture, health, medicine and mathematics. A famous example of these is the *Bencao gangmu* (*Systematic Materia Medica*), compiled by Li Shizhen (1518–93), which appeared in 1596. Li Shizhen collected information on mineralogy, metallurgy, botany, zoology and drug formulae and read exhaustively; his bibliography listed 932 titles. His work included new data about drugs and diseases, including references to maize and sweet potatoes and to syphilis, which he traced back to the late fifteenth century in Guangdong province. To classify materia medica, Li practised what was called the 'study of the investigation of things'. However, his investigations never progressed from the accumulation of knowledge to objectivist science – a development which, according to Benjamin Elman, only came about after the arrival of the Jesuits bringing with them Western learning.[13] Song Yingxing (1587–1666), whom Joseph Needham called 'the Diderot of China', took this accumulative tendency even further. He compiled the *Tiangong taiwu* (*The Exploitation of the Works of Nature*), an illustrated work covering a wide range of manufacturing and technological skills, including agriculture, nautical science, textile manufacturing and the production of weapons which used gunpowder.

The growth of industry and of urbanization brought with it attendant social problems, but did not precipitate an industrial revolution. Explanations of why this did not occur recall the debate concerning economic development under the Song. In the case of the cotton industry, it has been suggested that a combination of factors – a sufficient but not abundant supply of raw cotton, gradual technological improvements, an excellent commercial network and the availability of cheap labour – prevented the development of bottlenecks which might have forced a switch to factory production.

The Ming government rarely intervened in the operation of this economy. However, its policies relating to currency and taxation are of some relevance in this context. Under the Yuan, paper currency had circulated widely, and in the late Yuan period the reckless issue of paper notes had led to inflation and a silver shortage. Whereas the Mongols had understood that a paper currency should be convertible and should therefore be backed by silver reserves, Hongwu was oblivious to this need and issued large quantities of nonconvertible paper currency. By 1425 paper notes were worth only one fortieth of their face value, and by the end of the fifteenth century paper currency had ceased to have any commercial value. As a consequence, the monetary system was restricted to copper coinage and unminted silver.

The main sources of Ming government revenue were the land tax, which included labour services, and the salt monopoly. Hongwu's tax reforms, and in particular his establishment of a tax-quota system, had ensured that revenue would prove inadequate for future state needs, and from 1528 onwards the Ming government treasury was in deficit. To increase revenue a wide variety of supplementary taxes were levied, with the result that the land taxes of the late Ming period have been called 'as complex as personal income tax in the twentieth-century United States'.[14] It was this situation which prompted the ambitious measures dubbed the 'Single-Whip' reform, a pun on its correct title, the 'reformed single entry system'. Starting in 1531, on the initiative of two surveillance commissioners whose task was to rectify abuses in the tax system, measures were introduced to consolidate the land-tax and labour-service requirement into a single payment, to be paid in silver, not in kind. Between 1570 and 1590 these arrangements were extended to all parts of the empire.

These reforms have been cited as an important step towards the development of a monetary economy and 'the beginning of the modern land tax system'.[15] They may have been significant in shifting the incidence of taxation from the household to the land-holder, and thus have taken some cognizance of the fact that rural society had moved beyond a subsistence economy, and that the modest land-lord class of the early Ming had given way to the larger estates and the commercial landlordism of the later Ming. However, the reforms were never carried through in their entirety, the payment of tax in kind continued, labour services were still required in some areas, and the land tax became more rather than less complicated.

The outcome of the Single-Whip reform is an indication of both the strength and the limitations of the state in the Ming period. Timothy Brook has suggested that China had acquired many of the characteristic features of a modern state before such a development had occurred in Europe. The Ming state could impose new administrative divisions, revolutionize the fiscal system, intervene in the agricultural economy by trying to extend wet-rice cultivation north of the Yangzi, control the distribution and content of books and regulate Buddhist monasteries. These interventions appear to indicate the despotic nature of the state, and indeed the state did have very considerable powers of enforcement. However, if state initiatives were to be effective, they had to be supported by the local elite and they had to be adapted to suit local circumstances.[16]

*   *   *

It was during the Ming period that the status group known as the gentry emerged fully. The term gentry is used to translate *shenshi*, which means 'officials and scholars'. The term implies that entry into the group was achieved by success in the examination system or by the purchase of rank, and that the group existed to provide a reservoir of talent to support a bureaucratic system of government. However, this group owed its emergence as much to the economic and social changes of the Ming period as it did to the formal process of examination. The commercialization of the economy and the attendant rise in land prices encouraged the formation of a stratum of wealthy upper gentry who controlled land and credit. It had also brought into being a larger group of families prosperous enough to educate their sons for the examinations and to participate in the activities of gentry society. Viewed from this perspective, the gentry were not an adjunct of the bureaucracy, but rural elites 'with a wide and flexible repertoire of strategies at their disposal, in which land-owning, education, and degree-holding were usual but not necessarily indispensable elements'.[17]

This picture has been fleshed out in a number of studies. Hilary J. Beattie investigated Tongcheng county in Anhui and found that the families which produced degree-holders depended less on obtaining office – always a high-risk strategy – and more on the acquisition of land and the systematic use of marriage with other powerful lineages.[18] Timothy Brook has shown how gentry society maintained its position not only through economic and political means, but also through its cultural domination, expressed in literary and artistic pursuits. John W. Dardess, in a study of Taihe county, Jiangxi, suggested that although gentry society had deep local roots, even in the early Ming period the 'great talents' of the county had no intention of staying at home but were anxious to play their part on the national stage. For him, gentry society would not have existed if its values had not been confirmed by the national context into which it was embedded.

These studies invite a reconsideration of the amount of social mobility which existed in China at this time. The classic study by Ho Ping-ti assumed that social mobility derived from the examination system, which ideally provided equal opportunity for all but the 'mean people', who included slaves, the children of prostitutes and all boat people. He categorized the 14,562 men who had obtained the *jinshi*, the highest degree, between 1371 and 1904 according to whether their families had produced degree-holders in the three preceding generations. He found that in the early Ming period

57.6 per cent of *jinshi* came from families which had not previously produced a holder of a higher degree, and that the proportion remained as high as 49.5 per cent for the entire Ming period, but fell to 37.6 per cent under the Qing. He concluded that this was evidence of an unparalleled instance of upward social mobility in a major society prior to the industrial revolution.[19] Hilary Beattie's study, however, suggested that the important lineages of Tongcheng were well established by the middle of the Ming period and there was little subsequent movement up or down. John W. Dardess showed that in the early Ming the number of elite families in Taihe county was increasing in response to the availability of land and the high rate of bureaucratic recruitment, but by the mid-fifteenth century the opportunity for rapid expansion had gone. Then the excess children of elite families were 'purged'; that is, they either migrated to other regions, or they lost their elite status and became artisans or, in the case of daughters, concubines and maids.

THE LATE MING PERIOD

After the Tumu incident of 1449, the Ming dynasty pursued defensive and generally conciliatory policies towards the steppe tribes. The Jiajing emperor (*r.* 1522–66) had to deal with the rise of a new Mongol confederation under Altan Khan, who raided Chinese territory to obtain supplies for his campaigns against the Oirat to the west. In 1550 Mongol forces besieged Beijing and looted the outer suburbs. Despite efforts to buy off the Mongols and to strengthen the defensive walls, these raids continued until 1571, when Altan accepted a peace treaty. Nevertheless, China's military weakness had been exposed and her northern borders continued to be threatened by the Mongols until the end of the sixteenth century, when a new threat from the Jurchen, or Manchus, appeared.

The same defensive stance characterized Ming maritime affairs. Foreign relations were governed by the tribute system and took the form of embassies, the exchange of gifts and grants of trading rights. Private trade and unofficial contacts were discouraged. From early in the sixteenth century these conventions came under challenge. In 1514 the first Portuguese reached China and in 1517 Tomé Pires, who had been appointed Portuguese ambassador, arrived at Guangzhou and was eventually permitted to travel to Beijing. In the

1550s the Portuguese were allowed to establish a trading station at Aomen (Macao), but were ordered to remain apart from the Chinese population. In the meantime, Japanese traders and pirates had appeared in numbers along the south-east coast of China and had breached the restrictions on foreign trade. Large-scale attacks by *wokou*, or Japanese pirates, exposed the inadequacy of the coastal defences. In the 1550s raiding parties established bases on the coast of Zhejiang, threatening the whole region. In 1554 Songjiang, the centre of the cotton industry, was attacked and its magistrate killed. Official measures and regular forces having proved ineffective, Qi Jiguang, an unconventional Chinese commander, drilled a volunteer force, used firearms as well as traditional weapons and denied the raiders any respite. It was only when the ban on Chinese participation in foreign trade was rescinded in 1567 that peace was restored. Ten years later, Alessandro Valignano arrived in Macao and obtained permission for the Jesuits to establish a mission on Chinese soil. In 1598 his successor, Matteo Ricci, reached Beijing.

This failure to sustain frontier policies was an indication of the weakness of the Ming dynasty, rather than the cause of its fall. That has been explained in a variety of ways, beginning with the process of the dynastic cycle, with its emphasis on the inadequacy of emperors and the machinations of ministers and eunuchs. The Jiajing emperor (*r.* 1522–66) became obsessed with Daoism and the search for the elixirs of immortality, which eventually led to his death by poisoning. From 1549 to 1562 the most powerful official was Yan Song, whose long survival was based on obsequiousness towards the emperor and avoidance of the pressing issues of the day. The Wanli emperor's reign (1573–1620) began more promisingly, for he had the support of Zhang Juzheng, a man committed, albeit vainly and controversially, to raising government efficiency and improving the financial administration, but after Zhang's death in 1582 government fell into the hands of the eunuchs. The reign of the incompetent Tianqi emperor (1621–7) saw the rise of the eunuch dictator Wei Zhongxian; and that of the Chongzhen emperor (*r.* 1628–45), who was active and well intentioned, was marred by the service of untrustworthy officials.

Modern historians have looked beyond and below court politics to explain the Ming decline. One line of investigation concerns the response of the elite to the social and economic changes of the late Ming period. Timothy Brook described how Hongwu's ideal, of a society in which owner-cultivators worked within a subsistence economy, was subverted by the growth of a wealthy land-based gentry in the early sixteenth century. The gentry, finding that the competition for examination success had increased and the risks associated with a bureaucratic career had multiplied, turned away from a 'state-centered vision of gentry life', with its emphasis on engagement with public affairs, in favour of embracing Buddhism, pursuing economic rather than political power, involving themselves less with the state and more with the locality.[20]

The relationship between the state and the gentry was also damaged by a Confucian revival which later engendered violent factional disputes at court. In the late sixteenth century a number of private academies were established, where scholars and ex-officials bemoaned the decline of Confucian standards and the political immorality of the court. In 1577 Zhang Juzheng, Wanli's grand secretary, was criticized by the Confucianists for failing to observe the period of mourning after his father's death. In the same year he ordered a personnel evaluation which resulted in the discharge of a number of officials. Discharged officials joined academies, the most notable example being the Donglin academy, founded in 1604, which was based near Wuxi in the Yangzi delta. Its location supports the suggestion that the Donglin movement had a regional basis. Alternatively, it may have represented the interests of a land-owning class resentful of Ming absolutism. Donglin sympathizers were kept out of government until Wanli's death in 1620. In the early years of Tianqi's reign a group of officials, known to have Donglin connections, briefly dominated the court, and had the temerity to charge Wei Zhongxian, the eunuch dictator, with 'twenty-four crimes'. But Wei Zhongxian regained power and procured the arrest and murder of twelve leading members of the academy. Until the dynasty fell, factionalism deriving from the Donglin movement weakened the government. Officials and scholars were alienated and thus susceptible to changing their allegiance when the dynasty collapsed.[21]

In the late Ming period, and in particular between 1626 and 1640, China experienced unusually severe weather marked by low temperatures, drought and floods. The population, which for two centuries had been growing steadily, stagnated or went into decline. By the early seventeenth century the economy was being supported by a vast inflow of silver to pay for Chinese exports. However, a European trade depression in the 1620s, and the interruption of trade with the Philippines and Japan in the 1640s, reduced the inflow of silver, damaged the silk industry and drove up the price of grain. A decline in the influx of silver was cited as a major factor in the fall of the dynasty, but this view was challenged by Richard Von Glahn, who pointed out that the sharpest phase in the decline occurred in the 1650s, after the dynasty had fallen.[22]

The collapse of the dynasty was precipitated by peasant rebellions. James W. Tong has shown that the incidence of rebellions and banditry was far higher in the second half of the Ming dynastic period than in the first. These incidents were not a response to social change, because they were more common in the less commercialized parts of the country. Nor were they a response to the grosser examples of misgovernment, because the rise in incidents of violence was gradual and incremental. Tong concluded that the main reason for the increase was the decline of the coercive capacity of the state. This encouraged peasants, in times of hardship, to suppose that their best chance of survival was to become outlaws.[23]

Tong's conclusion was supported by the record of the rebellions which began in 1628 in northern Shaanxi and eventually caused the downfall of the dynasty. Shaanxi was an impoverished province which may have been more severely affected by the deteriorating climate than the south of the country. The security of the area, in so far as it depended on military garrisons, had broken down. The situation was exacerbated by administrative shortcomings: many official posts were vacant and the officials present failed to organize relief to combat a disastrous famine. The result was a rebellion that might have been defeated if the pacification programme had not been interrupted, in 1629, by the first major Manchu raid into China. After the Manchu withdrawal, government troops crushed the most obvious manifestations of rebellion, but the survivors became mobile raiders and the centre of rebel activity moved south to the area between the Yellow and Yangzi rivers.

In the late 1630s, when the rebellions again seemed on the verge of extinction, further Manchu raids diverted attention to the north. The leaders of the two main rebellions, Li Zicheng in Henan and Zhang Xianzhong in Sichuan, began to display political ambitions. Li Zicheng, who was ascetic in his lifestyle, attracted members of the gentry to his side, and after he had captured Xiangyang in 1643 he established an administrative structure and announced tax reductions. The following year he declared the foundation of a new dynasty and marched on Beijing. Even at this point it should have been possible for the Ming to offer effective resistance, but it had lost control of large areas of the country, its military forces had collapsed, it was bankrupt and the will to resist had almost disappeared. On 24 April 1644 the rebels entered Beijing and that same night the emperor hanged himself.

THE MANCHU INVASION

The Manchus were descendants of the Jurchen tribes who had founded the Jin dynasty in 1122. By the sixteenth century the Jianzhou Jurchen, who in 1635 were to adopt the name Manchu, were living in the vicinity of the Changbai mountains in the east of present-day Jilin. There they hunted, practised agriculture and traded extensively with the Chinese. By the late Ming period the area occupied by the Changbai Jurchen was designated a 'commandery', implying that it had been incorporated into the frontier defence system, although in truth Chinese control of the area depended largely on the exploitation of vendettas between the Jurchen tribes.

The transformation of the Changbai Jurchen territory into the Manchu state was largely the work of Nurhaci (1559–1626). He unified the Jurchen tribes through a mixture of aggression and marriage alliances and then cultivated relations with the Chinese. In 1589 he was granted a title by the Wanli emperor and in the following year he headed a tribute mission to Beijing. Through the 1590s he traded profitably in ginseng and horses, and took advantage of the disruption caused by Hideyoshi's invasion of Korea. In 1599 he began to organize the entire Jurchen population into banners. Groups of 300 households were designated a company and 50 companies formed a 'banner', the name referring to the patterned flag carried by each group. Initially there were four banners, later the number was increased to eight Manchu banners, and in addition there were eight Mongol and eight Chinese banners. In peacetime the banners served as administrative units and in times of war they formed the destructive cavalry forces of the Manchus.

By 1603 Nurhaci's rapid rise to power had alarmed the Chinese, and a boundary was defined between his lands and those of Chinese settlement. In the years that followed, Nurhaci, by employing Chinese officials and by adopting bureaucratic methods of government, transformed his confederation of Jurchen tribes into a Manchu state. At the same time he obtained the allegiance of the Jurchen tribes who had yet to place themselves under Chinese protection. In 1616 he announced the foundation of the Latter Jin dynasty and two years later, having justified his actions in a document entitled the 'Seven Great Vexations', he seized the important trading post and garrison town of Fushun, near present-day Shenyang. Nurhaci awarded the Chinese commander of the town a high military rank and married him to his granddaughter. A large Chinese force was dispatched to recover the town, but it was routed. By the end of 1621 Nurhaci controlled the whole of Liaodong and was appealing to Chinese officials and settlers to come over to his side.

The Manchu advance then stalled for eight years. After the occupation of Liaodong, the Manchus were ruling perhaps one million Chinese. Some important Chinese families switched to the Manchu side, but others were treated as slaves or were forced to accept Manchu bannermen into their households. In 1623 a Chinese attempt to poison the Manchus' food and water supplies was punished harshly. Two years later the Chinese revolted and Nurhaci concluded that he could not rely on the Chinese population to support him. At about the same time, the Ming strengthened their defences by deploying cannon supplied by the Portuguese to defend their garrisons beyond the Great Wall. Meanwhile the Manchus had started to manufacture their own firearms.

When Nurhaci died in 1626, the Chinese used the opportunity to negotiate peace terms. The new ruler, Hung Taiji (1592–1643), placated the Liaodong Chinese and the Manchu advance resumed. In 1629, in a spectacular raid, he crossed the Great Wall, captured four Chinese cities and reached the walls of Beijing. It was this raid which disrupted the pacification campaign directed against the peasant rebellions in Shaanxi. By 1631 the Manchus were manufacturing large, European-type cannon and these were used to defeat the Ming forces in the siege of Dalinghe.[24] In 1634–5 Hung Taiji, having subdued the Chaha Mongols, claimed the succession to Genghis Khan and the Yuan dynasty. In 1638 he led a force which defeated the Korean Yi dynasty and forced it to send tribute to the Manchus.

Hung Taiji realized that the Chinese could not be subjugated by military force alone, and from 1631 he began to adopt features of Chinese government, including the Six Boards and the Censorate, alongside Manchu institutions. He introduced an examination system and made increasing use of Chinese collaborators in government and Chinese troops, now organized into banners. That his ambitions exceeded those of his father was made clear in 1636 when he dropped the dynastic name of Jin in favour of Qing, signifying 'clear' or 'pure', a challenge to the Ming, or 'bright' dynasty. His adoption of Chinese practices led Franz Michael to declare, 'It was the Chinese system, Chinese officials and Chinese ideas that enabled the Manchus to conquer China.' However, by the mid-1630s Hung Taiji had become wary of excessive sinicization and had insisted on the maintenance of Manchu values and tribal virtues.

What I fear is this: that the children and grandchildren of later generations will abandon the old [Manchu] Way, neglect shooting and riding, and enter into the Chinese Way.[25]

In 1643 Hung Taiji died and, after a succession dispute, it was agreed that the throne should go to his 5-year-old son, with the new emperor's uncles Dorgon and Jirgalang acting as regents. By now the Ming dynasty, faced with uncontrollable peasant rebellions, was on the verge of collapse. The two regents had to decide whether to continue Hung Taiji's policy, which concurred with the aristocratic tribal traditions of the Manchus, of remaining in the Manchu homelands and raiding China when they pleased; or whether to abandon that stratagem and occupy China. Dorgon, ambitious to increase his power, favoured the latter course. It was at this point that the issue of Chinese collaboration became a crucial factor.

The most powerful Chinese commander on the north-east frontier was Wu Sangui. When the rebel leader Li Zicheng captured Beijing, he immediately attempted to persuade Wu Sangui to come over to his side. However, according to a popular story, Li Zicheng had already seized and violated Wu Sangui's concubine, the famous courtesan Yuanyuan, and for this reason Wu Sangui decided to reject Li's overtures and to negotiate with the Manchus. A less romantic explanation of Wu Sangui's decision is that his failure to respond promptly to Li Zicheng's invitation led Li to suspect that the general was not to be trusted. He therefore ordered the slaughter of all members of Wu Sangui's family to be found in Beijing, and it was for this reason that the general turned to the Manchus. Dorgon may have calculated that he could not defeat the combined forces of Wu Sangui and Li Zicheng, but with the former on his side he could inflict a crushing defeat on the rebel leader's forces.

In June 1644 Dorgon entered Beijing and issued an edict reassuring the population that the Manchus had avenged the overthrow of the Ming by those he described as 'roving bandits'. He added:

> In the counties, districts, and locales that we pass through, all those who are able to shave their heads and surrender, opening their gates to welcome us, will be given rank and reward, retaining their wealth and nobility for generations. But if there are those who resist us disobediently, then when our Grand Army arrives, the stones themselves will be set ablaze and everyone will be massacred.[26]

The Manchu forces quickly drove Li Zicheng's troops out of north China, and before the end of 1645 both rebellions had been defeated. The rump Ming court made Nanjing its capital and attempted to negotiate a settlement with the Manchus. The Manchu response was to launch an attack on the Yangzi provinces. This stage of the conquest witnessed the most spirited Chinese resistance and the fiercest Manchu reprisals. At Yangzhou, near the junction of the Grand Canal and the Yangzi, opposition to the Manchu advance was headed by Shi Kefa. After their first attack had been repelled, the invaders used cannon to breach the city walls and then sacked the city as a deterrent to further defiance. Modern nationalist writers have taken the ten-day massacre at Yangzhou as proof of Manchu ruthlessness and have regarded Shi Kefa as the epitome of patriotic Chinese resistance.

At Jiangyin, about 100 miles upriver from Shanghai, the initial reaction of the elite to the Manchu advance was to comply with the demand that the tax and population registers should be handed over. However, in June 1645 news reached the city that the Manchus were requiring men to wear their hair in the Manchu style; that is, with the forehead shaved and the hair at the back grown long and braided into a queue. This gave rise to a resistance movement in which elite and popular elements came together in a brief alliance. The Manchus stamped out opposition ruthlessly. At Jiangyin the elite was divided in its resistance and the slaughter was actually perpetrated by Chinese troops. Scenes such as these prompted Lynn A. Struve to challenge the view that the Ming–Qing transition was relatively short and smooth, both institutionally and culturally.[27]

Nanjing fell to the Manchus in June 1645 and the Ming court fled south. The Manchus then paused to quell a rebellion among their supporters and to consolidate their position in the Yangzi valley. The invasion of the south began in 1649 and in the following year Guangzhou was captured and sacked by Shang Kexi, a Chinese bannerman who had switched to the Manchu side in 1634. Resistance in mainland China had now effectively ended. The last Ming emperor fled to Burma and was captured and executed in 1662.

In the meantime, a challenge to the Manchus had come from Zheng Chenggong, known in the West as Koxinga, a man who was both pirate and patriot, who had established his base near Xiamen. Zheng Chenggong commanded a large naval force, which he used to dramatic effect in 1659 when he sailed up the Yangzi and besieged Nanjing. However, he had expended little effort on obtaining support from the Chinese population and a Manchu attack on his forces besieging the city forced him to withdraw. Despite this defeat, Zheng Chenggong remained a serious threat. To deny him economic support, the Manchus ordered the coastal population of the provinces of Guangdong, Fujian and Zhejiang to move several miles inland. Zheng Chenggong died on Taiwan in 1662, but resistance from his family and supporters continued for a further twenty years.

THE CONSOLIDATION OF MANCHU RULE

From the moment that Dorgon had committed the Manchus to the conquest of China, the question of how the Manchus should behave as rulers had been raised. Dorgon had read the history of the Jin dynasty, and was well aware of the tension which could arise between a sinicized emperor supported by a Chinese bureaucracy and a non-Chinese nobility accustomed to the use of military power. Moreover, he knew that the Chinese bureaucracy itself was split between those who accepted the Manchu presence and those who did not.

Dorgon's response was to perform a balancing act directed at reassuring the Chinese while retaining the confidence of the Manchus. When he entered Beijing he ordered a mourning service and funeral for the last Ming emperor. The heavy taxes of the late Ming period were reduced and tax concessions were given to war-torn areas. He declared 'The empire is a single whole. There are no distinctions between Manchus and Hans', and he initiated a Manchu–Chinese diarchy by inviting all Ming metropolitan officials to remain in their posts and to perform their duties alongside Manchu appointees. An extensive programme of reforms proposed by Ming officials was adopted. The examination system was continued, in a form advantageous to northerners, who had long suspected that the system favoured men from the south. On the other hand, care was taken to assert Manchu dominance. Although the Manchu–Chinese diarchy suggested parity, the top metropolitan posts were held by Manchus, and of the Chinese appointed many were bannermen who had submitted to the Manchus before the conquest. Although some tax relief was offered to the Chinese population, this economic gain was outweighed by the need for land on which to settle banner troops. Up to one million acres of land was confiscated from Chinese farmers in Zhili, who were forced to move to other parts of northern China. Ironically, this measure did not benefit the Manchu bannermen greatly, for they lacked knowledge of agricultural techniques and many soon became destitute.

By the early eighteenth century nearly 100 Manchu garrisons, each with its own separate compound, had been established around Beijing and across the country. Manchu communities were expected to remain separate from the Han population. Manchu men had to train to be skilled horsemen, adept in the use of the bow and arrow. Manchu women wore their hair in a distinctive style and did not bind their feet, instead wearing 'horse-hoof' shoes which induced a tottering walk. They were not permitted to marry Han civilian males and Manchu men almost invariably took Manchu women as their principal wives.[28]

Dorgon had been an ambitious and scheming ruler, and after his death in 1650 the Manchu court was beset by a period of intense factional rivalry. At first Jirgalang became influential, but from 1653 a dominant faction grouped itself around the Shunzhi emperor, who by now was old enough to play a role in government. The young emperor was a vigorous if erratic ruler, who encouraged a reform programme initiated by 'twice-serving ministers'; that is, officials who had previously served under the Ming. Shunzhi died in 1661, probably of smallpox, leaving a will which is now recognized as a partial forgery. The self-deprecatory remarks inserted in the will show that Shunzhi had aroused the opposition of the Manchu conquest elite to activities regarded as too favourable to the Chinese.

He admitted to having reversed Dorgon's policy of restricting the political influence of the eunuchs, by creating the Thirteen Offices, a personal bureaucracy of eunuch advisers. Shunzhi's purpose in this may have been to assert his authority against his Manchu opponents. He confessed to spending too much time with Buddhist monks, to allowing the German Jesuit Adam Schall to exercise too much influence, to favouring Chinese officials and Ming institutions, and to disregarding the Manchu advisers and bondservants[29] who had served his predecessors. Moreover, he had shown greater devotion to his consort, posthumously known as the Empress Xiaoxian, who to his grief had died in 1660, than to his mother. The will named his 7-year-old son as his heir, who was to reign as the Kangxi emperor, and prescribed that during his minority power was to be exercised by a regency composed of four Manchus from the imperial bodyguard.

The four regents, of whom the best known was Oboi, held power until 1669. In that period they reversed some of the legacies of Shunzhi's reign and attempted to reassert Manchu dominance. The Thirteen Offices were abolished, the late emperor's Buddhist advisers were expelled and a persecution of Jesuit missionaries was commenced. In the metropolitan government, Manchu institutions such as the Council of Deliberative Officials, the membership of which included the commanders of the Manchu and Mongol banners and the Manchu and Mongol presidents of the Six Boards, were given greater responsibility at the expense of Chinese institutions such as the Grand Secretariat.

In the provinces, the task of enforcing Manchu dominance was more difficult to complete. Few Manchus were proficient enough in Chinese, let alone experienced enough in administration, to discharge the duties of a provincial appointment. As a consequence, the regents continued Dorgon's policy of appointing Chinese bannermen to senior provincial positions, although their first move was to replace many of those already in post. Later in the regency some Manchus were appointed as governors and governors-general, but as these appointments were of Oboi's close associates they were resented by other Manchus.

Another problem concerned the relationship between the Manchu conquerors and the Chinese elite. The Hunanese scholar Wang Fuzhi (1619–92) at first supported the Ming cause, but later retired to live as a hermit. In seclusion he wrote anti-Manchu works, such as the *Yellow Book*, which denounced the mixing of Chinese and barbarians.

His writings were rediscovered in the nineteenth century and were used as a source for nationalist polemics.[30] Gentry who lived in the great commercial and cultural centres along the southern stretch of the Grand Canal initially acquiesced to Manchu rule, but this attitude concealed a persistent Ming loyalism and a resentment over what they perceived to be unfair treatment on matters such as official appointments and taxation. In 1661, a protest outside the Confucian temple in Suzhou over the ruthless collection of tax resulted in the trial and execution of 18 members of the gentry on charges of treason, and the subsequent deprivation of many gentry of their degrees. Two years later at Hangzhou, all involved in the production of a history of the Ming dynasty, which contained phrases construed as critical of the Manchus, were the victims of a violent persecution.

The regency suffered from persistent factionalism, with Oboi eventually emerging as the winner, and he continued to dominate the government after 1667 when Kangxi reached his majority. Two years later, the emperor arraigned Oboi and his supporters on charges of usurping his authority and many other faults. Oboi was imprisoned and died soon afterwards. Kangxi thereupon assumed full responsibility for government.

Shortly after Kangxi's accession, the Qing dynasty faced the most severe threat of the period of consolidation. The tension between a metropolitan desire to centralize control and a provincial or regional desire for autonomy has been a recurrent theme in Chinese history. At the end of the Han and Tang dynasties, and again after the fall of the Qing, China had fragmented into independent states or warlord regimes. A similar fragmentation threatened the Qing in the 1660s. The origin of the threat lay in the reliance the Manchus had placed on Chinese collaborators at the time of the conquest. Four collaborators, all of whom came from Liaodong, were of particular importance. Three of them, Shang Kexi, Kong Youde and Geng Zhongming, had crossed to the Manchu side in the 1630s. The fourth, Wu Sangui, had famously changed his allegiance in 1644. For their services they had been granted the title of prince and had been commissioned to pacify the south. Kong Youde had been cut off by Ming forces at Guilin in 1652 and had committed suicide, but the others completed the pacification and then carved out for themselves semi-independent fiefdoms, Wu Sangui in Yunnan and Guizhou, Shang Kexi in Guangdong and Geng Jingzhong, the grandson of Geng Zhongming, in Fujian. Such was the power of these three 'feudatories', as they are called, that Wu Sangui, for example, not only enjoyed virtual suzerainty over the two provinces he controlled directly, but could also make administrative appointments in neighbouring provinces and claim a subsidy of 10 million taels a year for the upkeep of his army.

In 1673, Shang Kexi requested permission to retire and to pass control of Guangdong to his son. The Council of Deliberative Officials accepted his retirement, but refused to make the appointment, effectively abolishing the feudatory. This put pressure on the other feudatories to resign. Both Geng Jingzhong and Wu Sangui tendered their resignations, but it was the view of the majority of the Council that Wu Sangui did not expect his resignation to be taken seriously and that it would therefore be prudent to refuse it. Instead, the Kangxi emperor decided to accept the resignation and disband the three feudatories, knowing that this was likely to precipitate a civil war.

In December 1673, Wu Sangui ordered the murder of the governor of Yunnan, decreed the revival of Ming customs and proclaimed the Zhou dynasty. He obtained the support of four provinces so quickly that the rumour circulated around Beijing that the Manchus were about to withdraw to the north east. However, Kangxi was made of sterner stuff. He put down unrest in the capital and ordered Wu Sangui's son, who had been kept in Beijing as a hostage, to commit suicide. Nevertheless, the rebellion continued to spread and by the end of 1674 virtually all the south and west of the country were in rebel hands, with only Shang Kexi in Guangdong remaining loyal. Kangxi personally directed the military campaign against the rebels, relying on Chinese rather than Manchu commanders, who in many cases had proved incompetent. Through his efforts, and through adroit diplomacy, the rebellion was slowly confined and, after Wu Sangui's death in 1678, gradually extinguished. A factor in the defeat of the rebellion was the use of cannon cast under the supervision of the Jesuit missionary Ferdinand Verbiest. More important than any military consideration was the contest for Han Chinese support, however. Even Ming loyalists found it difficult to support Wu Sangui, who was regarded as a double traitor. The lower Yangzi, the key economic area where previously resentment of the Manchu presence had been strongest, was won over through the remission of taxes and the restoration of gentry status to those who had lost it as a punishment for the 1661 protest.

After the defeat of the rebellion, one further task remained to be completed before the empire was secure. This was the subjugation of Taiwan, which until 1681 had been held by the son of Zheng Chenggong, who had joined the rebellion of the Three Feudatories and had for six years established an enclave on the mainland. In 1683 a large Manchu fleet, led by a former supporter of Zheng Chenggong, captured the Penghu (Pescadores) islands and then occupied Taiwan. In the following year Taiwan was incorporated into the empire as a prefecture of Fujian province and the policy of removing the coastal population was finally rescinded.

THE LATER YEARS OF KANGXI'S REIGN, 1684–1722

In the remaining years of Kangxi's long reign, the Manchu rulers became accepted as a legitimate Chinese dynasty and Manchu–Chinese antagonism ceased to be an important factor in politics. This was achieved by Kangxi committing himself whole-heartedly to the business of being a Chinese emperor. He was extremely hard-working, reading and commenting on an average of 50 memorials a day, as well as holding audiences and performing routine tasks such as reviewing death sentences. He also travelled extensively and recorded his impressions.

> On tours I learned about the common people's grievances by talking with them, or by accepting their petitions. In northern China I asked peasants about their officials, looked at their houses, and discussed their crops. In the South I heard pleas from a woman whose husband had been wrongly enslaved, from a travelling trader complaining of high customs dues, from a monk whose temple was falling down, and from a man who was robbed on his way to town of 200 taels of someone else's money that he had promised to invest – a complex predicament, and I had him given 40 taels in partial compensation.[31]

Kangxi prided himself on his military knowledge, gained through his direction of the campaign against the rebellion of the Three Feudatories. In the 1690s he took the field in two campaigns against the Zunghar. The background to this situation was Russian expansion across Siberia, the establishment of a Russian trading station at Nerchinsk and, in 1656, the construction of a fort at Albazin on the Amur river. At that time the Manchu position in China was too insecure to risk driving the Russians out, but in 1685 Kangxi concluded that the moment had come and he ordered an attack on Albazin. However, he recognized the danger of the Russians allying with the Zunghar, the western branch of the Mongol tribes. As soon as Albazin had been captured, he sought a settlement with Russia. The negotiations between the two states were handled by Jesuit missionaries and resulted in the Treaty of Nerchinsk in 1689, the first treaty signed by China which accepted the principle of diplomatic equality with another state. The treaty demarcated the frontier between China and Russia, keeping the Amur river in Chinese hands. Kangxi could now attack the Zunghar, whose leader Galdan was threatening to unite the Mongol tribes. The emperor led campaigns in 1696 and 1697 which resulted in the defeat of the Zunghar and the alleged suicide of Galdan. The Zunghar remained a threat throughout Kangxi's reign, but in 1717 they rashly invaded Tibet and this gave Kangxi a pretext to intervene and establish a Chinese presence in Lhasa.

Kangxi's government for the most part continued the practices of the Ming, but there were three significant innovations. One of these was the development of the Imperial Household system. Before the conquest the Manchus had kept household or agricultural slaves, many of whom were ethnic Chinese, and their descendants became hereditary slaves or bondservants. From 1615 the bondservants of the emperor and of the Manchu princes were organized into banner companies. The Imperial Household was derived from the bondservant companies of the banners commanded directly by the emperor, with the supervising officials becoming his officials and the rank and file his personal servants. The development of the Imperial Household had been interrupted by Shunzhi's decision to revive the eunuch-controlled Thirteen Offices. In 1661 Kangxi formally established the Imperial Household Department to supervise the eunuchs and to manage the emperor's affairs. By the late eighteenth century the Imperial Household, which was situated in the Forbidden City, employed some 1600 officials and engaged in a wide variety of administrative and commercial activities on the emperor's behalf.

The Imperial Household belonged to what was known as the 'inner court', the realm of the emperor, as opposed to the 'outer court', the realm of the bureaucracy. The outer court operated in accordance with statutory provisions and administrative precedent, but the inner court operated according to the emperor's will. The outer court communicated with officials through open channels, whereas the inner court – and this was the second innovation in the Kangxi period – used the 'palace memorial' system, a means of communicating directly and secretly with correspondents in the provinces. Many of these correspondents were bondservants serving in the provinces, often in the south, who supplied the emperor with confidential information on provincial affairs and the conduct of officials.

The third significant innovation of Kangxi's reign was the extensive employment at court of foreigners, in particular European Jesuits. The Jesuit mission in Beijing had been established in the closing years of the Ming dynasty, and although the Jesuits had supplied the Ming with cannon, their technical expertise enabled them to retain their position in China after the Manchu conquest. Shunzhi had been impressed by the German Jesuit Adam Schall, who was a noted astronomer. During the Oboi regency the Jesuits fell out of favour with the Manchu elite because of their association with the Shunzhi emperor, and with those Chinese who recognized the challenge they presented to Chinese culture. For a time during Kangxi's reign the Jesuits at court enjoyed a position of trust similar to that of Chinese bondservants. The vulnerability of their position was demonstrated in 1664 when Adam Schall, who was responsible for preparing the imperial calendar, was accused of inaccuracy amounting to treason and sentenced to death, the sentence later being rescinded. Schall died in 1666 and his position was taken by Ferdinand Verbiest, who more than restored the Jesuits' position by defeating his Chinese opponent with a display of superior skill in a further dispute over the calendar. Kangxi employed other Jesuits as architects, mathematicians and artists, and as diplomats in the negotiation of the Treaty of Nerchinsk.

In 1692, after Jesuit missionaries had successfully treated the emperor for malaria by prescribing quinine, Kangxi issued an 'edict of toleration' permitting the teaching of Christianity and he commissioned Jesuits to make a cartographic survey of the empire. However, the Jesuits were being attacked by other Christian groups for their willingness to compromise with the Chinese practice of ancestor worship, as required by Kangxi. The Pope sent Charles Maillard de Tournon as a special legate to the Qing court to resolve the issue. He was received in audience by Kangxi, but the emperor would not allow a representative of the Pope to reside in Beijing, nor would Maillard de Tournon accept the Jesuit accommodation on the matter of rites. When the papal legate indicated that Jesuits who observed the compromise were liable to be excommunicated, the emperor ordered all missionaries either to accept the compromise and agree to remain in China for life or to leave the country. After Kangxi's death further negotiations took place, but no agreement could be reached and in 1742 the papal bull *Ex Quo Singulari* forbade Christians to perform the Chinese rites. Some European missionaries remained in Beijing, but the proselytization of Christianity was forbidden and its practice by Chinese converts was driven underground, although it continued to make progress in some provinces, for example in Sichuan.

One of the most memorable of Kangxi's decisions in the later years of his reign was his announcement in 1712 that the number of *ding*, or tax-collection units, should be frozen permanently and should not take account of the rise in the population. This decision was represented as an act of benevolence, as a peace dividend and as fulfilment of the sentiment that 'the hallmark of good government is to keep the burden of taxation light'.[32] Although Kangxi may have been pleased to view his policy in that light, the reasons for his action were less estimable. Since the conquest the dynasty had been faced with mounting problems over the collection of tax. In the early years an attempt had been made to simplify and centralize the tax system, but it remained extremely complex and vulnerable to under-collection and corruption. Moreover, when young, Kangxi had been made aware of the political risks of enforcing tax payments and thereafter had found it expedient to act leniently on these matters. On several occasions he granted generous tax amnesties, failed to deal sternly with cases of official corruption and ignored the problem of 'hidden land'; that is, recently reclaimed land which did not appear on the tax registers.

Kangxi's later years were clouded by worries over the succession. In 1676 he had followed the Chinese imperial custom and had named the 18-month-old Yinreng, his second son and his only son born to an empress, as his heir apparent. At first the relationship between father and son was good and in 1696, when Kangxi left Beijing to campaign against Galdan, he appointed Yinreng as regent. But soon after his return Kangxi heard reports that Yinreng was engaging in immoral behaviour, and for the next 15 years the emperor vacillated between denouncing his son and reinstating him as his heir. Finally in 1712, Yinreng was declared insane and deposed. Until he lay on his deathbed, Kangxi refused to name who should succeed him. Then, according to one version of events, he nominated his fourth son, who was to reign as the Yongzheng emperor. However, the new emperor was accused of having usurped the throne, which should have gone to Kangxi's fourteenth son, and to have poisoned his father, accusations that may have had their origin in the factional infighting which marked court politics during the long succession crisis.

THE YONGZHENG EMPEROR

The relatively short reign of Yongzheng (*r*. 1723–35) was notable for the emperor's energetic attempt to introduce reforms. In September 1723, he introduced a succession system which departed from both the Chinese tradition of appointing the eldest son born of an empress, and the Manchu custom of selecting the heir from the ruler's sons according to merit and with the approval of influential members of the imperial family. Now the emperor was to select his heir from any of his sons and put the candidate's name into a sealed box. His choice would not be revealed to anyone, including the candidate himself, until after the emperor's death. Another reform, also directed at curbing the power of the Manchu princes, was the bureaucratization of the banner system. The background to this measure was the sharp decline in the value of the banner forces as military units and the emergence of strong cliques within the Five Inferior Banners, headed by the Manchu princes. Yongzheng deprived the princes of control of companies within the banners and placed the banners under uniform administrative rules. He established banner schools, which aimed at preserving the distinctive elements of Manchu and Mongol culture, and took steps to improve the economic condition of the bannermen. He sought to revive what was known as the 'Manchu Way' by criticizing bannermen for extravagance, for forgetting that 'The ordinary disposition of us Manchus is to be pure and plain' and for allowing their use of the Manchu language to decline.[33]

The emperor also reformed the dynastic governmental machinery. The palace memorial system, referred to above, undermined the censorial system by enabling the emperor to access confidential information directly. To complement this arrangement Yongzheng developed the 'court letter', a direct and confidential instruction to provincial officials. This change was part of a much more important reform, which had its origins under Kangxi and which was to be developed further by Yongzheng. The reference is to the Grand Council, the inner-court council comprising equal numbers of high-ranking Chinese and Manchu officials, which met daily in the presence of the emperor and enabled him to deal efficiently with the greatly increased volume of business requiring his attention. Although the Grand Council, as a permanent body vested with broad powers, did not appear until early in Qianlong's reign, in 1729 Yongzheng created a forerunner body to co-ordinate the campaign against the Zunghar, the most important war of his reign.

The Kangxi emperor had bequeathed to his successor a state treasury that was nearly empty. The reason for this was not Kangxi's extravagance, nor was it excessive military expenditure, but the large deficit between the amount of tax levied and the amount of tax received. This deficit had two main causes: loss at the point of collection and the proportion retained at the provincial level of government. Whereas Kangxi had adopted a relaxed attitude on fiscal matters, Yongzheng immediately instituted a crusade against official corruption. More originally, he initiated a reform connected with the 'meltage fee', a surcharge on the land tax which supposedly compensated for losses when silver collected as tax was melted down into standard ingots. The excessive imposition of this surcharge, which might add 40 per cent to the land tax, was both an abuse and an indication that officials were grossly underpaid. Oertai, a Manchu official noted for his frugality, contrasted his salary as a governor-general, which amounted to 180 taels per annum, with his expenses in office, which amounted to 6000 taels. Yongzheng acknowledged this problem and legalized the meltage fee to supplement official salaries and to provide public funds for projects such as replenishing community granaries. His reform, however, did not touch on the fundamental weakness of the fiscal system, which was that it was not able to extract more than 5 per cent of the gross national product of a predominantly agrarian economy, a proportion inadequate to discharge the responsibilities of a modern government.

Yongzheng involved himself energetically in many other aspects of ruling. He was determined to enforce ideological conformity among the literati, and he followed his father in promoting neo-Confucianism in the form of the school of Principle, which favoured moral imperatives such as the total subjection of women, the authority of fathers and the unquestioning loyalty of subjects to rulers. In 1670 Kangxi had circulated his *Sacred Edict*, which expounded these principles in the form of 16 maxims. In 1724 Yongzheng reissued the edict with his own amplified instructions. Examination candidates were required to memorize the maxims and scholars expounded them twice monthly at Confucian temples. Yongzheng took up the case of Zeng Jing, a Hunan scholar who had described the Manchus as barbarians and Yongzheng as an usurper. After he persuaded Zeng Jing to write a confession of error, he pardoned him and used his case as propaganda to support the claim that the mandate of heaven had been transferred to the Manchus because of the degeneracy of the Ming dynasty.[34]

Another example of Yongzheng's vigorous approach to ruling concerned the ethnic minorities in the south. In the past, imperial policy towards these groups had relied on the *tusi* or tribal headman system, whereby minorities were ruled by their own tribal leaders, who were given official ranks, and the people themselves were left alone. In the eighteenth century, with the Han Chinese population increasing steadily, pressure on areas occupied by ethnic minorities increased and incidents multiplied. Yongzheng found the tribal headman system incompatible with the principle of universal and absolute rule, and he began the process of bringing the minority groups into the provincial administrative system. This involved the 'pacification' of minority groups such as the Miao and their subsequent enforced sinicization.

Yongzheng's reputation as a ruler is mixed. He stands accused of having usurped the throne and of having disposed ruthlessly of his brothers, who threatened to contest his claim. On the other hand, he has been hailed as 'the greatest centralizer and stabilizer' of the Qing dynasty, who 'revitalized the state administration, and fostered a time of economic prosperity'.[35] He ruled as an autocrat, largely freeing himself from dependence on the bureaucracy and reliance on the Manchu princes. Yet his objective was not simply power, for he showed compassion for his subjects, notably in his efforts to emancipate the 'mean' people, occupational groups such as prostitutes and actors and the Tanka or boat people of south China, who were excluded from public service and were not allowed to marry members of the 'good' population.

THE QIANLONG EMPEROR

The Yongzheng emperor was succeeded by his fourth son, to be known as the Qianlong emperor (*r.* 1736–95). Yongzheng had concealed the name of his heir, and the future emperor and his half-brother closest to him in age were given the same education and administrative experience to prepare them equally for the throne. Both attended the Palace School for princes and studied Manchu texts and Confucian classics, and both learned painting, calligraphy and writing poetry, received instruction in archery and the use of firearms, and went hunting.

When he became emperor, Qianlong continued the autocratic tendencies of his father's government. In the early years of his reign the Grand Council took its definitive shape. The imperial princes lost their seats on the council, their places being taken by Manchu and, for the first time, Chinese officials in the approximate ratio of two Manchu appointments to one Chinese. Ironically, in the course of the reign the Grand Council became so effective a decision-making body that the need for the emperor to direct its deliberations declined. A willingness to appoint Chinese officials, as opposed to Chinese bannermen, was also evident in provincial appointments. In most other respects the operation of the bureaucracy remained unchanged. The examination system continued in full force and appointments to the civil service were dominated by degree-holders. Competition for official appointments became severe and success in the examinations went increasingly to families which had previously placed a member in the bureaucracy, or which could afford to use the purchase system to gain an advantage. Notwithstanding the autocratic tendencies at the centre, the bureaucracy was now too large, and its procedures too complex, to be a simple instrument of the emperor's will, a situation which the Qianlong emperor apparently understood. Iona D. Man-Cheong has suggested that by the eighteenth century, when the Manchus were ruling a vast, multi-ethnic empire, the purpose of the examinations extended beyond the recruitment of able and indoctrinated officials and became a key process in the creation of a centralized state. The examinations legitimized the hierarchical relationship between the throne and the educated elite, contributed to the constitution of state power and perpetuated the imperial system. At the same time, the process of taking the examinations introduced candidates to 'a horizontal web of intersecting ... networks in which a proto-nation-space can be discerned'.[36]

* * *

During the eighteenth century the Qing empire doubled its territorial size and became a multi-ethnic state. Qianlong's contribution to this massive expansion came principally in Tibet and Xinjiang. A Chinese presence in Lhasa had been established during his grandfather's reign, but Chinese influence was undermined by Zunghar intrigues, which in 1750 led to a civil war. Qianlong's response was to instate the Dalai Lama as the temporal ruler of a state enjoying internal autonomy, while at the same time declaring a Chinese protectorate over the country. Qianlong showed particular respect for Buddhism and for Tibetan lamas, and in return was portrayed as a reincarnation of Manjushri, the bodhisattvas of Wisdom. In 1793, in a further assertion of China's dominant role, Qianlong decreed that the future Dalai Lama should be chosen by lot and sent a golden urn to Lhasa for that purpose.

The continued independence of the Zunghar was viewed with suspicion by the Qianlong emperor. After the death of the Zunghar leader Galdan Tseren in 1745, the Zunghar state was riven by internal divisions. In 1755 the Qianlong emperor backed Amursana, one of the contenders for the leadership, and authorized the despatch of two armies to the region. They gained an easy victory, but found a political settlement more difficult to achieve. Two years later Amursana headed a major revolt against the Qing. A large force was sent to the region and the emperor ordered: 'Show no mercy at all to these rebels. Only the old and weak should be saved. Our previous campaigns were too lenient.' As a result of the genocide, the Zunghar disappeared as a state and as a people.[37]

Manchu rulers demonstrated a willingness to experiment in matters of foreign relations. To conduct relations with their Inner Asian subjects, they established the *Lifan Yuan*, the Ministry for Governing the Outer Domains, and used a range of approaches, including political marriages, religious patronage, commerce, diplomacy and war.[38] With reference to other states with which China had relations, Qianlong generally followed the practices of the tribute system. The most developed form of the system applied to relations with Korea, which on average sent a tributary mission to China three times a year. The tributary relationship was regarded as providing benefits to both parties, with China granting commercial privileges in exchange for recognition of China's claim to be the Middle Kingdom. China also accepted some responsibility for the well-being of tributary states, for example in 1788 a Chinese force was dispatched to Annam to assist the king to put down a rebellion.

The Qing court valued foreign trade more than is commonly supposed, but it was also mindful of the potential dangers of foreign contacts in the south, a region of suspect loyalty. In 1684 restrictions on foreign trade were eased, but it remained under close regulation. A superintendent of maritime customs, known to Europeans as the Hoppo, was stationed at Guangzhou. Only those Chinese merchants who belonged to the monopolistic group known as the Cohong were allowed to take a share of the trade, and they were required to guarantee the debts of the foreign traders. At first foreign trade was permitted at a number of southern ports, but this proved difficult to regulate and from 1760 maritime trade was confined to Guangzhou. By the eighteenth century, by far the most important participant in this trade was Great Britain. British trade was monopolized by the East India Company, which handled the tea trade, China's most substantial export.

In Qianlong's reign the economy appeared to be thriving. Its basis remained agriculture, with rice, wheat and millet the most important crops, although in some regions cotton, silk and tea were of major significance. Commerce was well developed, with perhaps 20 to 30 per cent of agricultural production reaching the market. Exchange banks, known as 'Shanxi banks' because many were operated by merchant families from Shanxi, transferred government and private remittances from one part of the country to another. Some industries, in particular the iron, cotton and ceramic industries, were large and sophisticated. These industries had been well established by the early seventeenth century and it has been suggested that China was then on the verge of an industrial revolution, but that development was delayed by the Manchu invasion. Marxist historians have also descried the 'sprouts of capitalism' appearing in the eighteenth century and have claimed that an impending industrial revolution was aborted by the impact of Western imperialism.

This view has been rejected by most Western historians. Albert Feuerwerker described the eighteenth-century industrial growth as 'a few possibly proven instances of fairly large-scale handicraft enterprises', but noted that these did not represent the first stage on the road to modern industrial production.[39] Mark Elvin summed up the state of the Chinese economy as 'quantitative growth, qualitative standstill'. He considered various explanations for China's failure to industrialize at this stage, including those of inadequate capital and political obstruction, but rejected them in favour of what he termed the 'high-level equilibrium trap'. He pointed out that the Chinese economy had achieved a high level of sophistication within the confines of traditional technology. However, in the eighteenth century the population had grown from an estimated 150 million persons to double that figure. Little new land was available for cultivation, and yields per acre were nearly as high as could be achieved using the available technology. At some point between 1750 and 1775 the amount of food available per capita began to decline, which led to a reduction of demand per person for goods other than those needed for bare survival, and a fall in the cost of labour. Under these circumstances there was no case for investing in technological improvements.[40]

These views continue to carry a good deal of weight, but two recent studies suggest that they may understate the Qing government's interest in the management of the economy. One refers to the state granary system which the Qing dynasty, like its predecessors, operated to store grain for distribution to peasants in time of famine. Previously Qing famine-control measures had been described as 'useful up to a certain point' but 'never free from the effects of official ineptitude, indifference, and corruption'.[41] However, a recent study has concluded that the granary system demonstrated not only that the state wished to intervene positively in people's lives, but also that it had the capacity to do so.[42] Another study analysed the eighteenth-century debate on the issue of state intervention in the management of the economy, as opposed to reliance on self-regulating market mechanisms. An example of this was Qianlong's decision in 1737 to promulgate a ban on liquor preparation in northern China, on the grounds that fermenting grain 'wasted' it and aggravated the risk of famine. The ban proved difficult to enforce and fell into disuse, but not before it had been criticized on the grounds that, for some poor peasants, converting part of their grain to liquor was a vital source of cash income and intervention was not in their best interests. Later in Qianlong's reign, government policy became more favourable to legitimate commercial operations and some officials suggested that economic liberalism benefited society as a whole.[43]

The debate on China's 'failure to industrialize' was reignited with the publication in 2000 of Kenneth Pomeranz's *The Great Divergence: China, Europe and the Making of the Modern World Economy.* Pomeranz argued that until the end of the eighteenth century the most advanced Chinese regions (he cited the Yangzi delta) and parts of Japan, India and South-east Asia were as developed economically as were comparable regions in Europe. But then two fortunate factors enabled the West to industrialize: coal reserves to replace exhausted supplies of wood; and overseas colonies, which provided virtually free calories from sugar plantations worked by slaves and silver to buy Indian cotton and Chinese china. Philip Huang took issue with the argument that agriculture in England and the Yangzi delta were roughly comparable. He pointed out that in the Yangzi delta agriculture experienced ever-greater labour intensification and diminishing marginal returns, and that there was a reluctance to use agricultural machinery. In his view, England and the Yangzi delta were 'virtually at opposite poles in a continuum from development to involution'.[44]

* * *

This description of Qianlong's reign has emphasized its stability and achievement, and indeed that is how it was regarded at the time. Manchu identity was closely related to a successful military culture. Toward the end of his reign Qianlong styled himself 'Old Man of the Ten Complete Victories', emphasizing the importance of his military victories.[45] Later writers, including supporters of the 1911 Chinese revolution, identified his reign as marking the beginning of dynastic decline. Recently Western historians, using Manchu records, have offered a new assessment. Mark Elliott found much to praise in the Manchu stewardship of the Chinese state. He cited the demographic expansion, 'unprecedented in world history', accompanied by 'a substantial increase in cultivated land and a steady growth in the national economy, buoyed by a remarkably stable political order administering a realm perhaps twice as populous as all the states of Europe combined'. He suggested that the most important legacy of the Qing period was the unification of China Proper with vast, newly conquered territories to the north and west, the unification of the 'inner' and the 'outer', which created the vast, multi-ethnic empire which is modern China.[46]

This appraisal challenged a long-established view of the nature of Manchu rule. In 1967 Ho Ping-ti argued that the key to Qing success was the adoption, by early Manchu rulers, of a policy of systematic sinicization. In 1994, in a review of the sixth volume of the *Cambridge History of China*, Mark Elliott took issue with the use of the term 'sinicization' because it implied that acculturation and assimilation were unidirectional, that the Manchus had become civilized through their acquisition of Chinese culture. Elliott's point was developed by Evelyn Rawski, who suggested that recent work on Manchu-language documents had shown that the Qing rulers, rather than having become sinicized quickly, had superimposed a separate conquest elite on the Han Chinese bureaucracy, an elite which had continued to participate in the highest councils of state until the mid-nineteenth century. Such an arrangement was not unusual in Chinese history, for previous regimes, including the Liao, Jin, Xixia and Yuan, had employed Han Chinese in the government service, but they themselves had resisted sinicization. Rawski's article prompted a response from Ho Ping-ti, who claimed that under the Qing systematic sinicization of the Manchu imperial clan had taken place. All imperial princes had to undergo years of instruction in Chinese. The Kangxi emperor performed the kotow before Confucius's tablet: 'If this was not a ritualistic expression of the highest possible degree of 'sinicization," I do not know what was.' It was this sinicization, he added, which gained the Manchu rulers the loyal support of the overwhelming majority of their subjects.[47]

The view that the Manchus became sinicized has been challenged indirectly by James Millward. He pointed out that Western historians have commonly made only passing reference to Qing activity in Inner Asia. However, the expansion westwards in the century and a half prior to 1800 was a striking change from the policies of the late Ming and merits the use of the term 'Qing imperialism'. This expansion, which was costly, needed to be reconciled with the Manchus' concern for their subjects in China Proper, and this was done by claiming that there was a 'forward defense dividend' and that the new acquisitions, notably Xinjiang, were self-financing. In fact, once the Zunghar had been defeated, neither of these benefits was significant. What was important to the Qing rulers was the position they now occupied: they were not sinicized rulers of China, nor did they regard China Proper as the centre of their empire. According to the Qianlong emperor, this consisted of five linguistic or ethnic blocs, Muslim, Mongol, Manchu, Tibetan and Han. Each of these blocs was related to the others in various ways, but none was superior to any of the others.[48]

Despite these indications of authority and capability, during Qianlong's reign major social and cultural changes were occurring, signs of dynastic decline had appeared, and some of these changes implied not only the collapse of a dynasty but also the beginning of the end of the imperial system of government. To consider these changes in greater depth three issues will be explored: literary and intellectual life, including the development of writing by women; popular religion and the rise of rebellion; and bureaucratic corruption.

The Qianlong emperor posed as a patron of the arts. He wrote poetry and commissioned scholarly enterprises, the most ambitious of which was the compilation of the *Complete Library of the Four Branches of Literature*, a collection of the 3500 works deemed to be the best in the Chinese literary tradition. The selection and editing of this collection provided employment for an army of scholars. However, the enterprise had a darker side, for it was also a literary inquisition aimed at identifying and destroying any literary works which contained disrespectful references to the Manchus. Because scholars were involved in collecting, rather than in original scholarship, and because they were forced to collude in a form of censorship, the whole project was repressive and stultifying. This accusation of intellectual sterility was challenged by Benjamin A. Elman, who argued that the main emphasis of scholarly activity, the careful textual studies of the Confucian classics, required the use of empirical methods and exact scholarship, the basic tools of research and scientific investigation.[49]

Some of China's most famous novels appeared in the eighteenth century. *The Scholars*, written by Wu Jingzi in the 1740s, contained an ironic description of misplaced intellectual activity, which involved an examination system that concentrated on literary skills and a system of appointment which promoted officials who were more concerned with pleasing their superiors than improving the lot of the common people. He also introduced themes relating to the condition of women, by attacking widow suicide and portraying women as capable of intelligence and cultural refinement, often at the expense of boorish men.[50] In the 1760s early versions of *Hong Lou Meng, The Dream of the Red Chamber*, also known as *The Story of the Stone*, attributed to Cao Xueqin, began to circulate in Beijing. The novel provided both a realistic description of a great family in decline and a complex allegory on the nature of reality and illusion.[51] The poet and essayist Yuan Mei (1716–98) was a great admirer of the novel. He gained notoriety by associating with young married women poets and for asserting that the best poetry was spontaneous and intuitive and that women were more likely than men to produce it.[52] He made no secret of his homoerotic tendencies and many of his poems were addressed to song boys and actors.[53]

Yuan Mei's comment on the literary abilities of women was a recognition of changes which had occurred in the role of elite women by this time. Dorothy Ko, referring to late Ming and early Qing society, has shown how urbanization, commercialization and the print culture brought women's voices into the historical record and how, through reading and writing, women had developed new spheres of influence, a progression which was bridged, rather than interrupted, by the change of dynasties.[54] Susan Mann, referring in particular to the large corpus of poetry written by women in the lower Yangzi region, explained how in the eighteenth century women had expanded the domain of learning and creative expression of their Ming predecessors. She also put forward a broader thesis:

> Far from being an era of unremitting female oppression, the Ming and Qing periods were dynamic and diverse centuries of social, political, and economic change with profound consequences for gender relations in China ...[55]

Her assessment has been supported by the publication of *The Red Brush*, a remarkable collection of women's writing throughout the imperial period. According to Wilt Idema, the last decades of the eighteenth century and the first of the nineteenth century were a second high point in the development of literature written by elite women. He notes in particular the emergence of a poetic form known as 'plucking rhymes', the beginning of a narrative literature in which women expressed their frustrations and aspirations.[56] However, Kathryn Bernhardt has pointed out that the decline in the legal status of women had occurred between the Tang–Song and the Ming–Qing transitions, because of 'a greater legal incorporation of a woman into her marital family and the concurrent weakening of her legal ties with her natal kin'. For her, the period from the late Ming to the mid-Qing was not a turning point in women's history, but a crystallization of trends in evidence since the end of the Song.[57]

The second theme concerns the importance of popular religion and popular culture to the mass of the people, an importance obscured by the dominance of Confucian ideology and of literati culture. A vivid example of this was the 'sorcery scare' of 1768. A rumour swept the lower Yangzi region that sorcerers were stealing men's souls by clipping off their queues. The rumour grew so strong that the emperor, suspecting that queue cutting masked sedition, ordered officials to arrest suspected sorcerers. Although the rumour had died down by the autumn, it had revealed incipient social strains which may have derived from a changing economy, population pressure, increased migration and the growth of an underclass of displaced persons.

Among popular religions, the most widespread was the White Lotus religion, whose adherents worshipped a supreme deity called the Eternal Mother. The religion suffered from periodic state persecution and as a consequence it had no central organization, being composed of small communities linked only by visits from peripatetic teachers. The White Lotus religion found many of its converts among recent migrants and other less settled groups in society and it had a particular appeal to women. For the most part the religion existed to satisfy the spiritual needs of the believers and to provide them with social support, but it also contained a millenarian message which predicted a coming apocalypse marked by the arrival of the Maitreya Buddha, the emissary of the Eternal Mother. The White Lotus religion provided the inspiration for the uprising led by Wang Lun in Shandong in 1774. The rebels were soon defeated, but not before they had exposed the incapacity of the Chinese Army of Green Standard and the Manchu banner troops sent against them. Twenty years later the White Lotus religion provided the inspiration for the first major popular rebellion to threaten the dynasty. This arose in the mountainous region between the upper waters of the Yangzi and Yellow rivers, an area which had received many recent migrants. The rebellion was not suppressed until the government had permitted local gentry to raise militia forces and employ mercenaries, and had sanctioned the movement of the population into strategic hamlets, thereby denying the rebels food and fresh recruits.

The third issue, that of bureaucratic corruption, was commonly cited as a cause of dynastic decline. Yongzheng had attempted to treat what he regarded as the root cause of corruption, the inadequate salaries paid to officials, by providing extra stipends for the 'cultivation of incorruptibility'. In Qianlong's reign these reforms were modified so that, according to Madeleine Zelin, officials were even more handicapped than they had been 50 years previously and 'corruption became a threat to the very survival of the unified Chinese state'.[58] The increase in corruption was illustrated by reference to a Manchu bannerman named Heshen, who was Qianlong's favourite throughout the last 25 years of his life. Heshen was to be accused of having built up an extraordinary network of patronage which corrupted a large part of the civil and military establishment and contributed to the growth of unrest and the rise of rebellion. It was claimed that during the White Lotus rebellion (1796–1804) Heshen had allowed the emperor to believe that the campaign was achieving success, while he embezzled the money intended for military supplies. For this, Qianlong's successor, the Jiaqing emperor, had Heshen arrested and then allowed him to commit suicide. Heshen's career would seem to prove the seriousness of corruption, although it must be said that the White Lotus rebellion had other causes and that the difficulty in suppressing it was only partly Heshen's fault. Albert Feuerwerker has pointed out that corruption was probably no more prevalent under the Qing than under earlier dynasties, and has suggested that corruption might be described as the use of inducements to make a bureaucratic system of government work.[59]

5

China in the Late Qing

In 1792 Great Britain, concerned about the security of its tea trade with China and keen to expand British commercial activity throughout Asia and into the Pacific, sent an embassy to China headed by Lord Macartney. Macartney had been instructed to negotiate a treaty of commerce and to obtain permission for Great Britain to accredit a resident minister at the Qianlong emperor's court. He was told to request the opening of ports additional to Guangzhou and the provision of a base for British merchants which was closer to the tea- and silk-producing areas than was Guangzhou. Macartney took with him as gifts samples of British manufactures, including a planetarium, chandeliers, two howitzers, three carriages and items of Wedgwood pottery, hoping thereby to secure new markets in China for British products.

Macartney was granted an audience with the emperor, but he refused to follow the protocol governing tribute missions and perform the kotow. In two edicts addressed to the king of England, Qianlong rejected all Macartney's requests. He was told that to allow a British national to reside in Beijing to take care of trade was 'contrary to all usage of my dynasty and cannot possibly be entertained'. The existing arrangements relating to trade were confirmed. The emperor supposed that Macartney had requested freedom to propagate Christianity – which he had not done – but such a concession was refused. Finally, the emperor referred to the gifts which Macartney had brought. These, he said, would be accepted out of consideration for the spirit in which they had been sent, but he added:

> As your Ambassador can see for himself, we possess all things. I set no value on objects strange or ingenious, and have no use for your country's manufactures.[1]

Various explanations have been advanced for why the mission returned empty-handed. Macartney opined that the Chinese, having once been very civilized, were now when compared to Europeans a 'semi-barbarous people'. For J. K. Fairbank the reason the Qing court clung so tenaciously to the performance of the kotow was because it functioned to legitimize its rule. Many writers have implied that the Qing court insisted on maintaining ceremonial supremacy because it could not adjust rationally to the demands of a new commercial age. James L. Hevia rejected that as a Eurocentric view and pointed out that in practice the Qing dynasty did not insist on a fixed ritual. Friction occurred on the occasion of the Macartney embassy because court officials failed to organize the ritual process properly. Only later was Macartney's embassy to be described as a failure and that conclusion used to justify Britain forcing China to accept foreign trade and foreign representation.[2] In a review of Hevia's interpretation, Joseph W. Esherick accepted that the kotow was not the issue, for it was probable that a modified form of the ceremony had been agreed. However, he reiterated that the embassy was a failure because it achieved none of its principal objectives, since the Qianlong emperor had refused all requests relating to trade and diplomatic representation.[3] Recently Joanna Waley-Cohen has challenged what she sees as a myth, propagated by Westerners since the eighteenth century, of China's isolationism. China did engage in substantial foreign trade, and the Qianlong emperor's declaration of China's self-sufficiency was disingenuous, being intended to forestall criticism from a domestic audience and to assert China's superiority over foreigners.[4]

In the early eighteenth century, British trade with China had been monopolized by the British East India Company and had comprised the exchange of Chinese tea for British woollen and metal goods. By the 1760s the value of tea exports greatly exceeded that of British imports and the balance had to be made up with silver. In 1784 the British government passed the Commutation Act, which cut tea duties sharply. The demand for tea increased and tea duties continued to provide a large proportion of the British government's revenue. To offset the trading deficit, raw cotton was exported from India to China on board 'country ships' owned by private British merchants. Alongside this legal commerce there was a small but lucrative trade in opium, which was grown on the Company's territory in Bengal and smuggled into China.

Although the Qing court had eventually allowed the resumption of maritime trade, it remained suspicious of foreign intercourse. It was for this reason that from 1760 foreign maritime trade was confined to Guangzhou, and Chinese participation in it was restricted to the group of merchants known to Westerners as the Cohong. As they were held responsible for the debts of foreign merchants, they protected themselves by setting aside a share of their profits in what was known as the Consoo fund. Foreign traders were subject to the Eight Regulations which defined the conditions of their residence in Guangzhou. Foreign women and guns could not be brought to the city and they were only allowed to remain in Guangzhou during the trading season. Relations between British and Chinese merchants were generally good, but in 1784 an unfortunate incident occurred which revealed the disparities between Chinese and Western concepts of legal responsibility and of legal process. A British merchant ship, the *Lady Hughes*, fired a salute and accidentally killed two Chinese officials. Chinese law required that the person responsible should be surrendered to the authorities. The unlucky gunner was handed over reluctantly and immediately strangled. As time passed the confinement of trade to Guangzhou became increasingly irksome to the private traders, and it was they who promoted the idea of sending a mission to China, which resulted in the Macartney embassy.

After the Napoleonic Wars, which had confirmed Britain's position as the world's leading naval power, several events increased tension between Britain and China. In 1816 Lord Amherst headed a second embassy to the Manchu court, but his requests for improvements in the arrangements for trade were rejected abruptly. Opium smuggling began to escalate, one reason being a reduction in the price of Bengal opium. By the 1820s the value of the drug being imported was so large that the balance of trade shifted against China and the deficit had to be made up in silver, which, it was believed, was causing a silver drain and making it more difficult for peasants to pay land taxes, which had to be rendered in silver. Evidence of the growth of addiction prompted Ruan Yuan, the governor-general of Guangdong and Guangxi, to take vigorous action. He drove the opium smugglers out of Aomen, but this only resulted in the trade extending along the coast eastwards and led to the greater involvement of secret societies in its operation.

In 1834 the East India Company's monopoly of the China trade, which had long been the subject of criticism by free traders, came to an end. The British government now assumed responsibility and Lord Palmerston, the British Foreign Secretary, appointed Lord Napier as superintendent of trade in China. Palmerston instructed Napier that on arrival in China he should open direct communication with the authorities in Guangzhou, with a view to discussing improvements in the arrangements for trade. Napier proceeded to Guangzhou without waiting to receive permission, as Chinese regulations required, and with only two frigates in support. There he was refused a meeting and only allowed to leave under humiliating circumstances. This debacle strengthened the contention of those in favour of free trade – notably William Jardine, the most successful trader in opium, and the Manchester Chamber of Commerce – that China should be forced to open additional ports.

While this was happening, a debate was taking place between officials and degree-holders in Beijing on how to stop opium smuggling. One group argued that, as the smuggling could not be prevented, the only practical response was to legalize and tax the importation of opium and to allow the growth of the opium poppy in China. This proposal aroused the fury of a group of degree-holders known as the Spring Purification circle. This group, formed in the 1830s, modelled itself on the Donglin academy of the late Ming period and claimed that scholars had the right of *qingyi*; that is, of moral censure. In 1836 the Spring Purification circle played a part in persuading the Daoguang emperor to reject the proposal to legalize the opium trade and to support a moral crusade against opium consumption. This crusade would involve the gentry of Guangdong and would threaten addicts with the death penalty if they did not give up the habit.

In December 1838, Lin Zexu, the governor-general of Hubei and Hunan and a supporter of the Spring Purification group, was appointed imperial commissioner with instructions to proceed to Guangzhou and carry out a comprehensive suppression of the opium trade. When Lin reached Guangzhou, he immediately enlisted local gentry in a campaign against consumers and ordered the arrest of 60 notorious opium dealers. He then turned to deal with the foreign suppliers, first writing a letter to Queen Victoria (which was never delivered) in which he pointed out that as opium was prohibited in her country, she should use her influence to prevent its production in territories under her control. On 18 March 1839 Lin ordered the Cohong merchants, whom he regarded as no better than wealthy smugglers, to call on the foreign merchants to hand them their stocks of opium within three days and to sign a declaration stating that they would either cease trading in opium or suffer death. In the meantime, foreign trade was suspended and the foreign merchants were kept under house arrest in the trading area outside Guangzhou known as the Thirteen Factories. Lin also attempted to arrest Lancelot Dent, whose firm Dent and Co. was heavily involved in opium smuggling. Charles Elliot, the new superintendent of British trade in China, advised the British merchants to surrender their opium and sign the declaration. He sent an urgent dispatch to Palmerston informing him that the foreign community was being kept under duress, and that he had guaranteed that the merchants would be compensated for the loss of their opium stocks. After having been kept in detention for seven weeks, the foreign community was allowed to go to Aomen. In July some drunken British sailors killed a Chinese farmer. Elliot, recalling the *Lady Hughes* case, refused to hand over the culprits. Lin Zexu responded by forcing the Portuguese authorities in Aomen to request that the British depart, whereupon they moved across the Pearl river estuary to Xianggang (Hong Kong).

Palmerston learned of the detention of British subjects and Elliot's guarantee on 21 September 1839. Prompted by William Jardine, on behalf of the opium interest, and by other British merchants keen to sell textiles to China, he obtained agreement for the dispatch of an expeditionary force to China with instructions to compel the Chinese to abolish the Cohong, to cede an island base and to compensate British traders for the loss of opium.

The war which ensued fell into two phases. In the first phase the expeditionary force, headed by Charles Elliot and his cousin Admiral George Elliot, blockaded Guangzhou and then moved north, seizing the island of Zhoushan and threatening Tianjin and Beijing. At this point the emperor dismissed Lin Zexu and authorized Qishan, the Manchu governor-general of Zhili, to negotiate with Elliot. In January 1841, Elliot and Qishan agreed the Convention of Chuanbi, which accepted British demands, including the cession of the island of Xianggang. This agreement was rejected by both sides as having conceded too little or too much. Qishan was disgraced and Elliot was replaced by Sir Henry Pottinger.

While a larger British expeditionary force was being assembled, an obscure but significant episode occurred near Guangzhou. After the agreement had collapsed, Elliot landed troops north of Guangzhou. As he knew that he had not got enough men to occupy a city of half a million people, he coerced the city authorities into promising the British a ransom of six million dollars for refraining from attack. In the meantime, local gentry leaders had raised a militia and were harrying the British troops. On 29 May 1841, near the village of Sanyuanli, they ambushed a British patrol, killing one man and injuring several others. This skirmish came to represent the beginning of Chinese popular resistance to foreign invasion, and was later contrasted with the Manchu court's self-interested willingness to compromise with the imperial powers.

In the second phase of the war, Pottinger moved up the coast and captured Xiamen, Zhoushan and Ningbo. In May 1842, having received reinforcements, he captured Zhapu, overcoming heroic resistance by Manchu soldiers whose families preferred death to capture. After Shanghai had been occupied and Pottinger had begun to move up the Yangzi, the emperor authorized Qiying, a Manchu imperial clansman, to conduct the negotiations which resulted in the Treaty of Nanjing. The treaty, which was signed on 29 August 1842, provided for the opening of five ports, Guangzhou, Xiamen, Fuzhou, Ningbo and Shanghai, to British trade and residence; the cession of Xianggang to Britain; the abolition of the Cohong; equality in official correspondence; and agreement on a fixed tariff. In addition, China was to pay Britain $21,000,000 to cover the costs of the war and the value of the opium which had been confiscated. The treaty made no reference to the opium trade.

The Treaty of Nanjing was the first of the treaties between China and the West which have been dubbed 'unequal treaties', because they conferred benefits on the Western powers without offering advantages to China in return. These treaties had four characteristic features: the opening of treaty ports; extraterritoriality, that is the removal of foreigners from the jurisdiction of Chinese courts; external tariffs fixed by treaty; and the 'most favoured nation' clause, which guaranteed that signatories of unequal treaties would share all benefits granted to other powers. The Nanjing settlement was supplemented by the Treaty of the Bogue, which provided for extraterritoriality and contained a most favoured nation clause. In this treaty, import tariffs were fixed at an average 5 per cent of the value of the goods. Similar treaties were negotiated by the United States and France. France also obtained an imperial edict which granted toleration to Roman Catholicism, a concession which was extended shortly afterwards to other Christian sects.

An extensive historiographical debate has arisen about the origins of the Opium War. Karl Marx, in articles for the *New York Daily Tribune* written in the 1850s, asserted the centrality of the opium trade to the origins of the war. However, modern Western historiography was long dominated by the view expressed by the Harvard historian John K. Fairbank that opium was 'the occasion rather than the sole cause' of the war, which he argued arose essentially from a conflict between Eastern and Western cultures.[5] More recently the importance of the opium trade to Britain has been re-emphasized. According to D. K. Fieldhouse, 'it formed an integral part of the pattern of British economic activity in India and was in some ways fundamental to it'.[6] For Carl Trocki, the opium trade made war inevitable: 'sooner or later the Chinese would have felt themselves required to take forceful action against the trade. Conversely, it is hard to find a moment when Britain might have turned things around and given up the trade.'[7]

FROM THE FIRST OPIUM WAR TO THE *ARROW* WAR OF 1856–60

Both sides soon expressed their dissatisfaction with the Nanjing settlement. On the British side, there had been high hopes that the opening of additional ports would lead to a large increase in trade, but after a short improvement the anticipated bonanza did not occur. Although a report made to the House of Commons in 1847 suggested that this was because of the lack of demand in the Chinese market, the suspicion remained that the real reasons were the obstructiveness of Chinese officials and the imposition of internal transit duties. Immediately after the conclusion of the Treaty of Nanjing, Pottinger and Qiying enjoyed a diplomatic honeymoon, but after 1844, when Pottinger was replaced by J. F. Davis, relations between Britain and China began to deteriorate. A particularly contentious issue was the 'Guangzhou city question', a dispute over whether the Treaty of Nanjing had given British subjects the right of trade and residence within the walls of Guangzhou and, if it had, when they would be allowed to exercise that right. In 1847 Davis lost patience and ordered the capture of the forts guarding the approaches to Guangzhou. Qiying was forced to promise entry into the city in two years' time.

On the Chinese side, the years immediately after the first treaty settlement were marked by the imperial court's willingness to be conciliatory in the management of 'barbarian affairs'. This policy was endorsed by Muchanga, the Daoguang emperor's chief minister. As Muchanga and Qiying were both Manchus, this willingness to appease the foreigners was later attributed to a Manchu desire to preserve the dynasty at the expense of the Chinese national interest. However, conciliation was a risky policy, as it conflicted with the anti-foreignism of the majority of Chinese officials and of the local gentry around Guangzhou. In 1848 the emperor dismissed Qiying and appointed Xu Guangjin as governor-general of Guangdong and Guangxi and commissioner for foreign affairs. Xu, a Chinese, had already shown that he was responsive to local opinion. Ye Mingchen, who took over as governor of Guangdong, was also known for his xenophobia.

As April 1849, the agreed date for British entry into Guangzhou, approached, Xu Guangjin abandoned the conciliatory policy and allowed local gentry to raise militia to oppose the entry. He then took the even more desperate gamble of forging an imperial edict ordering him to respect the will of the people. Sir George Bonham, the new governor of Xianggang, accepted a further postponement, a concession which was greeted by the Chinese as a victory and commemorated by the granting of imperial honours to Xu Guangjin and Ye Mingchen, but which was deeply resented by the local British community. The anti-foreign direction of Chinese policy became even more marked after the Daoguang emperor's death in 1850, for his successor, the Xianfeng emperor, dismissed Muchanga and in 1852 promoted Ye Mingchen to the positions held by Xu Guangjin.

These incidents, and this hardening of attitudes, might have led to a second war in the early 1850s, but other considerations prevailed. The rise of rebellion – the Taiping rebels captured Nanjing in 1853 and the Red Turbans rebels overran Guangdong in 1854 – forced the Chinese authorities to act circumspectly. British diplomats had assumed that the Treaty of Nanjing would be subject to revision after 12 years – that is, in 1854 – and it was only then that they realized that the Chinese had no intention of reopening questions which they regarded as settled. The outbreak of the Crimean War in March 1854 provided another reason for delaying what was now regarded as an overdue settlement of issues with China.

In October 1856 Chinese officials boarded the *Arrow*, a small ship claiming British registration, and seized the crew on suspicion of piracy. This incident was treated by Sir John Bowring, the Governor of Xianggang, as an insult to the British flag and he sanctioned a naval attack on Guangzhou. In response, Ye Mingchen suspended foreign trade, the foreign factories were burned down, and rewards were offered for the killing or capture of an Englishman. When news of these events reached London, Lord Palmerston, now prime minister, was criticized for his handling of affairs in China and his government was defeated in a vote of censure. However, Palmerston won the ensuing election and obtained a mandate to send an expeditionary force to China. This force, headed by the Earl of Elgin, included a French contingent dispatched to obtain compensation for the judicial murder of a French missionary.

After a delay occasioned by the need to divert forces to help suppress the Indian Mutiny, Elgin captured Guangzhou, sent Ye Mingchen as a prisoner to India, and placed the city under an allied government headed by the thrusting British consul, Harry Parkes. The allied forces then moved north, seized the Dagu forts and reached Tianjin, at which point the emperor decided to negotiate. In the Treaty of Tianjin, concluded in June 1858, China agreed to open ten more treaty ports; to allow foreigners, including missionaries, to travel in the interior of China; to accept changes relating to external tariffs and new arrangements governing transit duties; to legalize the opium trade; and to accept a resident British minister in Beijing. The opening of the treaty ports on the Yangzi was to be deferred until the Taiping rebellion had been defeated.

Treaties containing similar terms were signed between China and France, the United States and Russia. American interest in the Pacific had been growing rapidly in the 1850s. It was an American expedition which in 1853 had forced Japan to end the policy of seclusion. Russia's involvement stemmed from the forward policy in Siberia, which it had pursued since the late eighteenth century. In 1849, N. N. Muraviev, the governor-general of eastern Siberia, dispatched an expedition to explore the Amur river valley. Finding it devoid of Chinese garrisons, he established a trading post, which he named Nikolaevsk after the tsar. During the Tianjin negotiations the Russian diplomat Count Putiatin pretended to act as a mediator between China and the Western powers. In the meantime, Muraviev took advantage of China's weakness to obtain the Treaty of Aigun, which ceded to

.ll land north of the Amur river and provided for Sino-Russian .stration of the territory between the Wusuli river and the sea. June 1859 the allied representatives returned to China to ratify the treaties. When they attempted to pass the Dagu forts, they found the river blocked and in the action which followed the allies suffered heavy casualties. When news of this victory reached Beijing, hardliners at court advocated the abrogation of the treaties and the renewal of the war. In the following year the allies returned with a much larger force, outflanked the Dagu forts and marched on Beijing. A group of British and French diplomats and soldiers, headed by Harry Parkes, was captured and maltreated. In revenge, Elgin ordered the burning of the Summer Palace, the collection of buildings designed by Jesuits in the eighteenth century. Elgin then entered Beijing, where he signed an additional convention which committed China to opening Tianjin as a treaty port, to ceding the Jiulong (Kowloon) peninsula opposite Xianggang to Britain and to paying an additional indemnity. One month later, in November 1860, China was manoeuvred into ceding to Russia the vast expanse of territory east of the Wusuli river. This allowed Russia to establish a naval base at Vladivostok.

THE RISE OF REBELLION

Between 1850 and 1873, China experienced a sequence of rebellions and uprisings which came close to overthrowing the Qing dynasty. The greatest of these was the Taiping rebellion (1850–64), which for much of its course was centred on Nanjing, thereby splitting the country in two. The Nian rebellion (1853–68) had its base area in northern Anhui. In Yunnan (1856–73) and Gansu (1862–73), Muslim rebels threatened the secession of these provinces from China. In 1853 secret society members captured Shanghai and Xiamen and in the following year the Red Turbans nearly captured Guangzhou. Between 1854 and 1873 the Miao or Hmong were in revolt in Guizhou, and between 1865 and 1877 Yakub Beg, a Uighur from present-day Uzbekistan, ruled over much of western Xinjiang.

In Confucian historiography, the rise of rebellion marked a stage in the dynastic cycle. When dynasties were founded, they were headed by virtuous rulers who enjoyed the mandate of heaven. Inevitably, their successors could not maintain the standards which their predecessors had set and the quality of government declined. Rebellions arose which overthrew the dynasty and the dynastic cycle began again under a new leader. Some modern historians have adapted this concept, explaining the dynastic cycle in administrative rather than in moral terms. Dynasties were founded by active rulers supported by a modest court and an efficient bureaucracy. They exercised effective military authority and extended the frontiers of the empire. Later in the cycle, the court became extravagant and the bureaucracy corrupt. The armed forces deteriorated and could no longer defend the over-extended frontiers. The burden of taxation increased and was heaped ever more oppressively on those least able to pay, thereby provoking the rebellion which was to overthrow the dynasty.

These rebellions are commonly described as 'peasant rebellions', a term which may imply that they arose from peasant immiseration, that the leaders were peasants or that the great majority of the partici-pants were peasants. However, the term has also acquired a politi-cal implication. Mao Zedong described the hundreds of uprisings which had punctuated Chinese history as 'peasant revolutionary wars'. They arose because of the ruthless economic exploitation of the peasantry by the landlord class and were therefore an expression of the class struggle. Moreover, these wars 'alone formed the real motive force of China's historical evolution'.[8]

The mid-nineteenth-century rebellions have been located in the downward phase of the dynastic cycle. The White Lotus rebellion of the late eighteenth century, which became a major threat because of the ineffectuality of the armed forces and the misappropriation of funds by Heshen, the Qianlong emperor's favourite, weakened the dynasty. But the Qing court in the first half of the nineteenth century was not moribund, it was faced with situations of unprecedented complexity. Qianlong's successor, the Jiaqing emperor, attacked corruption, attempted to curb court extravagance, and tried and failed to resolve problems associated with the grain tribute system, which arranged the delivery of rice from the south to Beijing. In 1824–6 his successor, the Daoguang emperor, had to deal with a major crisis: the breaching of the Gaojia Great Dyke and the consequent flooding and disruption of traffic along the Grand Canal. Jane Kate Leonard, assessing his response to the crisis, asked whether the 'emperor, indeed the whole imperial state [was] as tentative and faltering at this time' as scholars have tended to assume. Her answer was that the crisis, a geophysical problem compounded by neglect, was inves-tigated thoroughly and the emperor's conclusion, that the difficulty could not be resolved but could be alleviated by greater use of sea transport, was sensible.[9]

Twenty years later, two disastrous floods of the Yellow river taxed the capabilities of the court to the extreme. According to Randall Dodgen, by this time the system of river control was 'more extensive, technologically sophisticated, fiscally demanding, and administratively challenging than it had been at any earlier time'. The Xiangfu flood of 1841–2, which left the city of Kaifeng cut off for a long period, did prompt a remarkable effort to repair the breaches. But the Taiyuan flood of 1842–5 'exposed Qing river engineering at its most disorganised and inept' and anticipated the river's shift to its northern course a decade later. The court's response to these events led Dodgen to conclude: 'The crisis that created the river's shift in the 1850s signalled neither dynastic decline nor an irresistible natural cycle, but the administrative, technological, and economic limits of the late imperial state.'[10]

Perhaps the most important factor undermining the dynasty was that in the eighteenth century the population of China had doubled, increasing from about 150 million to about 300 million people. This rise had occurred in a period of prolonged peace, at a time when there were no major outbreaks of epidemic disease. Until the end of the eighteenth century population growth had been matched by increases in the food supply, part of which came from the slow diffusion of new crops, notably maize, sweet potatoes and peanuts, which had been introduced into China from America in the late Ming period. Population increase encouraged extensive migration away from densely populated delta regions to less exploited hilly regions. A notable example of this movement occurred in the Yangzi highlands, where migrants known as 'shack people' cleared hillsides and planted the new crops, their activities causing serious erosion and flash floods. Migration weakened administrative control, because migrant communities were unstable and unruly and could not readily be incorporated into the *baojia* framework. In some areas, for example in southern Guangxi, friction arose between the established Chinese population and recent arrivals, who were often Hakka or *kejia* ('guest people') Chinese, who spoke a different dialect. Population growth also led to a rise in the number of candidates in the official examinations and heightened the already fierce competition for bureaucratic appointments. Administrative tasks became more complex and officials took on supernumerary personnel to enable them to fulfil their duties. They were paid by increasing the unofficial levies imposed on taxpayers.

A number of connections have been identified between the Opium War, Western imperialism and the rise of rebellion. Karl Marx, writing in 1853, attributed the rise of the Taiping rebellion to the effects of defeat. 'Before the British arms', he wrote, 'the authority of the Manchu dynasty fell to pieces.'[11] It has been suggested that the opium trade, and the consequent outflow of silver, altered the exchange rate between copper and silver, thereby increasing the land tax paid by poor farmers. It may also have exacerbated the contraction of the economy between 1825 and 1850, which led to a rise in unemployment. The opening of Shanghai as a treaty port put out of work many thousands of porters and boatmen who had been employed in transporting tea to Guangzhou. One of the tasks of the British navy, after the seizure of Xianggang, was to expel the pirate fleets from local waters. Some moved up the Xi (West) river, where they joined the rebels in the early stages of the Taiping rebellion.

In north China, rebellion was often associated with the White Lotus religion. In the south, the more common association was with the secret societies known in the West as the Triad. These had originated on Taiwan in the seventeenth century and had as their claimed political objective the overthrow of the Qing and the restoration of the Ming. In times of peace they provided mutual support for their members, who engaged in criminal activities such as piracy, smuggling and racketeering. When disturbances occurred, the societies were quick to take advantage of the situation. In the eighteenth century the societies spread across southern China, gaining recruits among mobile groups, such as porters and boatmen, and among bandits, smugglers and pirates. From about 1840, when feuding between rival lineages became increasingly commonplace, the societies began to gain recruits from the settled peasantry of the Pearl river delta.

THE REBELLIONS

Hong Xiuquan (1814–64), the future leader of the Taiping rebellion, was a Hakka Chinese who came from the district of Huaxian in Guangdong. In 1836, when in Guangzhou for the provincial examinations, he was handed a collection of Christian tracts entitled *Good Words to Admonish the Age*. The following year, having again failed the examinations, he fell ill and had a series of dreams in which a venerable man presented him with a sword with which to extermi- nate demons, and a middle-aged man, whom he called elder brother, fought at his side against devils. In 1843 Hong failed the examina- tions for a fourth time and, after returning home, picked up the tracts he had been given seven years previously. They seemed to provide him with the key to his dreams: the venerable man was God the Father, the middle-aged man his son, Jesus Christ, and Hong himself was God's Chinese son, who had been entrusted with the task of restoring the true faith to China.[12]

Hong began by announcing his vision to his family and making his first converts, who included his cousin Hong Ren'gan and a fellow schoolteacher, Feng Yunshan. They removed the Confucian tablets from the village school, and the hostility which this aroused may have prompted them to travel to Guangxi and make converts among the Hakka living there. In 1847 Hong returned to Guangzhou and for some months attended the church run by a fundamentalist Southern Baptist missionary, Issachar J. Roberts. When he returned to Guangxi, he found that Feng Yunshan had assembled a congrega- tion of some 2000 Hakka peasants and miners, known as the God Worshippers' Society, who were bound together not only by reli- gion but also by the experience of the communal strife between the Hakka and the earlier Chinese settlers. After Feng Yunshan had been arrested on a charge of planning rebellion, two new leaders emerged: Yang Xiuqing, a charcoal burner later known as the Eastern king, and Xiao Chaogui, a poor hill farmer, who became the Western king. Both claimed spirit possession, Yang as the mouthpiece of God the Father and Xiao as that of Jesus Christ.

In the summer of 1850, the God Worshipper movement entered a millennial phase. In anticipation of an imminent second coming, the adherents abandoned their houses and assembled near the village of Jintian. There they deposited their valuables in a sacred treasury and practised segregation of the sexes. In January 1851, after having been attacked by gentry-led militia and government troops, Hong Xiuquan declared the establishment of the *Taiping Tianguo*, the Heavenly Kingdom of Great Peace, and he himself assumed the title of the Heavenly king.

The rebellion which followed went through several phases. In September 1851 the Taipings captured the small walled city of Yongan and over the next few months they created a military organization, established a collective leadership and, using a captured printing press, published various documents including a new calendar. Yongan was besieged by government troops, but in April 1852 the Taipings broke out and began a spectacular northern advance, during which they collected a following estimated at over a million people. In March 1853 they captured Nanjing and massacred the 30,000 Manchus they found there. They made the city their capital, which later proved to be a strategic error. Later that year a northern expedition came close to capturing Beijing. A seven-year stalemate ensued, with the rebels occupying the middle Yangzi and government troops and gentry-led militia being unable to dislodge them.

In 1856 a power struggle within the collective leadership resulted in the death of the Eastern king and many of his followers. In 1859 Hong's cousin, Hong Ren'gan, rejoined the movement. Under his leadership and that of Li Xiucheng, the Loyal king, the Taipings' most successful military commander, the rebellion revived and in 1862 the rebels nearly captured Shanghai. Then the tide turned, the rebels losing control of the Yangzi above Nanjing to forces raised by gentry leaders, and of the Yangzi delta region to similar forces supported by the British. In July 1864 Nanjing was recaptured and Hong Xiuquan committed suicide.

The Taiping rebellion had many aspects and has been the subject of numerous interpretations. Like nearly all great rebellions in Chinese history, it had a religious inspiration. In the early years its followers were required to refrain from the use of tobacco, opium and alcohol, the practice of gambling and engaging in sexual relations. The Christian elements in Taiping religion at first raised hopes among Protestant missionaries that the movement presaged the mass conversion of China. Later most Westerners found fault with Taiping religion, which they regarded as blasphemous, and they alleged that the rebel leaders were hypocrites and their followers did not observe the religious tenets. The rebellion has been hailed as an expression of a nationalist spirit, directed against Manchu oppression and committed to achieving 'a complete reform of China's social, economic, political, and military institutions', an allusion in particular to the ambitious programme of reform proposed by Hong Ren'gan but never implemented.[13] According to Pamela Crossley, Taiping rhetoric introduced a new hostility towards the Manchus, who were 'the personal representatives of Satan'. The language used against them was adopted by Chinese nationalists at the time of the 1911 revolution.[14]

The rebellion is often described as a revolution, a reference to the ambitious plans to remake society contained in a document entitled *The Land System of the Heavenly Dynasty.* This prescribed that land should be classified according to its fertility and then divided up among the population, with equal shares for men and women. Each family would be allowed to retain such proportion of the produce that it required for its own consumption, and the rest would be deposited in the public granary. The population was to be divided into groups of 25 families, each headed by a sergeant, who would be responsible for the religious education of the children. The same system provided the military organization of the Taiping state and defined the arrangements for the promotion and demotion of individuals.

This land system, which has been attributed to Yang Xiuqing, the Eastern king, displayed revolutionary intentions which accord with the interpretation of the rebellion as a class movement directed against landlords. However, there is little evidence of its implementation. In areas under Taiping control some attempt was made to introduce the 25-family system, but no redistribution of land took place. In the later stages of the rebellion when the Taipings occupied Jiangnan, although they did not redistribute land, they did improve the position of tenants by requiring them to pay the land taxes – which gave them a claim to the ownership of land in cases where the landlord had fled – and by enforcing a reduction in the rent payable. This did not amount to a complete restructuring of property relations in the countryside, but it was a blow struck at the dominance of rural landlords.

The Nian rebellion (*nian* simply means group) arose in the harsh terrain north of the Huai river, an area affected by the White Lotus rebellion half a century previously. Nian groups of bandits gained influence throughout the area by establishing mutually advantageous relationships with the leaders of local communities. In 1851 the Yellow river began to shift to its northern course and two years later the Taipings established themselves at Nanjing. The Nian chieftains profited from both developments to set up local defence organizations, which purported to be loyal but in reality were an extension of Nian influence. In 1856, perhaps following the example of the Taiping rebellion, the Nian chiefs chose Zhang Luoxing to be their leader and adopted elements of a political programme, claiming that they had risen up 'to rescue the impoverished, eliminate treachery, punish wrongdoing, and appease the public indignation'.[15] In 1857 they made an informal alliance with the Taiping rebels, with Zhang Luoxing being given the title of a Taiping king.

One reason for the Nian rebels' success was their use of cavalry, and it was to combat this strength that in 1860 the Mongol Prince Senggelinqin was given the task of defeating them. By spring 1863 he had captured and executed Zhang Luoxing and had driven the other Nian leaders out of their 'nest area' in northern Anhui. This provoked the Nian to adopt a new strategy of hit-and-run raids. In 1865, when in pursuit of the Nian rebels after such a raid, Senggelinqin was ambushed and killed.

In the meantime, two major Muslim rebellions had arisen in south-west and north-west China. In both cases the underlying cause was the discriminatory treatment of the large Muslim population and the failure of imperial officials to curb the excesses of the local Han Chinese settlers. In the south west, in Yunnan, the so-called Panthay Rebellion had its origins in the tension caused by Han immigration into Yunnan and subsequent competition over resources – between 1775 and 1850 the population of Yunnan rose from approximately four million to about ten million. In 1856 after a massacre of Hui (Yunnanese Muslims) by Han Chinese in Kunming, the disorder turned into open rebellion, with the Hui and other ethnic and religious groups headed by Du Wenxiu establishing an independent state with its capital at Dali. Du Wenxiu ruled with the assistance of a Chinese bureaucracy and entertained some hope of recognition by Britain and France.[16] In the north west, many Muslims had adopted the New Teaching, a mystic form of Islam, which had brought them into conflict with other Muslims and with Han Chinese. Rebellion broke out in 1862 after a Taiping detachment had traversed the area, provoking both Muslims and Han Chinese to form armed corps. By 1864 Muslim rebels headed by Ma Hualong had occupied much of Gansu and dominated the trade routes to Mongolia.

THE DEFEAT OF THE REBELLIONS

In 1860, when the Taipings were on the verge of capturing Shanghai and the Western allies were marching on Beijing, the Qing dynasty appeared to be on the verge of collapse. Its recovery and survival for a further half-century were due to a variety of factors, including the limitations of the rebellions and the eventual marshalling of an effective opposition to them.

From its inception, the Taiping rebellion had suffered from internal problems. The religious fanaticism of its leaders had denied it popular support and had brought about the internecine strife of 1856. Hong's religious vision caused him to adopt Nanjing as his capital when an all-out assault on Beijing might have succeeded. In 1861 the failure of Li Xiucheng, the Loyal king, and Hong Ren'gan, the Shield king, to co-ordinate their campaigns led to the loss of the key city of Anqing on the middle Yangzi and to the eventual military defeat of the Taiping movement. The other rebellions did not even claim the coherence or the dynastic pretensions of the Taiping Heavenly Kingdom and, apart from the brief liaison between the Taiping and the Nian, no effort was made to co-operate in the overthrow of the Qing.

Such an account of the shortcomings of the rebellions suggests that it was remarkable that they lasted so long. In many respects the rise and persistence of rebellion demonstrated the limited capacity of the traditional forces of the Manchu dynasty. The main response was to mount an ineffective blockade of Nanjing, a tactic which left them vulnerable to the Taiping counterattack of 1860, which virtually destroyed the imperial command. Nevertheless, when Nanjing fell in 1864, the court was quick to claim credit for the defeat of the rebellion.

Western historians, writing in recent years, have ascribed the main role in the defeat of the rebellions to the new military formations known as the regional armies. When the Taipings swept across Hunan in 1852, the only resistance came from local defence organizations led by the gentry. It was obvious that better-trained and better-equipped forces were needed to oppose the rebels, and it was at this point that the famous Hunanese scholar-official Zeng Guofan (1811–72) began to play a key role. In 1852 he was permitted to return home to observe the customary mourning period for his mother, and soon after was ordered by the emperor to raise and drill a militia. Zeng exceeded his instructions and began to recruit mercenaries and to organize an army based on the principles enunciated by Qi Jiguang, who in the sixteenth century had played a notable part in defeating the Japanese pirates. Zeng's army, to be known as the Hunan army, was organized like a Confucian family, with senior officers recruiting their followers on the basis of personal links and with moral exhortation taking the place of impersonal discipline. To pay for this force, at first Zeng obtained permission to sell ranks and titles. However, from 1853 he began to utilize the *lijin*, a new tax on goods in transit, to pay his troops at a rate higher than that paid to regular soldiers. The Hunan army played a crucial role in preventing the Taipings from occupying Hunan in 1854 and in recapturing Anqing in 1861.

In 1862 Li Hongzhang, a former assistant of Zeng Guofan, organized the Anhui or Huai army on the pattern of the Hunan army, although he paid more attention to the adoption of Western arms and military drill. This force assisted in the defence of Shanghai and subsequently achieved the defeat of the Nian rebellion. A reorganized branch of the Hunan army, under the command of Zuo Zongtang, was instrumental in the suppression of the north-west Muslim rebellion.

When the Taiping rebellion broke out, the British government adopted a policy of strict neutrality between the rebels and the insurgents. However, the 1858 Treaty of Tianjin opened the Yangzi as far as Hankou to foreign trade once the rebellion had been suppressed; a provision which made a Manchu victory advantageous to Britain. Active intervention only began in 1862, when British forces assisted in the defence of Shanghai and British ships transported Zeng Guofan's troops down the Yangzi. In Shanghai the foreign community raised a force to be known as the 'Ever-Victorious Army', at one time commanded by Captain Charles Gordon, which co-operated with Li Hongzhang's Huai army in recovering the cities of the Yangzi delta.

THE TONGZHI RESTORATION

During the Tongzhi emperor's reign (1862–74) a 'restoration' – that is to say, a temporary reversal of the dynasty's decline – was claimed to have taken place. The first stage of this development came in September 1860 when, after the disastrous defeat at the battle of Baliqiao, Prince Gong, the sixth son of the Daoguang emperor, was ordered to negotiate a settlement with Britain and France. When the Xianfeng emperor died in August 1861 the throne passed to the Tongzhi emperor, who was a minor. A regency was set in place, but in November the emperor's mother, the Empress Dowager Cixi, and Prince Gong carried out a coup which eliminated the anti-foreign faction at court.

The task of restoration encompassed the defeat of the rebellions, the recovery of dynastic authority and the repair of the damage caused. The last of the rebellions, the north-west Muslim rebellion and the Miao uprising in Guizhou, were finally defeated in 1873. However, Yakub Beg was still in power in western Xinjiang and in 1871 Russia had occupied the Ili valley in north-west Xinjiang. Any loss of territory in Inner Asia implied a betrayal of the achievement of the earlier Manchu emperors. Some senior officials, including Li Hongzhang, argued that priority should be given to coastal defence, and that a deal should be done with Yakub Beg. Nevertheless, the decision was taken that Xinjiang must be recovered. The task was given to Zuo Zongtang, vast sums of money were raised and an enormous task force was assembled. Although Yakub Beg's forces had some modern weapons, his forces had become demoralized and when he died in mysterious circumstances in 1877, his regime collapsed.

There remained the issue of Ili. An initial agreement was repudiated by China and the crisis was only settled in 1881 with the withdrawal of Russia under the terms of the Treaty of St Petersburg. Three years later, the region became Xinjiang province. Many of the officials appointed to administer the new province were Chinese and Chinese immigration into the province was encouraged. This led James Millward to observe:

> During its last decades the Qing dynasty struck a bargain to remain in power in China and for security of the borders. The price of that security might be called 'Hanization' of the empire. This was not sinicization, the idealized notion that peoples in propinquity to China spontaneously acculturated to its superior civilization, but rather a concrete and traceable process by which Han replaced Manchus and Mongols in positions of authority ... and Han Chinese population settled frontier regions in increasing numbers.[17]

The Manchus had originally placed severe restrictions on Chinese emigration to present-day Manchuria. However by the early nineteenth century Chinese migrants had spread through Liaoning and Jilin, the southern and central provinces of the area. By the middle of the century restrictions on emigration were no longer applied and the wave of Chinese migrants became a flood. In 1820 the population of Manchuria was approximately three million; by 1910 it had risen to eighteen million.[18]

The recovery of the dynasty's authority in China Proper was a more difficult objective, and the extent to which it was achieved has become one of the main points of debate in late Qing history. In this debate two distinct but overlapping issues have emerged, namely the position of the gentry and the emergence of regional power centres.

In the early nineteenth century the gentry, by strict definition the holders of degrees and titles obtained by examination or purchase, numbered about 1.1 million. Only a small minority of them held office, but the remainder performed a vital role in ensuring local control, assisting officials in the performance of their duty and maintaining ideological conformity. In return for their services, the gentry occupied a privileged position with regard to the payment of taxes and access to officials. The Qing dynasty recognized the importance of maintaining control of the gentry group. It did this by regulating the quota of candidates who would pass the examinations, by restricting the sale of titles and by requiring the gentry to pursue what has been called 'a life of examination'. It also excluded the gentry from certain key roles: the organization of the mutual security system known as the *baojia*, the collection of taxes and engagement in military activity unless expressly required to do so.

The mid-nineteenth-century rebellions had a profound effect on the gentry's position. To raise funds, the court relaxed restrictions on the sale of degrees and titles. It later rewarded provinces where gentry had contributed to the defeat of rebellion, by raising quotas. As a consequence, the total number of gentry rose to about 1.45 million, the largest percentage increases being in those awarded higher degrees and those who obtained degrees by purchase. The gentry's exclusion from the collection of taxes was compromised by the introduction of the *lijin* tax. The prohibition on gentry involvement in military activities had been infringed, since endemic disorder and the effects of the Opium War had encouraged the development of *tuanlian*, gentry-led village defence organizations, an early stage in the increasing militarization of Chinese society. The *tuanlian* were supplemented by mercenary forces hired by gentry associations and eventually by the regional armies, which, although not the instrument of the gentry, owed much to gentry support. The consequent reduction in the dynasty's ability to control the gentry was reinforced by a gentry demand for 'local self-government'. Before the rebellions the view was expressed that the administration of the district magistrate had become corrupt and ineffective, and that its functions would be discharged more efficiently by the gentry. This case was taken up at the time of the restoration by the distinguished scholar Feng Guifen, who was an adviser to Li Hongzhang, the governor of Jiangsu. As a result of these changes, although no formal transfer of responsibilities took place from the traditional bureaucratic system to the gentry as a group, a shift in the balance of power at the local level became apparent.

The application of the term 'regionalism' to late Qing China implies that the rebellions brought about a transfer of power from the centre to the regions and into the hands of semi-independent regional leaders. Regionalism was a recurrent feature of periods of dynastic weakness. Symptomatic of its onset was the failure of the dynasty to enforce the rules devised to ensure its dominance, notably the rotation of officials, the 'law of avoidance', the freedom to make appointments and, most importantly, the separation of civil and military offices. It has been argued that these rules were flouted by Zeng Guofan and Li Hongzhang, who combined the holding of official positions with the command of regional armies. Zeng Guofan held office in his home province of Hunan and was said to have secured the appointment of his protégé Li Hongzhang to the governorship of Jiangsu. Li Hongzhang was later appointed governor-general of the metropolitan province of Zhili, in which position he served for the unprecedentedly long term of 25 years. Both Zeng and Li played a leading role in establishing military industries and Li Hongzhang went on to found a commercial empire. However, it is questionable whether their accumulation of influence amounted to regionalism. Both men remained ideologically committed to the support of the dynasty, and the breaches of the system of control were exceptions rather than the rule and may be interpreted as a response to the circumstances created by the rebellions and the challenge of the West.

The rebellions, and their suppression, caused enormous loss of life and severe economic dislocation. Some areas, for example parts of southern Anhui, were almost completely depopulated. Several million lives were lost in Gansu as a result of the north-west Muslim rebellion. Westerners living in China at the time of the Taiping rebellion estimated that it had cost 20 to 30 million lives, a figure which Ho Ping-ti has since rejected as too low. The rebellions brought some relief from population pressure, particularly in the lower Yangzi region, and this effect was evident even a century later. But the population of China as a whole recovered quickly and probably surpassed its 1850 peak before the end of the century.[19]

After the defeat of the rebellions, the Qing government introduced various measures to relieve the needy and to rehabilitate the agricultural economy. Areas of abandoned land were repopulated by sponsored migration, settlers were supplied with tools and planting materials and irrigation schemes were repaired. Gentry leaders were encouraged to open or reopen schools and to refurbish libraries. The examination system, which had been discontinued in areas affected by rebellion, was reinstated and it was estimated that after the restoration some two million candidates were presenting themselves annually for examinations at various levels. Education officials were given special instructions to ensure that the *Sacred Edict*, the series of maxims first produced by the Kangxi emperor, was expounded regularly. As it was believed that the burden of the land tax had played an important part in inciting the common people to support the rebellions, taxes were remitted or cancelled in areas which had suffered badly. In a widely publicized gesture, the grain tribute paid by the Susongtai circuit in Jiangsu province, which was levied at an exorbitant rate, was slashed.

Such is the evidence to support the case that a genuine restoration did take place. Mary Wright, who wrote the classic study of the restoration, remarked:

> not only a dynasty but also a civilization which appeared to have collapsed was revived to last for another sixty years by the extraordinary efforts of extraordinary men in the 1860s.[20]

However, no effort could reverse the changes in the role of the gentry and even the achievements of the restoration were a double-edged sword. After the restoration, a rapid expansion of charitable public schools and local academies, particularly in the Lower Yangzi area, produced a surfeit of *shengyuan*. According to Barry Keenan these men, lacking any opportunity for official appointment, began to assume an increasingly important managerial role, notably in the field of education. As a consequence, he suggests, the very success of the restoration guaranteed the social restlessness of the early twentieth-century reform movement.[21] The economic measures taken showed that the restoration leaders had no concept of an economy which was other than agrarian and self-sufficient. The only political change introduced was the establishment, on a temporary basis, of the office known as the Zongli Yamen to deal with foreign affairs. Furthermore, the much-vaunted reduction of the Susongtai grain tribute had more to do with achieving an advantageous accommodation between the local elite and the bureaucracy than with relieving the plight of poor peasants.

SELF-STRENGTHENING

In 1842 Wei Yuan, a scholar and adviser to Lin Zexu, expressed concern about the superiority of the West in terms of military technology and outlined a plan for maritime defence. He noted the traditional strategy of 'using barbarians to control barbarians', but also recommended 'building ships, making weapons, and learning the superior techniques of the barbarians'.[22] In 1860 Feng Guifen, the essayist referred to above as an adviser to Li Hongzhang, called for the adoption of Western knowledge, the manufacture of Western weapons and the establishment of translation offices and institutions where students would study Chinese classics and also Western languages and mathematics. This led him to enunciate a famous principle:

> If we let Chinese ethics and famous [Confucian] teachings serve as an original foundation, and let them be supplemented by the methods used by the various nations for the attainment of prosperity and strength, would it not be the best of all procedures?[23]

Later in the century, Zhang Zhidong encapsulated the same sentiment in the phrase 'Chinese learning as the base, Western studies for use'. This became the slogan of *ziqiang* or 'self-strengthening'.

In the 1860s the most prominent exponents of self-strengthening were the three senior provincial officials, Zeng Guofan, Li Hongzhang and Zuo Zongtang, all of whom had played a leading role in the defeat of the rebellions. They received some support from Prince Gong and from the Zongli Yamen, the 'office for general management', which had been established in March 1861 to handle relations with the Western powers and *yangwu* or 'foreign matters'. Their activities did not amount to a national policy and *yangwu* remained peripheral to the mainstream of intellectual activity in China until the 1890s.

The first self-strengthening projects included the establishment of foreign-language schools in Beijing, Shanghai, Guangzhou and Fuzhou. The first principal of the Tongwenguan, the Beijing school, was W. A. P. Martin, an American missionary who later translated many important Western-language texts into Chinese. At about the same time, a number of arsenals were set up which pioneered the introduction of Western technology. In 1862, having captured Anqing, Zeng Guofan set up an arsenal there to manufacture weapons to use against the rebels, and he also made the first, albeit unsuccessful, attempt at building a steamship.

The manufacture of weapons and ships to standards comparable with those of the West was a tall order, and to accelerate the process attempts were made to buy in foreign technology. In 1863 Zeng Guofan sent Rong Hong (Yung Wing), the first Chinese to receive a degree from an American university, to the United States to purchase 'machines to make machines'. Buying in foreign technology was not only expensive, but also entailed a risk of dependency. In 1861 Robert Hart, who later became inspector-general of the Imperial Maritime Customs, suggested to Prince Gong that China should buy a steam flotilla from Britain. Only after the flotilla, known as the Lay-Osborn flotilla, had reached China was it disclosed that it would remain subject to British control, whereupon it was sent back to Britain.

In 1865 two more ambitious self-strengthening projects were commenced. The Jiangnan arsenal in Shanghai consolidated a number of smaller ventures initiated by Zeng Guofan and Li Hongzhang. The arsenal was equipped with machinery purchased in the United States and it employed Halliday Macartney, a British doctor, as a technical adviser, and a number of Western technicians. Its first task was to supply small arms and ammunition to Li Hongzhang's Huai army for its campaign against the Nian rebels. It later concentrated on launching steamships, which incorporated much Western technology, but which proved very costly to build. In the 1870s it also manufactured Remington rifles under licence, but these were both more expensive and less accurate than rifles produced in the West. The other venture was the establishment of a shipyard at Fuzhou by Zuo Zongtang. This combined a complete ship-building facility with a naval school. The project used French technicians and was funded from the revenues of the Fuzhou customs. By 1874 the shipyard had launched 15 ships, but these were costly to produce and technically obsolescent.

In 1872 Li Hongzhang sent a memorial to the court in which he argued that the self-strengthening programme should be widened to include industrial ventures and transport facilities to support them. This was the beginning of the *fuqiang* or 'wealth and power' stage of self-strengthening, marked by the establishment of profit-oriented ventures. The first of these was the China Merchants' Steam Navigation Company, founded by Li Hongzhang to compete with foreign shipping, which was taking over China's coastal and riverine commerce. This venture was organized as a *guandu shangban*, an 'official-supervision merchant-management' enterprise, a form of organization to be adopted in other *fuqiang* ventures. In these enterprises officials were appointed to the management, but merchants supplied the capital and operated the company. Typically the enterprise was granted a monopoly to ensure its profitability. The China Merchants' Steam Navigation Company had a monopoly for the sea transport of tribute rice from the Yangzi delta to Tianjin.

At first the company operated quite effectively under the management of Tang Tingshu, who was an official in that he had acquired a title by purchase and was an expectant subprefect. His real expertise derived from his having been a compradore, or Chinese agent, of Jardine, Matheson and Company in Shanghai, and he had considerable experience of operating a joint-stock steamship enterprise. In 1876 the China Merchants bought the merchant fleet of the American-owned Shanghai Steam Navigation Company. However, after the dismissal of Tang Tingshu, Sheng Xuanhuai was appointed director-general. Sheng, who came from a family of officials and who had come to prominence as Li Hongzhang's deputy in economic matters, concentrated on protecting his and the company's financial interests, and under his direction the opportunity to establish a genuine modern company was lost.

In 1872 Li Hongzhang had pointed out the importance of establishing heavy industry in China, and six years later he followed this up by opening the Kaiping coal mines at Tangshan, 60 miles north east of Tianjin. The project, which was managed by Tang Tingshu, employed British engineers and introduced the latest Western technology, including gas lighting. It began production in 1881 and its output soon began to offset the cost, in foreign exchange, of imported coal. However, from the outset the mine encountered difficulties.

Mining was believed to harm the *fengshui*, the spirits of wind and water, and miners were regarded as a subversive group. The problem of transporting coal from the pithead to Tianjin had not been solved, because a request for permission to construct a railway had been withdrawn in anticipation of a refusal by the court. In the event a tramway was constructed, and a locomotive christened the 'Rocket of China' was built surreptitiously. The project was given retrospective approval, and so became China's first permanent railway.

A number of other self-strengthening enterprises deserve a brief mention. In 1877 Zuo Zongtang established a woollen mill at Lanzhou in Gansu province, which pioneered the application of steam power to industry in China. Sheng Xuanhuai was largely responsible for the establishment, in 1880, of the Imperial Telegraph Administration, which created a national network of telegraph lines. The largest industrial enterprise, another venture initiated by Li Hongzhang, was the Shanghai Cotton Cloth Mill, which was given a ten-year monopoly of the use of foreign textile machinery. In 1892 the mill produced 4 million yards of cloth, but the following year it was destroyed by fire. The mill was not insured and the loss was very heavy. Nevertheless, the enterprise had demonstrated that it was profitable to invest in modern machinery to produce textiles.

Most accounts of self-strengthening present it as an inadequate policy which initiated some rather unsuccessful ventures. A comparison is sometimes made with the Japanese government's role in pioneering successful enterprises, which the government later sold and which became the nucleus of the *zaibatsu* industrial empires. The evidence of China's failure is detected in the short term in the exposure of China's military weakness in the Sino-Japanese War of 1894–5, and in the long term in the delay before China eventually established a modern industrial base.

Having concluded that self-strengthening was a failure, many writers have then sought to explain why this occurred. Some cite the strength of China's cultural tradition and the incompatibility of Confucianism with the priorities of a modern state. Reference is made to the famous objection made in 1866 by Woren, a Mongol Grand Secretary, to the proposal that the Beijing language school should open a department of mathematics and astronomy, and that students should be encouraged to study these subjects by offering them increased stipends and rapid promotion. Woren replied, 'Your slave has learned that the way to establish a nation is to lay emphasis on propriety and righteousness, not on power and plotting.'[24] Alternatively, Chinese obscurantism is held responsible, the often-quoted example being the case of the short stretch of railway which was built to connect Shanghai and Wusong. This railway, constructed by a British consortium in 1876, was later bought by Chinese officials and destroyed. Their action was derided as irrational and superstitious, but it has been shown that they destroyed the railway because it had been built on Chinese soil by Westerners who had not obtained official permission, and because a fatality on the line had aroused local peasants and threatened disorder.

A second line of explanation concerns the role played by central government. The Qing court has been castigated as obstructive, and the Empress Dowager has been accused of being preoccupied with her own selfish interests. It has frequently been alleged that she misappropriated funds allocated for the purchase of naval ships and used them to refurbish the Summer Palace and to build the famous marble barge still to be seen there. However, most of the expenditure on the palace came after the disastrous naval defeat of 1894, and that debacle was occasioned principally by the inadequate training of the sailors and the faulty tactics of the fleet. The argument that the Chinese government was indifferent towards, or even hostile to, industrial and commercial undertakings has also been challenged, and in recent years arguments have been put forward which suggest that government economic activity, though falling far short of management of the economy, was more constructive and more extensive than has hitherto been recognized.

Albert Feuerwerker suggested that the 'official-supervision merchant-management' system itself played a part in China's failure to transform the economy in the last four decades of the Qing dynasty. He argued that it encouraged regionalism; that it relied too heavily on raising capital from Chinese merchants in the treaty ports – merchants who looked for quick profits and whose capital was always inadequate; that it continued bureaucratic practices and failed to introduce modern management techniques; that it ensured that the enterprises were vulnerable to official exactions; and that it gave the enterprises an unfair advantage over private activity by the provision of monopoly privileges.[25]

A further line of explanation, one which will be dealt with more comprehensively in the next section, is that self-strengthening was inhibited by Western imperialism. The military threat from the West forced China to concentrate, in the first instance, on the establishment of modern military industries. Defeat in war weakened the authority of central government and burdened it with indemnities, so curtailing investment. However, the self-strengthening enterprises also benefited from the Western presence. A number of foreign experts were employed to establish shipyards and mines. The missionary John Fryer translated technical and scientific texts for the Jiangnan arsenal and edited the *Chinese Scientific Magazine*, which appeared between 1876 and 1892. Foreigners taught in the language schools and Chinese students were sent to America. Benjamin Elman has noted the role that the shipbuilding industry played in the emergence of late Qing industrial enterprises: 'China's first lathes and furnaces to produce molten steel were created at Jiangnan and Fuzhou.' During the First World War, workers from the Fuzhou shipyard built China's first aeroplane. Those who had trained in the shipyards and arsenals became the architects, engineers and technicians of the industries of the early twentieth century.[26]

WESTERN IMPERIALISM IN THE LATE QING PERIOD

After the conclusion of the Treaty of Tianjin and the Convention of Beijing in 1858–60, the Western powers occupied a privileged position in China. Recognizing the impossibility of altering that situation in the short term, through the 1860s the Chinese government, as represented by the Zongli Yamen, the prototype foreign office, pursued a policy of co-operation. However, the increased Western presence in the country, particularly in the form of missionaries, was a constant cause of friction. In 1870 a massacre of French nuns at Tianjin was punished by the execution of officials held responsible and the imposition of an indemnity. In 1876 the murder near the Burmese frontier of Augustus Margary, a British official, was settled by the Zhefu Convention, which opened the upper Yangzi to foreign trade.

In the meantime, the imperial powers were encroaching on China's periphery. The loss to Russia in 1858–60 of the territory north of the Amur and east of the Wusuli rivers has already been mentioned. In 1871, some 54 inhabitants of the Liuqiu islands who had been shipwrecked on the Taiwan coast were murdered by aborigines. Three years later Japan sent a punitive expedition to Taiwan to avenge the murders and then laid claim to the Liuqiu islands, which were incorporated into Japan.

In 1862, France forced the ruling Nguyen dynasty to cede to her the southern part of Vietnam, known as Cochin China. France then obtained the right to navigate the Red river in north Vietnam and in 1874 negotiated a treaty which described Vietnam as an independent state which was willing to accept French protection. In 1880, after Jules Ferry had become premier, France established fortresses on the Red river and took steps to bring the country under French control. China, in the person of Li Hongzhang, responded cautiously, merely encouraging the irregular force known as the Black Flags, composed in part of former Taiping rebels, to harass the French. But then in 1882 Henri Rivière, a French naval officer commanding a minute force, seized Hanoi and precipitated a direct confrontation.

Between 1883 and 1885, France and China fought a sporadic campaign for the control of north Vietnam. After a year of conflict, Li Hongzhang and a French naval captain, F. E. Fournier, agreed that if China would withdraw from Vietnam and recognize French treaties with that country, France would not demand an indemnity, would not invade China and would not make disparaging remarks about China in future treaties. Both countries immediately rejected the agreement. For France it implied that China would retain suzerainty over Vietnam. In China the settlement was denounced by a hardline pressure group known as the *qingliu*, or 'party of purists'. There followed a second phase of the conflict, which was notable for three incidents. The first was the heroic defence of the Chinese outpost at Bac Le, which convinced *qingliu* supporters that China had the capacity to repulse Western troops. However, the second incident, a French attack on the Fuzhou shipyard and the destruction of all but two ships of the Fujian fleet, revealed China's naval weakness only too clearly. Negotiations had resumed when a third incident, the recapture of Langson from the French, precipitated the fall of the French government and made it easier for Li Hongzhang to obtain a settlement. By the Treaty of Tianjin of 1885, China recognized the French protectorate over Vietnam and offered France economic opportunities in south-west China.

China's most important and most regular tributary relationship was with Korea. Korea, like Japan, had adopted a policy of international seclusion, but this policy came under threat after Japan had been 'opened' by the United States in 1853. From 1867 the Zongli Yamen began to suggest to the Korean court that resistance was not practical and that Korea should open its ports voluntarily.

As a consequence, in 1876 Korea signed an unequal treaty with Japan. From 1879 Li Hongzhang took charge of Chinese relations with Korea, and with his encouragement Korea signed a treaty with the United States, thereby denying Japan exclusive access. He also secured a commercial treaty and despatched a young soldier, Yuan Shikai, to create a modern Korean army. In the meantime, Japan had also become involved in Korean internal affairs, encouraging the modernizing faction at court, whereas Chinese support went to its more conservative members. In 1884, while China was involved in war with France, pro-Japanese Koreans headed by Kim Ok-kyun attempted a coup, which failed. This prompted China and Japan to conclude the Tianjin Convention, under which the two countries agreed to withdraw their troops from Korea, to cease training the Korean army and to forewarn the other party of any intention to send troops to Korea. In effect, China surrendered its claim to exclusive suzerainty in Korea, which now had the status of a co-protectorate of the two countries.

This compromise survived until 1894, when two events occurred. In March Kim Ok-kyun, the leader of the pro-Japanese group, was murdered in Shanghai by the son of a victim of the 1884 coup. His body was returned to Korea in a Chinese warship, an arrangement which was found offensive by the increasingly vociferous proponents of expansionism in Japan. Meanwhile the threat of a popular movement, the Tonghak insurrection, led the Korean government to appeal to China for assistance. These events gave Japan a pretext for sending troops to Korea. Li Hongzhang attempted to negotiate a settlement, but when the Japanese navy sank the *Kowshing*, a Chinese troopship bringing reinforcements to Korea, war became inevitable.

Despite expectations of a Chinese victory, the contest was brief and one-sided. On land, units from Li Hongzhang's Huai army were defeated at Pyongyang. In September 1894, 12 ships from Li Hongzhang's Beiyang fleet engaged 12 Japanese warships off the mouth of the Yalu river. Four Chinese ships were incapacitated and the remainder took refuge at Weihaiwei, where they were later destroyed. These defeats ruthlessly exposed the limitations of military self-strengthening. China was forced to accept the humiliating terms of the Treaty of Shimonoseki, under which China recognized the independence of Korea and ceded Taiwan, the Penghu or Pescadores islands and the Liaodong peninsula in southern Manchuria to Japan. Japan also acquired unequal treaty rights in China, and these were supplemented by the right to establish industry in the treaty ports, a right which, by the most favoured nation principle, devolved to the other treaty powers.

China's defeat, and the terms of the Treaty of Shimonoseki, precipitated a scramble for China. In 1891 Russia had started to construct the Trans-Siberian railway to strengthen its position in East Asia. The cession of the Liaodong peninsula to Japan threatened these plans and provoked the Triple Intervention, whereby Russia, abetted by France and Germany, forced Japan to relinquish the peninsula in exchange for a larger indemnity, a humiliation which was to play a part in the coming of the Russo-Japanese War a decade later. In return for this support, in 1896 Li Hongzhang negotiated a secret alliance with Russia which permitted construction of a railway across Manchuria to Vladivostok. It also provided for mutual assistance in the event of a Japanese attack on China, Korea or Russian possessions in East Asia.

Prussia had negotiated an unequal treaty with China in 1861 and, after unification, German economic interest in China had grown steadily, being surpassed only by that of Britain. In the 1890s Germany became committed to a drive to world power and in China this was translated into a desire to obtain a naval base and a sphere of influence. The murder in 1897 of two German Catholic missionaries provided justification for the seizure of Qingdao in Shandong province. China was forced to grant Germany a 99-year lease on Jiaozhou bay and concessions for the construction of railways and the extraction of coal. France, not to be outdone, obtained commercial concessions in south-west China and a lease on Guangzhouwan, on the mainland opposite Hainan island. Hitherto Britain, as the satisfied power, had opposed the division of China into spheres of influence. It now sought compensation in the form of a lease on Weihaiwei in Shandong, guarantees for its economic interests in the lower Yangzi and a 99-year lease on what became known as the 'New Territories', on the mainland opposite Xianggang.

The scramble for concessions was accompanied by a rapid increase in foreign investment in China. For example, France took a large share in the Russo-Chinese Bank, which financed the Chinese Eastern Railway, the line constructed across Manchuria; and Belgium played an important part in the finance and construction of the Beijing–Hankou railway, which was completed in 1905. After the Treaty of Shimonoseki had permitted the establishment of industries in the treaty ports, foreign investment increased quickly. The treaty had imposed a large indemnity and for the first time China began to borrow heavily on the international money market.

One of the most extensive and acrimonious debates in modern Chinese history has concerned the economic effects of Western imperialism. According to Karl Marx, and to subsequent generations of Marxist writers, its effect was disastrous. Marx, writing in 1853, noted that the opium trade had caused a silver drain and that the importation of British cotton goods had disrupted the Chinese handicraft industry. The provision in the unequal treaties for foreign control of China's tariffs has been condemned as a device to prevent China imposing import duties to increase revenue and to protect new industries. In the treaty ports, Western commerce and industry enjoyed legal protection and other advantages, and were thus able to outstrip Chinese enterprises. Having defeated China in war, the imperial powers imposed indemnities which encumbered the Chinese government, and extorted concessions which gave them a stranglehold over China's heavy industry and communications.

In response to this indictment, some Western economic historians have argued that the evidence of exploitation is either misunderstood or grossly exaggerated. Referring to cotton textiles, Albert Feuerwerker remarked that foreign imports did not destroy the handicraft industry, which in the 1930s was still producing 61 per cent of the cotton cloth woven in China. Instead, it forced it to evolve. He pointed out that much of the handicraft industry was the result of rural poverty, which obliged peasant families to use their surplus labour to supplement their incomes by any means possible. When the import of cotton yarn and cotton cloth began to increase significantly after the treaty settlement of 1858–60, it was machine-made yarn which was in greater demand, because it was both cheaper and stronger, and for this reason it displaced locally produced yarn. Cloth woven with machine-made yarn, at first imported but later made in China, became widely accepted. The import of foreign-made cloth did increase, but at a lower rate and its principal market was in urban areas. At the same time, the distribution of the cotton textile industry changed and more advanced machinery was introduced.[27]

A similarly complex interaction has been traced by Robert Gardella with reference to the tea industry. In the eighteenth century tea was China's most important export and until the 1880s exports grew rapidly and prices rose. However, by 1900 dominance of the black tea market in Britain and the British Empire had passed to India and Ceylon. In 1908 a provincial assemblyman from Fujian, a major tea-producing area, identified a number of reasons for this disastrous decline. He alleged that Westerners applied the principles of nationalism to the tea industry. Not only did they employ mechanization to greater effect and use better planting methods, their newspapers also slandered the Chinese tea industry as unsanitary. In China, however, commercial knowledge was not well disseminated, the commercial spirit was dissipated and the Chinese were unable to organize and deal with foreign obstacles. In the twentieth century, attempts were made to revive the tea trade by reducing taxation, by making greater use of machinery in planting and processing, by organizational innovation and by improving quality control, but the lost markets were never recovered. From this, Robert Gardella concluded that although the opening of China to world trade initially had a beneficial effect on tea production, the pre-modern state of the Chinese economy prevented the transformation of the tea industry. On the other hand, the production and marketing revolution initiated by the corporate plantations of India and Ceylon responded effectively to rising world demand and brought China's tea boom to an end.[28]

Two recent studies of China's economic achievement in the nineteenth century have moved on from the limitations of self-strengthening and the burden of Western imperialism. In *The Merchants of Zigong*, Madeleine Zelin investigated 'the one-hundred-year rise and decline of China's first privately-owned high-capital, high-throughput industrial enterprises', the salt-manufacturing firms of Zigong, Sichuan. These firms mobilized capital, utilized technology – including pumping brine from deep wells and using natural gas for distilling the brine in salt pans – captured markets and sustained corporate business organizations. In all this the state, which has often been portrayed as a stifling influence, played a relatively benign role. When the Taiping rebellion cut off trade between central China and the salt-producing regions of the east coast, the Zigong salt industry expanded rapidly. By the late nineteenth century Zigong was the largest industrial centre in China. However, the two key factors which enabled that development, relatively political stability and moderate levels of taxation, then ceased to apply and despite further technological advances, including the use of steam engines, by the early twentieth century the industry had gone into decline.[29]

Another study looked at China's agricultural development. In Western economies an agrarian revolution had preceded an industrial revolution. In China, however, it appeared that the development of a capitalist form of agriculture had been inhibited either by the concentration of too many people on too little land, or by a social structure which prevented fundamental change. To test these explanations, James Reardon-Anderson investigated the economic development of Manchuria in the late nineteenth and early twentieth centuries. Here Western economic imperialism played a very limited role, land was plentiful and the waves of new immigrants were not constrained by social relations. Nevertheless, in Manchuria, as in the rest of China, agriculture experienced growth without development. Reardon-Anderson accepted that environmental factors, for example the fear of banditry and the volatility of markets, played a part in discouraging Chinese migrants from being more entrepreneurial. However, he concluded that the main reason they did not change their economic behaviour was that they persisted with the practices inherited from China Proper; that is to say, pursuing 'small-scale, short-term, low-risk opportunities'.[30]

CHRISTIAN MISSIONARIES IN CHINA

Christian missionaries have been described as the cultural arm of Western imperialism and stand accused of having denationalized many Chinese converts and having disintegrated both the body and the spirit of the nation.[31] This sweeping indictment by a Nationalist writer is testimony to the bitterness which Christian mission activity in China has aroused.

Until the early nineteenth century, Christianity had made little progress in China. The Catholic mission, which the Jesuits had initiated in the sixteenth century, had by the eighteenth century become subjected to restriction and persecution, although in some provinces, for example Sichuan, Christian communities had survived and expanded. Robert Morrison of the London Missionary Society, the first Protestant missionary sent to China, reached Guangzhou in 1807, but only made his first convert seven years later. In the 1830s a few missionaries were sent to China by several European Protestant mission societies and others came from the United States, a notable early arrival being Dr Peter Parker, the first medical missionary to China, who established a hospital in Guangzhou.

The position of Christian missionaries in China was transformed by the provisions of unequal treaties and associated agreements. In 1844 and 1846, France obtained edicts which removed many of the restrictions on Christian activity. In the settlement of 1858–60 the French treaties contained clauses which allowed missionaries to move freely about the country and to purchase or rent sites for missions in the interior. By virtue of the most favoured nation clause, these rights devolved to the other treaty powers, and the extraterritorial agreements protected not only Western missionaries but also mission property and mission converts. Under these conditions, mission activity increased rapidly. In 1844 Roman Catholic missions claimed to have only 240,000 converts; by 1901 this figure had risen to over 720,000; and it had doubled again by 1912. Protestant missionaries always asserted that their criteria for conversions were more stringent than those of the Catholics. In 1853 there were only 350 Protestant communicants; by 1889 the figure had risen to over 37,000; and by 1914 to over a quarter of a million. By that time over 5000 foreign missionaries were working in China, missions had been established in all of China's 18 provinces, at least 250 medical missions and hospitals were operating and over 2000 mission schools, some of which educated girls, had been opened. Missionaries had also started secondary schools and had founded universities which offered a Western curriculum. During the disastrous North China famine of 1876–9, Timothy Richard of the Baptist Missionary Society played a significant role in organizing relief and obtaining foreign assistance. He later became an advocate of reform and had some influence on Zhang Zhidong and other reformers.

Despite the sincere endeavour of many missionaries, the Chinese response to their religious message and social activities was at best disappointing and at worst violently hostile. The bitterest opposition came from the gentry, who reacted against what they saw as a threat to their position in rural society. Christianity had long been rejected by Confucian scholars as intellectually spurious. Zeng Guofan attacked the Taiping rebels for having plagiarized a foreign religion and for having precipitated an unprecedented crisis in the history of traditional Confucian moral principles. In 1861, a pamphlet entitled *A Record of Facts to Ward Off Heterodoxy* began to circulate, which set out to arouse hostility to Christianity by alleging, for example, that Christian missionaries habitually sexually abused children placed in orphanages.

From the 1860s anti-missionary incidents became commonplace. In 1862, an attempt to re-establish the French Lazarist mission at Nanchang resulted in a riot incited by members of the local gentry. In 1868, the Protestant China Inland Mission, whose leader, Hudson Taylor, was appalled by the thought that a million Chinese were dying every month without God, opened a station at Yangzhou. The building was soon attacked by a mob and Taylor called for assistance. Four British gunboats were sent to Nanjing and Zeng Guofan, the governor-general, was forced to dismiss the officials held responsible for the disorder. In 1870, the Catholic orphanage in Tianjin was attacked by a crowd which believed that the orphans were being abused. Some 19 foreigners were killed and the incident nearly provoked a war between France and China. After incidents such as these, the Chinese government had to agree to humiliating terms of settlement. After the Tianjin massacre the senior Chinese officials involved were sentenced to life-long exile, 18 Chinese were executed and a fine of 280,000 taels was levied.

NATIONALISM AND REFORM

The later Manchu rulers had copied the model of a Confucian emperor so closely that by the beginning of the nineteenth century, although anti-Manchu feeling had not entirely disappeared, it had ceased to be a political issue. However, the Opium War aroused xenophobia and defeat raised questions about the extent of the Manchu commitment to the national interest.

The development of nationalist sentiment can be traced by referring to various incidents. The skirmish at Sanyuanli in 1841 had briefly encouraged the notion that the Chinese people, led by the gentry, could resist the foreigner. This event has been taken as an example of proto-nationalism. In 1859, the defiance at the Dagu forts showed that foreign naval strength could also be challenged, even though that might lead to further humiliation. However, after 1860 the court followed a co-operative policy with the Western powers and the leaders of the self-strengthening movement adopted a pragmatic attitude towards borrowing from the West. This aroused the anger of scholars and officials such as Woren, who rejected any compromise

with the West. In 1875 they protested against the dispatch of Guo
Songtao to London to apologize for the murder of Augustus Margary.
The first settlement of the Ili crisis in 1879 was opposed by Zhang
Zhidong, a leading member of the *qingliu* or 'party of the purists'.
During the Sino-French War, Zhang Zhidong, now governor-
general of Guangdong and Guangxi, inveighed constantly against Li
Hongzhang, accusing him of being willing to betray China's national
interests. The disastrous defeat in the Sino-Japanese War destroyed
the credit of the self-strengtheners and raised acute fears for the
nation's survival. In its aftermath, in response to the scramble for
China, a determination to embrace all practical means to preserve
China may be observed, for example in the rights recovery movement, which brought together officials, gentry and merchants in
endeavours to recover concessions granted to the foreign powers.
From these incidents and from the social changes which occurred in
the late nineteenth century, there developed the sentiment which may
properly be called Chinese nationalism.

THE 100 DAYS' REFORMS, 1898

Defeat in the Sino-Japanese War and the subsequent scramble
for China had a momentous effect on Chinese intellectuals, who
responded violently to what they perceived as the threat of national
extinction. A few – the most notable example being Sun Zhongshan
(Sun Yat-sen) – abandoned not only the Manchu dynasty, but also
the system of imperial government and began to plot a revolution.
Others were so shocked that they proposed radical reforms to the
system. Among them was Kang Youwei, a scholar from Guangdong,
who had already achieved notoriety for his reinterpretation of the
classical texts. When the terms of the Treaty of Shimonoseki became
known, Kang Youwei circulated a petition which called for the rejection of the treaty and the introduction of a wide range of reforms. At
the same time some senior provincial officials, for example Zhang
Zhidong, the governor-general of Hunan and Hubei, pressed ahead
with a range of practical reforms, such as the introduction of electric
lighting to Changsha and the inclusion of Western subjects in the
syllabus of the *shengyuan* degree.

   Kang Youwei's chance came two years later. By this time he had
published another disquisition on the classical texts, in which he had

argued that Confucius, although claiming to revive the past, had in fact been a reformer. Kang's reputation as a radical thinker gained him an audience with the young Guangxu emperor, who since 1889 had exercised nominal authority, the Empress Dowager having retired officially. At that meeting Kang Youwei suggested to the emperor that he might bring about a 'revolution from above', similar to that achieved by the Meiji government in Japan 30 years previously. His suggestion was received and for 100 days, starting from 11 June 1898, the emperor, with the assistance of Kang Youwei and two other reformers, Liang Qichao and Tan Sitong, promulgated 40 edicts proposing wide-ranging reforms. These included the abolition of the formal examination composition, the 'eight-legged essay'; the creation of a ministry of agriculture; the phasing out of the Army of the Green Standard and the raising of a national conscript army. The only political reform proposed was to extend the right to send memorials to the emperor, a right hitherto granted only to senior officials, to all subjects.

On 21 September the Empress Dowager brought the reform programme to an abrupt halt. With the backing of Yuan Shikai, who after his service in Korea had organized the Beiyang Army in Zhili, she ordered the arrest and execution of the leading reformers on the grounds that they had been plotting a coup. Kang Youwei and Liang Qichao escaped, but Tan Sitong was among those executed.

The obvious reason for the failure of the reform programme was the opposition of the Empress Dowager, who has been portrayed as an implacable opponent of reform. However, her long-term support of Li Hongzhang suggests that she did not object to reform if it did not threaten her position. Many writers have accepted the view put forward by H. B. Morse, that the emperor and Kang Youwei were impractical reformers, whose over-ambitious reform programme threatened a wide variety of vested interests, including the gentry who were uneasy about the change in the examinations, senior officials who were dismayed by the loss of their privileges and Manchus who resented the loss of their sinecures.[32] Undoubtedly the reforms were handled in a politically inept manner, but reform per se was not the issue. Starting in 1895 a reform programme had been introduced in Hunan, which included industrial undertakings and the publication of the *Hunan Gazette*. These reforms had provincial support and the reform movement there only collapsed after the Empress Dowager had crushed the reformers in Beijing.[33] Jack Gray has suggested that the real reason for the Empress Dowager's intervention was because the 100 Days' reforms threatened to remove her power of patronage, and because the changes in the rules relating to communications raised the spectre of 'people's rights'.[34]

THE BOXER UPRISING

Scarcely had the repercussions of the 100 Days' reforms died down before the Qing court was faced with a very different sort of crisis, a major peasant uprising in north China.

The origins and objectives of the Boxer Uprising have been subject to a variety of interpretations. The event has often been referred to as a rebellion, implying that the Boxers were anti-dynastic. In fact the Boxers never rebelled against the Qing and in 1900, when threatened with a foreign attack on the capital, the court declared its support for the Boxers.[35] The Boxers have been described as descended from the White Lotus rebels of the early nineteenth century, but the Boxers were regarded as a new phenomenon and they did not share the White Lotus belief in the Eternal Venerable Mother or the coming of the Maitreya Buddha. Nor is there a clear connection between the Boxers and the martial arts associations which were common in Shandong, where the uprising had its origins.

The Boxer movement arose in Zhili and Shandong, provinces at the centre of the great drought famine of 1876–9 which had caused the death of between nine and thirteen million people. In 1898 the Yellow river burst its banks and caused extensive flooding. Two years later another prolonged drought inflicted further loss of life. The region had also suffered from Western economic imperialism, for example the importation of machine-spun yarn had affected the cotton-growing areas in the west. Several missionary societies were active in the area, the most aggressive being the German Steyl Society. The murder of two missionaries had served as the pretext for the German seizure of Jiaozhou bay in 1897. Banditry was an endemic problem, and to combat it the governor of the province had permitted the formation of militia forces. This provided a cover for the emergence, in the south of the province, of the Big Sword Society, a martial arts society which became prominent in the conflict between Christian congregations and the rest of the population.

The Boxers derived from a group calling itself Spirit Boxers, which appeared in north-west Shandong in 1896. They professed the simplest ethical principles – 'respect your parents, live in harmony with your neighbours' – and engaged in ritual boxing, which was not a martial art but an activity originally associated with healing, and later developed as an invulnerability ritual which provided protection against the power of the Christians. They also practised spirit possession, believing that any adherent who was pure in heart could become possessed of a particular spirit. From about 1898 the Spirit Boxer movement began to grow and to threaten Christian converts. The following year the name of the movement was changed to 'Boxers United in Righteousness' and clashes between the group and Christians became increasingly common and violent.

At first, provincial officials attempted to maintain an even-handed policy towards the Christians and the Boxers. However, as the situation deteriorated some officials – including Yu Xian, the governor of Shandong – were accused by foreigners of complicity with the Boxers. Late in 1899 Yu Xian was dismissed and replaced by Yuan Shikai, but by this time the court's policy was beginning to change. In January 1900 the Empress Dowager, alert to the danger of seeming to be hostile to a popular movement, issued an edict which urged officials to distinguish between outlaws and those law-abiding citizens who practised ritual arts to protect themselves.

By May 1900, groups of Boxers were appearing on the streets of Beijing and Tianjin. Most were young men, but a group known as the Red Lantern Society comprised young women, who it was said could ride on clouds and kindle fire to burn the warships of the Westerners. By June the threat to foreigners was so serious that Britain sent a force of 2000 men under Admiral Seymour to protect the legations in Beijing. The Boxers cut the Tianjin–Beijing railway line and forced Seymour to withdraw. In retaliation, the Western powers seized the Dagu forts.

On 21 June, the Empress Dowager threw in her lot with the Boxers and issued a 'declaration of war', which blamed the disorder on foreign aggression. In some parts of north China officials came out on the Boxers' side, the most notorious example being Yu Xian, now governor of Shanxi, who rounded up and executed 44 men, women and children from missionary families. However, in Shandong Yuan Shikai suppressed the Boxers and in other parts of China senior officials distanced themselves from events in the north.

In Beijing the foreign population was besieged in the legations for 55 days. The siege was raised on 14 August when a relief expedition reached Beijing. There followed an orgy of looting. The allies sent out punitive expeditions under the German Field Marshal von Waldersee, which inflicted heavy punishment on towns which had been the scene of Boxer activity. The Boxer Protocol, setting out the terms acceptable to the allies before they would withdraw, provided that ten officials, including Yu Xian, should be executed, and that others should be required to commit suicide or to suffer banishment. It also stipulated the dispatch of apology missions to Germany and Japan, the destruction of the Dagu forts and the suspension of the examinations for five years in cities where the Boxers had been active. Finally an indemnity of 450 million taels was levied, payable in instalments over 39 years. To facilitate payment, the tariff on external trade was raised.

The Boxer Uprising had several important consequences. The indemnity imposed a heavy and long-lasting financial burden, although the United States took the lead in waiving payment and using part of the proceeds to establish Qinghua University in Beijing. While the allied powers were marching to the relief of the Beijing legations, Russian troops had occupied Manchuria. After the settlement, Russia failed to withdraw as promised and this aroused Chinese nationalist feeling and contributed to the rise of tension between Japan and Russia. The uprising left a contradictory legacy: foreigners in the 1920s used the spectre of Boxerism to delegitimize Chinese nationalism, but writers sympathetic to that cause invoked the Boxers as 'a dramatic example of ordinary Chinese peasants rising up to rid China of the hated foreign presence'.[36]

THE LATE QING REFORMS

When the allied forces entered Beijing, the Empress Dowager and the court fled ignominiously to Xi'an. In January 1901, after having reflected on the gravity of the situation, Cixi issued a decree calling on senior officials to submit proposals for reform. The most important submission came from Zhang Zhidong and Liu Kunyi, two of the most senior provincial officials. They suggested a programme of reforms relating to education, the military, the economy and the operation of government. This was adopted as a basis for action and a start was made even before the Empress Dowager returned to the capital in January 1902.

Educational reform began in 1901 with the abolition of the 'eight-legged essay'. An edict required all prefectures to establish middle schools and all districts to establish primary schools. In these schools, Western subjects would be taught alongside the traditional syllabus. Another edict approved the sending of students to study abroad and provided that on their return they would be eligible for the award of degrees. In September 1905, after the defeat of Russia in the Russo-Japanese War, the Empress Dowager took the momentous step of announcing the immediate ending of the imperial examinations.

The need for military reform had been made abundantly clear by the defeats of the Sino-Japanese War, and in the years after that disaster new armies had been raised, notably by Yuan Shikai, whose Beiyang Army, based at Xiaozhan near Tianjin, was China's best-trained and best-equipped force. In 1901 the traditional military examinations were abolished and the first steps were taken to disband the Army of the Green Standard and to replace it with a new national army. In 1906 an army ministry was created, as part of a process intended to impose central control over all the armed forces in the empire. After the death of the Empress Dowager and of the Guangxu emperor in 1908, Prince Chun, the new emperor's father, made a determined effort to place Manchus in leading positions in the army and navy.

Several reforms with economic implications were introduced, although nothing like a programme for economic development was attempted. A change of attitude towards merchants was evident in the promulgation of a commercial code and the establishment of a ministry of commerce. This new ministry was responsible for railway construction, which hitherto had been the field of action of provincial merchant and gentry groups that had recovered rights alienated to foreign interests. In 1911 the government negotiated a loan from a consortium of British, French, German and American banking interests, to be used to develop Manchuria, to reform the currency and to buy out the provincial railway companies, and in particular the company which held the right to build the Guangzhou–Hankou railway. This issue was to be one of the precipitating factors of the 1911 revolution.

The case for a constitutional monarchy had been argued persuasively by the reformer and writer Liang Qichao who, after the failure of the 100 Days' reforms, had fled to Japan. In 1905, after the Japanese victory over Russia had seemed to betoken the victory of constitutionalism over autocracy, the Empress Dowager announced her conversion to constitutionalism and sent missions abroad to study constitutional systems. In 1908 a programme was announced which provided for the promulgation of a constitution in 1916 and for the convening of a parliament in the following year. In the meantime, provincial assemblies were to be elected by an electorate composed of men over the age of 25 who either had an educational qualification or owned property. Frederic Wakeman once described the membership of these assemblies as dominated by higher gentry, but recent studies indicate that young men, some of whom were journalists or Christian converts, whose political experience had often been gained through membership of various reform societies, were the dominant group.[37] The provincial assemblies were only supposed to discuss a limited range of topics and to make recommendations to the provincial authorities, but when the assemblies met in 1909 they became a forum for critical comments on the policies of central government. Pressure on government to accelerate the reforms led in 1910 to a decision to promulgate the constitution in 1912 and to convene the parliament in the following year.

The late Qing reforms were once dismissed as a futile attempt by a dynasty to defer its inevitable fall. More recently, several writers have argued that the reforms contributed to that debacle. Frederic Wakeman noted how the reforms accelerated the formation of new elites who were to play a large role in the fall of the dynasty.[38] He was referring to the educational reforms, which destroyed the basis of the dynasty's control over the gentry and created a new category of educated youth, and to the military reforms, which led to the recruitment of soldiers inspired by nationalism and apprehensive of Manchu dominance. Other writers have emphasized the negative impact of the reforms. Additional taxes imposed in 1908 to finance new administrative departments were a significant factor in several uprisings. The reforms were often ineffective and fell far short of the hopes of those who had looked forward to the establishment of a genuine constitutional monarchy. According to Edward Rhoads, the inability of the late Qing court to meet the rising expectations of its own reforms, in particular the demands for a 'responsible cabinet' and an elected legislature, estranged the reformist elite. He pinpointed three particular causes of affront: 'recentralization', a determined effort to recover some of the court's political and military authority which had been lost to provincial officials; 'reimperialization', the appointment of Manchu princes to political and military positions; and failure to eliminate 'differences between Manchus and Han', referring to matters such as the disbandment of the provincial banner garrisons and the removal of the ban on Manchu–Han marriage.[39]

6

Republican China, 1911–49

On 10 October 1911, a date thereafter known as the 'Double Tenth', a mutiny headed by New Army officers broke out at Wuchang. They seized the city and obtained the support of the Hubei provincial assembly, which declared the province independent from the empire. By December all the provinces of central and southern China had followed suit. A republic was declared and Sun Zhongshan (Sun Yat-sen) was invited to become provisional president. The Qing court appealed to Yuan Shikai, the most influential military commander in the north, to come to its aid, but instead he decided to support the republic and to force the emperor to abdicate.

Between 1912 and 1916 Yuan Shikai ruled, first as president and then as emperor. His death in 1916 left a political vacuum and until 1928 the government in Beijing exercised only symbolic authority over the country, real power resting in the hands of warlords. During these years several important events took place: the May Fourth Movement, the political and cultural movement which climaxed in 1919; the founding of the Chinese Communist Party (CCP) in 1921; the reorganization of the Guomindang, or Nationalist Party; and the Northern Expedition of 1926–8 which led to the nominal reunification of the country.

Between 1928 and 1937 the Guomindang attempted to transform China into a modern state, while at the same time harassing the CCP, with which it had split in 1927. In 1931 Japan seized Manchuria, but Jiang Jieshi (Chiang Kai-shek), now leading the Guomindang, refused to respond. He preferred to pursue the Communists, who set out on the Long March in 1934. By 1936 Japanese encroachment on north China forced Jiang Jieshi to agree an united front with the Communists, and in the following year the Sino-Japanese War broke out. After an initial period of heroic resistance, the Guomindang retreated to Chongqing while the Communists fought on from their base at Yan'an. After the defeat of Japan in 1945, the Guomindang and CCP fought a civil war, which resulted in the Communist victory of 1949.

THE SOCIAL BACKGROUND TO THE REVOLUTION

By the beginning of the twentieth century major changes were taking place in Chinese society, particularly in the treaty ports but also in inland cities such as Chengdu, the provincial capital of Sichuan. There the city administration adopted a New Policies reform programme, established a modern police force and co-ordinated economic development projects such as an electric lighting plant and a telephone system. New buildings were erected, some streets were paved and public parks and shopping arcades were laid out.[1]

The gentry, the traditional elite, no longer relied on the examination system to justify their position. Wealthy gentry families moved into the cities and employed lower gentry to manage their rural estates. Although they affected to despise trade, many engaged in commercial activities and on occasion joined with merchants, forming what has been described as a 'merchant–gentry alliance'.

The opening of China to world trade and the emigration of thousands of Chinese to the Americas and South-east Asia had created a new merchant class. This included compradores, a term first used to describe the agents of Western firms who handled the Chinese side of the business, but later applied to those who engaged in foreign trade or utilized their familiarity with Western business methods. It also included wealthy Overseas Chinese who invested part of their fortunes in China. The great majority of the new merchant class were owners of small enterprises which were affected by the changing economic environment. To protect their interests they formed chambers of commerce, which in 1904 were given official recognition. These chambers quickly outgrew their officially designated role, and their members began to express their views on issues such as currency reform, taxation and government expenditure.[2]

The late Qing educational and military reforms also contributed to the process of social change. The number of modern schools rose from 35,787 with an enrolment of 1,006,743 pupils in 1907, to 87,272 schools with an enrolment of 2,933,387 pupils in 1912.

It has been said of these schools, where ill-prepared teachers taught a syllabus which was divorced from Chinese reality, that they 'did more to encourage protest and demands than to consolidate the imperial monarchy'.[3] A small but influential group of students went overseas, many to Japan, where they studied a variety of subjects, but the main lesson they learned was the importance of nationalism, for they received continual reminders of the strength of Japan and the weakness of their own country.

Since the formation of the regional armies, the status of the military, which by tradition was very low, had begun to rise. After the abolition of the traditional military examinations and the creation of the new armies, a new class of professional soldiers began to appear. Young men from good families went abroad to study, usually to Japan, where they encountered the idea that the army might take the lead in defending and regenerating the nation. When they returned to China they became officers in the New Army units, of which the most prominent were the Beiyang Army, formed by Yuan Shikai in the north, and the Self-Strengthening Army, raised by Zhang Zhidong at Nanjing.

In the years before the 1911 revolution other autonomous groups began to play a significant role in politics, indicating the beginning of a new phase in the development of civil society. The Treaty of Shimonoseki had permitted the establishment of foreign-owned industry in the treaty ports. In Shanghai and a few other cities an industrial proletariat had begun to form, numbering about 661,000 by 1912. Workers, many of whom were women, were often recruited as contract labour, which left them entirely dependent on the contractor to negotiate their conditions of work, which were usually very poor. Between 1895 and 1919 women were the main participants in 57 strikes. The largest stoppage occurred in 1911 when 3000 women working at a Chinese-owned silk filature struck over a wage cut. Women workers were often divided by different geographical origins, and this inhibited their role in the development of a labour movement.[4]

Apart from organized labour, two other groups deserve particular mention: journalists and Christian converts. In 1904 *Shibao*, known in English as *The Eastern Times*, began publication in Shanghai. Many of its journalists had received a classical education, but they put themselves forward as representatives of a 'new middle level' in society, representing a fresh area of negotiation between ruler and ruled, and seeking to transform the people from passive subjects of the dynasty to active citizens of a new constitutional order. They called for educational, industrial and institutional reform and took up the common people's grievances over matters such as the taxes imposed to implement the 'New Policies' of the late Qing reforms.[5] Another group, that of Christian converts, has been depicted as denationalized and dependent for their position on Western missionaries. However, a recent study of converts in Fuzhou has shown them to have been an important part of the emerging professional sector. The Fuzhou branch of the Young Men's Christian Association, founded in 1907, played a key role in various reformist activities and made common cause with the progressive elite in the city. Christian converts also contributed to the development of the nationalist movement by introducing to China political ideas and political symbols often derived from the United States.[6]

Cities became the forum for mass political protests. In 1905 a boycott was organized in Shanghai and several other cities to protest against the restriction of Chinese immigration into the United States. In 1908, after the Chinese government had been forced to apologize abjectly over an incident concerning a Japanese ship, the *Tatsu Maru*, street demonstrations took place in Guangzhou and Japanese goods were burned. Among the demonstrators were many women, who urged their supporters to wear rings engraved with the words 'National Humiliation'.

As early as 1882, Kang Youwei had asserted that the binding of women's feet was not compatible with the needs of a modern nation-state. He later claimed that his words had prompted the founding of indigenous anti-foot-binding societies. Some foreign missionaries supported this view and in 1895 Mrs Archibald Little, the wife of a British merchant, organised a Natural Foot Society in Shanghai. In 1898, in a memorial to the throne, Kang Youwei denounced foot-binding: 'To cut off the feet was an ancient way of punishing criminals … What crime have women committed that they should invariably suffer this same punishment?' The proposal disappeared with the rest of the reform programme, but in 1902 the Empress Dowager herself issued an edict abolishing the custom. Abolition was not supported by all women – the writer Xue Shaohui opposed it as a naive response to Western prejudices – and the custom survived for some years in rural areas.[7]

In June 1906 an imperial edict announced a campaign to eradicate opium cultivation over a ten-year period. In Fujian, where the anti-American boycott had mobilized activists, an Anti-Opium Society was established, with Lin Binzhang, grandson of Lin Zexu of Opium War fame, as its first chairman. Opium dens were forced to close and opium and the apparatus for opium smoking were confiscated and burnt in public bonfires. These occasions were used for parades and for speeches on the evils of opium use and how opium users were betraying the nation.[8]

These signs of change were referred to as 'Young China'. Young China, of course, was an urban phenomenon; rural China remained, if not unchanging, at most only remotely affected.

THE REVOLUTIONARY MOVEMENT

In the Guomindang version of the history of the 1911 revolution, the revolutionary movement, headed by Sun Zhongshan, played a key role in the overthrow of the Manchus. Modern historians have been less convinced of the centrality of the revolutionaries in the events that led to the fall of the Qing dynasty and the collapse of the imperial system. Mary Wright suggested that at most the revolutionary movement created a revolutionary tradition. In 1911 it was too frail an instrument to be able to bring about a revolution on its own.[9]

Despite this disclaimer, the record of the early revolutionaries and their organizations is of interest. Sun Zhongshan (1866–1925), the founder of the first revolutionary group, was born near Guangzhou and studied in Xianggang, where he was baptized a Christian. He lived for a time with his brother in Hawaii before returning to Xianggang to study medicine. Having become interested in politics, in 1894 he offered his services to Li Hongzhang, but his offer was ignored and thereafter he abandoned thoughts of reform and turned to revolution. He formed a revolutionary organization in Honolulu and in the following year he was involved in an abortive attempt to capture Guangzhou. In 1896 he was kidnapped by the Chinese authorities on the streets of London and would have been smuggled back to China for trial and execution had he not contacted friends, who publicized his plight in the *Globe* and secured his release. Sun came into contact with Kang Youwei and Liang Qichao, the leading Chinese nationalists in exile in Japan, but he did not accept their plans for a constitutional monarchy or their links with the gentry reform movement. Instead, he preferred to seek funds from Overseas

Chinese and to attempt uprisings with the help of secret society members.

Nationalist accounts of the revolution have emphasized the contribution of Sun Zhongshan at the expense of that of other revolutionary figures. Zou Rong (1885–1905), like many other Chinese students living in Japan, became a revolutionary when Russia failed to withdraw troops from Manchuria after the Boxer Uprising. His manifesto, *The Revolutionary Army*, published in the comparative safety of the International Settlement of Shanghai, contained a violent attack on the Manchus. He was imprisoned for issuing inflammatory writings and died in jail at the age of 19. Huang Xing (1874–1916), a more conventional revolutionary, came from Hunan. After studying in Japan he returned to his home province, where he established the Society for China's Revival. A feature of this society was its early recognition of the importance of infiltrating the armed forces.

Qiu Jin (1875–1907), modern China's most renowned female revolutionary, left her husband and children to go to Japan to study and pursue her political destiny. She believed that the eradication of foot-binding and the promotion of women's education were essential steps to combat national weakness. She challenged the traditional identity of Chinese women by cross-dressing and riding astride on horseback. She insisted that a fundamental change in the condition of women would only be achieved in conjunction with China's political liberation. While in Japan, she joined organizations committed to overthrowing the Qing and trained in bomb-making. On her return to China, she joined the Zhejiang Restoration Society, became involved in an attempted revolutionary coup and was arrested and executed. Even in the manner of her death she defied her gender – whereas women criminals were dismembered or hanged, she was beheaded like a man. In her life and death she became 'an icon of the late Qing revolutionary struggle'.[10]

In 1905 Sun Zhongshan, with the support of Huang Xing, formed the Tongmenghui, or Revolutionary Alliance, in Tokyo. The alliance, which brought together several revolutionary organizations, adopted a manifesto written by Sun which contained a four-point programme: drive out the Manchus, restore China, establish a republic and equalize land ownership. The first revolutionary stage would be a military dictatorship, which would be followed by a period of one-party government or 'political tutelage', and eventually by the introduction of democracy.

Over the next few years several abortive revolutionary incidents occurred. In 1906, at Pingliuli in eastern Hunan, the Gelaohui or Elder Brother Society, in conjunction with dissident miners and soldiers, attempted an uprising. Some students from the Revolutionary Alliance took part and the rebels variously called for the establishment of a republic or the restoration of a Chinese Empire. However, the rebels were no match for well-armed government soldiers. In 1910, Huang Xing and other revolutionaries organized a mutiny in the ranks of the Guangzhou New Army, but the mutiny broke out prematurely and was easily suppressed. Nine months later the Alliance was involved in the Guangzhou revolt, which turned into a devastating defeat for the Guangdong revolutionaries.

THE 1911 REVOLUTION

Although the revolutionary attempts had dramatized the challenge to Manchu rule, at the beginning of 1911 there was no expectation that China was on the verge of a revolution. However, two incidents precipitated a crisis and exposed the weakness of the Manchu dynasty and the frailty of the imperial system.

The first incident derived from the issue of railway construction. In 1908 Zhang Zhidong had begun to negotiate an international loan, part of which was to finance the construction of a national railway network, a plan which threatened the interests of the consortia formed by merchants and gentry to build provincial railway lines. Zhang Zhidong died in 1909 and was replaced by Sheng Xuanhuai, a bureaucratic capitalist who had previously run the Hanyeping Coal and Iron Company at Hanyang. Sheng, a leading exponent of railway nationalization, already stood accused of selling out China's rights by borrowing from foreigners. In May 1911 Sheng proposed the nationalization of all non-completed railways for which provincial gentry and merchants had raised capital. When investors learned that they would only recover part of their investment, loud protests were expressed, particularly in Sichuan. The Sichuan Railway Protection League, a body with strong links with the provincial assembly, was established, mass meetings were held and a campaign of civil disobedience began. The governor-general of the province arrested the League's leaders, broke up demonstrations and called for military reinforcements. Nevertheless, by September local militia and secret societies, led in some cases by members of the Revolutionary Alliance, virtually controlled the province.

The second incident had its origins in the military modernization which began after the Sino-Japanese War and continued with the late Qing reforms. The new armies recruited better-educated soldiers, many of whom were susceptible to nationalist propaganda. After revolutionary attempts like the Pingliuli uprising had demonstrated that it was futile to oppose the new armies, revolutionaries tried to infiltrate them. This was done most successfully in Hubei, where the New Army units were stationed at Wuhan, the triple city on the Yangzi, which included Hankou with its important foreign concession. In 1908 a group calling itself the Political Study Society, which had links with the local treaty-port press, was formed among soldiers of the 41st Regiment of the Hubei Army. The society was broken up, but the revolutionaries regrouped in early 1911 to form the Literature Society.

In 1911 other events contributed to the development of a revolutionary atmosphere. Central China, and Hankou in particular, had suffered from an economic depression. Severe flooding of the Yangzi and Han rivers had cost an estimated 2,500,000 lives. In April one of the much-vaunted constitutional reforms at last came into effect: the appointment of a responsible cabinet. However, it was composed of eight Manchus, one Mongol and only four Chinese. Then came the controversy over the nationalization of the railways, which resulted in some units of the Hubei Army being sent to Sichuan to suppress a movement for which many soldiers felt some sympathy.

By October, it has been said, 'Central China lacked only the spark that would light the prairie fire'.[11] The Literature Society, together with other revolutionary organizations in Hubei and Hunan, had planned an insurrection for the middle of the month. The plot was discovered and this forced the revolutionaries to advance the date to 10 October. With surprising ease they seized Wuchang, on the opposite bank of the Yangzi from Hankou, and set up a military government, which was supported by the Hubei provincial assembly. Having declared independence from the empire and the establishment of a republic, they sent messages to other provincial assemblies and New Army units inviting them to follow suit. In cities across China attacks on Manchu populations and Manchu garrisons began. In Wuchang, revolutionary soldiers killed anyone suspected of being a Manchu, the test being whether their 'head was flat in the back' or whether they could say the number 6 correctly in Chinese (Manchus said *niu* rather than *liu*). The bloodiest incident came after the capture of the Manchu garrison at Xi'an on 24 October, when about 10,000 Manchus were massacred.[12]

By early December 1911, all the provinces of south and central China had seceded from the empire. The fate of the Qing dynasty, however, remained undecided. The most important of the new armies, the Beiyang Army, which was stationed in the north, was less responsive to revolutionary propaganda and did not react immediately to events in central China. Yuan Shikai, the army's creator, had been dismissed in January 1909. In November 1911 the Manchus invited him back to serve as prime minister. Yuan, who had also been approached by the revolutionaries, accepted the offer from the court. Imperial forces recaptured Hankou but were repulsed at Nanjing, and this reverse may have convinced Yuan that the future lay with the revolution. He encouraged the Qing dynasty to abdicate with the promise of a generous settlement, and in March 1912 he succeeded Sun Zhongshan as president of the new republic.

Many aspects of the 1911 revolution have been the subject of debate, not least whether the event – which was followed soon after by the decline of the republic into warlordism – should be counted as a genuine revolution. Two issues are of particular interest: the motivation of the gentry and the part played by the revolutionaries. In the past, the gentry group had transferred its allegiance to a new dynasty when it felt that the old dynasty could no longer secure its interests. It has been suggested that in 1911 some gentry leaders, particularly those who had played a prominent role in the provincial assemblies, were motivated by constitutionalism; that is to say, their main aim was constitutional reform and the establishment of a parliament. They abandoned the dynasty because they lost faith in the Qing commitment to political reform. However, for many other members of the gentry dynastic decline, the rise of violence, the activities of the secret societies, all spelled out danger. They sided with the revolution because they believed that the New Army units could best preserve order, and because they saw in the situation the opportunity to enhance their own power at local and provincial level.

The role of the revolutionaries was ambiguous. The Revolutionary Alliance did not contribute directly to the Wuchang coup. Sun Zhongshan himself was in the United States and read of the event in a newspaper. The Wuchang rebels persuaded Li Yuanhong, a New Army brigade commander who was not a revolutionary, to head the government. By November, almost all the revolutionary leaders had concluded that Yuan Shikai held the key to the success of the revolution. When Sun Zhongshan returned to China in December, he was apprehensive that more fighting might lead to foreign intervention and he too, albeit reluctantly, turned to Yuan and resigned the presidency to him. From this sequence of events one might deduce that although the revolutionaries and Sun Zhongshan had helped create the political atmosphere in which the 1911 revolution took place, they had little control over the events which ensued.

THE PRESIDENCY OF YUAN SHIKAI

The critics of Yuan Shikai have accused him of betraying the 1898 reformers, of deserting the Qing dynasty and of abandoning the republic to make himself emperor, at all times acting on selfish motives. His biographer E. P. Young, while admitting that Yuan had faults, has suggested that throughout his presidency he pursued policies which he believed to be in the best interests of his country. Apprehensive of foreign pressure on China's sovereignty, he set out to centralize the administration through reforms, which were introduced in stages to reduce the risk of disorder.[13]

According to the constitution of the new republic, the president exercised considerable power, but was required to share that power with the prime minister and the provisional parliament. Tang Shaoyi, the first prime minister and four other cabinet ministers were members of the Revolutionary Alliance, which also held about one third of the seats in the provisional parliament. This arrangement soon proved unmanageable. In June, Tang and the other Alliance members of the cabinet resigned after a row over a foreign loan. In August, Yuan Shikai announced that the first parliamentary elections would take place at the end of the year. In preparation, the Alliance amalgamated with four minor parties and renamed itself the Guomindang, or Nationalist Party. In the elections the Guomindang, headed by Song Jiaoren, who had drafted the constitution, won a majority in both houses of parliament. The new party immediately began to criticize some of the actions of Yuan's government, particularly its willingness to take foreign loans, and demanded that the power of parliament should be increased. Yuan Shikai's response was to have Song Jiaoren assassinated.

There followed the event known as the Second Revolution. In April 1913 Yuan Shikai, without the prior consent of parliament, contracted a 'Reorganization Loan' of $25,000,000 from a British, French, German, Russian and Japanese consortium. The loan, which was secured on the revenue of the salt monopoly, was ostensibly intended to refinance China's existing debts and to pay for a reform of the administration. However, Yuan's opponents were sure that he intended to use it to bankroll a campaign of suppression against his political opponents. This suspicion was confirmed in June, when Yuan dismissed three military governors, including Li Liejun, the governor of Jiangxi, with whom he had already clashed. Li Liejun thereupon declared his province independent and tried to rally military support. But Yuan had anticipated the danger and, although his opponents captured Nanjing and threatened Shanghai, by September the attempted revolution had been crushed.

After the Second Revolution Yuan established himself as a dictator. Martial law was declared, newspapers were closed down, opposition members of parliament were arrested and many thousands of people were killed. The Guomindang members of parliament were expelled and the party itself proscribed. Yuan then dissolved the provincial assemblies, thereby tampering with the interests of the gentry. At the same time, Yuan introduced several measures, some of which, for example his attempt to revise the fiscal relationship between the province and central government, continued his policy of centralization. Other reforms, including one which aimed to provide education for all Chinese boys and another which sought to raise standards of agriculture, hinted at a wider agenda of social improvement.

At the time of the Second Revolution, Yuan had justified his actions on the grounds of national unity. In 1915 his commitment to that cause was tested severely by the presentation by Japan of the notorious document known as the 'Twenty-one Demands'. When the First World War broke out, Japan opportunistically declared war on Germany and seized the German base at Qingdao in Shandong. In January 1915, the Japanese government presented to Yuan Shikai 21 demands divided into five groups, which included the transfer to Japan of all German interests in Shandong, the extension of Japan's lease on the Liaodong peninsula, the grant of further commercial rights in Manchuria and joint Sino-Japanese control of the Hanyeping industrial complex. The fifth group required the Chinese government to use Japanese advisers in its military, police and financial administrations, thereby turning China into a 'second Korea'. The document was leaked to the Chinese press and an outburst of patriotic protests followed. Britain and the United States expressed concern, but advised that China would have to accept the ultimatum. On 7 May 1915, Yuan acceded to the first four groups of demands, but deferred agreement on the fifth group. That day was to be commemorated as the day of national humiliation and Yuan's prestige was never to recover from his compromise on the issue.

Yuan's willingness to compromise has been attributed to his desire to become emperor. His opponents had long suspected him of cherishing that ambition, but he only became committed to it in 1915 after the presentation of the Twenty-one Demands. He believed that a restoration was the preference of the mass of the population, which had never accepted the republic. He was encouraged in this view by Dr F. J. Goodnow, his American political adviser, who argued that China's history and traditions made it more suited to a monarchy than to a republic. Despite evidence of opposition to his plans, in December Yuan accepted an invitation from his supporters to become emperor and on 1 January 1916 his reign began.

The monarchical venture was not a success. Intellectual criticism was led by Liang Qichao, once an advocate of a constitutional monarchy, but who now believed that the mystique of the monarchy had been destroyed irrevocably. Japan and the Western imperial powers expressed doubts about the wisdom of the move, and Japan began to supply funds to Yuan's political opponents. The most serious opposition came from a group of military men headed by Cai E, the military governor of Yunnan. Having protested in vain against Yuan's monarchical plans, in December 1915 Cai E declared Yunnan independent, and in the following month he led his troops into Sichuan. Yuan dispatched units of the Beiyang Army, which should have been able to defeat Cai E easily, but a combination of Cai E's enterprising military tactics and the defection of Yuan's supporters led to the loss of Sichuan. By now support for Yuan Shikai was crumbling rapidly, and in March he abandoned his claim to the monarchy. Three months later he died.

THE WARLORD ERA, 1916–28

Yuan Shikai's death left a political vacuum which in the short term proved impossible to fill. His rejection of the republic had discredited parliamentary democracy, but his ventures into dictatorship, and his restoration of the monarchy, had shown that neither alternative had enough support. In the ensuing period, the central government ceased to exert national authority, and effective power fell into the hands of military governors or warlords.

The origin of warlordism has been the subject of a lively debate. Franz Michael argued that Chinese history showed a pattern of recurrent decline in the authority of the central government and the development of regionalist power centres; that the nineteenth-century rebellions had left a legacy of regionalism; and that the collapse of the empire completed the disintegration and ushered in the era of warlordism.[14] Other writers, for example Jerome Ch'en, have suggested that warlordism in China was a modern phenomenon which could be traced to the effects of military modernization. According to Ch'en, Yuan was the founder of the Chinese modern army and his legacy to the republic was a large number of warlords. When he was alive, they supported him; when he was dead, they fought among themselves.[15] Edward A. McCord has pointed out that warlords emerged during the continuing crisis of political authority which followed the fall of the imperial system, a crisis which revolved around issues such as the relative powers of president and parliament and the relationship between civil and military power.[16]

Yuan Shikai was succeeded as president by Li Yuanhong, the 1912 constitution was revived and there was a brief period of national unity. This was destroyed by disputes between Li and Duan Qirui, a general in the Beiyang Army, in the first instance over the validity of the 1912 constitution, which in some eyes had been superseded by the constitution introduced by Yuan Shikai in 1914, and secondly over whether China should enter the war against Germany. In July 1917, the vacillations of the Beijing government encouraged Zhang Xun, known as the 'pigtailed general' because his troops had retained their queues, to march into Beijing and restore the last Manchu emperor. He was quickly expelled and Duan Qirui regained control. However, Li Yuanhong was forced to resign the presidency, his place being taken by Feng Guozhang, another former commander under Yuan Shikai. In 1918 Duan Qirui outraged nationalist opinion by accepting the 'Nishihara loans' provided by Japanese interests to advance their claims in Manchuria.

From this point onwards the Beijing government, although it continued to receive the recognition of the foreign powers, ceased to exercise effective authority over the nation. Over the next decade, the distribution of power was fluid, but it may be indicated in broad outline by saying that initially north and central China was divided between the supporters of Duan Qirui, who formed the Anhui or Anfu clique, and the supporters of Feng Guozhang, who formed the Zhili clique. In 1920 the Zhili clique, with the support of the Fengtian or south Manchurian clique headed by Zhang Zuolin, otherwise known as the Old Marshal, defeated the Anfu clique. The Zhili and Fengtian cliques then fought two wars; the second, in 1924, was a major conflict which resulted in the break-up of the Zhili clique. From 1924 a somewhat more stable situation emerged, the principal warlord regimes being those of the Old Marshal in Manchuria; that of Feng Yuxiang, the 'Christian General', in the north west; Yan Xishan, the 'Model Governor', in Shanxi; Sun Chuanfang, a former member of the Zhili clique, in the lower Yangzi provinces; Wu Peifu, the 'Philosopher Marshal', in the middle Yangzi; and in the south west the Guangxi clique. Around Guangzhou, Sun Zhongshan, with the consent of the local warlord Chen Jiongming, maintained a precarious existence.

Although warlord regimes were extremely diverse, they did have some common features. Most warlords had a military background and many had previously been military governors of provinces. They all maintained armies which were personally loyal to them, and all – with the exception of Feng Yuxiang, who has been described as a 'mobile warlord' – commanded a territorial base. Armies had to be paid and warlords used a variety of levies to supply their financial needs. Part of their revenue came from taxes which were normally payable to the government, for example the land tax. Another part derived from monopolies on consumer goods, the sale of opium and charges on businesses and railway companies. Warlords were frequently short of funds and they used unorthodox methods to supplement their income, for example printing their own currency.

Warlords did differ in terms of the ideologies they projected. James Sheridan identified three main categories: conservative warlords, for example Wu Peifu, who was a committed Confucianist; reactionary warlords, for example Zhang Xun, who attempted to restore the Qing; and reformist warlords, who included Feng Yuxiang and Yan Xishan. The former, who had become a Christian in 1914, insisted that his troops should not drink, gamble, use opium or visit prostitutes. He selected recruits on the basis of physical fitness and expected his men to train vigorously. The latter, who controlled the poor province of Shanxi, promoted primary education and literacy, and initiated campaigns against foot-binding and prostitution.[17]

The warlord period has usually been regarded as a disastrous episode in China's history. Central government had collapsed, Outer Mongolia and Tibet had become semi-independent, intellectuals had withdrawn from public service, warfare was endemic, the economy was neglected and Western imperialism continued to make inroads. Wen Yiduo, one of China's best-known modern poets, wrote bleakly in the late 1920s:

This is a ditch of hopelessly dead water.
No clear breeze can raise half a ripple on it.
Why not throw in some rusty metal scraps,
Or even some of your leftover food and soup?[18]

Nevertheless, the warlord period had some positive aspects. Despite their self-seeking tendencies, most warlords subscribed to the cause of Chinese nationalism. During the First World War, largely because of the preoccupation of the European powers with the conflict in Europe, China's exports had boomed and modern industries had expanded sharply. This trend continued after the war, with the index of industrial production rising by 300 per cent between 1916 and 1928. The traditional emphasis on ideological conformity was replaced by intellectual freedom, which enabled the cultural change known as the May Fourth Movement to take place. The political disintegration left the way open for the emergence of new political parties, and it is in these years that the Chinese Communist Party (CCP) was founded and the Guomindang was reorganized and began its bid to reunify China.

On 4 May 1919, the news reached Beijing that the Paris Peace Conference had decided that the former German interests in Shandong, which had been seized by Japan during the war, should not be returned to China but retained by Japan. A crowd of 3000 students assembled at the Tiananmen (the front gate of the former imperial palace) and marched on the foreign legations. The march was blocked by the police, so the students diverted to the house of Cao Rulin, the minister of communications who had negotiated the Twenty-one Demands and arranged the Nishihara loans, and burned it down. The police arrested 31 students, one of whom later died of his injuries. The incident rapidly turned into a national protest, with demonstrations occurring in many other cities and a boycott of Japanese goods being declared. The government responded indecisively, at first arresting more students and then capitulating to their demands. Cao Rulin resigned from the government and the government itself fell shortly afterwards. The Chinese delegation at Versailles refused to sign the concluding agreement.

In Shanghai, the news of the Versailles settlement prompted businesspeople and students to organize a Citizens' Association, which called for a boycott of trade with Japan, the removal of the three pro-Japanese officials and the release of the students arrested in Beijing. In early June groups of workers began to come out on strike, with workers in Japanese mills forming the single largest contingent of strikers. This combined action of students, businesspeople and workers became known as the triple stoppage, and the participation of workers was identified as the first political strike and first general strike in the history of China.[19]

These events precipitated the intellectual or cultural movement known as the May Fourth Movement. Its main themes were an attack on Confucianism, an enthusiasm for new ideas and a literary revolution. The movement emerged at a time of rapid social change, marked by the growth of the coastal cities and the rapid increase in the number of students at universities and colleges; by 1919 about 4,500,000 students had received an education which included some Western-style studies. Beijing National University, which had been founded in 1898 as a training centre for officials, had been transformed by its chancellor Cai Yuanpei (1868–1940) into the leading academic institution committed to the promotion of liberal ideas. He brought to the university several leading academics, including Hu Shi (1891–1962), who had studied with the philosopher John Dewey at Columbia University, and Chen Duxiu (1879–1942), who had founded the journal *New Youth* in Shanghai in 1915. Its first editorial had called on the youth of China to cast off the conventions of the past and to embrace the individualism and utilitarianism of the West. Chen Duxiu and Li Dazhao (1888–1927), the university's librarian, were to be the joint founders of the Chinese Communist Party.

The 1911 revolution had dismantled the political framework of the Confucian state, but the Confucian tradition remained dominant in the family, particularly in the wealthy extended families from which many of the first generation of Westernized intellectuals came. This tradition was now attacked fiercely in the pages of *New Youth*.

In December 1916, Chen Duxiu, who came from a prosperous Anhui family and who had failed the provincial examinations, published an article entitled 'The Way of Confucius and Modern Life'. In it he criticized Confucian teaching on filial piety and on the subservience of women, noting in particular the prejudice against the remarriage of widows. Confucius, he remarked, lived in a feudal age and the ethics, social mores and political institutions that he advocated belonged to a feudal age. Confucius's view recorded in the Book of Rites, that 'to be a woman means to submit', enshrined principles of proper social conduct which were incompatible with a modern way of life, which rested on the concepts of equality and independence. Chen Duxiu's essay ensured that issues relating to women's emancipation were to be prominent through the May Fourth era.[20]

Classical Chinese literature was written in a condensed and allusive form which made it accessible only to those with a classical education. By the end of the nineteenth century, the demand for newspapers, popular fiction and translations of Western works had resulted in the production of a large amount of writing in the vernacular, but the classical form continued to be used for all serious literature. In 1917 Hu Shi published an article in *New Youth* in which he called for a 'literary revolution', which would supplant the classical style with the vernacular for all forms of literary expression. The following month Chen Duxiu demanded:

> Destroy the aristocratic literature which is nothing but literary chiselling and flattery, and construct a simple, expressive literature of the people.[21]

The consequence was the emergence of a true vernacular literature. One of the first and greatest exponents of this was Lu Xun (1881–1936), whose short story 'A Madman's Diary' appeared in *New Youth* in April 1918. In 1921 the ministry of education decreed that the vernacular should be used in all primary school texts.

The third strand in the intellectual ferment of the May Fourth Movement was the diffusion of a wide range of ideas from the West. By the late nineteenth century many of the key concepts of Western thought, including Social Darwinism and socialist and anarchist ideas, had been translated into Chinese. In November 1918, in an article in *New Youth* entitled 'The Victory of Bolshevism', Li Dazhao attempted to explain the tenets of Bolshevism, and in the following year he used an entire issue of the magazine to discuss Marxism. In January 1919, Chen Duxiu was still arguing that only science and democracy could 'cure the dark maladies in Chinese politics, morality, learning and thought',[22] but he, like many others, lost faith in Western democracy after the betrayal of China at Versailles. Hu Shi adopted the pragmatic philosophy of John Dewey, who was lecturing in China between 1919 and 1921. This made him doubt that ready-made ideologies such as anarchism or Marxism, which he called 'isms', could provide the solution to China's problems. He asked rhetorically what the sole aim of this new thought was. His answer was: to recreate civilization, but civilization was not created *in toto,* but by 'inches and drops'.[23] His leaning to gradualism contrasted with the revolutionary preferences of Li Dazhao and Chen Duxiu, an indication that the intellectual unanimity of the May Fourth period, brought about largely by the nationalistic fervour of the times, would not last.

THE FOUNDING OF THE CHINESE COMMUNIST PARTY AND THE REORGANIZATION OF THE GUOMINDANG

Many Chinese were to be proud of having belonged to the May Fourth generation, for they regarded those years as the starting point of modern Chinese history. Among them was Mao Zedong (1893–1976), who came from Hunan, where his father had begun life as a poor peasant. Mao was a student at the time of the 1911 revolution and a political activist when the May Fourth incident occurred. By 1920, Chen Duxiu and Li Dazhao had started a Marxist study group at Beijing University and Mao Zedong had begun his own group in Changsha, the provincial capital of Hunan. In April of that year Grigori Voitinsky, representing the Third Communist International, visited China to assist in the formation of a Communist party. First a Socialist Youth League was organized and contact was made with the group of students from Hunan and Sichuan – among them Deng Xiaoping – who were being sent to France on a scheme that was part study, part work. In July 1921, at a girls' school in the French Concession in Shanghai, the First Congress of the CCP was held. Neither Chen Duxiu nor Li Dazhao was present on that occasion, though Chen Duxiu was chosen as secretary-general of the Party in absentia. There is some uncertainty about the decisions taken at that meeting, but probably it was agreed that the Party should concentrate on promoting the labour movement.

Between 1921 and 1923, China experienced what has been described as 'the first big wave of labour struggles'.[24] Communist historiography has claimed that the CCP played the major role in directing the struggle, but Guomindang activists also played their part and the rise of unrest was apparent before the CCP had been formed. The most successful industrial action was the Xianggang seamen's strike, which began in January 1922 and had as its central issue the discrepancy between the wages of white and Chinese seamen. The strike spread to Guangzhou and Shanghai, eventually involved 120,000 workers and resulted in the Xianggang seamen receiving a wage rise of 15 to 30 per cent. Later that year the Communist-supported Labour Secretariat organized a congress in Guangzhou which was attended by delegates who claimed to represent 300,000 workers. But then, when the labour movement seemed about to take off, a strike of railway workers on the Beijing–Hankou line led to disaster. The local warlord, Wu Peifu, perhaps with the encouragement of the Western powers, broke up the strike, killing 35 of the strikers, including the branch secretary of the union of the Jiangnan depot in Hankou, who was beheaded on his own station platform.

After the Guomindang had been expelled from the Beijing parliament in 1913, it moved to Guangzhou, where it maintained a shadowy existence with the unreliable support of Chen Jiongming, the local warlord. It was these circumstances which made Sun Zhongshan receptive to the overtures of Maring, the Comintern agent whom he met in 1921. In the previous year, Lenin had persuaded the Comintern (the Communist International, the Moscow-based organization committed to promoting revolution) that in colonial countries, a term which included China, Communists should collaborate with bourgeois-democratic movements. Maring concluded that the Guomindang should be regarded as such a movement, and he obtained Sun Zhongshan's agreement that members of the newly formed CCP should be allowed to join the Guomindang as individuals and that an united front should be formed by the two parties. In later years this assumption of a common interest between the two parties was derided. However John Fitzgerald, whose concern was nation-building in China in the 1920s, has suggested that the division between the Nationalists and Communists was not a struggle between nationalism and Marxism-Leninism, but a struggle between two phases of nationalism:

> a conflict over membership of the nation at a time when the nation was still under negotiation. Institutionally, it was a struggle between two highly-competitive state-building parties ...[25]

Sun Zhongshan had already begun a reorganization of the Guomindang. A new constitution had been adopted which refined the manifesto commitment of the Revolutionary Alliance to three principles: nationalism, democracy and the people's livelihood. Now the Comintern, in the person of Mikhail Borodin who had arrived in Guangzhou in October 1923, assisted in making further changes. The party was reorganized on Bolshevik lines, although Sun Zhongshan retained personal leadership, a diversion from the Leninist model. Through the efforts of Sun Fo, Sun Zhongshan's son, who was mayor of Guangzhou, a significant improvement was made to the party's finances. Most importantly, in May 1924 a military academy was opened at Huangpu (Whampoa), south of Guangzhou. The academy, headed by Jiang Jieshi (Chiang Kai-shek; 1887–1975), who had recently returned from Moscow, was to train a National Revolutionary Army which would be used to reunify China.

In the meantime the Guomindang, with Communist support, was attempting to organize mass movements. Liao Zhongkai, leader of the left wing of the Guomindang, promoted a revival of the Guangzhou labour movement, which led to a series of strikes and a strengthening of union discipline. One notable protest, the Shamian affair of July 1924, was directed against Western imperialism and the unequal treaties. Contact was made with the peasants, now recognized as an important component in the revolutionary struggle. In 1922 Peng Pai, the son of a landlord, who had joined the Socialist Youth League, began to work among the peasants of his home district in eastern Guangdong. Two years later the Guomindang established a Farmers' Bureau, headed by Peng Pai, which organized peasant associations and supported peasants in disputes with landlords.

However, the more successful the Guomindang was in creating a mass following, the more it alienated the merchants and landlords who provided its principal support. This situation was illustrated dramatically in the autumn of 1924, when a group of Guangzhou merchants, infuriated by the heavy taxes imposed by the Guomindang and its encouragement of the labour movement, raised a militia and smuggled arms into the city. Ironically, this militia was defeated by soldiers from the Huangpu military academy, although their commander, Jiang Jieshi, had already voiced his suspicion of the infiltration tactics of the CCP.

In March 1925, Sun Zhongshan, who had long been a sick man, died of cancer. His death was commemorated in services nationally, but memory of him might then have faded if an incident had not inflamed nationalist sentiments in China. On 30 May 1925, police commanded by a British officer fired on Chinese demonstrating in the Nanjing Road in Shanghai, killing 12 people. Protests followed in cities throughout China. In Guangzhou, on 23 June, British troops fired on a rally and killed 52 demonstrators. This precipitated the Guangzhou–Xianggang strike, which lasted 16 months and seriously disrupted the trade and services of Xianggang.

Since 1924, discussions had been taking place in Guomindang and CCP circles of a northern expedition to reunify China. In the autumn of that year the defeat of Wu Peifu, the dominant figure in central China, by the combined forces of Feng Yuxiang, the Christian General, and Zhang Zuolin, the warlord of Manchuria, encouraged Sun Zhongshan as he had made an agreement to share power with the latter. However, Borodin advised that the military strength of the northern warlords was still too great, and the expedition was postponed.

The Northern Expedition was eventually launched in July 1926. By then the National Revolutionary Army and its allies had some 150,000 men and was assisted by Russian military advisers. Against it were arrayed the large but inferior forces of Wu Peifu in central China, Sun Chuanfang in the east and Zhang Zuolin in the north. The Nationalist forces advanced rapidly through Hunan, and only encountered stiff resistance from Wu Peifu's army as they approached Nanchang, the provincial capital of Jiangxi. According to Harold Isaacs, a left-wing American journalist, this rapid progress was due to the help given to the Guomindang forces by the mass movements. Other writers have been more sceptical, arguing that it was only after the revolutionary armies had arrived that the mass movements, which had been kept in check by the warlords, began to play an important role.[26]

Whether the response came before or after the arrival of the Nationalists, there is no doubt that the Northern Expedition did set off a wave of popular movements. In the Hunan countryside the number of peasants belonging to peasant associations rose dramatically. This prompted Mao Zedong, who had been head of the Guomindang Peasant Movement Training Institute in Guangzhou, to return to Hunan in December 1926 and make his celebrated investigation into the peasant movement. In his report he predicted that 'in a very short time, several hundred million peasants ... will rise like a tornado or a tempest'.[27] The arrival of the Nationalist armies in the Yangzi cities also brought about a surge of revolutionary spirit in the cities, made manifest in a wave of industrial strikes and heightened student activism.

The relationship between the Guomindang and the CCP was already under severe strain. In March 1926, Jiang Jieshi, suspecting that the crew of a gunboat named the *Zhongshan* were about to kidnap him, seized the boat and then carried out a purge of Communist supporters in Guangzhou. Borodin calmed things down and persuaded the CCP to continue the united front with the Guomindang. The Northern Expedition exposed the different agenda of the two parties, and the likelihood of an open disagreement increased as Jiang Jieshi and the eastern wing of the National Revolutionary Army approached Nanjing and Shanghai. On 24 March the expeditionary force entered Nanjing and some of its troops looted the foreign consulates and killed several foreigners. In response, British ships laid down a protective barrage which killed a number of Chinese. Jiang Jieshi, determined not to antagonize the Western powers, blamed the Communists for the attack and executed some of the soldiers held responsible for looting. In Shanghai, Communist leaders, including Zhou Enlai, future prime minister of the People's Republic, had mobilized city workers, in particular those of the Commercial Press and the Shanghai Post Office, against the warlord Sun Chuanfang. In March 1927 they seized control of the city. Jiang Jieshi then entered Shanghai and immediately began to use his contacts with the Western powers, with wealthy bankers and industrialists and with underworld figures such as 'Smallpox Jinrong', leader of the Green Gang, to raise a force of mobsters to strike at the labour unions. On 12 April they killed several hundred union members and handed the city over to Jiang Jieshi.

Notwithstanding the events in Shanghai, in Wuhan the united front between Guomindang and Communists survived. One reason for this was that Stalin, currently engaged in his power struggle with

Leon Trotsky, had staked his ideological reputation on continuing the alliance with the 'bourgeois-democratic' Guomindang, and as a consequence Borodin and the Comintern had to support that policy. Another reason was that the leader of the Guomindang government in Wuhan was Wang Jingwei, regarded by many as Sun Zhongshan's heir, who was on the left wing of the party. The key political issue was whether the two parties should carry through an agrarian revolution and, if so, from whom should land be confiscated and to whom should it be distributed. Confused and ill-informed instructions from Moscow threw the CCP into disarray. The threat of a rural revolution lost the Guomindang support and at the same time the deteriorating military situation forced Wang Jingwei to act. In July, Communists were expelled from the Guomindang, Wuhan was placed under martial law and a repression of the CCP began.

The CCP, with Comintern encouragement, now turned to armed revolt. On 1 August, National Revolutionary Army units sympathetic to the Communist cause seized and briefly held Nanchang. They then marched south, apparently hoping to find support in eastern Guangdong, where Peng Pai had achieved success with the peasant associations. In the meantime Mao Zedong had been instructed to organize a peasant insurrection in Hunan. The event, known as the Autumn Harvest uprising and celebrated as evidence of Mao's inspired recognition of the role that poor peasants were going to play in the revolution, turned into a disaster. The peasant forces were easily defeated and Mao and the few survivors were forced to flee into the mountains. Despite these reverses, in December the CCP Politburo, with encouragement from the Comintern, promoted an insurrection in Guangzhou which has become known as the Guangzhou Commune. The uprising was ill prepared, there was little popular support and Zhang Fakui, commander of the Nationalist forces, put down the revolt with great severity. This incident, it has been claimed, 'turned Chinese public opinion against the Communist Party and Soviet Russia'.[28]

The events of 1927 discredited Wang Jingwei and the left wing of the Guomindang, and enabled Jiang Jieshi to consolidate his position. In April 1928, having secured the co-operation of two important warlords, Feng Yuxiang and Yan Xishan, he recommenced the Northern Expedition against the remaining warlord armies headed by Zhang Zuolin, the warlord of Manchuria. The second half of the expedition, now simply a military campaign, was marked by two important incidents. In late April the Nationalist forces captured Jinan, the provincial capital of Shandong, which had a substantial number of Japanese residents. The Japanese government had already warned that the Northern Expedition might endanger Japanese interests in China. The arrival of the Nationalist forces at Jinan prompted the despatch of two Japanese divisions to protect Japanese nationals. A clash between Nationalist and Japanese troops followed, but Jiang Jieshi, ignoring Chinese protests against this infringement of China's sovereignty, patched up the incident and the National Revolutionary Army continued its advance on Beijing. Then the Guandong Army, the force safeguarding Japanese interests in Manchuria, attempted to influence events. Suspecting that the warlord Zhang Zuolin would oppose any extension of Japanese influence in Manchuria, on 4 June Guandong Army officers assassinated him by blowing up his train. However, his son Zhang Xueliang took his place and supported the Nationalists. Before the end of June, Nationalist forces entered Beijing, so completing the Northern Expedition.

THE NANJING DECADE, 1928–37

The Guomindang made Nanjing its capital because the southern capital was closer to its main power centre on the lower Yangzi. Beijing was now renamed Beiping; that is, 'Northern Peace'. The ten-year period between 1928 and the Japanese invasion in 1937 is known as the Nanjing decade. The record of the Guomindang in these years provides the evidence on which to judge the success of its attempt to create a modern nation-state.

China in the Nanjing decade was a country of startling contrasts. In the coastal cities the indications of modernization and Westernization were widespread, if superficial. In Shanghai in 1929 there were 2326 factories employing nearly 300,000 workers, 70 per cent of whom were women or children. In 1933 more than 80 per cent of Chinese-owned industry was located in the eastern and southern coastal provinces and in Manchuria.

In contrast, the pattern of rural life appeared to be unchanging, although allegations were being made that China was facing an agrarian crisis. The evidence for this is contradictory. According to Albert Feuerwerker, until 1937 the total output of agriculture probably kept pace with the growth of population, which he considered a creditable performance in view of the lack of significant technological improvements.[29] However, Chen Han-seng, who observed conditions in Guangdong in the early 1930s, recorded that some peasants were reduced to such abject poverty that they sold their daughters, or joined those who had migrated to work in the European colonies of South-east Asia. Chen's study suggested that the main causes of peasant immiseration were the exploitation of landlords and the effects of Western imperialism. A modern study of the peasant economy of Hebei and Shandong in the same period concluded that peasants' living standards were rising and that the main obstacle to their increased prosperity was not landlord exploitation, but the absence of any coherent programme for improving agricultural technology.[30]

The Guomindang, following Sun Zhongshan's political programme which had assumed that China was not yet ready for democracy, established a one-party dictatorship. In 1931 it issued a provisional constitution which created a five-branch system of government, comprising the executive, legislative, judicial, examination and control bureaux. This structure was a curious mixture of traditional and modern features. The examination bureau, which supervised entry to the civil service, and the control bureau, which supposedly stamped out corruption, were reminiscent of the imperial system, whereas other aspects of the government displayed Western influence. The Guomindang's Central Political Council nominally exercised executive control, but after 1930 Jiang Jieshi obtained such dominance that both the Guomindang and the government lost authority.

Jiang's dominance was achieved by manipulating factions within the army, the party and the government. In the army his support came from former cadets at the Huangpu Military Academy, where he had been commandant. Within the party Jiang Jieshi was aided by the 'CC clique', led by his close friends the Chen brothers, whose influence derived in part from their involvement with the secret police. A less formal grouping, known as the Political Study clique, provided Jiang with support from professional organizations. Jiang also benefited from other personal connections. In 1927 he had married Song Meiling, the sister of Sun Zhongshan's widow, and he later converted to Christianity. Song Meiling's other sister was married to Kong Xiangxi (H. H. Kung), a leading banker, and her brother Song Ziwen (T. V. Soong) was a Harvard graduate and a noted financial expert. Because of these nepotic connections, the Communists described the Nanjing government as the rule of the 'Four Big Families'.

The ideological stance of the Nanjing government was also ambiguous. Although many of its supporters were of the May Fourth generation and had participated in the attack on Confucianism, Jiang Jieshi remained a follower of Zhu Xi, the twelfth-century neo-Confucianist. Whereas Sun Zhongshan had admired Hong Xiuquan, the Taiping leader, Jiang Jieshi extolled the achievements of Zeng Guofan, who had led the opposition to the rebellion. During the Nanjing decade Confucianism was reinstated and Confucius's birthday was made a public holiday. Confucianism was also an important element in the New Life Movement, which Jiang Jieshi launched in 1934. This encouraged the practice of the four Confucian virtues of propriety, justice, honesty and self-respect, while at the same time it disseminated Western ideas on hygiene. In Nanjing the 'Movement to Eliminate the Three Evils' targeted prostitution, opium-smoking and gambling in an explicit attempt to revive the country and protect the health of the nation.[31] The New Life Movement also had a Christian content, with Jesus being held up as a model to emulate and members of the Young Men's Christian Association (YMCA), which was very active in social work in Chinese cities, being asked to give it support.

In 1931 a group of Huangpu officers formed an elitist organization later known as the Blue Shirts, because they wore Chinese-made cotton cloth as a demonstration of their commitment to China's national interest. They aimed to revive the Guomindang and make Jiang Jieshi a dictator. They also played a leading role in the New Life Movement. The Blue Shirts' open admiration of Mussolini, their strident anti-Communism and their use of violence led to them being described as a fascist organization and to Jiang Jieshi being accused of harbouring fascist sympathies. This issue was revived in the 1980s with the publication of information about a highly secret organization, the Lixingshe or 'Society for Vigorous Practice', which was the core group of the Blue Shirts. This group has been described as 'a military freemasonry that admired fascism and pledged itself to carry out Sun Yat-sen's [Sun Zhongshan's] Three People's Principles under the guidance of its supreme leader, Chiang Kaishek [Jiang Jieshi]'. Frederic Wakeman coined the term 'Confucian Fascism' for the Blue Shirts, which he described as a remarkable blend of Chinese and Western components. Nevertheless, he did not equate it with European fascism, because Jiang Jieshi never intended to create a mass movement.[32]

The economic record of the Nanjing government has been the subject of conflicting assessments. In 1957, Douglas S. Paauw argued that as the government had neither developed the agricultural sector nor encouraged saving and investment in the modern industrial sector, the overall picture was one of economic stagnation.[33] On the other hand, Thomas G. Rawski calculated that China's annual rate of per capita output growth exceeded 1 per cent during the interwar years, a rate comparable with that achieved by Japan between 1897 and 1931.[34]

The most impressive aspects of the economic record concerned financial institutions, communications and the growth of the modern industrial sector. In the 1920s China still lacked a unified currency, and foreign exchange and banking facilities were largely in the hands of foreigners. In 1927, Jiang Jieshi had asked his brother-in-law Song Ziwen to develop a financial strategy for the government. Among Song's achievements were the rescheduling of China's foreign debts, the introduction of a Chinese silver dollar and the abolition of the the *lijin,* the tax on internal trade. He also established a central bank and specialized banks to deal in foreign exchange, to provide credits for peasants and to finance the development of transportation.

His reforms were not entirely successful, however. Throughout the Nanjing decade, because of heavy military spending, government revenue covered only about 80 per cent of its expenditure. The financially sound way to increase government revenue was to tax the agricultural sector efficiently, but the Guomindang lacked the authority and the trained personnel to achieve this. To cover the deficit the banks sold large quantities of heavily discounted government bonds, very often to officials, thereby increasing government liabilities and diverting private investment into speculation. Bureaucratic capitalism became even more marked after Song Ziwen was replaced in 1933 by Kong Xiangxi. Faced with the crisis caused by the United States' Silver Purchase Act of 1934 (which was intended to stabilize the price of silver), the Bank of China was forced to issue new shares and to exchange these for government bonds. As a consequence, the government holding of bank assets rose from 20 per cent to over 70 per cent.

At the beginning of the Nanjing decade China had about 8000 miles of railway track and about 18,000 miles of motorable road. Ten years later a further 5000 miles of railway had been built, the length of motorable roads had increased to 69,000 miles and a further 10,000 miles of road were under construction. In addition, a national airline operated scheduled services and carried airmail. This expansion of modern communications created work and investment, helped to integrate economic regions and strengthened the sense of national identity. In other respects the achievement was less creditable. Much of the labour used was conscripted and peasants were often not permitted to use the new roads because they had been built for military purposes. Over half the new railway mileage had been built in Manchuria, which from 1931 was under Japanese control.

During this period the modern industrial sector grew rapidly from a small base. Impressive advances were achieved in new industries, for example electricity generation, and in older industries such as coal, where output grew at 7 per cent per annum. However, this growth was heavily concentrated in the treaty ports and in Manchuria, a high proportion of the larger enterprises were foreign owned and much of the Chinese share of modern industry was in consumer goods, with perhaps three-quarters of the output by value being in textiles and foodstuffs.

Of fundamental importance to China's economic regeneration was the raising of output and the improvement of productivity in the agricultural sector. Reference has been made to the issue of an agrarian crisis during the interwar years. To add to peasants' difficulties, between 1931 and 1935 they suffered a sharp fall in income occasioned by the world depression and the outflow of silver to the United States. The Guomindang was aware of the problem of peasant immiseration and it took some steps to relieve it. In 1930 it passed a land law which restricted rent to three-eighths of the main crop, but this was never enforced. A National Agricultural Research Bureau was set up in 1932 and measures were introduced to extend credit to farmers through the agricultural co-operative movement. However, most of the loans went to landlords and little of what they borrowed was invested in the land. In retrospect these measures appear woefully inadequate and the commitment of the Guomindang to a transformation of the countryside is suspect.

The Guomindang had signalled its intention to develop education as a means of creating a modern nation-state. When it came to power it passed detailed laws covering all forms of schooling, and in 1930 Jiang Jieshi himself became minister of education. Advice was received from the League of Nations on a national plan of educational reform and 1940 was chosen as the date for the introduction of compulsory education. The educational record during the Nanjing decade was very uneven. The proportion of children attending primary and secondary schools increased, but the provision was much better in the cities than in the countryside. In 1932 only 15 per cent of the children enrolled in primary schools were girls. Many private schools continued to operate and missionary societies ran over 3000 primary schools. The most ambitious attempt to extend educational opportunities was made by the National Association for the Promotion of Mass Education, led by Dr James Yen, an American-educated Christian. The literacy campaign it promoted was part of a broader rural reconstruction movement pioneered at Yen's centre at Ding Xian in Hebei.

Colleges and universities were concentrated in the coastal cities. Universities made heavy use of staff who had trained abroad and who based their teaching on foreign texts and examples. Many universities were underfunded and their students suffered economic hardship. The Guomindang clamped down on political activity in universities, but students were frequently involved in protests, notably in 1935 and 1936 when a wave of nationalism swept the campuses. Nevertheless, a scholarly community grew up, which engaged in research and publication. A notable achievement was the founding in 1928 of the Academia Sinica, a national research institute.

The Guomindang had come to power on a wave of nationalist sentiment and it had declared that it intended to get rid of the unequal treaties. However in 1927, in Hankou, in Nanjing and yet again in Shanghai, it strove to avoid antagonizing the Western powers, and after it came to power it used diplomatic measures rather than threats of violence to achieve its aims. In 1928 the United States took the lead in returning tariff autonomy and between 1929 and 1931 Britain voluntarily surrendered concessions in Hankou, Jiujiang, Zhenjiang and Xiamen, and the leased territory of Weihaiwei. Other concessions remained in foreign hands and negotiations to end extraterritoriality had made little progress before the outbreak of war with Japan changed the priorities of China's foreign relations.

In 1929 the Nanjing government had passed the first sports law in Chinese history, which stated that it was the responsibility of every young man and woman to pursue physical exercise. The slogan 'Use sports to save the nation' was coined. The connection between sport and nationalism was to be tested at the 1932 Los Angeles Olympic Games. Initially China was not intending to participate, but then the news was leaked that Manzhouguo, the Japanese puppet state, intended to send Liu Changchun, China's best sprinter, as a competitor. Although the news was false, it provoked nationalist outrage. Liu Changchun went to Los Angeles as the sole athlete representing China, and China took an important step into the international arena.[35]

In the 1970s the assessment of the achievements in the Nanjing decade was distinctly unfavourable. Lloyd E. Eastman entitled his influential study of the years 1927 to 1937 *The Abortive Revolution*. James E. Sheridan's equally influential review of the Republican era, *China in Disintegration*, reiterated that judgement. Recently that assessment has been challenged, however. For Robert E. Bedeski the republican government's major contribution was the establishment of a new and sovereign Chinese state system, which implied the expansion of state sovereignty, the creation of national institutions and the improvement in China's international stature. Julia Strauss described Nationalist China as 'a weak state operating in a hostile environment'. Nevertheless in the 1930s it was surprisingly successful in developing critical components of state-building, for example building up and resourcing an effective military establishment, and developing foreign relations to create a less precarious international environment. In *Reappraising Republican China*, Richard Edmonds remarked how researchers, who now had access to mainland Chinese records, were describing the Republican era as 'part of a continuous transition during which China modified its traditional society and adapted to new roles in world affairs – sometimes with considerable success'.[36]

THE CHINESE COMMUNIST PARTY, 1928–35

The series of disasters which had overwhelmed the CCP in 1927 forced a re-evaluation of the Party's strategy. At the Sixth Party Congress, held in Moscow in June 1928, Li Lisan took over as secretary-general from Qu Qiubai, who was condemned for his 'leftist opportunist deviation'. A surprisingly optimistic view was taken of the situation in China, but for the time being it was agreed to concentrate the Party's efforts on the countryside. When Li Lisan returned to China he acknowledged the importance of the rural bases which Mao Zedong and others had established, but his commitment remained to the cities and to the industrial proletariat. His authority was weakened by the presence of the 'Twenty-eight Bolsheviks', a group of Moscow-trained Chinese Communists who considered it their task to rebuild and redirect the Party.

Perhaps because of the weakness of his position, or perhaps because he believed that the world depression and the Guomindang's involvement in a war with the warlords Feng Yuxiang and Yan Xishan meant that the time was ripe, in 1930 Li Lisan embarked on another attempt at an armed uprising. The plan was to foment strikes and demonstrations in Changsha, Wuhan and Nanchang, and then for the newly formed Red Army to capture those three cities. The coup was launched in the summer of 1930, and the greatest success was achieved at Changsha, which was held for ten days. However, the Red Army was inadequate for the task, the popular response was half-hearted and the support of some rural-base leaders, notably that of Mao Zedong, was withheld. The result was a disaster. In 1931 Pavel Mif, the new Comintern representative, arrived in China. Under his direction, Li Lisan was condemned for blind opportunism and the Twenty-eight Bolsheviks took over leadership of the Party.

After the failure of the Autumn Harvest uprising, Mao Zedong had retreated to the mountain range on the borders of Hunan and Jiangxi known as the Jinggangshan, where he joined up with two bandit chiefs. In April 1928 Zhu De brought in the survivors from the attack on Nanchang. Later Peng Dehuai, a future minister of defence, arrived with a group from Hunan. These forces, the nucleus of the Red Army, were soon called into action to repel Guomindang attacks. Before the end of the year Mao had concluded that the Jinggangshan area was too small and too rugged to be a suitable base area, and in January 1929 he moved east to Ruijin in southern Jiangxi.

The Ruijin area became the most important of several Communist rural bases. For Mao Zedong, possession of a rural base was an essential part of his revolutionary strategy. He likened a base to a person's buttocks: without buttocks one would be unable to sit down and recover one's strength. At the Ruijin base he began to put into practice three key policies, the first of which was to make the Red Army a disciplined and politicized force. Already at Jinggangshan Mao had enunciated the basic principles of guerrilla warfare – 'The enemy advances, we retreat; the enemy camps, we harass; the enemy tires, we attack; the enemy retreats, we pursue' – and had required every soldier to know the Three Rules – to obey orders, to take nothing from the peasants and to pool all captured goods. However, it was evident from remarks made by Mao at the Gutian conference held in December 1929 that many Red Army soldiers still lacked discipline and did not understand the aims of the revolution or the role that the army was expected to play. In future, political officers were appointed to help the army mobilize the masses and set up new regimes. At least one in three soldiers had to be a Party member. The army was intended to be democratic, the soldiers wore no badges of rank, all received the same pay and all shared in the discussion of any proposed action.

The second policy concerned revolutionary land reform; that is, the confiscation of land from landlords and its redistribution to poor peasants. This policy had only been adopted by the CCP at its Fifth Congress in April 1927, on the eve of its split with the Guomindang, and there was no agreed line on whether land should also be confiscated from rich peasants, those who owned more land than they could farm with their own labour. At the Ruijin base Mao Zedong introduced a moderate policy which allowed rich peasants to retain their land. Villages were encouraged to form revolutionary committees, which first classified the inhabitants of the village as landlord, rich peasant, middle peasant and poor peasant, and then applied the agreed redistribution of land.

The third policy concerned social reform and in particular the position of women. At the time of the May Fourth Movement, Mao Zedong had criticized arranged marriages and during his investigation of the peasant movement in Hunan he had written approvingly of the formation of women's associations which challenged the authority of husbands. In 1930 he carried out a study of Xunwu in south-east Jiangxi to provide himself with recent and detailed information on a rural community. Among the matters he studied was the effect of permitting freedom of marriage and divorce. In his report he argued that male peasants opposed the emancipation of women only because they were uncertain of the outcome of land reform.

Mao's position in the Jiangxi soviet was unchallenged until 1931, when members of the Central Committee abandoned their undercover existence in Shanghai and moved to Ruijin. Later that year the Chinese Soviet Republic was established at Ruijin, with Mao Zedong its first president, although his authority and policies were now being challenged by the Twenty-eight Bolsheviks. The Soviet Republic immediately passed a radical land law which provided for the confiscation not only of landlords' land but also that of rich peasants. It also approved a marriage law which defined marriage as 'a free institution between a man and a woman'. Both men and women could apply for a divorce and divorced women were given some economic protection. There immediately followed a spate of divorce petitions.

The survival of the rural soviets was threatened by developments from both within and without. In December 1930 the Nationalist Army made its first determined attack on the Communist bases in southern Jiangxi, but was forced to withdraw. The attack coincided with the Futian Incident, which involved the alleged infiltration of the Jiangxi action committee by the pro-Guomindang Anti-Bolshevist League. There followed a mutiny in a Red Army unit and a purge by Mao Zedong of his suspected opponents. In July 1931, Jiang Jieshi took personal command of the Nationalist forces investing the Communist bases, which now numbered 300,000 men, and he was making good progress when the campaign was called off because of the Japanese occupation of Manchuria. This respite, and a Comintern declaration that the world depression would lead to a global revolutionary upsurge, encouraged the Twenty-eight Bolsheviks to denounce Mao Zedong's tactics of mobile guerrilla warfare as over-cautious. Mao lost his place on the Party's Military Council and the strategy promoted by Zhou Enlai of positional warfare and capturing cities was adopted.

In the Jiangxi central base the CCP had begun to apply its revolutionary land policy. Many landlords were dispossessed and others were killed, but it soon became apparent that some landlords and rich peasants were concealing the extent of their land-holdings. In June 1933 a Land Investigation movement was launched, originally with Mao Zedong's support, to identify cases of evasion. Later Zhang Wentian, one of the Twenty-eight Bolsheviks, took charge and the investigation became increasingly oppressive. In November 1933 the Guomindang Nineteenth Route Army, stationed in Fujian province, mutinied in protest against Jiang Jieshi's failure to oppose Japanese encroachment on China. Whereas Zhou Enlai was in favour of assisting the rebels, Mao Zedong counselled caution. While the Communist leadership was arguing, Jiang Jieshi stepped in and crushed the mutiny and a great opportunity for the Communists was lost.

In October 1933, Jiang Jieshi commenced his fifth encirclement campaign. This comprised both a major military offensive and a comprehensive political campaign. The Nationalist Army, which now numbered over 750,000 men in the field, was supported by German advisers and equipped with heavy guns and aeroplanes. To counter the Communist tactic of mobile warfare, it had ringed the Jiangxi central base with 15,000 blockhouses. On the political front, the Guomindang attempted to match CCP propaganda by requiring the officers in its armies to wear the same uniform and eat the same food as their men. The population of the areas around the Communist bases was compelled to support a blockade of all essential supplies. It was at Nanchang in 1934, while he was planning the fifth extermination campaign, that Jiang Jieshi launched the New Life Movement, which was in part a response to the threat of Communism.

The CCP's decision to abandon the Jiangxi base and set out on the Long March was probably taken in May 1934, although the departure was delayed until October. The main reason for going was the deteriorating military situation, although it has been suggested that the over-zealous application of the Land Investigation movement had lost the Party much popular support. Approximately 86,000 people set out from the Jiangxi base, while some 20,000 sick and injured and a force of 30,000 soldiers remained behind. After breaking through the Guomindang blockade with surprising ease, the Red Army marched due west and crossed into Hunan and then Guangxi. The first major engagement was the crossing of the Xiang river north east of Guilin, where the Red Army lost about half its strength. In January 1935 the Communists captured Zunyi in northern Guizhou, and there an important conference took place. The main issue was the military failure, which had resulted in the abandonment of the Jiangxi base. The policies pursued by the Politburo and by the military leadership, which included Otto Braun, the Comintern military adviser, were criticized and by implication those advocated by Mao Zedong were endorsed. Although Mao did not become Party leader at this point, his rise to power had begun.

The marchers left Zunyi with the intention of joining up with Zhang Guotao's Fourth Front Army, which had moved from its original base in Anhui to Sichuan. Various final destinations were under discussion, with Mao Zedong proposing a move north to oppose the Japanese. First the upper waters of the Yangzi river had to be traversed, which meant marching far to the west to shake off the Nationalists, and finally crossing the Jinsha or Golden Sands river. The marchers turned north, through areas inhabited by sometimes hostile minority groups. Then came the most celebrated incident of the march, the crossing of the Dadu river by the Luding Bridge, an ancient chain suspension bridge guarded by a Guomindang machine-gun post. The next obstacle was the Great Snowy Mountain, where hundreds of men died from exposure. In June the two main branches of the Red Army met at Mao'ergai in north Sichuan. On the surface the reunion between Mao Zedong and Zhang Guotao was cordial, but past differences and political rivalries soon appeared; whereas Zhang Guotao chose to move west to Tibet, Mao Zedong continued northwards through Gansu, where he encountered one final physical challenge, the vast swamp of the Great Grasslands.

In October 1935, Mao Zedong and the First Front Army reached the north Shaanxi rural base. The Long March had extended over 5000 miles and fewer than 20,000 of those who had set out arrived at its final destination. Many years later, Mao Zedong was to speak sadly of the thousands who died, and the obligation felt by the survivors that their sacrifice should not have been in vain. As a result of the march, the main theatre of Communist operations was transferred from the south to the north. But for the outbreak of war with Japan, their cause would probably have perished there.

THE SINO-JAPANESE WAR, 1937–45

After having occupied Manchuria in 1931, Japan continued to encroach on north China. In the following year China and Japan fought an undeclared war in Shanghai, and the Chinese Soviet Republic in Jiangxi declared war on Japan. However, Jiang Jieshi, recognizing the weakness of his position, refused to allow China to be drawn into hostilities, declaring that the Japanese were a disease of the skin, but the Communists were a disease of the heart. By 1936, Hebei and Inner Mongolia had established autonomous governments under Japanese protection.

Protests against Jiang Jieshi's policy came from various quarters and were particularly vociferous on university campuses. The Guomindang treated student political movements with suspicion, on the grounds that as the nationalist revolution had been completed, student agitation must be fomented by the Communists. The student movement of 9 December 1935 challenged this view. It began when Beiping police attempted to suppress a student protest against

Japanese plans to turn areas of north China into autonomous regions, and it then spread to many other cities. Pressure on Jiang Jieshi to change his mind also came from the National Salvation Association, founded by the journalist Zou Taofen. Among the supporters of the association was Zhang Xueliang, the 'Young Marshal' of Manchuria, whose father had been killed by the Guandong Army in 1928. Zhang had moved his forces into north China and had reluctantly taken on the task of suppressing the Communists in Shaanxi. In December 1936, Jiang Jieshi flew to Xi'an to encourage Zhang to campaign more vigorously. However, the Young Marshal took him prisoner and detained him until Jiang Jieshi had agreed to end the civil war and lead the resistance to Japan.

Early in 1937, the Guomindang and the CCP negotiated a second united front. The Communists agreed to abandon armed insurrection and cease confiscating landlords' land. In return, the Guomindang undertook to end the attacks on Communist bases, release political prisoners and prepare to resist Japan. On 7 July 1937, an incident at Lugouqiao (Marco Polo Bridge) near Beiping led to full-scale war between China and Japan.

The first phase of the war, which lasted until October 1938, was marked by a rapid Japanese invasion and some heroic Chinese opposition. In north China, Japanese troops advanced along the main railway lines and Chinese forces fell back in disorder. In Shanghai, Chinese resistance was better organized and more determined. Chinese ground forces surrounded the Japanese settlement and, in a tragic error, Chinese aeroplanes bombed the International Settlement. The battle for Shanghai continued for three months, until Japanese troops landed on the coast to the south of the city and forced the Chinese forces to fall back to Nanjing. Jiang Jieshi had ordered that the capital should be defended to the last man, but his orders were ignored and on 12 December Japanese troops entered the city and perpetrated the atrocities known as the 'rape of Nanjing'. At the post-war military tribunals in Tokyo and Nanjing, five Japanese officers, including General Matsui Iwane, the commander of the Japanese forces, were executed for committing war crimes or for failing to stop them. At the Nanjing trial the death toll was put at over 300,000.

After the Communist victory in 1949, a critical view of Japan's wartime record in China was likely to be condemned as pro-Communist. But then, in the 1970s, the Japanese journalist Honda

Katsuichi wrote a series of articles on atrocities committed by Japanese soldiers during the war. This sparked off vehement rebuttals from Japanese nationalists. In the 1980s the death toll of 300,000 was described as a fabrication and an agency of the Japanese government downgraded the description of the atrocity in school textbooks to an 'incident'. In 1997 Iris Chang's *The Rape of Nanjing*, which described the event as a holocaust, became a runaway bestseller in the United States. This provoked further denials in some, but not all, sections of the Japanese press.[37]

In November 1937 the Nationalist government transferred its capital to Chongqing, a thousand miles up the Yangzi river. From January to October 1938 the centre of Chinese resistance was at Wuhan, to where many thousands of refugees had fled. There the Nationalists and the Communists set up an united front government, while competing for political support. The press was free, there was an upsurge of cultural activities, and foreigners, including the poet W. H. Auden and the photographer Robert Capa, were welcomed.[38] Chinese troops continued to fight and in April 1938 obtained a significant victory, when forces under Li Zongren defeated a large Japanese force at Tai'erzhuang, near Xuzhou. In June, in an attempt to delay the Japanese advance on Wuhan, Jiang Jieshi ordered the Yellow river defences near Kaifeng to be breached, at the cost of some 900,000 lives and making some four million people homeless.[39] However in October, after a prolonged siege during which the Japanese suffered their heaviest losses of the war, Wuhan fell, and in the same month Guangzhou was occupied.

In December 1937 Japan had offered Jiang Jieshi peace terms, but he refused them because they required recognition of Manzhouguo, the puppet regime which had been established in Manchuria under the last Chinese emperor. As Japan could not force Jiang to surrender, the alternative solution was to establish puppet regimes in the parts of China now under Japanese control. In Wuhan the collaborationist administration was headed by Zhang Renli, the son of Zhang Zhidong, the leading reformer in the late imperial period. In December 1938 Wang Jingwei, leader of the left wing of the Guomindang, defected from the Nationalist side and offered himself as leader of a collaborationist regime which had its capital at Nanjing. In 1940 this became the Reorganized National Government, which claimed to exercise authority over much of central and south-east China. It maintained diplomatic relations with Japan and Germany and had its own armed forces and the trappings of a government. However, its dependence on Japan was never in doubt and when Wang died in 1944, the regime had ceased to be relevant.

Until very recently the history of wartime collaboration in China has been a closed book. For the Communists, collaborators were traitors and their collaboration should be condemned rather than discussed. For Nationalists, who in 1949 had ordered the release of all collaborators serving jail sentences shorter than life imprisonment, collaboration was an awkward topic and one best ignored. For Westerners, limitations on the source material available and disregard for the significance of puppet regimes meant that very few historians took an interest in them. However, with the passing of the Maoist era, the Communist Party has released key documentary collections. Studies of this period based on this material are now beginning to appear and to reveal a much more complex picture than earlier stereotypes of collaboration and the character of puppet regimes have suggested.[40]

The Nationalist government claimed to govern an area containing nearly half the population of China, although in truth its political authority was weak. It had lost control over the lower Yangzi provinces, its main political base, and now it had to rely on local power-holders, for example Long Yun in Yunnan. This weakness was not immediately apparent, for at the beginning of the war the Guomindang and Jiang Jieshi enjoyed a wave of national and international support. Before the move to Chongqing, Jiang Jieshi had been given the title of director-general of the Guomindang, and he was also chairman of the Military Affairs Commission. In a gesture towards broadening the basis of the Guomindang's support, a People's Political Council was formed which contained representatives of minor parties and even Communists. In addition, the Three People's Principles Youth Corps was created to mobilize the nation's youth and revitalize the Guomindang. However, Jiang Jieshi 'did not understand this form of modern pluralistic politics'.[41] In 1942, after independent members of the People's Political Council had criticized the government, the Guomindang was given the majority of the seats on the council, which thereafter was of little importance.

Relations with intellectuals and students also soured. When Japan invaded China, universities migrated to areas outside Japanese control. Staff and students from Beijing National University, Qinghua, and Nankai University, Tianjin, made their way to Kunming in Yunnan, where they formed the National South-West Associated University. However, the university's liberal values were not acceptable to the increasingly autocratic rule of the Guomindang, and the Three People's Principles Youth Corps had cells on the campus and spied on the staff and students. Before the end of the war the political strains within the Guomindang were evident. At the Guomindang's Sixth Party Congress, the government was described as corrupt and inefficient and Jiang Jieshi was accused of having become increasingly dictatorial.

To conduct a war of resistance, the Nationalist government had to establish a war economy within the Free Zone, as the area under its control was called. This was a demanding task, as much of the region was economically backward. Nevertheless, at the beginning of the war a heroic attempt was made to shift industrial plant and skilled workers from areas threatened by the Japanese invasion to the Free Zone. The government established a National Resources Commission, which took control of heavy and technical industry. Between 1939 and 1943, industrial output grew rapidly, coal output doubled, over 1000 miles of rail track were built, electricity production increased sevenfold and, after the closing of the Burma Road in 1942 had cut petroleum supplies to the amount which could be brought in by air, ingenious attempts were made to produce liquid fuels from alternative sources. However, the industrial growth began from a very small base, industrial output was insufficient to satisfy demand and the rate of growth declined sharply after 1943, when the Free Zone began to experience an industrial crisis.

The industrial crisis was a symptom of a deeper economic malaise which manifested itself in inflation. During the Nanjing decade the government had been unable to balance its budget and had borrowed heavily. With the move to Chongqing it had lost its main sources of revenue, in particular customs duties, and it now incurred heavy wartime expenditure. It tried to recover control of the land tax from the provincial authorities and, in order to secure food supplies for its troops, it began to collect taxes in grain, but these measures did not solve the problem of inadequate revenue. Between 1942 and 1945, inflation rose at over 230 per cent annually. Official salaries declined sharply and this encouraged corruption. Because of the shortage of commodities, in particular petrol, a flourishing black market grew up.

The vast majority of the population of the Free Zone were peasants. To fight a war of resistance effectively their co-operation was essential, as the Communists were to show. However, the policies which the Guomindang pursued alienated peasant support. Inflation generally benefits primary producers, but because government regulations required grain to be sold at fixed prices and transported to collecting stations, poor peasants incurred costs which more than doubled their tax burden. As the gap in incomes between rich and poor in the countryside widened, landlord–tenant conflicts reached epidemic proportions. The consequences of the government's imposing heavy exactions to feed its troops were revealed in the Henan famine of 1942–3, which left five million people starving, many to death. Peasants also bore the main burden of conscription, which nominally applied to all males between the ages of 18 and 45, but which inevitably fell most heavily on poor families.

After the heroic resistance of the first year of the war, the main Nationalist forces were withdrawn to the Free Zone to regroup and retrain. Thereafter the Nationalist armies remained largely on the defensive, although the casualty record shows that the fighting between Nationalists and Japanese never stopped. Between 1939 and 1941, Chongqing and other cities held by the Nationalists were bombed incessantly. The only land link with the outside world available to the Nationalists was the Burma Road, which had been built at immense human cost in 1938 and was to close in 1942 after the Japanese invasion of Burma.

At the beginning of the war, the Nationalists and Communists had reached agreement about the zones in which the Red Army would operate. In addition to its forces in the north, now renamed the Eighth Route Army, the CCP raised the New Fourth Army in Jiangxi. In October 1940 Nationalist commanders, who regarded the Communist operations south of the Yangzi as an infringement of the agreement on zones, ordered the New Fourth Army to move north. Its failure to comply fully led to fighting between Nationalist and Communist forces, which effectively ended the united front.

The Japanese invasion of China was condemned by the United States, and from December 1938 American aid began to reach the Nationalist side. After the Japanese attack on Pearl Harbor in December 1941, the two countries became allies. General Joseph W. Stilwell ('Vinegar Joe'), a former military attaché to China, was sent to Chongqing with the task of encouraging Jiang Jieshi to go on the offensive against Japan. However, to Stilwell's annoyance, Jiang Jieshi refused to commit his troops to support the British in Burma and keep the Burma Road open. Nor would he agree to Stilwell's suggestions on how the Nationalist army, which numbered about 3,800,000 men, might be made more effective. In April 1944, when it seemed that the war in China had reached stalemate, Japan launched Operation Ichigo. The short-term objective was to disable the best National armies and to deny the United States the use of Chinese airfields. The longer-term strategy was to establish a land supply route across China to Hanoi, to ensure that even if Japan lost the war with the United States, it could not be evicted from China. The operation resulted in a major Japanese victory, which exposed the corruption and inefficiency of the Nationalist government. It 'pushed Jiang's regime almost to the edge, depleting its resources and crippling its leadership'.[42]

THE CCP DURING THE SINO-JAPANESE WAR

At the end of the Long March, Mao Zedong had established his headquarters at Yan'an, a city in north Shaanxi. There the CCP developed political, social and economic policies which transformed the Party and gained it mass support.

At Yan'an, Mao Zedong consolidated his position as Party leader. His two main rivals were Zhang Guotao, the veteran Party leader whose disagreement with Mao on the Long March has already been noted, and Wang Ming, the most influential of the Twenty-eight Bolsheviks. Zhang Guotao, having lost much of the New Fourth Army, finally reached Shaanxi in late 1936. Although his disagreements with Mao were patched up, his defection to the Nationalists in April 1938 was no great surprise. Wang Ming's position rested on the support he received from the Comintern, and at first his political influence outweighed that of Mao Zedong. However, he held no military command and he had no experience of conducting a rural revolution, and after the outbreak of war he lost influence.

Mao Zedong also strengthened his position by claiming the ideological leadership of the Party. In 1938–40 he wrote three key works: 'On the New Stage', 'The Chinese Revolution and the Chinese Communist Party' and 'On New Democracy'. In the first he called for the 'sinification of Marxism', arguing that if Marxism was to mean anything to China it had to be imbued with Chinese peculiarities: 'We must put an end to writing eight-legged essays on foreign models.' In the second he reviewed Chinese history, emphasizing the key role of peasant revolts, and pointing out that earlier peasant revolts had failed because they had not been led by the proletariat and the Communist Party. In 'On New Democracy' he repeated Lenin's argument that in colonial societies revolution would be accomplished in two stages, the first of which would be bourgeois-democratic and the second socialist. 'New democracy' was the term used by Mao Zedong to denote the point – which he identified with the May Fourth Movement – when the revolution began to be led not by the bourgeoisie alone, but by a 'joint revolutionary-democratic dictatorship of several revolutionary classes'. After the Communist victory, which he now began to anticipate, there would be a place in the new state for the bourgeoisie, or at least that part of it which had not allied with feudalism or imperialism.

During the Sino-Japanese war the CCP underwent a drastic reorganization. At the beginning of the war, as refugees flocked to Yan'an, its membership had soared to 800,000. Many of the new members knew little of Marxism and did not accept Party discipline. In February 1942, after a series of military setbacks and political disagreements, Mao Zedong launched a rectification campaign. Cadres (trained leaders) were required to attend a Party school, at which Mao gave lectures in which he identified the main errors threatening the Party, including 'subjectivism', by which he meant the claim to superiority by cadres who had theoretical knowledge but no down-to-earth experience. In another lecture he argued that art and literature must serve the masses. The rectification campaign did not amount to a purge, but a number of intellectuals were forced to make a self-criticism and all cadres were expected to study Mao's writings and to strive to improve the quality of their work.

*   *   *

Yan'an was the capital of the Shaanxi–Gansu–Ningxia (Shaan-Gan-Ning) Border Region. By 1944 the Communists claimed to control four 'border regions', which stretched across much of China north of the Yellow river. There were also about a dozen other 'liberated areas', most of which were in central China. In the border regions representative governments were established. All men and women over the age of 16 could vote and the 'three-thirds' system was adopted, which meant that the Communists restricted themselves to one third of all elected positions, the rest being shared between 'progressive' (petty bourgeois) and middle-of-the-road (middle bourgeois or enlightened gentry) candidates.

Like the Guomindang, the CCP had to develop a self-sufficient wartime economy. Shaanxi was a very poor area which had suffered badly in the 1928–33 famine, when many peasants had been forced to sell their land. Before the Long Marchers had arrived the local soviet had already begun to confiscate and redistribute landlords' land. Under the united front agreement the CCP had agreed to stop confiscations, and throughout the war it adhered to that policy, except in the case of landlords who collaborated with the Japanese. Instead, from 1942 it promoted a Rent and Interest Reduction campaign. A rent ceiling of 37.5 per cent of the crop – the figure endorsed but never applied by the Guomindang – was enforced strictly. A programme of land registration was introduced and security of tenure was improved, measures which threatened the privileged position of landlords and rich peasants. The Border Region government was desperate for tax revenue and by 1941 the tax burden was heavy, although it had eased by 1943. In that year a campaign was launched to develop a more productive economy organized on co-operative principles. At the same time, attempts were made to increase industrial production using primitive technology and surplus labour.

At Yan'an, important experiments were made in the delivery of mass education. Many primary schools were *minban* schools; that is, schools paid for and run by the people, who hired the teacher and suggested the curriculum. Their priority was for the pupils to become literate, but literacy was closely connected with the needs of the world of work, and schools closed at harvest time. In secondary schools, courses were reduced from six to three years, the curriculum was simplified and all students did at least 20 days of productive labour a year. In 1941 Yan'an University was founded, and here too study was combined with productive labour and emphasis was placed on political study.

While these policies were being pursued, the Communists were also fighting a war. In 1937 the Eighth Route and New Fourth armies had 92,000 men. Although these troops did engage the Japanese forces at the time of the invasion, for the next two years they restricted themselves to guerrilla tactics, leaving the Nationalist armies to take the brunt of the Japanese attack. Faced with an elusive enemy, the Japanese commander General Tada instituted a 'cage policy', sealing off the Communist areas within a cage of block-houses and trenches. In 1940 the Communist forces, now numbering 500,000 men, launched the Hundred Regiments' campaign, which broke out of the cage and inflicted heavy losses on the Japanese. Their response was to counterattack and to carry out ruthless reprisals against civilians suspected of harbouring the Communists. As a consequence, the population of the areas under Communist control fell sharply and the strength of the Eighth Route Army declined from 400,000 to 300,000 men.

The reason for the Communist change of tactics which turned into a disaster is disputed. The campaign may have been launched because the Nationalists were believed to be about to negotiate a settlement with Japan. An attack would have exposed the contrast between Communist patriotism and Nationalist defeatism. During the Cultural Revolution Peng Dehuai, who had led the attack, was held responsible and accused of megalomania. Whatever the reason for the change of tactics, thereafter the Communist forces reverted to guerrilla activity and small-scale attacks, frequently on the forces of the puppet regimes rather than on the Japanese army.

There is no doubt that the balance of power between Nationalists and Communists shifted during the Sino-Japanese War. One reason for this was that the Japanese invasion and Operation Ichigo gravely damaged the Nationalists' military capacity. Another was that Jiang Jieshi's government earned a reputation for being undemocratic, corrupt and inefficient, whereas the Communists at Yan'an took pains to project a contrasting image. In 1944 John S. Service, a member of an observer group from the United States, travelled from Chongqing to Yan'an. He was so struck by the contrast between the two regimes that when he reached Yan'an he wrote, 'we have come into a different country and are meeting a different people'.[43] This image was manipulated and the Communists were no democrats. In the 1942 rectification movement, the target of the Yan'an forum on literature and art was intellectual freedom. One of the victims of the rectification movement was Ding Ling, China's foremost woman writer, who in a story entitled 'When I was in Xia Village' had criticized male Communist cadres for having double standards on sexual morality. For this she lost her post of literary editor of the Yan'an newspaper *Liberation Daily* and was sent to work in the countryside for two years. Perhaps the most important consequence of this contrast of images was the increased scepticism of the United States toward Jiang Jieshi as a reliable ally.

The Communist success in the war years has been explained in a number of ways. In 1962, Chalmers Johnson observed that whereas before the war the Communists had made little progress in mobilizing the peasants on their side, during the war they obtained a mass following in the countryside. The alliance between the Eighth Route Army and the peasantry was born in the aftermath of the Hundred Regiments' campaign, when the Japanese adopted the 'three-all' policy – 'kill all, burn all, destroy all'. The alliance, according to Johnson, 'derived partly from nationalism (hatred of the invader), but to a large extent it was purely a matter of survival'.[44] Johnson's view was challenged by Donald G. Gillin, who argued that when the Red Army entered Shaanxi at the end of the Long March, it received popular support because it advocated revolutionary land reform. After the Japanese invasion, the elite responded to the appeal of nationalism, but peasants were happy to work for the Japanese, who paid good wages. Only when the Eighth Route Army resumed its attack on landlords did it recover popular support. His argument was developed by Mark Selden, who discussed the significance of the 'Yan'an Way', the range of reforms which the Communists introduced at Yan'an after 1942, which Selden described as a bold and effective response to the war-aggravated problems of rural society.[45]

The debate on how the Communists obtained popular support was reopened in the 1990s, when the archives of the border regions and base areas of north China became available to researchers both in China and in the West. Odoric Wou, utilizing research done by Chinese scholars in Henan, reasserted the importance of the role played by the CCP and also that of the intellectuals, urban workers and displaced students who had moved to the border areas, whose contribution had been understated for political reasons. Ralph Thaxton challenged Wou by asking: Did the Communists win the countryside or did the Nationalists lose it? He agreed that the CCP acted as a catalyst, but he did not accept that the revolution was the party's creation. The dynamic force behind the revolution was the moral outrage that peasants felt over the treatment they had received. His prime example was the case of the peasants who worked in the salt industry in the Hebei–Shandong–Henan area. In the 1930s the Nationalist government had attempted to put an end to the free marketing of salt and to reintroduce a government salt monopoly. The Nationalists alienated the 'marginalized peasants who marketed the salt of the earth for their existence' and thus presented the Communists with the opportunity to win their support.

Several writers have rejected a single-cause explanation of the Communist advance. Pauline Keating revisited Mark Selden's identification of the policies of the 'Yan'an Way', investigated villages in northern Shaanxi and concluded that those policies could not simply be applied in other parts of China. If they were not shaped creatively to suit different circumstances, the results were often disastrous. This conclusion has been supported in a number of other studies which take as their theme the 'social ecology' of revolution; that is, they begin by emphasizing the variety of conditions which prevailed in different base areas and border regions. David Goodman studied the Taihang base area in Shanxi and noted that a social revolution had begun in this area in the 1920s and 1930s, but the process of change differed in different counties. This differential was to affect the Communist Party's ability to implement its programmes of mobilization and social reform.[46]

CIVIL WAR AND COMMUNIST VICTORY

The bombing of Hiroshima and Nagasaki by the United States in August 1945 brought the Sino-Japanese War to an abrupt end and left the Nationalists and Communists jostling for advantages. Although, under the Yalta agreement of February 1945, the Japanese forces were to surrender only to the Nationalists, the Communists also occupied territory held by the Japanese and seized Japanese weapons. Immediately after the bombing of Hiroshima, the Soviet Union finally declared war on Japan and proceeded to occupy Manchuria. In response, the United States assisted the Nationalist forces to return to north-east China and to Manchuria, but by the time they arrived the Chinese Communists had already entrenched themselves in the countryside.

In December 1945, General George C. Marshall was sent as United States' ambassador to China, with a brief to encourage the creation of a unified China under a coalition government. In January 1946 he persuaded the Nationalists and Communists to agree to a ceasefire. A Political Consultative Conference was convened, at which a majority of delegates represented the 'Third Force', the 'democratic parties and individuals'.[47] A range of political and military issues were decided, and Jiang Jieshi announced that one quarter of the Nationalist army would be demobilized. However, neither Nationalists nor Communists were sincere in their search for a peaceful settlement, and there was no superior power to enforce the agreements they had made. The Soviet forces began to withdraw from Manchuria in March 1946, taking with them industrial machinery in lieu of war reparations. Chinese Communist troops took their place and by May the ceasefire had ended in Manchuria. General Marshall continued his peace mission until the end of the year, although well before then it was clear that both sides were using the pretence of negotiations as a cover for preparations for war.

At the start of the conflict, it appeared that the Nationalists held a clear advantage. They controlled China's major cities and the country's industrial base. Their armies numbered more than twice as many men as the Communists' and they were supported by an air force and a small navy. Although the United States placed an embargo on the shipment of arms to China in July 1946, this was rescinded within less than a year and the Nationalists were not short of weapons. Nevertheless, within three years they were driven from the mainland.

The civil war may be divided into three stages. The first stage, which lasted from July 1946 to June 1947, began with the Nationalists occupying the main cities of Manchuria as far north as Changchun and recovering large areas of north China, including Yan'an, which was captured in March 1947. The People's Liberation Army, as the Communist forces were now named, adopted new tactics, surrendering territory but harassing and destroying the Nationalist forces. Lin Biao, the commander of the Communist forces in Manchuria, carried out lightning attacks, which halted and then reversed the Nationalist advance.

In the second stage of the civil war, which began in June 1947, the People's Liberation Army overran much of Manchuria and north China, apart from the key cities and main lines of communication. In June, Communist forces crossed the Yellow river and cut off Xi'an, and then began to isolate concentrations of Nationalist forces. By March 1948 the Nationalists' hold on Manchuria was reduced to three cities. From the middle of the year the power balance had begun to shift in the Communists' favour; by now the People's Liberation Army had over 1,500,000 troops and had seized large quantities of weapons and equipment.

The final stage began in the autumn of 1948. By November Lin Biao had captured Shenyang, and Manchuria had fallen to the Communists. He then moved into north China and in January 1949 he took Tianjin. Each of these victories was accompanied by the surrender of thousands of Nationalist troops and the seizure of vast quantities of materiel. Between November 1948 and January 1949, in the area between the Huai river and the Longhai railway, the decisive battle of Huai-Hai was fought. Communist forces methodically cut off and then forced to surrender a Nationalist force of 300,000 men. After this battle, Nationalist resistance north of the Yangzi came to an end. In April 1949 Communist forces captured Nanjing, and in the following month Shanghai fell. In December, Jiang Jieshi and two million of his supporters, taking with them China's foreign reserves and art treasures, fled to Taiwan.

Various explanations have been given for the Communist victory. At the time, accusations were levelled against the United States for having failed to provide the Nationalists with sufficient military and economic aid. The change of American policy towards Japan, the 'reverse course', which began in 1947 and involved stimulating Japan's economic recovery and treating Japan as an ally against a Communist threat in Asia, further encouraged anti-American feeling and weakened popular support for the Nationalists.

The Nationalist defeat was a military disaster which can be explained in military terms. Major-General David Barr, writing in early 1949, gave his appreciation of why the Nationalists were losing on the battlefield. They had made a major strategic error in trying to recover Manchuria. The leadership of the Nationalist army was very poor and contrasted sharply with the brilliance of some of the Communist military leaders. The Nationalists had resorted to a defensive strategy which allowed them to be surrounded and forced to surrender. Finally, the morale of the Nationalist troops, who were poorly paid and badly treated, was very low and they frequently deserted. In a recent analysis, Christopher Lew has placed less emphasis on Nationalist military shortcomings and more on the Communist achievement. He argued that it was the Communists' ability to formulate strategy, seize the initiative, and outthink the Nationalists that won them the war.[48]

Clausewitz famously said that 'war is nothing more than the continuation of politics by other means'. The civil war had its origin in a political struggle and it was success in that struggle which was to determine the outcome of the war. The Nationalists, through errors and omissions, lost the political struggle, but the Communists profited from the Nationalists' mistakes and presented themselves as a moderate, efficient and patriotic alternative to Nationalist rule.

It may be argued that the Guomindang had begun to lose the political struggle during the Nanjing era, when it had failed to live up to the expectations of a modernizing government. Alternatively, it may be suggested that the Nationalists forfeited support during the Sino-Japanese war by ceasing to fight the enemy and by ignoring urgent political, social and economic issues. Recently Joseph Esherick has suggested a new line of inquiry, by pointing out that during the War of Liberation the Nationalist government introduced fundamental changes to aspects of Chinese society:

> The economy was planned and industry nationalized; the interior was developed; improved transport served national integration; education was expanded, centralized and given new practical and nationalistic content; modern media were developed and put under more direct state control; the state penetrated further into rural society; students and workers were organized and mobilized; and new egalitarian and nationalistic values were promoted.

These changes, he suggested, both transformed Chinese society and prepared it for Communist revolution.[49]

The war with Japan seriously weakened the Guomindang's position. It accentuated rural poverty, so providing the Communists with 'a social laboratory for land reform'. The high level of collaboration between Chinese in the coastal cities and the Japanese authorities split the Chinese elite, and the Japanese attack weakened the Guomindang's reserves of military power, economic resources and morale.[50]

After 1945, the Guomindang government made a series of mistakes which eventually destroyed its basis of support. The mistakes began as soon as the Guomindang government returned to Nanjing. Many expected that those who had collaborated with the Japanese would be punished, but only a few notorious collaborators were executed and others were allowed to retain their jobs. Guomindang officials were accused of commandeering Japanese property, whereas industrialists and merchants whose property had been seized by the Japanese received no compensation. When the Nationalists reoccupied Manchuria, such was their suspicion of the local leadership that they appointed outsiders to administrative posts and thereby presented the Communists with a grievance to exploit. When the Nationalists returned to Taiwan, which had been a Japanese colony for 50 years, they treated the native Taiwanese more harshly than the Japanese had done, and provoked a serious uprising.

Much of the blame for the outbreak of the civil war had fallen on the Guomindang. The most coherent criticism came from radical students, who believed that the Guomindang should have formed a coalition government with the Communists. They regarded the close links between the Nationalists and the United States with suspicion and particularly resented the continued presence of American troops on Chinese soil. In December 1946, two United States marines were accused of raping a student at Beiping University. This incident provoked a series of anti-American and anti-government demonstrations on campuses throughout the country. Student agitation continued throughout the civil war, and other issues, for example the economic hardships of students and intellectuals, helped to turn university communities against the government. The Guomindang insisted that this hostility was fomented by Communists and there probably was an underground Communist organization supporting the protests. However, the agitation could be explained readily by reference to government incompetence and the brutal suppression of student demonstrations.

Two other issues served to alienate the Guomindang's basis of support: the lack of political progress and economic mismanagement. Sun Zhongshan had prescribed that after a period of political tutelage by the Guomindang, a constitutional government would be introduced. A constitution had been drafted in 1936 and the Political Consultative Conference held in January 1946 had agreed to introduce it forthwith. However, the Guomindang commitment to constitutionalism was undermined by the Renovationist faction, which would not accept that the Guomindang should give up its monopoly of power. The constitution was promulgated on 1 January 1947 and elections for a National Assembly were held later in the year, but the elections were condemned as a farce and the sessions of the National Assembly ended in uproar. By now the Guomindang was regarded as too corrupt, too intolerant of minority parties and too indifferent to the issue of civil liberties to be able to introduce a constitutional form of government.

Monetary inflation had already set in during the war. It started to accelerate in 1946 and by mid-1948 the Shanghai wholesale price index (September 1945 = 100) had risen to 1,368,049 and the economy was on the verge of collapse. In August the government replaced the worthless *fabi* with the gold *yuan* note, without previously having attempted to balance the budget or to back the new currency with reserves. Hopes of a currency stabilization loan from the United States were dashed. When the new currency was issued, the rich were urged to turn over their gold and foreign currency holdings to the government in exchange for certificates. In October the government, in an attempt to reduce the budgetary deficit, raised taxes on consumer goods. This prompted a rush to stockpile goods, disastrous shortages and within three months the collapse of the currency reform. So disastrous was the gold *yuan* experiment that some observers at the time regarded it as the main cause of the government's fall.

* * *

The shortcomings of the Guomindang only supply half the explanation for the shift in the political balance. The other half lies in the CCP's success in winning the battle for hearts and minds, particularly in the countryside. Revolutionary land reform has been seen as the key factor in this success. During the war, the CCP had renounced land reform as part of the second united front agreement. However, on 4 May 1946 a directive was issued which authorized the seizure of land from collaborators, and the Outline Agrarian Law, published on 10 October 1947, provided for the confiscation of all land belonging to landlords and for its division among the total population. These measures sanctioned the violence against landlords already occurring in many villages in north China, which amounted to a rural revolution.

A programme of revolutionary land reform only attracted peasant support under certain conditions. When CCP cadres returned to Manchuria in 1945, they found that the simple promise of land was not enough to bring peasants over to their side. What was needed was an 'equation of revolutionary transformation', which meant convincing poor peasants that those who supported the Communists in the civil war, by supplying them with taxation, military and labour service and food, would receive a share of the landlords' land and would participate in new decision-making bodies after the revolution. This promise was only credible if the peasants were confident that the revolution would not be reversed. In many parts of north China it was not landlordism which afflicted poor peasants, but low wages, high taxes and the arbitrary exercise of power by the local elite. To obtain their support, CCP cadres had to awaken peasants to their condition of exploitation and give them the confidence to act against it. To do this, they organized 'struggle meetings' at which the poorest of peasants were given the opportunity to voice their grievances. Cadres would then encourage, but not lead, a movement to seize the goods of members of the exploiting class and to wreak vengeance on them.

The CCP also backed the formation of women's associations and implied that the revolution would lead to women's emancipation. Both the new marriage law, which gave women rights relating to divorce and custody of children, and revolutionary land reform, which gave women a share of the redistributed land, provided reasons why rural women should support the revolution.

It is not easy to determine the relative importance of the armed struggle and the mass campaigns in the CCP's victory in the countryside. No mass campaign could succeed if there was a risk of the Guomindang forces returning and the local elite recovering power, for if this occurred terrible reprisals would take place. In one Henan village, a returning landlord shot or buried alive a member of every family which had supported the Communists. Land reform, and more generally the overthrow of the system of exploitation, provided the motivation for peasants to join the revolution, but their participation depended on the Communists being able to convince them that their oppressors would not return.

In the 1930s, the Nationalist government had effectively suppressed Communist activity in the cities. However, the formation of an anti-Japanese national united front made it possible to revive the CCP, for example in Tianjin. Zhou Enlai, by avoiding physical confrontation and focusing on student unrest, the alienation of the intellectuals, corrupt and undemocratic government and chaotic economic conditions, undermined the urban authority of the Guomindang.[51] In August 1945 the Communists captured Zhangjiakou (Kalgan), 200 miles north west of Beijing. Here they engaged in an urban experiment to demonstrate that they could administer a city more effectively than the Nationalists. Collaborators were arrested, streets were cleaned and beggars and prostitutes were found alternative employment. The workers were unionized and their wages raised, but private businesses were left untouched. A reputation as honest and effective administrators served the Communists in good stead when the cities of north China fell into their hands. Beiping was occupied in January 1949 without a shot being fired. The People's Liberation Army enforced strict discipline and no looting took place. Workers and students co-operated in restoring production and maintaining essential services. The gold *yuan* notes were replaced with 'people's notes', or *renminbi,* and an attempt was made to curb inflation. Political groups opposed to the Guomindang were invited to participate in a coalition government. As the Nationalists fell back in disorder, the disciplined Communist approach allayed panic and ensured that the civil war was concluded swiftly.

7

· · · · · · · ·

Revolutionary China, 1949–76

Between 1949 and his death in 1976, Mao Zedong attempted to translate the revolutionary commitment of the CCP into practice. This led
to a sequence of policies referred to as the period of consolidation,
1949–52; the Soviet period, 1953–8; the Great Leap Forward and its
aftermath, 1958–65; and the Cultural Revolution, from 1966 to Mao
Zedong's death a decade later. Although these divisions obscure
major continuities throughout the period and beyond, they do provide
a convenient framework within which to examine developments.

THE PERIOD OF CONSOLIDATION, 1949–52

When, on 1 October 1949, Mao proclaimed the establishment of the
People's Republic, it appeared that he was inaugurating a new era in
Chinese history. However, several recent studies have pointed to the
continuities between the Nationalist and Communist eras. Among these
continuities were central government industrial planning, which demonstrated significant policy and personnel continuity, the origins and
evolution of the *danwei* (work unit), workers' rights and notions of the
family.[1]

Until 1952 the main effort of the new government was expended
on consolidating its control. No organized resistance remained in
China Proper after the Guomindang's precipitate departure from the
mainland. Nevertheless, there was a real danger of subversion and, to
guard against this, in September 1949 the country was divided into
six military regions and joint military and administrative commis-
sions exercised authority. The CCP referred to the border regions as
the 'old liberated areas' and the rest of China as the 'new liberated

areas'. In the old liberated areas the Communist leadership was already established, but in the new areas much remained to be done. Guangzhou, for example, was not occupied until two weeks after the establishment of the People's Republic of China. In the new liberated areas most senior Guomindang officials had fled, and the first task was to find people with the skill and political reliability to take over their posts and to keep essential services functioning. In this the student body played an important part.

Four tasks needed to be addressed immediately. The first was to define the political characteristics of the new state. In September 1949, a People's Political Consultative Conference was convened and an Organic Law and a Common Programme were adopted. The former established a 'democratic dictatorship' led by the CCP; the latter guaranteed basic human rights and promised equality for women, the continuation of revolutionary land reform, the development of heavy industry and safeguards of the rights of minority peoples. The second task was to gain control of the economy, which meant curbing inflation. This was achieved by increasing government revenue, by creating a unified fiscal system (for the first time since 1928, land taxes accrued to central rather than to provincial government) and by selling bonds. At the same time, various strategies were employed to keep government expenditure under control, for example requiring the army to be partly self-sufficient.

The new government was intent on asserting control over all territory deemed to be part of China. This, with one significant exception, was within the boundaries of the Qing empire. The Nationalist government had claimed to inherit the Qing domain, but it had been too weak to incorporate the diverse populations within these frontiers into an effective nation-state. Nor had it been able to to counter Japanese attempts during the war to manipulate the national aspirations of the non-Chinese minorities. To assert its claim to this inheritance became the objective of the People's Republic. The term *zhonghua minzu*, 'Chinese nationality', is used to describe an identity which is not synonymous with Han Chinese, an identity which transcends ethnic divisions and incorporates all peoples living within the boundaries of China.[2] The three provinces of Manchuria were now fully integrated into China. Tibet, which had been autonomous since 1913, was 'liberated' by the People's Liberation Army in 1950 and later became the Xizang Autonomous Region. Xinjiang, which between 1944 and 1949 had been known as the Eastern Turkestan

Republic, was persuaded to join the People's Republic of China. However, Outer Mongolia, which had become the Mongolian People's Republic in 1924, remained independent. As for Taiwan, in October 1949 a Communist force tried but failed to seize the island of Jinmen (Quemoy). The rebuff showed that an invasion of Taiwan would be a major operation, and the matter was postponed.

The fourth priority task concerned foreign relations. During the Second World War China had been treated flatteringly by the United States as a great power, but in the post-war period and the civil war, China's international status had declined to that of a client state. The CCP aspired to present China as an independent and unaligned power, but in 1949, in the atmosphere of the Cold War, it seemed that China must 'lean to one side', which meant seeking an alliance with the Soviet Union. In December 1949, Mao Zedong left China for the first time in his life to go to Moscow and negotiate with Stalin. Although there was a show of cordiality between the two, neither man fully trusted the other and the negotiations were prolonged and difficult. The outcome was the Sino-Soviet Treaty of Alliance and Mutual Assistance. Its most important provisions were a promise of mutual support in the event of an attack by Japan, and a Soviet advance of $300 million in credits to China.

The implications of the alliance with the Soviet Union soon became apparent. In June 1950, civil war broke out between North and South Korea. After North Korean troops had virtually overrun the south, the United Nations sent forces to assist South Korea. At the same time, the United States interposed its Seventh Fleet in the Taiwan Straits to prevent China using the opportunity to invade the island. By November 1950 the United Nations' forces had not only invaded North Korea, but were within 50 miles of the Yalu river, the frontier with China. China intervened on a massive scale and drove the United Nations' forces back to the 38th parallel, the boundary between North and South Korea. The war then reached stalemate and a truce was signed in June 1953.

China's decision to intervene was most probably occasioned by the collapse of the North Korean army and the threat of a United Nations' force, in effect a United States' force, becoming poised on its north-east frontier. Chinese participation in the war was significant in a variety of ways. Although the Chinese forces, led by Peng Dehuai, achieved remarkable success, the war exposed serious military weaknesses and a decision was taken to modernize the People's Liberation Army and to develop the air force. The war cost over 700,000 Chinese casualties, among them Mao Zedong's son, and China incurred very heavy debts to the Soviet Union for the purchase of arms. China's involvement also deepened the rift with the United States, which now became committed to the support of the Nationalists on Taiwan. In China the threat of war was used to whip up support for the regime, for example through the Resist America, Aid Korea campaign. It was also invoked to justify a harsher line against all persons suspected of not giving the regime their full support.

During these years the programme of revolutionary land reform was completed. The Agrarian Reform Law of 1950 extended land reform to the new liberated areas. Its purpose was explained by Liu Shaoqi, who was second to Mao Zedong in the Party hierarchy: it was not only to end the feudal exploitation of the landlord class, it was also to preserve a rich peasant economy to enable the revival of agricultural production. Land reform had been completed by 1952 except in areas occupied by national minorities, which were exempted. By then about 43 per cent of China's cultivated land had been confiscated and redistributed, with about 60 per cent of the rural population benefiting. Many poor peasants, who by definition owned little or no land and survived by selling their labour, now became middle peasants. The importance of this measure in terms of consolidating peasant support behind the regime cannot be underestimated. However, the reform was achieved at a high cost. Estimates of the number of landlords and rural power-holders who died range from 200,000 to 2,000,000. The redistribution on average gave a poor peasant just over a quarter of an acre of land, which did little to solve the problem of land shortage. Official estimates of grain production indicate that between 1949 and 1952 output rose by 12.6 per cent. The increase may reflect the post-war recovery and perhaps a greater effort from peasants, who no longer had to surrender much of their crop to landlords. Without fresh inputs, however, this rise in output could not be sustained.

During these years, several other measures helped to consolidate the CCP's position. In 1950 a Marriage Law was introduced which replaced the 'feudal' marriage system with the 'New Democratic' marriage system. Women were allowed to choose their partner freely and given equal rights relating to divorce, custody of children and property. After the law had been promulgated, women's associations led a mass campaign to publicize the changes and a sharp rise in the number of divorces followed. Nevertheless, in rural areas many features of the traditional marriage system survived.

Steps were taken immediately to increase educational opportunities for the masses. Those whose schooling had been interrupted by war were offered accelerated programmes of study and many millions of adults attended winter study classes and spare-time schools. Teachers were re-educated, school texts were revised and political study classes were held. Most Western missionary educators left the country and their schools and universities were nationalized. By 1952 about 60 per cent of children eligible for primary education were in school, and impressive increases had been recorded in the numbers attending secondary schools and colleges.

It was essential that the new government should gain the confidence of the industrial and business communities. At the time of the Communist victory, economic activity in the cities was virtually at a standstill and public utilities were out of commission. Once order had been restored, it was made clear that, for the time being, the more traditional sector of the economy would not be reformed. At the same time, the government took steps to discourage strikes and to negotiate moderate wage claims. However, the modern economic sector was immediately affected by the departure of most foreigners and those Chinese industrialists who had close links with the Guomindang. Their enterprises were immediately taken under state control. In April 1951, systematic confiscation of foreign assets began with the nationalization of the property of Shell Oil.

By early 1951, the period of reconstruction and moderation was coming to a close. The apprehension aroused by the Korean War was utilized by the CCP to justify the launching of mass campaigns, which were to have a profound impact on Chinese society. Three major campaigns were initiated: against suspected counter-revolutionaries, against corrupt cadres and, in the 'Five Antis' campaign, against capitalists. The campaign against counter-revolutionaries began with mass rallies and denunciations and was followed by arrests and executions. In the Guangzhou region alone over 28,000 people were executed, and in the country as a whole 500,000 to 800,000 people may have been killed. The campaign against corrupt cadres had its origin in the shortage of trained cadres when the CCP came to power. This had led to the recruitment of cadres whose class origin or personal commitment was unsatisfactory. Perhaps 10 per cent of

Party cadres were now weeded out. The Five Antis campaign was an attack on wealthy capitalists, who, it was claimed, were defrauding the public through a variety of economic crimes. Capitalists who were found guilty were forced to pay heavy fines and to accept state control of their enterprises. These mass campaigns mobilized the population and attacked the web of personal friendships and obligations (*guanxi*) which typified relationships within the business community.

Another indicator that fresh initiatives were imminent was the establishment in 1952 of the State Statistical Bureau and the announcement of a census on 30 June 1953. The declared result was that the People's Republic of China, excluding Taiwan and the Overseas Chinese, had a population of 582,603,417. From figures collected later, it has been calculated that the population was growing at about 2 per cent per annum. The census has been described as merely an enumeration of the population and the results have been disputed, but as there is no good reason why the results should have been falsified, they represent the best available evidence of the magnitude of China's population at that time.

THE SOVIET PERIOD, 1953–8

In 1953 the Communist leadership began to implement its policy of socialist transformation and economic development; that is to say, the transfer of ownership from private to public hands and the introduction of centralized economic planning. In September the First Five-Year Plan was introduced and the collectivization of agriculture began.

The influence of Soviet Russia on China was already apparent in a variety of forms, but now with the adoption of state planning the Chinese debt to Soviet Russia was even more noticeable. When selecting a development model which gave priority to heavy industry, which involved the construction of large-scale, capital-intensive and technologically advanced plants, and which assumed the institutional transformation of the agricultural sector, which was to supply much of the capital required, China was following the path recommended by Lenin and implemented by Stalin. That China should be willing to become so dependent on a foreign power was surprising, but only the Soviet Union was willing to contribute to the heavy investment which the Chinese leadership believed was an essential element in the country's transition to socialism.

China now received Soviet assistance in the form of expert advice, extensive economic aid and the introduction of Soviet methods, for example in industrial management. Initially 156 major industrial enterprises, including 7 iron and steel plants, 24 power stations and 63 machinery plants were supplied, many of them in kit form for assembly in China. Later another 125 projects were approved. Some 11,000 Soviet specialists were sent to China to supervise the installation and operation of plants and to provide technical assistance, and 28,000 Chinese students were sent to Russia to study.

The period of the First Five-Year Plan saw a number of other important initiatives. Hitherto most of China's modern industry had been concentrated in the coastal cities and the north east. Now, as a matter of policy, industrial complexes were sited in the interior. Major steel complexes were constructed at Wuhan and in Inner Mongolia, and an oil refinery was built at Lanzhou in Gansu province. To service these plants a large investment was made in new railways, including the construction of a line from Xi'an to the Xinjiang oilfields. In these new industrial complexes the Soviet model of 'one-man management' was introduced. This system, which was associated with centralized planning and the setting of production targets, replaced management committees and worker representation with an authoritarian system. Workers, who in the Yan'an period had responded to ideological incentives, now did piecework or were placed on steeply graded salary scales.

Soviet influence was also apparent in education, particularly in universities and colleges, which were reorganized on Soviet lines. Russian academic advisers assisted in the planning of courses and Russian textbooks were used widely. Expenditure on higher education tripled between 1952 and 1957 and the number of students, one third of whom studied engineering, rose sharply. Students from poor families received free tuition and maintenance grants. In return, many pledged themselves to the '8:1:50' schedule: eight hours of sleep and one hour of exercise a day and 50 hours of work a week.

*   *   *

The socialist transformation of society also implied the collectivization of agriculture. The arguments in favour of this step were both economic and political. One consequence of revolutionary land reform had been even greater fragmentation of agricultural holdings.

Peasants farming small, scattered holdings could not accumulate capital for investment and could not maintain the sustained rise in output and productivity needed to feed the growing population and to release surplus labour for industry. The Soviet Union had collectivized agriculture in the 1930s and it was capital derived from the agriculture sector which had provided investment in industry. It was also apparent that, since land reform, many poor peasants had sold the land they had been given. In 1955 Mao Zedong complained that there had been a spontaneous growth of capitalist elements in the countryside.

In the Yan'an period co-operative farming had been encouraged in the form of mutual aid teams, which pooled their resources in terms of labour and draught animals. After a period of experimentation, from 1954 mutual aid teams were encouraged to amalgamate to form agricultural producers' co-operatives. In these, families retained the titles to their plots, but their land was farmed co-operatively and crops were divided according to the amount of land and labour supplied by each family. On 31 July 1955, while this change was still under way, Mao Zedong called for a sharp increase in the rate of collectivization. In the winter of 1955–6 co-operatives began to be merged into Advanced Producers' Co-operatives. These were collective farms in which private land ownership was abolished and members were remunerated on the basis of their labour alone. By the end of 1956, the socialist transformation of agriculture was virtually complete.

China's experience of collectivizing agriculture has been compared favourably with that of the Soviet Union. Collectivization there was opposed by the rich peasants, or kulaks, and several million of them lost their lives. Various explanations for China's better record have been proposed, for example that China's rich peasants were neither as numerous nor as established a feature of rural society as were the kulaks. Perhaps collectivization in China was better timed, in that only a short period had elapsed since land reform and the capitalist tendencies in the countryside, against which Mao Zedong had warned, had not become firmly established. Collectivization, it has been claimed, appealed to the rational self-interest of peasants and was carried through by local cadres, who had a clear grasp of the situation.

At the time there was little sign of disagreement with the policy. It is now known that rapid collectivization was opposed by some members of the Party leadership and that Mao countered their opposition by seeking the support of provincial leaders. Since decollectivization other dissenting voices have been heard. In 1984 a Shandong farmer recalled:

> When we had advanced co-ops I was the head of one. Quite the little activist I was in those days. When the call went out to form co-ops I put everything my parents had bought – the land, the ox, the donkey and all – into the co-op. At night I was grieving over losing them, but during the day I was taking the lead, trying to talk other people into joining – and trying to talk myself into it too.[3]

Undoubtedly the achievements of these years of socialist transformation were impressive. During the First Five-Year Plan period China's industrial output doubled, the most spectacular increases being recorded in the output of steel, oil and chemicals. These rates of growth probably exceeded those of the Soviet Union at the time of its First Five-Year Plan, but it should be remembered that China owed the Soviet Union a share of the credit, as about 50 per cent of the industrial investment made during the First Five-Year Plan derived directly or indirectly from the Soviet Union. The debt included the Soviet provision of plant, blueprints and technicians, which has been described as 'one of the largest transfers of technology in world history'.[4] During the same period China collectivized agriculture and carried through an extensive programme of social reforms, notably in education. Between 1949 and 1956 primary school enrolment rose from 24.3 million to 64.2 million, middle school enrolment from 1 million to 6.2 million, and in higher education the number of students quadrupled to 441,000.

THE GREAT LEAP FORWARD AND THE SINO-SOVIET SPLIT

In 1958 China embarked on a radical, even utopian programme to 'complete the building of socialism ahead of time, and carry out the gradual transition to communism'.[5] Behind this rapid change of pace, if not direction, lay a complex set of interactions within the Party, the economy, industrial management, educational strategy and international relations.

One indication of the strain imposed by revolutionary change was the disillusionment of the intellectuals – that is to say, the educated elite – most of whom had welcomed the Communist victory in 1949.

At first the CCP had tolerated what was seen as the intellectuals' bourgeois individualism, but in 1955 a harder line was adopted. A mass campaign was launched against the poet Hu Feng, who had criticized the Party's insistence that culture should be proletarian. The campaign was used to warn intellectuals not to oppose the First Five-Year Plan or the collectivization of agriculture.

In 1956, Premier Zhou Enlai commented that to promote the economy and to reform the bureaucracy the Party needed the support of intellectuals. In May, Mao Zedong, who was engaged in the Party debate over the pace of co-operativization, endorsed the changed line by announcing: 'Let a hundred flowers bloom, a hundred schools of thought contend.' After some hesitation, intellectuals began to criticize the competence of cadres, for example for interfering in scientific research. When Mao heard of the Hungarian uprising of November 1956, he attributed it to the isolation of the Hungarian Communist Party from the masses and the intellectuals. In February 1957, in a speech entitled 'On the Correct Handling of Contradictions Among the People', he argued that 'non-antagonistic contradictions' could exist in a communist society and that their resolution by discussion would speed up progress to socialism. His ideas encouraged intellectuals to believe that the open expression of their opinions would be welcomed and many articles critical of the Party, of educational policies and even of Mao Zedong himself were published. Students from Beijing University put up posters criticizing officials on 'democracy wall', a stretch of wall near the Forbidden City. In May and June thousands of letters of criticism were sent to the government and some Party leaders were expressing concern that the matter had got out of hand. In July the CCP launched an Anti-Rightist campaign headed by Deng Xiaoping. The most outspoken critics of the Hundred Flowers movement were singled out for punishment and other intellectuals were forced to participate in their denunciation. One of the most famous victims was the writer Ding Ling, who was accused of having opposed the Party leadership in literary work. She refused to admit her faults and was sent to redeem herself through labour on a farm near the Soviet border. Wu Hongda, later known in the West as Harry Wu, was another victim of the campaign. He was arrested in 1960 for being a 'counterrevolutionary rightist' and was to spend eighteen years in *laogai* or labour camps.[6]

Some writers have accused Mao Zedong of treacherously encouraging intellectuals to criticize the Party and then siding with the Party in persecuting them. Merle Goldman has suggested that the Hundred Flowers movement developed a momentum of its own which went beyond the Party's intention and this dismayed Mao. Thereafter he rejected the intellectuals as the key to economic development and instead became concerned with what he saw as insufficient revolutionary consciousness among educated young people.[7]

Notwithstanding the economic achievements of the First Five-Year Plan, as an economic strategy it had serious shortcomings. Investment had been concentrated on heavy industry, which had grown at a rate five times faster than that of agriculture. The increase in agricultural output had done little more than feed the growing population. The industrial sector had not created the number of jobs needed to reduce unemployment in the cities. More jobs would be created if the consumer industries were expanded, but these were restricted by shortages of raw materials. In a speech entitled 'On the Ten Great Relationships', given in 1956, Mao Zedong had expounded a theory of relationships, or as he defined it 'contradictions', in economic development. The first contradiction was between industry and agriculture and between heavy industry and light industry. His conclusion was that although heavy industry must continue to be given priority, agriculture and light industry must also be developed, a strategy which was called 'walking on two legs'.

Other dissatisfactions included a reaction against the 'one-man management' system. This system had been associated with Gao Gang, the chairman of the State Planning Commission, who in 1954 had been accused of plotting against Liu Shaoqi and had committed suicide. At the Eighth Party Congress, which began in September 1956, the 'one-man management' system was criticized and replaced by a system of collective leadership with the Party in command. The extensive Russian influence on education was also challenged, and from 1956 attempts were made to speed up the expansion of education, particularly at junior middle school level.

Relations with the Soviet Union had improved after Stalin's death in 1953, and when Khrushchev and Bulganin visited China in 1954 it seemed that the two countries had formed a relationship of equality and mutual respect. However, in February 1956 Khrushchev delivered his secret speech denouncing Stalin. Mao Zedong resented Khrushchev's failure to give him warning of the speech, which Mao believed would cause dissension in the Communist world at a time when unity was essential. Disagreement on the issue exposed ideological differences, for example over the inevitability of war with the capitalist powers, which Khrushchev now denied. The attack on Stalin's personality cult may also have caused Mao Zedong to be concerned about his own posthumous reputation. Despite these differences, Mao Zedong visited Moscow for the second time in November 1957, soon after the Soviet Union had launched Sputnik, an achievement which led Mao to praise the achievements of the Soviet Union and to declare that 'The East Wind is prevailing over the West Wind'.

*   *   *

In late 1957, while a Second Five-Year Plan was being considered, indications began to multiply that the conservative economic strategy was about to be replaced by a radical programme. In the countryside a massive programme of irrigation using the labour of 100 million peasants was rushed through. In November, the *People's Daily* gave prominence to the slogan 'More, better, faster, cheaper'. In a speech given at the Supreme State Conference on 28 January 1958, Mao Zedong declared that 'It is possible to catch up with Britain in 15 years', and shortly afterwards production targets for agriculture and industry were raised dramatically. In that same speech Mao had stated: 'In making revolution one must strike while the iron is hot – one revolution must follow another, the revolution must continually advance.' This was his theory of 'permanent revolution', a process which embraced both the economic substructure and the social superstructure of society. The Great Leap Forward which soon followed, which has been described as 'more the product of a social vision than an economic plan', may be connected with Mao's concept of revolutionary change.[8]

In April 1958, 27 Advanced Producers' Co-operatives in Henan decided to amalgamate and form a commune. They did so without formal direction from the centre, although the encouragement given to the large irrigation schemes of the previous winter had implied tacit approval for the creation of larger units. Other co-operatives followed suit and in August communes received official approval. Before the end of the year, the 700,000 Agricultural Producers' Co-operatives had been reorganized into 24,000 People's Communes, each with an average of 5000 families. In the autumn, communes were also organized in urban areas. The model for these was the Zhengzhou Spinning and Weaving Machine Plant commune in Henan, which was centred on the factory but which also farmed some land.

The main economic benefit of communes was the mobilization of labour for large-scale labour-intensive projects. To maximize the release of labour, the private plots which peasants had been allowed to keep in the Agricultural Producers' Co-operatives were abolished and rural markets ceased to function. To enable women to participate in productive labour, crèches and nurseries were opened, collective kitchens were organized and a free food system was introduced. The labour thus made available was employed on major construction projects, such as the Ming Tombs Dam near Beijing, and also used to develop rural industry. Following reports of an abundant harvest, communes were encouraged to prospect for local sources of iron ore and to construct their own 'backyard steel furnaces'.

During the Great Leap Forward, vastly increased targets were set for industrial production. The target for steel output, fixed in February 1958 at 6.2 million metric tons, was already a 19 per cent increase on the previous year's production. In August, Mao endorsed raising it to 10.7 million tons and a few weeks later he even suggested 12 million tons. To achieve high targets over a range of industries, hundreds of new state projects were started. Between 1957 and 1960 the number of people employed in state industries doubled to over 50 million, which placed an immense strain on the system of food procurement from the countryside. This vast workforce was encouraged by ideological exhortation to work excessively long hours on plant which was over-used and under-maintained.

That the Great Leap Forward was more than a leap for economic growth was demonstrated by other aspects of the movement. In September 1958 a 'great leap' in education was announced. In part this meant rapidly expanding educational opportunity, particularly in the countryside. Primary school enrolment rose by 20 million and there were large increases in the number of students at secondary and tertiary level. Some 30,000 agricultural middle schools and about 400 'red and expert' universities were opened. At the same time, important changes took place in the operation of the educational system. The new schools were organized on the *minban* or 'run-by-the-people' principle, productive labour was introduced into the curriculum in all schools and at all levels, and students were encouraged to voice their criticisms of teachers. Another feature of the communes was the revival of the people's militia and the arming of the peasantry.

The need for military preparedness was justified by the crisis of August 1958 caused by the declaration that China intended to 'liberate' Taiwan. It was also a challenge to the professional leadership of the People's Liberation Army and a reminder of the 'people's war' fought in Yan'an days. Furthermore, the communes briefly offered women an escape from the double burden of domesticity and work. This was most warmly embraced in the urban communes where women, who in the past had been restricted to the home, took a leading role in organizing child-minding arrangements and other features of the commune which were a break from the traditional family structure.

The euphoria of the Great Leap in 1958 was followed by disillusionment and dissension in the following year. By then it had become apparent that reports of a bumper harvest had been exaggerated and that the industrial targets were unrealistic. The response was to reorganize the communes, making the production brigade, in effect the former Advanced Producers' Co-operative, the level at which ownership and decision making were fixed. Communal eating was ended and steps were taken to restore private plots and to reopen rural markets.

As the retreat from the Great Leap Forward began, the political conflict which had simmered under the surface at least since 1956 came out into the open. At the Party's Central Committee meeting held in Wuhan in December 1958, Mao agreed to step down as Chairman of the People's Republic, and in April 1959 that position was taken by Liu Shaoqi. Although Mao remained chairman of the Party, he later claimed that after the Wuhan meeting he was treated like a 'dead ancestor'. In July, at a conference held at Lushan, Mao Zedong received a letter from Peng Dehuai, a veteran of the Long March who was now Minister of Defence, warning him that the achievements of the Great Leap Forward were being exaggerated. Mao chose to publish the letter and to attack Peng Dehuai openly at the conference. As Peng had recently returned from Moscow, Mao accused him of having conspired with Khrushchev to criticize the communes and also to cancel the offer of nuclear aid for China. Subsequently Peng Dehuai was replaced at the ministry of defence by Lin Biao, a close supporter of Mao. Critics of the Great Leap Forward were intimidated and a second Great Leap began in 1960. A feature of the second Great Leap was the extensive introduction of urban communes, in an attempt to make urban areas more self-sufficient.

Mistaken agricultural policies, bad weather and the withdrawal of the Soviet technicians in July had by mid-1961 forced the abandonment of the second Great Leap.

The Great Leap Forward has excited controversy as an economic strategy and its failure has been seen as having momentous consequences for China. Before the full extent of the disaster precipitated by the Great Leap Forward was known, some Western economists, for example Alexander Eckstein, contended that the strategy of using China's under-employed labour to invest in agriculture, for example by promoting large-scale irrigation projects, was appropriate for a densely populated under-developed country. The reason for failure was not faulty strategy but hasty and ill-planned implementation and the adverse circumstances which have already been mentioned.[9] Nicholas Lardy was much more critical of the strategy, which he regarded as based on a misunderstanding of the constraints facing Chinese agriculture, a reference to Mao's belief that larger agricultural units would capture significant economies of scale. The projects undertaken by mobilized labour, most particularly the irrigation projects, were poorly designed and reduced rather than raised yields. In addition, the massive growth in the industrial workforce drove grain procurement in 1959 up to nearly 40 per cent of the harvest.[10]

The release of demographic data in the 1980s revealed that the Great Leap Forward had a disastrous effect on China's population. The decline in food production and the breakdown in the system of distribution had set off a famine described as the worst in human history. The cumulative increase in mortality has been estimated as somewhere between 16 million and 27 million deaths. The famine, which was at its height in 1960, was felt most severely in rural areas and in certain provinces, with Anhui alone suffering about 2 million deaths. These figures may be compared with the loss of life in the Soviet Union at the time of the collectivization of agriculture, which has been estimated at 5 million deaths. The Party's response to this tragedy was wholly inadequate. The system of gathering statistics had collapsed and had been replaced by grossly exaggerated claims of increases in output. Cadres persisted in enforcing government policy and even prevented peasants from resorting to their traditional methods of surviving famine.[11] Notwithstanding the seriousness of the crisis, many Party leaders, including Chen Yun, the Party's most senior economist, long remained silent.

The Great Leap Forward and its consequences played a significant role in deepening the Sino-Soviet dispute. The origins of the dispute go back to incidents in the history of the rise of the CCP, to the negotiation of the Treaty of Alliance and Mutual Assistance in 1950, to Sino-Soviet relations during the Korean War, to Khrushchev's secret speech denouncing Stalin in 1956, and to the tensions which had emerged during Mao's visit to the Soviet Union in November 1957. However, it was the Great Leap Forward which brought these tensions out into the open. The rejection of Soviet economic methods, the trumpeting of the initial achievements of the Great Leap Forward and the hailing of the communes as a short cut to communism, all threatened to deprive the Soviet Union of its claim to be the 'ideological and economic leader of the socialist camp'.[12] The tensions were heightened in 1958 and 1959 by various international crises, beginning with the United States' landings in Lebanon. On the day that Khrushchev arrived in Beijing, his cautious response to this crisis was criticized in *Red Flag*, the Party's journal. Soon after, the Chinese threat to 'liberate' Taiwan was treated coolly by the Soviet Union. The Tibetan revolt in spring 1959, and the flight of the Dalai Lama to India, posed a threat to China, but again the Soviet Union did not offer firm support.

The rupture followed shortly after. In June 1959, the Soviet Union rescinded the offer of nuclear assistance it had made two years previously. At the same time, reports of critical remarks made by Khrushchev about the communes reached Mao's ears. In April 1960, *Red Flag* openly criticized the Soviet Union's policy of peaceful co-existence. This, and its rejection of China's economic policies, led the Soviet Union to announce in July that its technicians would be withdrawn in two months. Thus began a diplomatic estrangement which was to last until 1985.

PRELUDE TO THE CULTURAL REVOLUTION

The years following the disaster of the Great Leap Forward were dominated by economic reconstruction and educational and political adjustment. Steps were taken to restore the agrarian economy. In 1959, the brigade had replaced the commune as the unit of accounting and private plots had been restored. Up to 30 million people were relocated from the cities to the countryside, so allowing a large reduction in cereal procurements. Under Chen Yun's direction, an 'agriculture first' economic strategy was developed. Believing that the mobilization of labour alone could not solve China's agricultural problems, Chen increased state investment in agriculture, expanded the production of agricultural machinery and chemical fertilizers and developed a 'high and stable yield' area policy, which encouraged regions which already produced large quantities of grain to concentrate on expanding cereal production. In the industrial sector, many state enterprises were closed down and a partial return was made to the one-man management practices of the First Five-Year Plan. As a result of these policies, by 1965 agricultural output had returned to the level achieved in 1957, although in the meantime the population had risen by 80 million. Industrial output recovered even more quickly and by 1963 a period of sustained growth had begun, aided by the development of new industries, most notably the petrochemical industry. This recovery was remarkable for two reasons: it was achieved when China was technologically isolated and when the development of nuclear weapons – China's first nuclear test took place in October 1964 – was absorbing high-technology resources.

In education, the principle of 'walking on two legs' – which in this context meant the provision of regular, quality schools and mass-based work-study alternatives, and the combination of study and productive work – was not abandoned, but it was modified extensively. The number of pupils in elementary schools fell from 93 million in 1960 to 69 million in 1962. Most of the agricultural middle schools, where students had studied the Chinese language and practical subjects in the morning and had worked in the fields in the afternoon, were closed. Likewise, few of the 'red and expert' universities survived, one exception being the Jiangxi Communist Labour University, which continued to serve as a model for work-study and agricultural education. Central authority over education was reasserted and the amount of productive work required of staff and students was limited. Significantly, 'keypoint schools', which had been introduced at the time of the Great Leap Forward, were retained. In them talented children were taught by selected teachers in a well-equipped environment.

*   *   *

In the post-Great Leap Forward period, political leadership was provided by Liu Shaoqi, supported by Deng Xiaoping (the general secretary of the CCP), the economist Chen Yun and Peng Zhen, the 'mayor' of Beijing. Mao Zedong had largely withdrawn from the day-to-day management of affairs, but his views were represented by his wife Jiang Qing, who was active in the field of cultural affairs, and by Lin Biao, the minister of defence. Zhou Enlai, the premier, remained uncommitted to either side.

The nature of the contest between these two groupings has been interpreted in a variety of ways. One way is to regard it as a power struggle between Mao Zedong and his critics. Although differences between Mao and other Party leaders can be traced back many years, it was only after the disaster of the Great Leap Forward that Mao Zedong found himself excluded from political power. Subsequent events – the Socialist Education movement, the promotion of Mao's personality cult, Lin Biao's reforms of the People's Liberation Army and the Cultural Revolution – may all be taken as an assault on Mao's political rivals, Liu Shaoqi and Deng Xiaoping.

Mao Zedong's relationship with the CCP had altered drastically since 1949. Then, when the Party was transforming itself into the government of China, Mao's authority and ideological leadership had been unchallenged. In 1956, at the Eighth Party Congress, the Party constitution was revised by deleting reference to Mao Zedong's thought as part of the CCP's guiding ideology and by making it easier for white-collar workers to become members of the Party. The Politburo was enlarged and important positions were filled by technocrats. Recognizing that the government was becoming more bureaucratic and increasingly divorced from the masses, a campaign for Party rectification was launched. The changes effected did not satisfy Mao and his hostility towards the Party was apparent in his speech 'On the Correct Handling of Contradictions Among the People', which he had given in February 1957. Among the contradictions he had identified was one between the leadership and the masses, which he described as a nonantagonistic contradiction. His hostility increased markedly during the period of recovery after the Great Leap Forward. At the 7000 cadres' conference held in 1962, he accused Party bureaucrats of being arrogant. By then he had concluded that the relationship between the Party, which for him represented privileged power-holders, and the masses was an antagonistic contradiction. As such a contradiction could not be resolved by rectification, the Party would have to be smashed.

Other interpretations of the origins of the Cultural Revolution emphasize differences in the revolutionary objectives of the two sides. Mao had managed to persuade many, though not all, Party leaders to support the launching of the Great Leap Forward. In 1962, when the true extent of the disaster became apparent, Deng Xiaoping openly criticized the communes and socialist relations of production and hinted at the abandonment of collectivized farming. Speaking at a Communist Youth League conference, he said that he favoured any form of production which would rapidly restore and increase agricultural output. Famously, he quoted a Sichuan proverb: 'Yellow or white, a cat that catches mice is a good cat.'[13] This issue, and other causes of dispute, earned Deng Xiaoping and Liu Shaoqi condemnation as 'capitalist-roaders', and led to their being accused of following the revisionist course set by Khrushchev in the Soviet Union. Mao Zedong's loss of confidence in the Party and its leaders led him to look to the next generation in his search for revolutionary successors.

The first rounds of the struggle were fought in the context of the Socialist Education movement, which was launched in 1963. Mao shared common ground with other Party leaders in believing that apathy and corruption among Party cadres in the countryside were widespread. In a document later known as the 'Former Ten Points', which Mao himself had drafted, poor and lower-middle peasant associations were given the task of investigating cadre corruption and restoring the collective principle in farming. In September Deng Xiaoping issued the 'Later Ten Points', which supported many of the anxieties voiced in the previous document, but which called for the formation of urban-based work teams to carry out the rectification. In the winter of 1963–4 Wang Guangmei, Liu Shaoqi's wife, spent six months incognito investigating examples of cadre abuse. In September of the following year Liu Shaoqi, using information gathered by his wife, produced a third document, the 'Revised Later Ten Points', which painted a gloomy picture of the situation and proposed that large work teams should visit selected communes, investigate them thoroughly and deal severely with cases of cadre corruption. The dispute separating Mao and Liu Shaoqi was now becoming clear: whereas Liu regarded the central issue to be cadre corruption and the appropriate action the reimposition of Party authority, for Mao the issue was the revisionism which had appeared at all levels in the Party. In January 1965, Mao convened a conference and issued yet another document, the 'Twenty-three Articles', which indicated that the target was not the corruption of local cadres, but the actions of those people holding positions of authority in the Party who were taking the capitalist road.

In the meantime, other controversies had widened the gap between Mao and his critics. Mao had long favoured the use of revolutionary models and in 1964 he promoted Dazhai Brigade in Shanxi as a model because its peasants, through their self-reliance and commitment to collective farming, had transformed the barren land they farmed and had raised its yields fivefold. The slogan coined was 'In agriculture learn from Dazhai'. Other brigades were called on to emulate the selfless commitment of the people of Dazhai and to adopt their work-point system, which rewarded political awareness as well as physical effort. Later that year, a work team investigating Dazhai concluded that the production figures had been grossly exaggerated, but Mao's influence protected the reputation of the brigade, which continued to serve as a model until Mao's death. Only in recent years has the full extent of the damage caused by the indiscriminate use of the Dazhai model in different environments been recognized fully. A particularly disastrous venture was the land reclamation project on the shores of Dian Lake south of Kunming. This involved 300,000 people and the moving of half a million cubic metres of earth. Valuable wetlands were destroyed and the microclimate was affected.[14]

Mao had greater success in mobilizing support in the People's Liberation Army. Peng Dehuai, who had been appointed Minister of Defence after the Korean War, had introduced a series of reforms intended to turn the army into a professional force. When he was replaced by Lin Biao in 1959, the latter had continued the modernization programme and in October 1962, when the border dispute between India and China turned into a war, the People's Liberation Army achieved a rapid and overwhelming victory. Lin Biao also supported the nuclear programme, which resulted in China detonating an atomic device in October 1964. However, Lin was also politically ambitious and he decided to make the armed forces an example of revolutionary zeal. He promoted the case of the model soldier Lei Feng, who had died in 1962 at the age of 20 when trying to help a comrade. In 1964 the army's political department produced an early version of the compilation which was to become the *Quotations from Chairman Mao Zedong*. In return for Lin's support, Mao endorsed a campaign based on the slogan 'Learn from the People's Liberation Army'. In 1965 Lin's article entitled 'Long Live the Victory of the People's War!' anticipated a confrontation between the United States and national liberation movements. In the article, he praised Mao Zedong extravagantly for his leadership in the war of resistance against Japan, which he described as a genuine 'people's war', in which the Party had relied on the masses, not on machines.

Two other issues were important in the years preceding the launching of the Great Proletarian Cultural Revolution, and were to be central to that event. The first was education, with particular reference to access and opportunity. In the aftermath of the Great Leap Forward, fresh emphasis had been placed on educational standards and the use of examinations. By the early 1960s the educational system was 'probably more elitist than it had been a decade earlier'.[15] In a speech given at the Tenth Plenum of the Eighth Central Committee in September 1962, Mao Zedong had warned 'never forget the class struggle'. However, it appeared that the experiments in mass education introduced during the Great Leap Forward had been forgotten and that a 'two-track' educational system, which worked to the advantage of urban children, in particular the children of Party cadres, had been established. Mao criticized these developments at the Spring Festival Forum of 1964. He argued that the current period of schooling was too long, that too much reliance was placed on examinations, that too much deference was paid to teachers and that a stronger link should be established between education and production.

The other issue was culture. In 1942, in his 'Talks at the Yan'an Forum on Literature and Art', Mao had argued that the arts should serve the revolution and should do so by endorsing proletarian values. In the early 1960s, a number of novels and plays had appeared which contained implicit comments on political issues. The most notorious example was an opera written by the historian Wu Han entitled *Hai Rui Dismissed from Office*. Hai Rui, an upright sixteenth-century Ming official, had been dismissed by the emperor because he had protested against the confiscation of land from peasants. The opera was widely recognized as a criticism of Mao's actions at the time of the Great Leap Forward.

In response, Mao called on his wife Jiang Qing, herself an erstwhile film star and Shanghai socialite, to formulate a policy statement on culture. She teamed up with Kang Sheng, a former member of the Politburo who had specialized in issues relating to revisionism and counter-revolution. She found allies among the Shanghai radicals, including the Shanghai Party chief Zhang Chunqiao, the literary critic Yao Wenyuan and Wang Hongwen, a factory worker whose rapid rise to prominence earned him the description 'helicopter' because he had gone straight up.[16] These three and Jiang Qing were later to achieve notoriety as the 'Gang of Four'.

In 1964 Jiang Qing's efforts seemed to have born fruit when a 'Group of Five', headed by Peng Zhen and including Kang Sheng, was formed to carry out a cultural rectification. However, it soon became apparent that the efforts of the Group of Five did not satisfy the radicals. In November 1965, Yao Wenyuan published a critical review of *Hai Rui Dismissed from Office* in *Liberation Army Daily*, the organ of the People's Liberation Army. He alleged that the play was a coded attack on Mao for having dismissed Peng Dehuai for criticizing the Great Leap Forward. Wu Han, who as deputy mayor of Beijing happened to be Peng Zhen's immediate subordinate, was forced to make a self-criticism. This political infighting set the stage for the Cultural Revolution.

THE CULTURAL REVOLUTION

The Great Proletarian Cultural Revolution, to give it its full title, began in May 1966 and its active phase lasted until April 1969. Its reverberations continued until Mao Zedong's death in September 1976 and the arrest of the Gang of Four in the following month.

The official launch of the Cultural Revolution was preceded by a period of manoeuvring. In the People's Liberation Army, Lin Biao was engaged in a struggle with Luo Ruiqing, his Chief-of-Staff. When the United States had started to bomb North Vietnam in February 1965, Luo Ruiqing had advocated a policy of improving relations with the Soviet Union and making preparations to give material support to North Vietnam. Lin Biao, on the other hand, argued that the Vietnamese should fight a 'people's war' and that China should only offer moral support. The difference of opinion between the two men resulted in Luo Ruiqing being forced to make a self-criticism, and to his dismissal. At the same time, cultural issues were becoming increasingly divisive. The Group of Five issued the 'February Outline', which aimed to limit consideration of the bourgeois tendencies in *Hai Rui Dismissed from Office* to an academic discussion. However, Mao Zedong complained that the Group had obscured class lines and had encouraged rightist sentiment.

He described Wu Han as an 'academic warlord' and Peng Zhen, the leader of the Group, as a 'Party warlord'.[17] This manoeuvring phase ended with the Politburo meeting which began on 4 May. Lin Biao used the occasion to accuse Luo Ruiqing and Peng Zhen of having plotted a coup against him and other radicals. At the end of the meeting, the Politburo issued the 'May 16 Circular', which alleged that the Party had been infiltrated by bourgeois revisionists. It also announced the dissolution of the Group of Five and the appointment of a Cultural Revolution Group to be led by Chen Boda, the editor of *Red Flag*, and including Jiang Qing and Kang Sheng.

In the 'Fifty Days' between 16 May and 5 August, two conflicting tendencies were apparent. Liu Shaoqi, whom Mao Zedong may already have regarded as a revisionist, was placed in charge of implementing the Cultural Revolution. At the same time, covert encouragement was given to radicals in the universities to challenge Party leaders. On 25 May, Nie Yuanzi, a philosophy teacher at Beijing University, put a big-character poster on the canteen wall which attacked the university president for having supported the February Outline. The university authorities tried to suppress the radical movement, but on 1 June Mao Zedong authorized the broadcasting of the contents of the poster. This resulted in a rash of big-character posters critical of educational leaders and educational policies appearing in schools and colleges throughout the country. Liu Shaoqi dispatched over 400 workteams to schools, universities and various government agencies to carry out a rectification campaign, and attempted to assert Party authority over the radical student movement. At Qinghua University in Beijing, the conflict between Party leaders and radicals was personalized. Wang Guangmei, Liu Shaoqi's wife, was a member of the workteam, whereas Jiang Qing lent her support to the radicals.

Up to this point Mao Zedong had remained in Hangzhou, distancing himself from the struggle. On 16 July he made his famous swim in the Yangzi river, covering nine miles downstream in 65 minutes. Two days later he returned to Beijing and on 1 August he indicated his support for the use of the term 'Red Guard', which had been coined in May by student radicals at Qinghua University Middle School. On 5 August he published his own big-character poster entitled 'Bombard the Headquarters', which accused the workteams of 'adopting the reactionary stand of the bourgeoisie'. On 8 August, at a meeting of the Eleventh Plenum of the Central Committee of the

CCP (from which some of Mao's opponents were excluded), a document known as the 'Sixteen Points' was adopted, which set out the purpose of the Cultural Revolution:

> to struggle against and overthrow those persons in authority who are taking the capitalist road, to criticize and repudiate the reactionary bourgeois academic 'authorities' and the ideology of the bourgeoisie ... and to transform education, literature and art and all other parts of the superstructure not in correspondence with the socialist economic base ...[18]

By now numerous Red Guard organizations had appeared in schools and colleges, and on 18 August Mao Zedong reviewed the first of many Red Guard rallies in Tiananmen Square. The impression given was that this was a movement united in its revolutionary purpose and adulation of Mao Zedong. However, the Red Guards also articulated deeply rooted tensions in Chinese society, in particular issues of power and domination characteristic of both traditional and twentieth-century Chinese political culture.[19] From an early stage the Red Guard movement was split by factionalism, which derived from the educational policies adopted after the Great Leap Forward. The main division lay between those students who came from the 'five kinds of red' family background – that is to say, the children of workers, peasants, soldiers, cadres or revolutionary martyrs – and those who came from 'bourgeois' backgrounds. The former, who had enjoyed preferential educational treatment in the 1960s, supported the work-teams which Liu Shaoqi had sent into schools, and by extension they supported the Party. The latter, who felt that they had been over-looked academically, began to form their own rebel organizations and to challenge the workteams.

At the end of the Eleventh Plenum, Mao Zedong had addressed a rally of Red Guards and had encouraged them to make revolution throughout the country. In schools and colleges, administrators and teachers were subjected to criticism. Teachers were identified as the 'stinking ninth category' – lower than eight other reactionary groups – and were held to blame for the faults of the 'old' education. They were publicly humiliated and the same treatment was meted out to some Party officials. Lin Biao had called for the destruction of the 'four olds': old ideas, old culture, old customs and old habits. Red Guard groups took this as an invitation to destroy anything which might be described as representing bourgeois culture, whether it be works of art, foreign clothing, hairstyles or even street names which made reference to the past. Red Guards also took advantage of free rail travel to visit Beijing and other parts of the country to attend rallies and to enjoy the experience of 'revolutionary tourism'.

By October, it was apparent that the Cultural Revolution Group intended to challenge the Party establishment and that a fierce power struggle lay ahead. The Group accused 'persons in authority' of having taken the capitalist road, and Liu Shaoqi and Deng Xiaoping were forced to make self-criticisms. Red Guard groups in the provinces, often incited to action by delegates from Beijing Red Guard organizations, attacked local Party officials. After the 'five red' qualification for Red Guard membership had been relaxed, Red Guard organizations became more daring. In November they were permitted to enter factories and communes and to challenge the Party monopoly of relations with peasants' and workers' organizations.

In January 1967, an incident known as the 'Shanghai storm' epitomized the collapse of Party provincial authority. The Shanghai workforce included many thousands of casual labourers and contract workers who enjoyed none of the benefits enjoyed by employees in the state sector. The tensions deriving from their economic situation were exploited by Shanghai radicals with the encouragement of the Cultural Revolution Group. On 6 January, the mayor and other municipal officials were forced to resign and rebel organizations, with the support of the People's Liberation Army, seized control of factories and offices. A new city government was formed, supposedly modelled on the Paris Commune of 1871. Its representatives were elected in a secret ballot by members of factory organizations. The Party authorities were swept aside. By the end of January, similar 'seizures of power' had occurred in cities throughout the country, although in some cases these had been stage-managed by Party officials.

The resultant confusion led Mao and the Cultural Revolution Group to reject the Paris Commune model and to endorse a new power structure, the revolutionary committee, which comprised representatives of the mass organizations, Party cadres and the People's Liberation Army. Each of these groups contained radical and conservative elements and in the first half of 1967 there was incessant infighting. Party cadres fought to protect themselves from criticism, the mass organizations struggled among themselves, and even in the armed forces radical and conservative elements were in competition. At the same time, the Red Guard press openly criticized Liu Shaoqi and Deng Xiaoping.

The danger of the situation was made manifest by an incident which occurred in Wuhan in July. The commander of the Wuhan Military Region, who had supported an organization of conservative workers known as the 'Million Heroes', was accused of repressing the radical mass organizations. A delegation from the Cultural Revolution Group, accompanied by Zhou Enlai, went to Wuhan and found in favour of the radicals, whereupon the Million Heroes attacked the delegation. To resolve the dispute, Zhou Enlai was forced to bring in outside military forces and to dismiss the Wuhan military commander. By the end of August China was on the verge of civil war. Red Guard and other mass organizations were obtaining arms and fighting pitched battles in the streets. Jiang Qing was criticizing leaders of the People's Liberation Army, thereby threatening to undermine the army's shaky authority. The foreign ministry, which was headed by Marshal Chen Yi, an ally of Zhou Enlai, was seized by the radicals, and the British legation in Beijing was burned down.

The crisis forced Mao Zedong, supported by Zhou Enlai and Lin Biao, to adopt measures to restore stability. Some of the radicals were purged from the Cultural Revolution Group and the People's Liberation Army was empowered to suppress disorder. The army encouraged the study of the 'little red book', the *Quotations from Chairman Mao Zedong*, to provide a basis for a revolutionary consensus. In September, the first steps were taken towards the reconstitution of the Party. After a further upsurge of campus violence in spring 1968, Red Guard organizations were disbanded. The process of forming revolutionary committees was accelerated and completed in September 1968. In the following month, at the Twelfth Plenum of the Central Committee, Liu Shaoqi was officially expelled from the Party. Finally, at the Ninth Party Congress, held in April 1969, a new Party leadership, with Lin Biao identified as Mao's successor, was agreed. A report from Lin Biao to the Congress marked the conclusion of the first stage of the Cultural Revolution.

Mao Zedong is reputed to have said that the Cultural Revolution consisted of 70 per cent achievements and 30 per cent mistakes. This estimate was based on the alleged aims of the event: reversing the trend towards revisionism, getting rid of bourgeois influences and placing 'politics in command'. Since Mao Zedong's death, however, few have regarded it so favourably. An account of the revolution published in Xianggang in 1986 concluded:

> For China the Cultural Revolution remains a colossal catastrophe in which human rights, democracy, the rule of law, and civilization were unprecedentedly trampled. Not only was the president [Liu Shaoqi] persecuted to death, tens of millions of innocent people were also attacked and maltreated.[20]

In some provinces of China mass killings took place, the largest group of victims being adults and their children who had been identified as 'class enemies'. In Guangxi province, two-thirds of all counties reported mass killings with as many as 2463 people being killed in one county. The killings were instigated by government authorities and carried out by members of the militia or mass organizations.[21]

Roderick MacFarquhar, who had been in China at the height of the Cultural Revolution, looked back over thirty years later and described it as a cataclysm, asserting that it was 'so great a disaster that it provoked an even more profound cultural revolution, precisely the one that Mao intended to forestall'.[22]

The direct impact of the Cultural Revolution on the economy was limited. Industrial and agricultural output only declined temporarily and by 1970 output was already surpassing previous peak levels. The indirect effects were more significant. For years it left China's planners 'severely constrained by fears of political reprisals'.[23] It had a lasting influence on industrial management. During the 'Shanghai storm', the conservative labour unions had been accused of trying to bribe the workers with the promise of higher wages. The radicals had countered this by introducing ideological incentives and by appealing to the *Quotations from Chairman Mao Zedong* for guidance. Other changes gave workers a share in management and required cadres to participate in labour. Soon after the Cultural Revolution material rewards were reintroduced, but the influence of the revolution could still be detected in a management style which sought to compromise between 'one-man management' and worker participation in management, resulting in management by revolutionary committee. Industrial strategy was also affected. In response to perceived threats from the Soviet Union and the United States, between 1964 and

1971 a massive programme of relocation of industry was initiated from coastal areas and from central China to the west, which was described as the 'Third Front'. For ten years, 40 per cent of the central government's total annual budget was committed to this end. By the late 1970s the rationale for this move no longer applied, but the relocated industries and their workforces were to be subsidized for years to come.

The Cultural Revolution left its most enduring imprint on education. Between 1968 and his death in 1976, Mao Zedong presided over a set of radical reforms which aimed to reduce the 'three great distinctions': between town and country, industry and agriculture, and mental and manual labour.[24] The school curriculum was shortened, more time was spent on political education, and all pupils and students were required to participate in manual labour. In the countryside, middle schools were run by communes and primary schools by production brigades. Primary school teachers were paid in work points based on the collective's annual income. National college examinations were abolished and colleges selected students from those recommended by their work units. A typical innovation of the time was the 'July 21 Workers' University', exemplified by the institute attached to the Shanghai Machine Tools Plant. There workers and peasants with good political credentials and extensive practical experience followed a shortened course which combined technology, political thought and manual labour. After graduation they returned to their original place of work.

After Mao Zedong's death, the official line was that 'not one good thing' could be said of these years of educational reform. Suzanne Pepper, however, has suggested that, like the French Revolution for Charles Dickens, they were both the best of times and the worst of times. On the positive side, the most important achievement was the expansion of educational opportunity. Between 1969 and 1977, primary school enrolment rose from 100 million to 146 million pupils and ordinary secondary school enrolment from 20 million to 67 million pupils. The disadvantages experienced by children who lived in rural areas were somewhat reduced by a redistribution of resources. The main negative criticism of the reform programme was that it lowered educational standards, the most severe impact being on tertiary education. Most universities and colleges did not resume regular intakes until the early 1970s. Some 4 million secondary students, who formed the 'Red Guard generation', were 'rusticated';

that is, sent to the countryside on rural assignments, where they remained for up to ten years. When tertiary education was resumed, the challenge to academic education continued. A notable protest was made in 1973 by a student named Zhang Tiesheng who, when taking the cultural test for entry to a provincial college, handed in a blank examination paper. His explanation was that he, unlike other entrants, had been unable to study because he had been working. His action was cited as a praiseworthy example of 'going against the tide' which was restoring academic standards.

FROM THE CULTURAL REVOLUTION TO THE DEATH OF MAO ZEDONG

During the Cultural Revolution, the People's Liberation Army had been called on to restore order and later to form a part of revolutionary committees. In 1967, People's Liberation Army officers headed 21 of the 27 provincial revolutionary committees. Two years later, at the Ninth Party Congress, Lin Biao, the minister of defence, was named as Mao's successor. A new Politburo was chosen, 55 per cent of the membership of which came from the military. Some Western observers suggested that in China, as in some other Third World countries, the army was in the process of displacing the Party.

Over the next two years Mao Zedong, motivated either by his belief that 'the Party should command the gun' or by his growing suspicion of Lin Biao, took steps to restore the authority of the Party and to undermine Lin Biao's standing. While the army continued to perform a political role, a start was made on reconstituting the Party and revising the state structure. In late 1969, the army was told to pay greater attention to military training, an indication that it would soon be relieved of its political responsibilities. In the meantime, differences had emerged between Lin and Mao over the future direction of China's foreign policy. Whereas Lin believed that in international relations China should ally with oppressed and revolutionary peoples, Mao now endorsed cautious moves towards a rapprochement with the United States. Finally, at the Second Plenum of the Ninth Congress, held at Lushan in September 1970, events occurred which may have convinced Mao that Lin was not a suitable successor. Some months previously Lin had proposed that Mao should become head of state. This position, which after 1959 had been held by Liu Shaoqi, was due to be abolished in the new state structure. Mao rejected the offer, but Lin raised the matter again at the Second Plenum, perhaps expecting that Mao would refuse once more and that the position would then be awarded to him to signify publicly that he was Mao's heir. The persistence of Lin Biao and his supporters, who included Chen Boda, a former member of the Cultural Revolution Group, earned a rebuke from Mao Zedong.

After the Plenum a campaign was mounted to discredit Chen Boda and in August 1971 Mao visited regional military commanders in central and south China to assure himself of their loyalty. According to allegations made later, Lin Biao realized that his time was up, so he authorized his son to devise the '571 plot', which involved killing Mao Zedong when he was aboard his special train. When the plot failed, the conspirators attempted to set up a rival regime in Guangzhou. That plan also having collapsed, on 13 September Lin Biao, his wife and his son fled the country. They died when their plane crashed in Mongolia.

While these dramatic events were occurring, a major realignment had taken place in China's foreign relations. At the time of the Cultural Revolution, China had become diplomatically isolated. In March 1969 fighting broke out with the Soviet Union over the ownership of Zhenbao (Damansky) island on the Wusuli river. Mao Zedong risked attacking a nuclear superpower without international support and when China's military forces were preoccupied. The Soviet Union responded with premeditated border incidents coupled with the despatch of diplomatic notes threatening wider action by the Soviet forces concentrated on China's frontier. To this tactic China had no reply, and in October talks began in Beijing to settle the border dispute. Before the end of the year, the possibility of improving China's relations with the United States was under discussion. In July 1971 Henry Kissinger, the United States' National Security Advisor, made a secret trip to China to prepare the way for a visit by President Nixon in the following year. From the Chinese point of view Nixon's visit was a great success, as it resulted in an agreement on peaceful co-existence between the two countries without China having to make concessions about the 'one China' policy and the claim to Taiwan.

After Lin's death, the main domestic political issue was the succession to Mao. The struggle lay between the more pragmatic senior Party members, who included Zhou Enlai and Chen Yi, the former foreign minister, and the radicals, who included Mao's wife Jiang Qing, Zhang Chunqiao and Yao Wenyuan, all from Shanghai. As Mao regarded none of them as a potential successor, he first promoted another Shanghai radical, Wang Hongwen, a former cotton mill worker, to the number three position in the Party hierarchy. Wang found that Zhou Enlai held all the key posts and this encouraged him to join Jiang Qing in the 'Criticize Lin Biao, criticize Confucius campaign', the real targets of which were Zhou Enlai and former victims of the Cultural Revolution who were being rehabilitated. However, Zhou had recently been diagnosed as having cancer and the campaign misfired. Thereupon Mao Zedong decided to turn to Deng Xiaoping – the man who in 1967 had been described as the 'number two person in authority taking the "capitalist road"' – because of his high reputation with the military and his political skills.

Deng Xiaoping was rehabilitated in May 1973 and over the next year he initiated a number of overdue reforms. These included reducing the size of the People's Liberation Army and defining a long-term economic policy, described by Zhou Enlai as the 'Four Modernizations', which referred to agriculture, industry, defence and science and technology. These reforms left him open to criticism from the radicals. When Zhou Enlai died in January 1976, Mao decided against appointing Deng as premier and chose instead Hua Guofeng, the former First Secretary of the Party in Hunan, who he believed was committed to the policies of the Cultural Revolution.

Jiang Qing, Zhang Chunqiao, Yao Wenyuan and Wang Hongwen, described by Mao as 'the Gang of Four', were infuriated by Hua Guofeng's elevation, and Jiang Qing criticized him openly. However, a demonstration in Tiananmen Square in April 1976 in memory of Zhou Enlai showed how unpopular the radicals were. Suspecting that the demonstration was connected with Deng Xiaoping, the Gang had it broken up ruthlessly, and Deng himself, on Mao's instruction, was removed from all his offices. In July an earthquake hit Tangshan, 160 miles south east of Beijing, killing nearly a quarter of a million people. The Gang misread the situation, which was one of extreme apprehension, and issued an official message to survivors that they should 'deepen and broaden' the criticism of Deng Xiaoping's revolutionary line.

Mao Zedong died on 9 September 1976. The Gang of Four assumed that the succession to Mao would fall to them and at the memorial service held in Tiananmen Square on 18 September, Jiang Qing stood beside Hua Guofeng when he read the eulogy. But on 6 October Hua Guofeng had the Gang arrested on the charge of plotting to usurp power. Four years later the Gang, and five military commanders who were accused of complicity in Lin Biao's attempted coup, were put on trial. Jiang Qing spoke in her own defence, arguing that she was merely 'Chairman Mao's dog'. She was given a suspended death sentence, later commuted to life imprisonment. She committed suicide in 1991.

The editorial of the *People's Daily* of 18 September claimed that 'Chairman Mao Will Live Forever in Our Hearts', but this uncritical assessment did not survive long. In June 1981 the Party accepted a wordy 'Resolution on Certain Questions in the History of Our Party'. Mao Zedong Thought, now described as the collective wisdom of the Party, was to remain 'a guide to action for a long time to come', but Mao himself was said to have made 'gross mistakes' at the time of the Cultural Revolution, although his earlier contribution to the Party's success far outweighed those errors.

Over the last thirty years many reassessments of Mao's achievement have been made, most of which have balanced positive and negative aspects of his career. Then in 2005, Jung Chang and Jon Halliday published *Mao: The Unknown Story*, a ferocious attack on the man and his motivation. He was portrayed as 'lacking either idealism or a clear ideology' and 'driven by a personal lust for power'. Through the use of terror he enforced his will on the Chinese people and his dream to dominate the world cost 38 million lives. The book provoked a fierce debate, much, though not all, echoing the hostility of the authors towards their subject.[25] A different reflection on Mao's revolutionary deeds was offered by Jack Gray. He wrote:

If I had been young and Chinese in 1958 I would have thrown myself into the Great Leap; and in 1966 I would have been out with the Red Guards, protesting against privilege and the abuse of power.

For Gray, the Great Leap Forward was an alternative strategy of development to deal with China's shortage of land, lack of capital and vast surplus of rural labour, and he found the text for the Cultural Revolution in a speech given by Mao in 1966 in Shanxi: 'The officials of China are a class, and one whose interests are antagonistic to those of the workers and peasants.'[26]

8

. . . .

From the Era of Deng Xiaoping to the Present Day

After Mao Zedong's death and the fall of the Gang of Four, Deng Xiaoping was restored to the offices he had held before the Tiananmen incident, but Hua Guofeng, who had previously been his subordinate, remained premier. Over the next four years, Deng Xiaoping campaigned to secure the rehabilitation of the victims of the Cultural Revolution, and by implication the rejection of Mao Zedong's legacy, of which Hua Guofeng claimed to be the guardian. In 1979, the poor performance of the People's Liberation Army when it invaded Vietnam in support of the Pol Pot regime in Cambodia weakened Hua Guofeng's position and in the following year he was forced to resign as premier. In the early 1980s, Deng delegated routine administration to two men from a younger generation: Hu Yaobang, who became Party secretary, and Zhao Ziyang, who succeeded Hua Guofeng as premier. Deng remained in control until 1987, when he resigned from the Central Committee, although he retained the chair of the Military Affairs Commission. He continued to dominate the political scene until his retirement from all official positions in 1990, and his influence was apparent until shortly before his death in February 1997.

Deng Xiaoping's political style was highly personalized and he was prepared to go to great lengths to settle private animosities. For example, he used his authority to secure a ten-year prison sentence for Nie Yuanzi, the philosophy teacher at Beijing University whose big-character poster had launched the Cultural Revolution. In Deng's opinion she was also responsible for the persecution by Red Guards of his son Deng Pufang, which led to him falling from a fourth-floor window at the university in 1968 and becoming paralysed from the waist downwards.

Deng was no advocate of democracy, but he accepted the case for some modest political changes. In 1980 the system of congressional elections, which had not operated since the Cultural Revolution, was revived and direct elections were held for some 2000 county-level congresses. Members of the National People's Congress, an indirectly elected body which hitherto had met sporadically to rubber-stamp Party decisions, were now allowed to cross-examine ministers on their work and to table suggestions for government action. The 1982 constitution provided for the Congress to establish standing committees to deal with foreign, economic and minority nationalities' affairs. In September 1985, a special Party conference was convened to force the retirement from the Politburo of some of its most aged members. An attempt to reduce the gerontocratic character of government was certainly desirable, but Deng's main motive may have been the settling of old scores.

These moves were subordinate to Deng's primary objective, which was to bring about a major shift in economic policy. In agriculture this implied the abandonment of collectivization and the adoption of a market economy. After the Great Leap Forward, modifications had been introduced to the communes, but the principles of public ownership of land, reliance on human labour as the main resource and restrictions on private enterprise had been retained. In the years from 1966 to 1978, the gross value of agricultural output had grown at 3.1 per cent per annum, sufficient to sustain the increasing population but quite inadequate to raise living standards to a significant degree.

In 1979, two reforms were instituted which were to transform the agricultural sector. The first encouraged peasants to maximize the use of their private plots and to sell their produce on the open market. By 1982 the private income of peasant families may have amounted to 38 per cent of family income. The second was the introduction in 1981 of the 'household responsibility system'. Although the collective ownership of land was retained, individual families could now take out contracts to cultivate plots of land with specified crops, and could retain or sell any surplus produced in excess of their contract. These measures injected an entrepreneurial spirit into farming. The slogan 'To get rich is glorious' was coined and the 'ten thousand yuan' household appeared. In the years immediately after the introduction of these reforms, the growth rate of grain output rose from 3.5 per cent to 5 per cent per annum. In 1984, China's grain output topped 400 million tons for the first time. The improvement in rates of growth could not be maintained without new inputs, which meant greater use of agricultural machinery, chemical fertilizer and electric power. Rural incomes might be increased further by diversifying production and by encouraging rural industry, but the fundamental problem of agriculture remained the shortage of arable land, which in 1987 amounted to only 0.1 hectare per capita.

In the ten-year period after 1979, China's gross national product grew at 9.2 per cent per annum. Part of this growth, as has been indicated, was achieved in the agricultural sector, and more came in the hitherto much underdeveloped service sector. The key area of growth, however, was industry. In the 1970s China's industry still retained many of the characteristics of the Soviet period. The Ten-Year Plan launched in 1976 had concentrated investment on large-scale heavy-industrial projects, which were set unrealistically high production targets. By the 1980s the need to improve incentives for workers was apparent. This forced a switch to the production of consumer goods, which in turn encouraged the importation of foreign technology and the growth of foreign trade. After a period of adjustment, China experienced an economic boom, and between 1981 and 1986 China's industrial output nearly doubled.

Although China's industrial sector had achieved an impressive rate of growth, it was still controlled by a centralized planning system which determined what an enterprise should produce, where it should obtain its raw materials and where and at what price it should sell its products. In 1984, while China was suffering the consequences of an energy crisis, economic policy began to shift away from centralized planning towards the greater use of market forces. Two years later, state-owned enterprises were removed from Party control and modern managers were installed. State price control was replaced with a dual-price system, with state-set prices being used to subsidize favoured firms, but market-set prices controlling demand for materials in short supply. Although these reforms freed up the market, they also accelerated inflation and encouraged corrupt practices in the allocation of goods at state-set prices.

The policy of national economic self-sufficiency had been abandoned in December 1978. China began to accept loans and foreign investments and joined the International Monetary Fund and the

World Bank. In 1980, four 'Special Economic Zones' were created at Shenzhen near Xianggang, Zhuhai north of Aomen (Macao), Shantou and Xiamen. Their task was to initiate a new stage in economic development, by attracting foreign capital and experimenting with economic reforms. The largest and by far the most important of these was Shenzhen. Foreign firms were offered advantageous terms for investment, suitable sites and a supply of cheap labour. Foreign direct investment quickly became substantial, most of it coming from Xianggang firms. It brought with it not only foreign exchange, but also new technology and management practices. In the 1980s, Shenzhen increased its GDP by an average annual rate of 50 per cent. Unskilled workers earned 500–700 renminbi (RMB) per month, compared with rates of 150–200 RMB for workers elsewhere in the Pearl river delta. By 1999, over 40 per cent of the value of Shenzhen's industrial output came from new and high-tech products. The success of Shenzhen and other SEZs was later confirmed by the opening up of the coastal cities of the Yangzi delta and subsequently of inland areas.[1]

Under Deng, new impetus was given to China's space programme. The programme had begun in 1955 when Tsien Hsue-shen, who had studied rocketry in the United States, returned to China. At first it depended on the acquisition of Russian rocket technology, which in turn derived from German V2 rockets. DF-1, the first Chinese version of a Russian rocket, made its maiden flight in 1960; DF-2, the first indigenously designed missile capable of carrying a nuclear warhead, was launched in June 1964. Two years later, a rocket with an atomic warhead exploded in Xinjiang, 1,000 miles away. The manned space programme began in 1968 and the first satellite was launched in 1970. After Lin Biao's death, the space programme was run down and Deng suspended the manned space programme, as he did not think that human space flight would promote economic development. Instead, the Long March launch vehicles were developed and China started to provide a commercial satellite-launching service. However then, in 1986, Deng announced that for China to keep up with advanced technologies, it must invest in high-tech research and development. The National High Technology Research and Development Programme – the 863 programme, the nation's major technology development programme – was established and the space programme accelerated.[2]

The 1953 census had shown how rapidly China's population was growing and a birth-control campaign was introduced, although this was abandoned during the Great Leap Forward. During the Cultural Revolution birth control was denounced as an anti-Marxist heresy. In the 1970s, partly in response to a government campaign which imposed economic sanctions on families with more than three children, the birth rate halved. Nevertheless, both Hua Guofeng and Deng Xiaoping believed that population growth still threatened China's modernization goals, and that more state intervention was essential. In 1980, the draconian 'one-child family' policy was introduced. Couples who accepted a one-child family certificate received a generous package of benefits, whereas those who had a second child were liable to lose a percentage of their income and forfeit their private plot or responsibility plot. Some exceptions were made in the case of children born with congenital defects, and the policy generally did not apply to minority groups.[3]

Many questions have arisen about the advisability of this policy. The need for drastic action was supported by the evidence of the 1982 census, which showed that China's population exceeded one billion. Nevertheless, the policy flew in the face of the deeply held belief that a family needed a son to preserve the ancestral line and to provide economic support. The enforcement of the policy involved the widespread use of abortion and sterilization and encouraged female infanticide. In 1984, it was recognized that the campaign was too coercive, and a wider range of exemptions was allowed.

The introduction of the one-child family policy revived the debate about the status of women in modern Chinese society. The 1950 Marriage Law had appeared to confirm the Communists' promise that under the new regime, women would occupy a position of economic and legal equality with men. Rural China remained a patriarchal society, however, and although educational opportunities for girls and employment opportunities for women improved, women still laboured under the double burden of child-bearing and work. During the Great Leap Forward, the provision of communal kitchens and nurseries offered women a brief glimpse of a less trammelled existence, but during the Cultural Revolution the class struggle was emphasized and feminist issues were dismissed as bourgeois preoccupations. In 1980, a new Marriage Law confirmed the legal rights of women and raised the minimum age of marriage for men from 20 to 22 and for women from 18 to 20. If the position of women in Chinese society today is compared with that which they occupied before 1949, the argument that they have been liberated would seem incontrovertible. Yet few women achieve senior positions in employment or occupy important political roles, and the one-child family policy has proved a sharp reminder of the misogynism which persists in Chinese society.

In the new constitution promulgated in 1982, it was reaffirmed that the People's Republic was a multinational state. This was in recognition of the fact that 8 per cent of China's population belongs to one of the 55 national minorities. The largest single group, the Zhuang, who live in the south west, number over 15 million. Other sizeable groups include the Hui, Chinese-speaking Muslims and the Uighur, to be found in the north west, and the Miao and the Tibetans in the south and west.

In 1992 Jiang Zemin, the General Secretary of the CCP, delivered a major speech on ethnic affairs. He made it clear that the government had no intention of yielding to any demands for independence from any minority group. However, he confirmed the policies of ethnic autonomy, helping the minorities to develop themselves and the promotion of economic development in ethnic areas. In 1999, the government committed itself more strongly to improving the economic and social life of the minorities, with the express intention of making them more content with their life in the People's Republic and less likely to support separatist movements.[4]

For the most part, China's minority nationalities occupy China's strategically important border regions. The territories in which they predominate have autonomous-region status, which affords them some economic and political freedom but does not give them the option of secession. Although the minority nationalities are encouraged to preserve features of their culture, the persistent migration of Han Chinese into these regions forces ethnic groups to adapt to the dominant Han Chinese presence. The process of absorption, typical of the historical relationship between Chinese and neighbouring peoples, is continuing, and this causes the keenest resentment.

In Xinjiang, where the largest minority nationality is Uighur, the proportion of Han Chinese in the population in 1949 was 5.5 per cent. By 1970 that figure had risen to 40 per cent. In 1980, conflict emerged within the Urumqi Military Region and there were Uighur calls for self-rule. Ten years later the Baren rising, a protest movement headed by Uighur nationalists, raised concerns about the security of southern Xinjiang. Some 8000 officials in rural work teams were despatched to stabilize the region and strengthen political organizations. Mosques were closed down and foreign preachers banned. In 1992, a proposal to settle in Xinjiang 100,000 Han Chinese displaced by the Three Gorges Dam led to an international outcry, which eventually forced the government to back down. In 1997, Uighur militants carried out a series of attacks. The Chinese government blamed the outbreak on separatists or 'splittists', Muslim radicals or terrorists, and applied a policy of 'Strike Hard, Maximum Pressure'. A prominent figure among the Uighur leaders is Rebiya Kadeer, who made a fortune from cross-border trading and became a member of the Chinese People's Consultative Conference. She founded the Thousand Mothers' Association and campaigned actively on a variety of social issues, but in 2000 she was imprisoned for revealing state secrets. On her release in 2005 she went into exile in the United States, and has been President of the World Uyghur Congress since 2006.[5]

Tibet came under Chinese political control in the eighteenth century and thereafter international agreements, for example the Anglo-Chinese agreement of 1906, acknowledged the region to be Chinese territory. In 1911, Outer Mongolia and Tibet seized the opportunity to break away from China. The Dalai Lama declared Tibet to be an independent state and this was recognized by Great Britain, but never accepted by China. In 1950 Tibet was 'liberated' by the People's Liberation Army commanded by Deng Xiaoping, and was designated the Xizang Autonomous Region. Assurances were given that the region would continue to administer its internal affairs and that its social system would be left intact. However, the Chinese presence in Tibet, and in particular the challenge this posed to Tibetan Buddhism, led to rising tension. The Tibetan revolt of 1959 resulted in Chinese military intervention and the flight of the Dalai Lama to India. During the Cultural Revolution, many Buddhist monasteries were destroyed, in some cases by Tibetan Red Guards. After the Cultural Revolution reassurances were offered about Tibet's economic and cultural autonomy. Nevertheless, Tibetan opposition to the Chinese presence continued, and in 1989 demonstrations in favour of Tibetan independence were crushed brutally.

During Deng Xiaoping's time as leader, the relationship between the People's Republic of China and the Republic of China on Taiwan changed from military and political confrontation to economic co-operation. After the Guomindang defeat on the mainland, Taiwan, under President Jiang Jieshi, became a bastion of Nationalist resistance and part of the United States' strategy for the containment of Communism. This arrangement collapsed in October 1971 when the People's Republic took the seat held by Taiwan at the United Nations, and in February of the following year when President Nixon visited China. Nevertheless, Jiang Jieshi persevered with the policy of confrontation with the mainland until his death in April 1975. He was succeeded by his vice-president and then, in 1978, by his son Jiang Jingguo, who initiated a policy of cautious political liberalization. He remained deeply suspicious of the People's Republic and his doubts about China's intentions increased in 1979, when relations between the United States and China were normalized. In 1981, Deng Xiaoping assured the people of Taiwan that China no longer planned to recover the island by force and that if it were reunited peacefully with the mainland, its people would be allowed to retain a high degree of autonomy. Although no negotiations on reunification took place, trade between Taiwan and China began to increase rapidly, and in 1987 Taiwan relaxed its foreign-exchange controls and removed its ban on travel to the mainland.

Deng Xiaoping also played a leading role in determining the future of Xianggang (Hong Kong). The island itself had been ceded to Great Britain in perpetuity in 1842, but the New Territories, which were essential for Xianggang's survival, had been leased to Great Britain on a 99-year term from 1898. After 1949 it was expected that the People's Republic would demand the immediate return of Xianggang, but Mao Zedong gave the matter a low priority. Twice over the next 20 years the security of Xianggang as a British colony appeared under threat. After the Great Leap Forward, Xianggang's resources were strained to the limit by an influx of thousands of refugees. In 1967, during the Cultural Revolution, Red Guards fomented the most serious disorder the colony had ever known. Notwithstanding these threats, the issue of Xianggang's future remained undecided.

When the colony's economy began to expand rapidly in the 1970s, this was so much to China's advantage that it seemed possible that the return of the territory to China would be postponed indefinitely. However, Deng Xiaoping had strong views on national unification, and he suggested that Xianggang should receive an offer similar to that which had been made to Taiwan in 1981. After reintegration the territory would be allowed to retain a high degree of autonomy, a concept which was later described as 'one country, two systems'. In 1982 Margaret Thatcher, the British Prime Minister, visited Beijing and began the negotiations which resulted in the Anglo-Chinese agreement of 1984. Under this, Xianggang would revert to China in 1997 and become a Special Administrative Region. Its people would be allowed to retain their own social and economic systems for 50 years after that date.

* * *

Deng Xiaoping's record as paramount leader was to be tarnished by his handling of the democracy movement, and by his role in the massacre which took place in the vicinity of Tiananmen Square on the night of 3–4 June 1989.

Since its foundation, the CCP's attitude towards democratic freedoms has been very mixed. In 1919, Chen Duxiu declared that only the two gentlemen 'Mr Science and Mr Democracy' could 'cure the dark maladies in Chinese politics, morality, learning and thought'. However, Comintern influence on the Party led to Chen being expelled and to members being subjected to Party discipline. At Yan'an, some intellectuals who had joined the Party ventured to criticize the lack of democratic rights. Mao Zedong responded in his 'Talk at the Yan'an Forum on Literature and Art'. Art, he said, must serve the masses, not the subjective interests of the artist. In protest against this denial of freedom, Wang Shiwei, a young Communist activist, wrote an essay entitled 'Wild Lily'. For his temerity Wang was put on trial and later executed. The term 'wild lily' came to denote democratic dissent, and Wang Shiwei was later described as the CCP's first dissident.

In 1957, when Mao Zedong launched the Hundred Flowers campaign, intellectuals were given a brief opportunity to express their opinions. On Beijing University campus a 'democracy wall' was started, with one student calling for true socialism with democracy. When the strength of dissenting views became apparent, Mao abandoned the intellectuals and called on Deng Xiaoping to lead an anti-rightist movement. During the Cultural Revolution, when Mao himself had declared that 'to rebel is justified', some Red Guards had published critiques of aspects of the Party in the Red Guard press. After the Cultural Revolution, millions of Red Guards were sent down to the country. Many of them felt betrayed, either because they had been deprived of their educational opportunities, or because the cause to which they had been committed was rejected after Mao Zedong's death.

This was the background of the new democracy movement which appeared in 1978. At first this was not primarily a movement of intellectuals, its main participants being state-employed manual workers and technicians, who were later joined by former Red Guards who had drifted back to the cities. The first manifestation of the movement was the appearance of posters on a wall along Chang'an Avenue in Beijing. Among the contributions was a poster headed 'Democracy, the Fifth Modernization' by Wei Jingsheng, an electrician at Beijing Zoo who was also studying at Beijing University. Wei Jingsheng argued that free enterprise was the only economic system compatible with democracy. Other contributors to the democracy movement remained committed to socialism and argued that China's problems stemmed from the shortcomings of its bureaucracy.

The democracy movement began soon after Deng Xiaoping had been reinstated. At first he regarded the activists as useful allies against the surviving Maoists and gave the movement his guarded support. However, his priority was economic modernization and in February 1979 he defined his political stance in 'four cardinal principles': that China should keep to the socialist road and that it should uphold the dictatorship of the proletariat, the leadership of the CCP and the authority of Marxism-Leninism and Mao Zedong Thought. At the same time, the 'four great freedoms' which had been formulated by Mao Zedong – to speak out freely, to air views fully, to hold great debates and to write wall posters – were removed from the 1978 constitution. When Wei Jingsheng and others protested, they were arrested and Wei was given a 15-year jail sentence.

In the early 1980s, the effects of China's increasing contact with the outside world alarmed the more conservative Party leaders. In 1983 a campaign was started against 'spiritual pollution', a reference to Western hairstyles, Beethoven's music and other examples of capitalist decadence. The leadership was not united in this condemnation and Hu Yaobang, who became general secretary of the Party in 1982, became known for making incautious remarks which were sometimes critical of Marxism or positive about aspects of the West. Some intellectuals, the most famous of whom was the astrophysicist Fang Lizhi, who had been a victim at the time of the Hundred Flowers and who was now vice-president of the University of Science and Technology at Hefei, were also bold enough to question the record of the CCP.

In December 1986, a student movement began at Hefei in protest against the alleged rigging of elections to the people's congresses. Whereas student movements had played a key role in national history in 1919 and again in 1935, this was 'the first sustained series of student demonstrations in the People's Republic not directly sponsored or explicitly encouraged by top party officials'.[6] The movement spread to Shanghai and Beijing, the students were joined by other social groups and banners were displayed calling for democracy. As the movement gained momentum, Party leaders became increasingly concerned. In January 1987, Fang Lizhi was dismissed and it was later revealed that in the same month Hu Yaobang had been forced to make a self-criticism and resign for allowing the demonstrations to get out of hand. Zhao Ziyang took over as Party secretary and in November 1987 Li Peng became acting premier. Under this new leadership, further efforts were made to implement the Four Modernizations, but political reform remained excluded from the agenda.

In April 1989 Hu Yaobang, who was popularly supposed to have been a supporter of democracy, died of a heart attack. Beijing students held demonstrations in his memory and at the same time protested about corruption and nepotism in government and the new restrictions on students' choice of employment after graduation. The seventieth anniversary of 4 May 1919, a date forever associated with democratic freedoms, was marked by massive unofficial parades in Beijing and in other cities. The Chinese leadership was surprised by the scale of these demonstrations, and Zhao Ziyang and Li Peng disagreed on how best to proceed. Tension rose when student demonstrators camping on Tiananmen Square began a hunger strike to force the government to make political concessions. The situation was complicated by the arrival of the Soviet leader, Mikhail Gorbachev, on 15 May for a state visit. That he could not be received on the square was a severe loss of face for the regime. On 18 May Li Peng met student leaders in the Great Hall, an occasion which was televised live. The students expressed their demands and refused to ask the protesters to leave the square until they were met, but Li Peng was in no mood to compromise. The following day, Zhao Ziyang visited the hunger strikers and gave the impression that he was sympathetic to their demands. Li Peng took a harsher line and he issued emergency orders banning demonstrations and empowering the People's Liberation Army to take appropriate action.

On the night of 22 May, and again two days later, Deng Xiaoping called together the Party elders to discuss the crisis. The leading advocate of decisive action was President Yang Shangkun, who argued that if the Party gave way it would fall from power and capitalism would be restored.[7] The student protesters remained resolute and on 29 May erected a statue of the Goddess of Democracy on Tiananmen Square. The first army units to arrive in Beijing appeared unwilling to use force against the demonstrators, but on the night of 3–4 June troops broke into the square and opened fire. It was later estimated that between 400 and 800 people had been killed, most of whom were not students and many of whom did not die in the square but in the surrounding streets.

Various explanations have been advanced for why the massacre occurred. The official version was that it was the suppression of an attempted coup by counter-revolutionaries who had foreign backing. The Party leadership was blamed, and Zhao Ziyang was dismissed for having failed to take a firm line with the students. Deng Xiaoping concluded that Li Peng was also at fault, for he had bungled the containment of the movement and then ordered its suppression in a blaze of international publicity. To distance himself from those implicated, Deng arranged that Jiang Zemin, the mayor of Shanghai, should be promoted above Li Peng as secretary-general of the Party. In broader terms, the tragic events of 3–4 June 1989 have been explained as a failure of China's political system. The economic reforms which began in 1978 might have eased tensions within the leadership and might have been accompanied by the development of institutions which would have promoted long-term political stability. Instead, the reforms provided further grounds for dispute between reformers and conservatives. Because of this rift, there was no agreement within the leadership on how to deal with the democracy movement, and policy seesawed between concession and violent suppression.

After the Tiananmen Square massacre, political activists who had not fled abroad were rounded up and imprisoned. For a time, international outrage in the West was so great that it seemed possible that the Chinese leadership might have to make political concessions. However, at the 1992 Party Congress, Deng's 'four cardinal principles' were reaffirmed and the need to suppress political 'turmoil' – a reference to the 1989 demonstrations – was reiterated. Nevertheless, economic reforms, which to hardline members of the leadership were the cause of political discontent, by now had become irreversible. Between 1989 and 1991 an attempt was made to restore centralized control of the economy, but in 1992 Deng Xiaoping, while making a tour of south China which included a visit to Shenzhen, proclaimed that China would adopt a 'socialist market economy', and this meant the end of price controls, a massive shakeout of workers in state enterprises and the encouragement of private enterprise.

In 2008, the dissident writer Ma Jian published *Beijing Coma*, a novel about Tiananmen. The main character is in a coma. He can remember the events but is unable to act, an indictment of what happened in June 1989 and the unresolved issues which still paralysed China's political progress. This state-enforced erasure of memory has been so effective that when Beijing students were shown the iconic photograph of a man confronting a tank in Tiananmen Square, they did not recognize it.[8]

CHINA AFTER THE DEATH OF DENG XIAOPING

Deng Xiaoping's death on 19 February 1997, at the age of 92, in one sense marked the end of an era, for he was nearly the last link with the early years of the CCP, but in other respects it brought little immediate change. The political leadership headed by President Jiang Zemin, which Deng had approved, remained in place. The economic modernization, Deng's enduring legacy, forged ahead. By the late 1990s it appeared that the authority of the Communist Party depended on economic growth, growth which was producing a society of gross inequalities which was riddled with corruption. To counter this, in February 2000 Jiang Zemin announced his 'Three Represents' theory, which claimed that the Party had always represented the most advanced productive forces, the most advanced culture and the fundamental interests of the overwhelming majority of the Chinese people. Jiang Zemin, who lacked personal influence with the military, also had to win the support of the People's Liberation Army by making judicious appointments, by pressing ahead with military modernization and by increasing the funding allocated to the armed forces.[9] At the time, Western observers belittled the Three Represents theory, but recently it has been described an 'important, even radical shift in party philosophy, party composition, and party orientation'. It was added to the CCP constitution at the Sixteenth Party Congress in 2002. The 'first represent' concerned recruitment to the party of entrepreneurs and intellectuals, rather than the previous emphasis on recruiting members of the proletariat.[10]

It has been said that the Party's strategy amounted to 'economic reform without political reform'. According to Zhang Wei-wei, a more subtle line was adopted: 'a process of significant economic reform together with lesser political reforms, aimed at political rationalization, not democratization'.[11] There has been some progress towards representation at village level. In 1979, after the collapse of the commune system, villagers in Guangxi created a village autonomy system and held elections. Village elections were formally introduced in 1987 under the Provisional Organic Law of Village Committees. In 1998, a New Organic Law of Village Committees provided for fairer and more open elections. It is usually accepted that the village leader is the party secretary, not the elected village head, but in some places the party secretary is now elected by party members and non-party villagers. In recent years some 600 to 900 million rural people have experienced semi-competitive elections. Nevertheless, the question of whether democracy can be fitted into a one-party state remains unanswered.

Market forces have changed economic and social structures and have brought sharp contrasts in the fortunes of various groups. For example, women, particularly older women, have borne the brunt of the layoffs in state enterprises. Nevertheless, a few women have become successful entrepreneurs, and top female graduates have challenged their male classmates in the pursuit of good jobs. Another consequence has been the rise of NGOs (non-governmental organizations). In 2001, according to official statistics, China had over 136,000 social organizations and 700,000 non-governmental and non-commercial enterprises. NGOs play an increasingly active role in economic and social development, but have almost no voice in political and religious issues. Since the 1990s the government has promoted certain types of NGO to support its reform agenda. However, all NGOs must follow the CCP's political ideology in order to exist.

The significance of the development of NGOs can be judged by reference to the All-China Women's Federation (AWCF). The Federation was formed in 1949 as a mass organization supporting and supported by the CCP. Until the 1980s, most of its staff were wives of CCP leaders and its primary task was obtaining women's participation in the CCP's socialist construction and political struggles. But then, with the introduction of major social and economic reforms, it began to change its objectives. At its 1988 National Assembly it defined its principal task as safeguarding the rights of women and children. It also made organizational changes, no longer serving as a government department in women's affairs and instead supporting the development of a network of female workers' committees within unions and women's friendship associations. The AWCF no longer relies exclusively on government funding and its staff members no longer enjoy civil servant status. In these respects the AWCF has achieved considerable autonomy, but it still gives its overt support to government policies, for example implementing birth-control policy and repressing the Falun Gong religious movement.[12]

THE PRESIDENCY OF HU JINTAO: POLITICS AND HUMAN RIGHTS

In November 2002, at the 16th National Congress of the CCP, the first peaceful and orderly leadership succession since the Communist revolution took place. The 'fourth generation', headed by Hu Jintao, had grown up during the Cultural Revolution. Many of its members were technocrats, economists or lawyers, rather than engineers like their predecessors. Hu became President in March 2003 and he and Premier Wen Jiabao have promoted a '*xiaokang* society'; that is, a society in which most people are moderately well off. The government's declared aim is not economic growth at all costs, but the promotion of measures which advance social equality and environmental protection. Its achievement of this aim depends on many factors, not least that of curbing corruption.

China's system of government, like all transitional systems, has not been able to escape corruption. Deng Xiaoping once commented that you cannot open the door without letting in a few flies. In the case of China, this has been more like a swarm. Corruption may take the form of the abuse of power for personal gain, for example doctors demanding fees for giving priority to certain medical services, teachers taking money for examination favours, minor officials extorting money from farmers by levying illegal taxes and the 'black whistles' of bribe-taking football referees. It may involve very senior officials, for example Liu Ketian, vice-governor of Liaoning, who in April 2005 was sentenced to 12 years in jail for taking bribes amounting to 1.3 million yuan. In recognition of the seriousness of the problem, in 2007 a National Bureau of Corruption Prevention was established to chase down the 'tigers', corrupt high-ranking officials, as opposed to the 'flies', officials in minor posts. An early success was the conviction of Chen Liangyu, the Shanghai Party boss, for involvement in a social security fund scandal.[13]

Recent reforms to the criminal justice system have guaranteed defendants the right to legal counsel before trial, and the presumption of innocence before conviction is now accepted. The absolute authority of the state over the individual has been diluted by allowing that, under certain circumstances, an individual can sue a government agency. In many other respects the law remains very harsh. In 2004, 90 per cent of the world's known executions took place in China. Amnesty International's monitoring system recorded that in 2006 1010 people had been executed, but the true figure was probably around 8000. That same year, perhaps in deference to world opinion and in anticipation of the Olympic Games, 'kill fewer, kill carefully' reforms were instituted, which gave the supreme court the right to overturn capital sentences handed down by lower courts. Only 'extremely vile criminals' were to be executed. Nevertheless, in 2008 reported executions numbered 1718.

* * *

Over the last two decades, progress on matters such as freedom of speech, fair trials and human rights has been limited. In 1993 Wei Jingsheng, the most prominent human rights activist in the Democracy Wall protests in 1978 and 1979, was set free as a gesture to support China's bid for the Olympic Games. That bid having failed, he was rearrested in December 1995 and given a further fourteen-year jail sentence. In November 1997, he was released on grounds of ill health and on condition that he went into exile in the United States. His release coincided with the temporary relaxation of control known as the 'Beijing Spring'. In March 1998 the government, perhaps prompted by the impending visit of President Clinton, signed the International Covenant for Civil and Political Rights, whereupon a number of political activists, headed by Wang Youcai, challenged the government by forming the China Democracy Party. For a few weeks this met openly, but immediately after Clinton's departure the party was harassed and its members put on trial, Wang Youcai being sentenced to eleven years' imprisonment. He was paroled on medical grounds in 2004 and allowed to go to the United States.

Since then, individuals and some small groups have challenged authority and have been labelled dissidents. The most common human rights issues they have taken up are freedom of expression, the rule of law, arbitrary detention, enforced disappearances and matters relating to Tibet and Xinjiang. In the past, their criticisms would have received short shrift. In recent years, the Party has presented suppression of dissidence as action taken as in the interests of the state and in accordance with the law. Occasionally it has paid some attention to international opinion.

What dissidents have campaigned for, and how they have been treated, can be illustrated by reference to four well-known dissidents. Lu Banglie from Hubei was a farmer and migrant worker who, after a disastrous harvest, petitioned central government to reduce the tax paid by his village. In 2003, he campaigned to remove the village chief who was accused of electoral irregularities and was elected in his place. In August 2005, he was asked by the villagers of Taishi in Guangdong to help them oust their village chief, who was accused of corruption. Taishi became a symbol for the fight for peasant rights, but Lu Banglie was beaten up, probably by thugs hired by the local authorities, and sent back to Hubei. In October 2007, it was reported that he had disappeared.

Liu Xiaobo, a former academic, spent twenty months in jail after the Tiananmen Square demonstrations and three years in a 're-education through labour' camp in the 1990s. In 2009, he went on trial on a charge of inciting the subversion of state power. This concerned his role in writing Charter 08, an appeal for democratic reform and greater civil liberties, which was modelled on Vaclav Havel's Charter 77 in Czechoslovakia. For this, Liu was sentenced to eleven years' imprisonment and two years' loss of political rights. In October 2010, to the fury of the Chinese government, he was awarded the Nobel peace prize for his 'long and non-violent struggle for fundamental human rights in China'.[14]

Gao Zhisheng, a Beijing human rights lawyer, acted in a number of controversial cases, including the implementation of family planning policies and offering legal help to Falun Gong practitioners. In 2006, he was given a three-year suspended sentence for subverting the state. On his release, he wrote an open letter describing how he had been tortured in jail. He later defended a man whose house had been requisitioned for the site of the Beijing Olympics. In February 2009, Gao Zhisheng disappeared from his home town in Shaanxi and his family fled to the United States. In March 2010, he contacted the media, saying that he had been living on Wutai mountain because he wanted a quiet life.

Until 2006, Hu Jia ran the Loving Source AIDS support NGO, but then resigned to become a full-time democracy activist. He is a Buddhist and an admirer of the Dalai Lama and has campaigned for an independent judiciary, free media and competing political parties, and has supported several environmental campaigns. In 2007 he was arrested with other human rights activists, and in 2008 he was imprisoned after he had protested against the Beijing Olympic Games.

* * *

The People's Liberation Army (PLA), with an estimated three million personnel, is the largest fighting force in the world. All men between the ages of 18 and 21 register for military service and men and women are liable to conscription, though in recent years high standards of education are required and only a minority of the draft is taken up. The PLA army today has sophisticated equipment and is well supplied with weapons. The Air Force has some 400,000 personnel and over 2000 combat aircraft and the navy has 225,000 personnel, 70 submarines, of which 10 are nuclear, and 72 combat ships.

China has intercontinental ballistic missiles with a single nuclear warhead capable of hitting targets in the United States, and is estimated to have between 100 and 200 nuclear warheads. Nevertheless, China has been wary of using its nuclear capacity as an overt threat. China acceded to the Nuclear Non-Proliferation Treaty in 1992 and to the Chemical Weapons Convention and the Comprehensive Test Ban Treaty in 1996. Recently China has played a role in limiting nuclear proliferation. In May 2010, Hu Jintao agreed to sanctions against Iran if it persisted in developing its nuclear capability.[15]

After Deng Xiaoping's death, the space programme was continued and accelerated. In September 1999, *Shenzhou* (Divine Vessel) 1, China's first unmanned spacecraft, was launched and on 15 October 2003, *Shenzhou* 5, with Yang Liwei on board, made fourteen orbits of the earth. When the success of this first manned flight was announced, China exploded with nationalistic fervour. In October 2007, China launched lunar explorer *Chang'e* 1, the first stage of a programme to put a man on the moon. The following year, *Shenzhou* 7 was launched for China's first spacewalk. There are plans to place an unmanned rover on the moon's surface by 2012 and a man on the moon before 2020.[16]

* * *

Xianggang was returned to China on 30 June 1997. Under the terms of the Sino-British Joint Declaration of 1984, which had agreed that there should be 'one country, two systems', Xianggang became a 'special administrative region' guaranteed an 'open and free plural society', with its own laws, institutions and freedoms, for fifty years. China rejected the progress the colony had made towards an elected government and arranged for its own candidate, Tung Chee-hwa, to succeed the governor as chief executive. Tung found it difficult to respond to both the dictates of Beijing and the hopes of the population of the former colony; having failed to get a new security law agreed, he resigned in March 2005, and was succeeded by Donald Tsang.

The political impasse over Tibet has continued. In 1996, the Dalai Lama proposed that Tibet should be granted 'genuine autonomy' within China, a proposal which was not accepted. An Amnesty International report of 2000 referred to the continuation of 'gross human rights violations' in Tibet, and Han immigration was cited as one of the main reasons for Tibetan discontent. According to the 2000 census, Han Chinese still number less than 6 per cent of the region's population, but in 'Greater Tibet' – the three historic Tibetan provinces of Amdo, Kham and U-Tsang – 7.5 million Chinese outnumber 6 million Tibetans. According to Chinese sources, tremendous changes have taken place in Tibet over the last fifty years. In 2005 the railway link to Lhasa through Qinghai was completed. This line is expected to bring 2.5 million tons of goods and a million visitors a year to Tibet. In old Tibet there were no modern schools, but in 2009 all Tibetan children received six years' compulsory education and in addition there were high schools and institutions of higher learning.[17]

Although the region's economy grew 13.8 per cent in 2007, tension rose because Tibetan nationalists felt that the benefits of investment were going to Chinese settlers. The approach of the Beijing Olympics gave them an opportunity to publicize their campaign. In March 2008, a demonstration in Lhasa commemorating the 49th anniversary of China's military intervention and the Dalai Lama's flight to India led to an outburst of violence and dozens of Chinese were reported to have been killed. China accused the Dalai Lama of instigating the violence, but the following month it agreed to meet his envoys, claiming that it was always willing to talk to him if he recognized Tibet as part of China and renounced violence. In February 2010, US President Obama risked China's wrath by meeting the Dalai Lama, but the talks were kept low profile and the Dalai Lama was referred to as Tibet's 'spiritual leader'.

At present, the separatist movement involving the Uighur in Xinjiang (properly the Xinjiang Uighur Autonomous Region) is seen by the Chinese government as posing a greater threat to China's territorial integrity than events in Tibet. The break-up of the Soviet Union, and the creation of the republics of Tajikistan, Kyrgystan and Kazakhstan, all of which have a common boundary with China, encouraged the revival of a Uighur separatist movement. In 1996, the Presidents of China, Russia, and the three new republics met in Shanghai to agree policies on 'Muslim extremists' and drug trafficking in the area. The following year there were large-scale demonstrations in Ili, which were crushed brutally. After the 11 September 2001 attack on the World Trade Center in New York, China took further steps against separatists in Xinjiang, claiming that Uighur were involved in the al-Qaida network. Reports from Human Rights Watch alleged that the Chinese government was using the fear of international terrorism to justify carrying out a systematic persecution of Uighur Muslims.[18]

In July 2009, riots described as 'the worst race riots in modern Chinese history' broke out in Urumqi. Under a government scheme to encourage migration from poor western provinces to rich eastern provincess, some 200,000 Uighurs had moved east to find work. Uighur exiles denounced this as a plot to deprive Xinjiang of its oil, gas, coal and young people – particularly young women. In May 2009 a large group of Uighurs started work at a toy factory in Shanguan, Guangdong. Their presence led to friction with the Chinese work force, to allegations of rape and to the killing of two Uighurs. News of these events was relayed to Urumqi. Violent clashes occurred which left 156 dead, most of whom were Chinese. The Chinese government alleged that the clashes had been planned by the World Uighur Congress and that Rebiya Kadeer was involved. On the ground, the issue was a complex mix of Uighur resentment of Han Chinese immigration, and Han Chinese resentment of the affirmative action policies in favour of the Uighur. The Chinese government tried to arbitrate a peaceful settlement and both Uighur and Han Chinese were prosecuted for their role in the riots.[19]

The relationship between China and Taiwan remains problematic. Mainland China's policy has long been that Taiwan might become a special region of China with its own system of government. The Democratic Progressive Party (DPP), which won the 2000 election, called for the total independence of Taiwan. In the 2008 elections the DPP was accused of corruption and swept aside by a revitalized Guomindang Party headed by Ma Ying-jeou. The new government was committed to reviving the economy and improving the relationship with the People's Republic. Today, travel and commercial intercourse between China and Taiwan have been freed up. Mainland China is Taiwan's most important market and most important destination for investment. Since the 1990s, a new Taiwanese identity has been forged. Many young Taiwanese regard themselves as members of a new independent nation with its own culture and history.[20]

THE ECONOMY AND THE ENVIRONMENT

Over the last thirty years, the most striking feature of China's record has been the headlong pace of economic growth. Between 1978 and 2005, China's real GDP grew at an average annual rate of 9.5 per cent. Before the end of that period, China had overtaken the United States as the world's largest recipient of foreign capital. The growth in industrial output was based, in the first instance, on the manufacture for export of low-technology products, including clothing, especially socks and shoes, and items such as zips, toothbrushes and children's toys. However, by 2005 China was manufacturing 25 per cent of the world's washing machines and 50 per cent of the world's cameras. The country had overtaken the United States in sales of television sets and mobile phones and was expected shortly to become the world's largest market for computers. Between 1978 and 2003 China's exports rose from US $8.8 billion to US $438 billion, of which 40 per cent went to the United States. In 2004 the United States had a trade deficit with China amounting to US $162 billion, the largest imbalance ever recorded with a single country. The United States has claimed that this imbalance derived from an artificially low exchange rate, which from 1995 was pegged at 8.27 yuan to the dollar and in July 2005 was slightly revalued at 8.11 yuan to the dollar. In 2008, to help Chinese exporters during the downturn in the world economy, the yuan was pegged to the dollar at a rate of 6.83. This was still regarded as too low, and in June 2010 China agreed to allow more flexibility in its currency.

Alongside the domestic expansion of the economy, China has invested heavily overseas to secure sources of raw materials, most importantly oil. In the Sudan, by 2005, China had acquired a

41 per cent stake in the national oil consortium as part of total investments of about £8 billion. During the Cold War, China had built the Tazara railway to link Zambia's copper belt with Dar es Salaam. In subsequent years the railway deteriorated and the copper industry declined. However, by 2006 the Chambishi copper mine was re-established with Chinese capital and was producing 50,000 tons of copper concentrates per annum. The China-Henan International Corporation was building roads in Zambia and many Chinese farmers had bought land there and were employing Zambians as labourers.[21] China has used its enormous trade surpluses to invest in other fields, for example in food production. By 2005, Brazil was a leading supplier of protein to China, in the form of soya bean. China has also used a fraction of its vast holdings of foreign currency to buy stakes in Western industries, for example purchasing Volvo, the Swedish car firm, in 2010.

Since the beginning of the twenty-first century, a construction boom in China has prompted a rapid growth in retail sales. Over 400 massive shopping centres have been opened, including the Golden Resources mall in West Beijing, which claims to have more than 1000 shops. There has been a sharp rise in the purchase of luxury items, ranging from Rolls-Royce cars to Prada shoes. This trend has prompted Credit Suisse First Boston to predict that by 2015, 'Chinese consumers will likely have displaced United States' consumers as the primary engine of global and economic growth'.[22] The growth is not confined to China, but is a feature of Greater China, a term used to refer to mainland China, including Xianggang, and Taiwan, which together have developed an integrated economy which now rivals the economies of the United States, Japan and the European Union.

By 2006, serious concerns were being voiced in the West about the extremely rapid growth of China's economy and of China's economic expansion overseas. It was suggested that the Chinese economy was overheating and this seemed probable when in 2007 the annual inflation rate tripled. But then in August 2007, the United States' subprime market collapsed, triggering a world banking crisis and recession. In 2008, with the decline of world trade, China's growth target was cut to 8 per cent per annum, a rate lower than that needed to provide jobs for new entrants to the labour market. The Chinese government injected 4 trillion yuan into the economy. However, the economic downturn and closure of factories left as many as 23 million migrant workers jobless. Some economists in the West suggested that the continued expansion of the Chinese economy would help bring the world out of recession. That is only conjecture, but it is true that after a short period of hesitation the Chinese economy continued to surge ahead. In August 2009, China announced a massive expansion of its high-speed rail links, which would create six million jobs. In January 2010, China overtook Germany as the world's largest exporter, and later that year China overtook Japan to become the world's second-largest economy.

An analysis of the characteristics of China's growth since 1979 would emphasize the development of the rural non-farming sector, and in particular of the rural township, village and private enterprises (TVPs), a feature of the Chinese economy identified as the source of China's economic 'miracle'. Rapid growth in this sector began with the introduction of the household responsibility system in 1981. A combination of private initiative and cheap labour accelerated growth, and the importance of TVPs was recognized in 1991 when the government ceased to discriminate against the nonpublic economy. By 2002, rural industry employed twice as many people as in the state sector. An outstanding example of success is the Haier company, based at Qingdao, which by 2008 was the fourth largest white goods manufacturer in the world.[23]

The liberalization of foreign trade and foreign investment has widened the urban–rural economic gap and has advantaged coastal provinces at the expense of inland ones. According to most estimates, mean per capita income in urban China is more than triple that in rural areas, one of the highest urban–rural income ratios in the world. Economic growth has lifted millions out of poverty and has enabled some entrepreneurs to make their fortune. However, millions of people, most of whom live in rural areas, still subsist on incomes equivalent to less than US $1 a day. One way of relieving their poverty has been to move to cities to find work, and from 1988, with the removal of restrictions, internal migration rose sharply. In 2001 the *hukou* or household registration system was further reformed and the rural-to-urban migration quota was abolished. However, although rural migrants can work in the cities, they live in designated areas and do not enjoy facilities, for example in education, equal to those of holders of urban *hukou*.

By 2006 the 'floating population', the transient migrants in urban centres, numbered between 80 and 120 million people. Many of the men work on building sites and in factories. Women, who comprise over a third of the migrants, work as poorly paid waitresses, maids, cleaners and prostitutes. Both men and women are paid irregularly and work long hours. The provisions of China's labour law, in effect since 1994, which sets out employers' responsibilities in terms of the length of the working week, overtime and the minimum wage, are widely ignored. Most migrants live in collective dormitories provided by their work unit or on construction sites. Most women workers are young. Their stay in urban factories lasts four to five years and they then return to their villages to get married. Much of their wage is remitted home. In 1997, migrant labourers from the poor inland province of Guizhou remitted home 5 billion yuan, a sum equivalent to 10 per cent of the province's gross domestic product.[24]

*   *   *

Rural protest, villagers protesting against officials whom they accuse of dishonest or unjust actions, has a long history in China. In recent years protests have occurred more frequently – it is claimed that there were 87,000 protests in 2005 – and have been on a larger scale and better organized. The most common cause of protest is the compulsory purchase of land from villagers for urban development. For example, in September 2004 the villagers of Xiangyang and three neighbouring villages in Guangdong province discovered that officials from the nearby town of Yunfu had seized 132,000 square metres of their land, ostensibly for the construction of a municipal power station. They dispatched petitioners to Beijing to argue their case, but in vain. This scenario has been repeated frequently all over China, the accusations usually being levelled against local cadres who are suspected of having profited from land deals. Decollectivization and the development of the market economy have made villagers wealthier, and the end of class labelling and mass political campaigns has made them less fearful. Protesters have become adept at using mobile phones to co-ordinate protests. They claim, with justification, that the law is on their side. Nevertheless, protests frequently fail, either because officials may use either legal or illegal methods to suppress the movement, or because the events which led to the protest cannot be reversed.[25]

Differences in education levels contribute 25 to 30 per cent of the gap.[26] Chinese children are entitled to nine years' free education, but not all are able to enjoy that entitlement owing to the effects of the *hukou*, the household registration system. The children of migrant labourers may be left with relatives in their home villages and go to school there. However, some 19 million children are living with their parents in the cities. State schools receive no funding for migrant children and as a consequence, many do not go to school at all. At the other end of the educational scale, China now spends 1.5 per cent of its GDP on higher education and more than 5 million students are enrolled on degree courses. China's top universities now aim to rank with, if not exceed, the most prestigious universities in the Western world.[27]

Concern over increasing rural–urban economic inequality played a part in bringing about a significant change in economic priorities in the new five-year economic programme announced in 2006. This promised to create a 'new socialist countryside' by increasing rural investment and agricultural subsidies by 20 per cent. So much agricultural land had been lost to industrial use that urgent measures were needed to preserve 120 million hectares for farming and to set a target of 500 million tons of grain a year, the amount required for national self-sufficiency. At the same time, peasants' main grievance, the agricultural tax, would be phased out and social services improved, by providing free education for rural children and an insurance scheme to subsidize medicare for those too poor to pay for treatment.

* * *

A major concern relating to China's recent spectacular economic growth has been the effect that this is having on the environment and the future quality of life. It has been estimated that one fifth of all crop land in China is suffering from heavy metal pollution. This has been blamed for an explosion in lead-poisoning cases and a dramatic rise in cancer. A high proportion of China's energy needs are supplied by burning unwashed coal, which has resulted in high particle levels and high levels of sulphur dioxide, causing severe atmospheric pollution in some cities. An extremely rapid increase in car ownership – in 2009 more new cars were sold in China than in the United States – has exacerbated the situation. Not only is the atmosphere polluted, China's water supplies are compromised. In 2007, the water quality of a third of the length of all China's rivers and three-quarters of lakes was described as 'heavily polluted'.

In 2004, China emitted 4.7 billion tons of carbon dioxide and was expected soon to exceed United States' emissions. Though not a party to the Kyoto Protocol, in July 2005 China made an agreement with India, the United States and South Korea to cut greenhouse gas emissions, and alternative energy programmes, notably the use of solar energy, were to be developed rapidly. In 2006, China announced a campaign to combat desertification, in particular the encroachment of the Gobi and Taklamakan deserts, a consequence of climate change and industrial demands for water, by planting 12 billion trees in the Great Green Wall project.

As the 2010 Copenhagen conference on climate change approached, China anticipated that the rapid growth of its carbon emissions would lead to international pressure to commit to significant reductions. To counter this, in November 2009 Hu Jintao promised a 45 per cent reduction in carbon intensity by 2020. At the conference, China blocked any proposal to cut emissions that threatened its capacity to expand, asserting that it had been agreed that developed countries should be set compulsory emission-reduction targets and developing nations would take voluntary mitigating actions. After the conference, there were accusations that China had deliberately wrecked any climate deal.

Construction of the Three Gorges Dam project, the extraordinarily ambitious programme promoted by Li Peng to control the Yangzi river, began in 1992. The reservoir started filling in 2002 and the turbines are now generating electricity. The main benefits of the project have been identified as flood control, the construction of the world's largest hydroelectric generating plant and improved navigation to Chongqing. The social costs include the relocation of over one million people and the destruction of up to 800 historic sites. Critics have suggested that there are risks of earthquake damage, pollution and erosion, and that several smaller dams along the Yangzi would have achieved comparable advantages without the dangers involved in implementing so vast a project. When the project was completed in 2006, it was cited as a textbook example of how not to build a dam. The hydroelectric scheme was threatened by silt, species of freshwater fish were endangered and there had been little consultation over the project. In 2001 another enormous undertaking, the South–North Water Diversion Scheme, was given the go-ahead. This is a 50-year, $62 billion plan to channel water on three main routes from the Yangzi to the Yellow river. The project is still in its early stages, but has already encountered major difficulties.[28]

* * *

For some years, commentators in the West have doubted whether China can maintain its headlong economic progress and have suggested that the country is heading for disaster. In 2002, Gordon Chang published *The Coming Collapse of China*, which cited the problems of state-owned enterprises, the burdens which their problems placed on banks, widespread corruption and the incapacity of the Communist Party to implement essential reforms as reasons for anticipating an early and catastrophic collapse. His views have been dismissed as exaggerated and ill informed, and there is no sign of imminent collapse. However, a more cautious and better-grounded assessment by Sung Yun-wing drew attention to serious underlying problems relating to China's economy. He argued that the spectacular economic growth 'is so inefficient that it is unsustainable'. The country is extremely wasteful in its use of energy and raw materials, and has become dependent on imports of petroleum and other essential supplies.[29] There are major structural and social problems which need to be addressed urgently, for example income maldistribution, regional inequality, corruption and the pressing need to reform services and banking. Chris Bramall, in an exhaustive survey of China's recent economic record, accepts that there has been a rapid increase in material living standards, but notes this has been achieved at a heavy human cost. For him, China has 'a capitalist system as vicious and malevolent as anything that has been seen across the globe'. An urban elite has emerged which has no intention of giving up its riches to the peasantry, and there is endemic discrimination against women and naked exploitation of China's colonies, Xinjiang and Tibet.[30]

SOCIETY AND THE ARTS

In 2000 China's population reached 1.266 billion, with well over one third of the total living in towns and cities. The one-child family policy was being applied, but in a modified form, with most rural families being allowed to have two children whereas in the cities one child was the norm. By the 1990s, ultrasound equipment capable of foetal sex determination was widely available and this had a marked effect on the sex ratio at birth. In 1995 there were 117.4 males born for every 100 females.[31] Today, the one-child family policy continues to cause controversy, for it has become symptomatic of the wealth gap. Wealthy families can afford to pay the fines for breaking the rules. In January 2008, for example, the footballer Hao Haidong was fined 50,000 yuan (£3500) for having a second child. His annual salary was 5 million yuan.

In the last thirty years China has experienced a 'demographic change of historic proportions'. Recent figures indicate that life expectancy for women has risen to nearly 75 years and for men to 71 years. By 2020, 11.8 per cent of the population will be over 65 years old. In 2007 the total fertility rate fell to 1.75, well below the level of 2.1 required to replace a population.[32] According to the Centre for Strategic and International Studies, by 2050 China will have 438 million people over the age of 60. Each would have just 1.6 working-age adults to support him or her, compared with 7.7 adults in 1975. In Shanghai the fertility rate has dropped to 0.88. In 2009 the city authorities, worried about the lack of young workers and an ageing population, announced the end of the one-child rule and urged couples to have a second baby.[33]

Until 1980, health care in rural areas was provided by communes and in urban areas by the factories and other enterprises where people were employed. Since that date, with decollectivization and the break-up of state-owned enterprises, for the most part health care has been privatized. It is against this background that the government's response to recent health crises should be assessed. The first and as yet the most serious is that of HIV/AIDS. HIV was first reported in Beijing in 1985. The condition was explained as a consequence of contact with the West and was called the 'loving capitalism disease'. By 1988, HIV had been reported in all 31 provinces, autonomous regions and municipalities. Then in 2000, a major scandal emerged in Henan: the sale of blood and blood products by poor peasants to illegal blood-processing companies, thereby infecting some 300,000 people. Only in 2003 did the government admit the seriousness of the situation. Hu Jintao and Wen Jiabao met people with AIDS, the national budget for diagnosis and treatment was increased, international donations were accepted and some non-governmental organizations were allowed to get involved in the campaign to control the condition. The government started a belated programme of education, advocating the use of condoms, supplying clean needles for drug addicts and providing some anti-retroviral drugs for HIV/AIDS patients. In 2007, UNAIDS estimated that between 390,000 and 1,100,000 adults aged 15 and over were living with

HIV in China and that between 90,000 and 310,000 deaths were due to HIV/AIDS, but that only 25 per cent of adults infected with HIV were receiving anti-retroviral therapy.[34]

Other recent health crises have raised concerns about the government's ability to deal with this type of challenge. In November 2002, cases of SARS (severe acute respiratory syndrome) were identified in Guangdong. Before the infection could be contained, there had been over 5000 cases of SARS in China and another 1700 in Xianggang, leading to more than 600 deaths. Passengers on aeroplanes took the disease worldwide, with cases reported in Australia, Canada and several other countries. The slow response to the outbreak of the disease led to a severe loss of confidence in the Chinese health authorities, both in China and abroad. Another crisis arose over the spread of the avian flu virus H5N1. In 1997, it was reported in Xianggang that avian flu had been transmitted to a human. The authorities responded by ordering a cull of 1.2 million chickens. In 2003, an outbreak of avian flu was reported in Vietnam which by February 2005 had caused 54 deaths. Then in May 2005, a flock of migrating geese in Qinghai was found to be infected with avian flu. The Chinese government ordered a campaign of compulsory vaccination of all poultry in the province. China has the world's biggest poultry population and the threat of further outbreaks of avian flu, with the risk of transmission of the virus from human to human, remains a major concern.

In September 2008, it was reported that 13,000 Chinese babies were in hospital after consuming milk powder contaminated with melamine, which had been added to increase the apparent protein content. The incident raised serious questions about the safety of Chinese food products. Sanlu, the main company involved, was forced into bankruptcy, a farmer and a milk salesman were executed, and a new food safety committee was formed to deal with widespread accusations of food contamination.

A separate health issue is an epidemic of obesity on a scale comparable to that occurring in the West. In 2008, it was estimated that there were 184 million people overweight in China and 31 million classified as obese. The threat is particularly evident among children of wealthy families living in urban areas. Here the single-child policy and the adoption of a fattier Western diet have resulted in a sharp rise in the number of obese children, with Shanghai having an obesity rate among primary school children of 15.2 per cent.[35]

China continues to pay a heavy price for natural and man-made disasters. In April 2008, an earthquake measuring 7.9 on the Richter scale hit Sichuan, causing 87,000 deaths and displacing 4.8 million people. In 1976, when the Tangshan earthquake occurred, China did not accept foreign assistance, but after the Sichuan earthquake teams of foreign specialists worked alongside Chinese emergency workers. The impression given to the world media was that the Chinese government had dealt efficiently with the effects of a natural disaster. However, when it emerged that a large proportion of the victims were children and that they had died in shoddily built schools, there was a public outcry, which was quickly suppressed.[36]

China still has a very high number of workplace accidents. In 2009 over 83,000 people died at work, or in road traffic accidents, the most dangerous occupation being coal mining.[37] In 2002, 6995 people were recorded as having died in mining accidents, though the figure was probably much higher because many accidents occurred in small, illegal mines. Since then, many small mines have been closed under the government's 'industrial consolidation programme'. By 2009, the official figure for mining accidents had fallen to 2631 deaths. However, in April 2010, 153 men were trapped underground by a flood at the huge Wangjialing mine in Shanxi. This incident would have cast serious doubts about the benefits of the consolidation programme but for the rescue of 115 of those trapped after eight days underground. In May 2010, the government announced that it was to invest nearly 500 billion yuan to reduce the country's notorious industrial accident rate.[38]

* * *

Over the last twenty years there has been an extraordinary outburst of creative activity across the whole field of the arts, even though the censorship of films and literature remains common practice. With reference to the cinema, China's best-known film-makers, Chen Kaige and Zhang Yimou, members of the 'Fifth Generation', have had their films banned, although in 1999, in a reversal of fortune, the government made Zhang Yimou's film *Not One Less*, which described the difficulties experienced by a primary school teacher, required viewing. Lou Ye, the new *enfant terrible* of the cinema, was given a two-year ban for his thriller *Suzhou River.* For *Summer Palace* (2006), a film which contained sex and full frontal nudity, the ban was extended to five years. The true reason for the ban was because the plot pivoted around the events of 1989.

In recent years there has been a tremendous outpouring of literature in China, much of it acceptable to the authorities, but a significant fraction critical of recent events. The critical literature, often in the form of novels, comes from authors whose books have been banned. Many of them have chosen to live abroad. The most distinguished of these is Gao Xingjian, whose *Soul Mountain* (1989), part memoir, part novel, described the author's long journey along the Yangzi 'to find the origin of Chinese culture, the source that had not yet been polluted by politics'. In 2000, he became the first Chinese writer to be awarded the Nobel prize for literature. More sharply critical of events in modern China are the novels of Ha Jin, who since 1985 has lived in the United States and who writes in English. In *Waiting* (1999) he described the life of an officer in the People's Liberation Army who had gone through an arranged marriage, but who then fell in love with a nurse in the hospital where he worked. In another novel, *War Trash* (2004), he recounted the experiences of Chinese soldiers captured in the Korean War and their reception on release. One of the most controversial novels of recent years is *Beijing Coma* (2008), by Ma Jian. In it the paralysed protagonist looks back over events in modern China, culminating in the Tiananmen Square massacre.

The fault line between literature which is acceptable to the authorities in China and the writings of dissidents abroad was exposed in October 2009, when China was invited as the 'guest of honour' to the Frankfurt Book Fair. Critics claimed that this would indicate acceptance of Chinese censorship. Ma Jian commented: 'There is little need for literary censors these days … Chinese fiction is in the main a fiction of compromise.' Ai Weiwei, the dissident artist, said that publishing was the most damaged area of expression in China and that 99 per cent of Chinese writers would not be read in a free society. However, such is the demand in the West for books about China that a compromise was reached, with events at the fair being split between 'official' and 'independent' strands.

During the Cultural Revolution, Western music had been condemned as bourgeois and musicians were singled out for contemptuous treatment. Ye Xiaogang, a leading composer and artistic director of the Beijing Modern Music festival, whose father, also a composer, attempted suicide during Cultural Revolution, described the trauma of those years as 'a giant fault line, ripping through China's musical life'. Nevertheless, classical music has made an astonishing comeback. The pianist Lang Lang has acquired an international reputation and played at the Nobel Peace Prize ceremony for Barack Obama. In China today, some 20 million children are learning the piano and 10 million the violin. In December 2006, the conductor Tan Dun conducted his opera *The First Emperor* at the New York Met. The emperor was played by Placido Domingo and the music attempted to combine, but not to fuse, Western and Chinese techniques. At the other end of the scale, in October 2007 Li Yuchun was voted winner of the Supergirl talent show. Dressed like a tomboy, she sings aggressive, loud songs to audiences of up to 400 million people. However, traditional music, in particular music played on traditional instruments, is in decline, despite efforts to reinvigorate it; for example, Wu Na has played jazz on the *guqin*, the Chinese zither.

The visual arts have experienced some striking developments and have provoked a curious reaction from the government. After the Tiananmen demonstrations in 1989, Beijing's radical artists relocated to the East Village, beyond the city's third ring road. Later the area was bulldozed and in 2001 the community had moved to a machine-tool plant known as Factory 798. There the government sanctioned a cultural quarter and permitted international investment, in the process transmogrifying itself from enemy to champion of free-thinking artistic culture. In March 2007, 'The Real Thing: Contemporary Art from China' opened at the Tate Liverpool in the UK, which led a critic to comment: 'China arguably has the most vital, imaginative and uncontainable art scene in the world today.' It is now quite difficult to provoke the authorities into closing an artistic exhibition, as the Chinese government seeks to co-opt contemporary art to advertise the productivity and tolerance of the new China.[39] Nevertheless, Ai Weiwei, China's most famous artist and contributor to the design of the Bird's Nest Olympic stadium, remains defiantly anti-establishment. His installation 'Sunflower Seeds', 100,000,000 hand-painted porcelain seeds spread over an area of 1000 square metres, went on display in London's Tate Modern Turbine Hall in October 2010.

*   *   *

Television broadcasting began in China in 1958 and television viewing surged in the 1980s. By 2000, some 1.1 billion people were watching television and China had the largest television network in the world. National television is dominated by China Central Television and the content of television broadcasting is monitored by the Propaganda Department of the Chinese Communist Party. China's first email was sent overseas in September 1987 and since then the use of the internet and of mobile phones has rocketed. By 2010, China Mobile claimed to have 518 million subscribers, about 70 per cent of the market. The Chinese government has encouraged these developments, believing that the use of information and communication technology will enable China to perform a 'developmental leapfrog', thereby accelerating the economic growth on which it has pinned its legitimacy.[40]

However, the government wants the benefits of information and communication technology while not losing its authoritarian grip. To prevent the dissemination of material regarded as politically suspect, it has created an 'internet police force', said to have about 30,000 members. With assistance from the United States' companies Microsoft and Google, it developed the 'Great Firewall', the most sophisticated internet control on earth. Banned phrases from news sites, blogs and instant messaging include independence, democracy, Taiwan, Tiananmen Square, freedom and the Dalai Lama. All bloggers and hosts of internet chat shows have to register with the authorities. These controls may be easy to circumvent, but journalists, editors and internet service providers choose to abide by the rules and to self-censor to stay in business. In 2008, just before the Beijing Olympics, there was some relaxation of the blocking of sites such as Amnesty International and Human Rights Watch. Chinese authorities threatened to install 'Green Dam' internet-filtering software on all computers from July 2009 to 'curb access to pornography', but in the following month the plan was shelved. In January 2010 the Google search engine, which had about one third of the market in China (the other two-thirds being claimed by the Chinese search engine Baidu), announced that it was withdrawing from China because it was no longer willing to censor search results on its Chinese website.

* * *

Under the 1954 constitution, the people of China were guaranteed freedom of religion on the condition that links with foreign churches were broken. According to Marxist theory, religion is supposed to wither away as socialism is established, but since the 1980s religious traditions in many parts of China have revived. There are government-approved forms of the five major religions. The National Daoist Association has presided over a resurgence of Daoism and the first ordinations of priests since the 1949 revolution were held in 1989. After 1949 Buddhist monasteries were destroyed, Buddhist land confiscated and many Buddhist monks and nuns were forced to return to lay life. However, a Chinese Buddhist Association has in recent years encouraged Buddhist studies and Buddhist monks again perform rituals at funerals. For the 20 million Muslims in China, there has been some relaxation of control; in the late 1990s over 6000 Chinese pilgrims went to Mecca.

As for Christianity, in 1949 Pope Pius XII forbade Catholics to co-operate with the new regime. A government-supported Catholic Patriotic Association was formed, but most Catholics refused to co-operate with it, Catholic leaders were imprisoned and most Catholics remained loyal to the Vatican. Nowadays there are between 10 million and 12 million Roman Catholics in China. Although some reconciliation has taken place recently between the official and unofficial branches of Catholicism, the standoff continues. Chinese Protestants are required to adhere to the Three Self Patriotic Movement, the state-sanctioned Protestant church in mainland China. However, most worship is in unofficial 'house churches'. According to recent estimates, there are between 25 million and 30 million Protestants. On any given Sunday, there are probably more Protestants in church in China than in all of Europe.

Many popular religious sects have revived and new ones have emerged. Among them are local community religions such as the cult of the Silkworm Mother in a village in Hebei province. In the 1990s two new sects, Zhong Gong and Falun Gong, which interwove traditional religious themes with *qigong* (systems of physical and mental training), gained large numbers of followers. At first their activities were tolerated, but in 1999 a large crowd of Falung Gong adherents demonstrated in Tiananmen Square and this triggered off a sharp episode of religious persecution. Around 50,000 members of Falun Gong were arrested, some 1200 of whom were Party cadres, and a vigorous campaign against their beliefs was launched. In January 2001 five members of Falun Gong, including a 12-year-old girl and her mother, set fire to themselves in Tiananmen Square, an act which enabled the government to condemn the movement as evil. Since then, Falun Gong has made extensive use of the internet to recruit members and to canvass for sympathy overseas.[41]

* * *

No survey of recent developments in China would be complete without reference to tourism and sport. In both instances, developments over the last thirty years, and in particular over the last decade, indicate a remarkable change in China's relationship with the outside world. Since the early 1970s, travel restriction on visitors to China have been lifted. In 1995 it was estimated that about 45 million visitors had come to China, of whom about 36 million were overseas Chinese, and that these visits had earned US $4.6 billion. By 2001 these figures had risen to 89 million visitors, earning US $17.8 billion. Domestic tourism has also increased sharply and some destinations have set restrictions; for example Jiuzhaigou, Nine Village Valley, in Sichuan, which was listed as an UNESCO World Heritage Site in 1992, has limited entry to a maximum of 28,000 tourists a day.[42] In 2005, China surpassed Italy as a tourist destination and it is estimated that by 2020 China will be the world's most popular destination. Until recently, Chinese could only travel abroad for business or study, but in 2005 the United Kingdom was granted approved destination status and 95,000 visitors from China arrived. By 2020, it is expected that Chinese will be among the top five nationalities coming to Britain.

China's involvement in modern sporting activity dates back to 1895, when the YMCA representative David Willard Lyon arrived in Tianjin. His arrival coincided with China's defeat in the war with Japan, a defeat which provoked a demand for the development of *shangwu*, a warlike spirit. This, it was believed, could be stimulated by the introduction of modern physical education and competitive sport. The value of sporting achievement in promoting the nation-state was recognized by the Republican government in the 1930s. However, the spread of football and other sports was delayed by war, revolution and then the Cultural Revolution. Only in the 1980s did professional sport begin to gain a large following and since then progress has been extremely rapid. Professional football leagues were established in 1994 and in 2002 China qualified for the World Cup. A super league was formed in 2004 and football matches attract large crowds and enormous television audiences. However, the sport has been marred by frequent allegations of corruption.

Alongside football and athletics, other sports have expanded rapidly. There are over 200 golf courses in China and many more under construction. China has earned a formidable reputation in table tennis and tennis is attracting an increasing following. Recently a craze for snooker has swept China. When in April 2005, Ding Junhui became the first Chinese snooker player to win a world-ranking event, it was estimated that 100 million people watched the match on television.

After the founding of the People's Republic of China, Beijing and Taipei treated sport as a vehicle for asserting their political legitimacy. In 1971, Zhou Enlai used the world table tennis championship being held in Japan to improve relations with United States; the visit of the United States' ping-pong team to China later that year initiated moves which led to Nixon's visit to China in 1972. A key issue was the representation of China at the Olympic Games and the 1976 Montreal Games nearly foundered on this issue. China participated in the 1984 Los Angeles Games and won its first gold medal. When in 2001 China bid successfully for the 2008 Olympics, the editorial of *Xinhua* commented:

> [this] is another milestone in China's efforts to enhance its international status ... the competition for hosting the Olympic Games is a test of a country's comprehensive international power, economic potential, scientific strength, and cultural attraction ... Whoever wins the bid has won the respect, trust and love of the world community.[43]

At the 2004 Athens Olympic Games, China won only slightly fewer gold medals than the United States. Xiang Lu's victory in the men's 110 metres hurdles in a time equalling the world record attracted global attention. Chinese women also won an impressive number of medals. Success for them in badminton and table tennis was not unexpected, but for a Chinese woman to win the 10,000 metres was a notable achievement.

In 2005, detailed plans for the 2008 Olympics were revealed. The cost was put at $40 billion, 200 miles of new streets were to be built in Beijing and 90 miles of new rail track were to be constructed. Norman Foster was to design a new airport terminal for Beijing and twelve new venues, including the Bird's Nest stadium and the Water Cube aquatic centre, were to be built. The slogan of the games was to be 'One World One Dream'.

When the Games were awarded to China, the conflicting claims of China's national prestige and international concerns relating to human rights in China were to dominate much of the debate. In April 2001, when China's bid for the Games was being adjudged, Liu Jingmin, vice-president of the Beijing 2008 Olympic Games Bid Committee, claimed 'by allowing Beijing to host the Games you will help the development of human rights'. However, in 2008 *Amnesty Magazine* declared that with less that a hundred days to go to the Games, a wave of repression had been instigated.[44] The 85,000-mile Olympic torch relay was subject to violent attacks in London and Paris, and there were threats to the proposal to take the Olympic flame up Mount Everest. In July 2008, the authorities set up three 'protest zones' in parks around Beijing, where protesters could express grievances as long as they had prior permission from the police. Nobody was given permission. Criticism was voiced about the displacement of tens of thousands of Beijingers because of the construction boom. Since Beijing is one of the most polluted cities in the world, work on construction projects during the Olympics was banned. Beijing's 3.3 million vehicles were only allowed on the road on alternate days during the Games.

The Games themselves were an extraordinary success. The opening ceremony, choreographed by film director Zhang Yimou, 'outdid all predecessors in numbers, colour, noise and expense'.[45] Athletes had come from 204 countries, including Palestine and 'Chinese Taipei'. The popular Chinese response to the Games was that of Cao Xiqing, aged 22, who said: 'This shows the greatness of our 5000 year history. I'm so proud I was born Chinese.' At the end of the Games, China headed the medal table with 51 golds.

* * *

The Beijing Olympics were always more than just a sporting competition. They were intended to showcase 'China's economic, technological, cultural, social and environmental achievements to the rest of the world'. They set the agenda for how China would be understood both within the country and throughout the world. In so doing, they still begged the question: What is, and what is not, the 'real China'?[46]

If it is difficult to summarize where China stands now, it is impossible to predict where this vast political entity will have progressed to over the next decades. In a recent study, David Shambaugh described the state of the Chinese Communist Party as a mixture of atrophy and adaptation. He compared political developments in former Communist states in eastern Europe with those in China and found many common symptoms of Party atrophy. However, he noted that in the 1990s the CCP had adapted to new circumstances and this had enabled it to survive. In 2009 it had 74 million members, up from

50 million in the 1990s. It no longer concerned itself with mass mobilization of the proletariat but with a 'technocratic leadership corps'. Alongside this development, Chinese citizens have carved out greater, variable space to criticize low-ranking officials, engage in public affairs, debate ideas and take part in emerging civil society. This, it is claimed, amounts to 'democracy with Chinese characteristics' – but it is not clear what that means.[47]

In May 2010, the Shanghai Expo 2010 opened. The city-wide makeover it entailed had cost £27 billion, including three new subway lines and a new air terminal. Nearly 200 countries were represented and the Expo was expected to receive more than 70 million visitors. Its ostensible purpose was to attract business on a massive scale. A Western critic commented that the real intention was to distract people from depressing issues: unemployment, the cost of living, official corruption and incompetence, access to good health care and escalating house prices. However, that is not how the average Chinese saw it. A sugarcane seller on the site said that she had been counting down the days until the Expo opened, commenting: 'It's the biggest thing that's happened in my lifetime.'[48]

Notes

CHAPTER 1

1. Robin Dennell, *The Palaeolithic Settlement of Asia* (Cambridge: Cambridge University Press, 2009), pp. 174–85.
2. Dennell, p. 399.
3. Kwang-chih Chang, 'China on the eve of the historical period', in Michael Loewe and Edward L. Shaughnessy (eds), *The Cambridge History of Ancient China* (Cambridge: Cambridge University Press, 1999), pp. 37–73.
4. See, for example, Pingfang Xu, 'Epilogue', in Kwang-chih Chang, Xu Pingfang, Lu Liancheng, et al., *The Formation of Chinese Civilization: An Archaeological Perspective* (New Haven: Yale University Press, 2005), pp. 283–8; and Barry Sautman, 'Peking man and the politics of paleoanthropological nationalism in China', *Journal of Asian Studies*, 60.1 (2001), pp. 95–124.
5. William G. Boltz, 'Language and writing', in Loewe and Shaughnessy (eds), pp. 74–123.
6. Robert L. Thorp, *China in the Early Bronze Age: Shang Civilization* (Philadelphia: University of Pennsylvania Press, 2006), pp. 21–61.
7. Robert Bagley, 'Shang archaeology', in Loewe and Shaughnessy (eds), pp. 124–231.
8. Thorp, pp. 136–7.
9. David N. Keightley, *The Ancestral Landscape: Time, Space, and Community in Late Shang China (ca. 1200–1045 B.C.)* (Berkeley: University of California Press, 2000), pp. 121–9.
10. D. C. Lau (trans. and ed.), *Mencius* (Harmondsworth: Penguin, 1970), p. 128.
11. Quoted in Derk Bodde, 'Feudalism in China', in Rushton Coulborn (ed.), *Feudalism in History* (Hamden, CT: Archon Books, 1965), p. 58.
12. Herrlee G. Creel, *The Origins of Statecraft in China: The Western Chou Empire* (Chicago: University of Chicago Press, 1970), p. 320.
13. Edward L. Shaughnessy, 'Western Zhou history', in Loewe and Shaughnessy (eds), pp. 292–351.
14. Xueqin Li, *Eastern Zhou and Qin Civilizations* (New Haven, CT: Yale University Press, 1985), p. 477.
15. Lionel Giles (trans.), *Sun Tzŭ on the Art of War* (London, Luzac & Co., 1910), chapter 1, paragraphs 18–19.
16. Raymond Dawson, *Confucius* (Oxford: Oxford University Press, 1981), p. 76.
17. Lothar von Falkenhausen, *Chinese Society in the Age of Confucius (1000–250 BC): The Archaeological Evidence* (Los Angeles: Cotsen Institute of Archaeology, University of California Press, 2006), pp. 1–3.

18. D. C. Lau (trans. and ed.), *Confucius: The Analects* (Harmondsworth: Penguin, 1979), pp. 74, 131.
19. W. T. de Bary, W. Chan, and B. Watson (eds), *Sources of Chinese Tradition*, 2 vols (New York: Columbia University Press, 1960), vol. I, p. 40.
20. D. C. Lau (trans. and ed.), *Lao Tzu: Tao Te Ching* (Harmondsworth: Penguin, 1975), p. 57.
21. Ibid., p. 59.
22. De Bary et al. (eds), *Sources of Chinese Tradition*, vol. I, p. 73.
23. Lau (trans. and ed.), *Confucius*, p. 143.
24. Lau (trans. and ed.), *Mencius*, p. 160.
25. De Bary et al. (eds), *Sources of Chinese Tradition*, vol. I, p. 104.
26. Nicola di Cosmo, *Ancient China and Its Enemies: The Rise of Nomadic Power in East Asian History* (Cambridge: Cambridge University Press, 2002), pp. 174–5.
27. Michael Loewe, *Crisis and Conflict in Han China, 104 BC–AD 109* (London: George Allen & Unwin, 1974), pp. 11–13.
28. Anne Behnke Kinney, *Representations of Childhood and Youth in Early China* (Stanford, CA: Stanford University Press, 2004), pp. 19–23.
29. Bret Hinsch, *Women in Early Imperial China* (Lanham, MD: Rowman and Littlefield, 2002), pp. 10–11, 44–6, 122–3.
30. Sadao Nishijima, 'The economic and social history of Former Han', *CHC*, 1, p. 589.
31. Hans Bielenstein, 'Wang Mang, the restoration of the Han dynasty and Later Han', *CHC*, 1, pp. 223–90.
32. Mark Edward Lewis, *The Early Chinese Empires: Qin and Han* (Cambridge. MA: The Belknap Press of Harvard University Press, 2007), pp. 3, 248–9, 253–5.
33. Hans Bielenstein, 'The institutions of Later Han', *CHC*, 1, pp. 491–519. For a systematic comparison of the two empires, see: Walter Scheidel (ed.), *Rome and China: Comparative Perspectives on Ancient World Empires* (Oxford: Oxford University Press, 2009).

CHAPTER 2

1. Patricia Buckley Ebrey, *The Aristocratic Families of Early Imperial China: A Case Study of the Po-ling Ts'ui Family* (Cambridge: Cambridge University Press, 1978), p. 18.
2. W. J. F. Jenner, *Memories of Loyang: Yang Hsüan-chih and the Lost Capital (493–534)* (Oxford: Clarendon Press, 1981), p. 28.
3. The Longmen grottoes are now a UNESCO World Heritage site.
4. Mark Edward Lewis, *China Between Empires: The Northern and Southern Dynasties* (Cambridge MA: The Belknap Press of Harvard University Press, 2009), pp. 118–27.
5. Mark Elvin, *The Pattern of the Chinese Past* (London: Eyre Methuen, 1973), p. 55.

6. W. E. Soothill, *A History of China,* rev. edn (London: Ernest Benn, 1950), p. 40.

7. Howard J. Wechsler, *Mirror to the Son of Heaven: Wei Cheng at the Court of T'ang T'ai-tsung* (New Haven, CT: Yale University Press, 1974), p. 84.

8. Arthur F. Wright, 'T'ang T'ai-tsung and Buddhism', in Arthur F. Wright and Denis Twitchett (eds), *Perspectives on the T'ang* (New Haven, CT: Yale University Press, 1973), pp. 239–63.

9. Mark Edward Lewis, *China's Cosmopolitan Empire: The Tang Dynasty* (Cambridge, MA: The Belknap Press of Harvard University Press, 2009), pp. 180–9, 211–14; Kang-I Sun Chang and Haun Saussy (eds), *Women Writers of Traditional China: An Anthology of Poetry and Criticism* (Stanford, CA: Stanford University Press, 1999), pp. 67–75.

10. G. W. Robinson (trans. and ed.), *Poems of Wang Wei* (Harmondsworth: Penguin, 1973), p. 30.

11. Elling O. Eide, 'On Li Po', in Wright and Twitchett (eds), pp. 367–403.

12. Arthur Cooper (trans. and ed.), *Li Po and Tu Fu* (Harmondsworth: Penguin, 1973) p. 184.

13. Michael Sullivan, 'The heritage of Chinese art', in Raymond Dawson (ed.), *The Legacy of China* (Oxford: Oxford University Press, 1964), pp. 165–233.

14. Denis Twitchett, 'Introduction', *CHC*, 3, pp. 37–8.

15. Sechin Jagchid and Van Jay Symons, *Peace, War, and Trade along the Great Wall: Nomadic-Chinese Interaction through Two Millennia* (Bloomington: Indiana University Press, 1989), pp. 1–23.

16. Charles Benn, *Daily Life in Traditional China: The Tang Dynasty* (Westwood, CT: Greenwood Press, 2002), pp. 53–64.

17. C. A. Peterson, 'Court and province in mid- and late T'ang', *CHC*, 4, pp. 464–560, at p. 487.

18. Arthur F. Wright, *Buddhism in Chinese History* (Stanford, CA: Stanford University Press, 1959), pp. 82–3.

19. E. Zürcher, 'Perspectives in the study of Chinese Buddhism', *Journal of the Royal Asiatic Society* (1982), part 2, pp. 161–76.

20. Marc S. Abramson, *Ethnic Identity in Tang China* (Philadelphia: University of Pennsylvania Press, 2008), pp. 52–82.

21. W. T. de Bary, W. Chan, and B. Watson (eds), *Sources of Chinese Tradition,* 2 vols (New York: Columbia University Press, 1960), vol. I, pp. 372–4.

22. Reigned 846–59, to be distinguished from his famous predecessor who reigned 712–56.

CHAPTER 3

1. Denis Twitchett and Klaus-Peter Tietze, 'The Liao', *CHC*, 6, p. 110.

2. Gungwu Wang, 'The rhetoric of a lesser empire: Early Sung relations with its neighbors', in Morris Rossabi (ed.), *China among Equals: The Middle Kingdom and Its Neighbors, 10th–14th Centuries* (Berkeley: University of California Press, 1983), pp. 47–65.

3. E. A. Kracke, *Civil Service in Early Sung China, 960–1067* (Cambridge, MA: Harvard University Press, 1953, 1968), pp. 68–70.

4. John W. Chaffee, *The Thorny Gates of Learning in Sung China: A Social History of Examinations* (Cambridge: Cambridge University Press, 1985), pp. 182–3.

5. Winston W. Lo, *An Introduction to the Civil Service of Sung China: With an Emphasis on Its Personnel Administration* (Honolulu: University of Hawai'i Press, 1987), pp. 92–3.

6. Mark Elvin, *The Pattern of the Chinese Past* (London: Eyre Methuen, 1973), pp. 113–99.

7. Charles O. Hucker, *China's Imperial Past: An Introduction to Chinese History and Culture* (London: Duckworth, 1975), p. 342.

8. Etienne Balazs, 'The birth of capitalism in China', in Etienne Balazs (ed. A. F. Wright), *Chinese Civilization and Bureaucracy* (New Haven, CT: Yale University Press, 1964), pp. 34–54.

9. Albert Feuerwerker, 'Chinese economic history in comparative perspective', in Paul S. Ropp (ed.), *Heritage of China: Contemporary Perspectives on Chinese Civilization* (Berkeley: University of California Press, 1990), pp. 224–41.

10. John Meskill (ed.), *Wang An-shih: Practical Reformer?* (Boston: D. C. Heath, 1963).

11. James T. C. Liu, *China Turning Inward: Intellectual-Political Changes in the Early Twelfth Century* (Cambridge, MA: Harvard University Press, 1988), pp. 81–104.

12. Richard L. Davis, *Court and Family in Sung China, 960–1279: Bureaucratic Success and Kinship Fortunes for the Shih of Ming-chou* (Durham, NC: Duke University Press, 1986).

13. Edward L. Davis, *Society and the Supernatural in Song China* (Honolulu: University of Hawai'i Press, 2001), pp. 4–7, 14–15.

14. Peter J. Golas, 'Rural China in the Song', *Journal of Asian Studies,* 39.2 (1980), pp. 291–325.

15. Robert P. Hymes, *Statesmen and Gentlemen: The Elite of Fu-chou, Chiang-si, in Northern and Southern Sung* (Cambridge: Cambridge University Press, 1986), pp. 210–18.

16. Patricia Buckley Ebrey, *The Inner Quarters: Marriage and the Lives of Chinese Women in the Sung Period* (Berkeley: University of California Press, 1993), pp. 4–6, 37–43, 199.

17. Kathryn Bernhardt, *Women and Property in China, 960–1949* (Stanford, CA: Stanford University Press, 1999), pp. 9–11, 40; Bettine Birge, *Women, Property, and Confucian Reaction in Sung and Yüan China (960–1368)* (Cambridge: Cambridge University Press, 2002), pp. 284–96.

18. Ping-chen Hsiung, *A Tender Voyage: Children and Childhood in Late Imperial China* (Stanford, CA: Stanford University Press, 2005), pp. 9–10.

19. David M. Farquhar, *The Government of China under Mongolian Rule: A Reference Guide* (Stuttgart: Franz Steiner Verlag, 1990), p. 5.

20. For the case against Marco Polo having gone to China, see: Frances Wood, *Did Marco Polo Go To China?* (London: Secker and Warburg, 1995). For a refutation of her case, see: I. de Rachelwitz, 'F.Wood's Did Marco Polo Go To China? A Critical Appraisal', http://dspace.anu.edu.au/bitstream/1885/41883/1/Marcopolo.html, accessed 4 February 2011.

21. Frederick W. Mote, 'Chinese society under Mongol rule, 1215–1368', *CHC,* 6, pp. 616–64, at p. 620.

22. Morris Rossabi, 'The reign of Khubilai khan', in *CHC*, 6, pp. 414–89, at p. 489.
23. Bayan of the Merkid, to be distinguished from Bayan of the Barin, the general who conquered the south.
24. Quoted in Hucker, *China's Imperial Past*, p. 400.
25. Ch'i-ch'ing Hsiao, 'Mid-Yüan politics', *CHC*, 6, pp. 490–560.

CHAPTER 4

1. Frederick W. Mote, 'The rise of the Ming dynasty, 1330–1367', *CHC*, 7, pp. 11–57, at p. 48.
2. Edward L. Dreyer, *Early Ming China: A Political History 1355–1435* (Stanford, CA: Stanford University Press, 1982), p. 87.
3. Sarah Schneewind, *Community Schools and the State in Ming China* (Stanford, CA: Stanford University Press, 2006), pp. 2–3.
4. F. W. Mote, 'The growth of Chinese despotism: A critique of Wittfogel's theory of Oriental Despotism as applied to China', *Oriens Extremus*, 8 (1961), pp. 1–41.
5. On Hongwu's posthumous reputation, see: Sarah Schneewind (ed.), *Long Live the Emperor: Uses of the Ming Founder across Six Centuries of East Asian History* (Minneapolis, MN: Society for Ming Studies, 2008).
6. Dreyer, *Early Ming China*, p. 182.
7. Edward L. Dreyer, *Zheng He: China and the Oceans in the Early Ming Dynasty, 1405–1433* (London: Pearson Longman, 2007).
8. The official salary of a county magistrate was about 5.2 taels per month.
9. Schneewind, *Community Schools*, pp. 1–5, 167–9.
10. Ray Huang, *Taxation and Governmental Finance in Sixteenth-Century Ming China* (Cambridge: Cambridge University Press, 1974), p. 60. A standard *mou* was approximately 6,000 square feet, or one seventh of an acre.
11. John W. Dardess, *A Ming Society: T'ai-ho County, Kiangsi, Fourteenth to Seventeenth Centuries* (Berkeley: University of California Press, 1996), p. 82.
12. Victoria Cass, *Warriors, Grannies and Geishas of the Ming* (Lanham, MD: Rowman & Littlefield, 1999), pp. 6–15.
13. Benjamin A. Elman, *On Their Own Terms: Science in China, 1550–1900* (Cambridge, MA: Harvard University Press, 2005), pp. 29–34.
14. Huang, *Taxation and Governmental Finance*, p. 82.
15. Fang-chung Liang, *The Single-Whip Method of Taxation in China* (Cambridge, MA: Harvard University Press, 1970), p. 1.
16. Timothy Brook, *The Chinese State in Ming Times* (London: RoutledgeCurzon, 2005), pp. 182–90.
17. Dardess, *A Ming Society*, p. 48.
18. Hilary J. Beattie, *Land and Lineage in China: A Study of T'ung-ch'eng County, Anhwei, in the Ming and Ch'ing Dynasties* (Cambridge: Cambridge University Press, 1979).
19. Ping-ti Ho, *The Ladder of Success in Imperial China: Aspects of Social Mobility, 1368–1911* (New York: Columbia University Press, 1967), pp. 92–105.

20. Timothy Brook, *Praying for Power: Buddhism and the Formation of Gentry Society in Late-Ming China* (Cambridge, MA: Harvard University Press, 1993), pp. 311–21.

21. John W. Dardess, *Blood and History in China: The Donglin Faction and Its Repression, 1620–1627* (Honolulu: University of Hawai'i Press, 2002).

22. Richard Von Glahn, *Fountain of Fortune: Money and Monetary Policy in China, 1000–1700* (Berkeley: University of California Press, 1996).

23. James W. Tong, *Disorder under Heaven: Collective Violence in the Ming Dynasty* (Stanford, CA: Stanford University Press, 1991), pp. 192–203.

24. Nicola di Cosmo, 'Did guns matter? Firearms and the Qing formation', in Lynn A. Struve (ed.), *The Qing Formation in World-Historical Time* (Cambridge, MA: Harvard University Press, 2004), pp. 121–66.

25. Joanna Waley-Cohen, *The Culture of War in China: Empire and the Military under the Qing Dynasty* (London: I. B. Tauris, 2006), p. 18.

26. Quoted in Frederic Wakeman, Jr., *The Great Enterprise: The Manchu Reconstruction of Imperial Order in Seventeenth-Century China*, 2 vols (Berkeley: University of California Press, 1985), vol. I, p. 317.

27. Lynn A. Struve (trans. and ed.), *Voices from the Ming-Qing Cataclysm: China in Tigers' Jaws* (New Haven, CT: Yale University Press, 1993), p. 2.

28. Mark C. Elliott, *The Manchu Way: The Eight Banners and Ethnic Identity in Late Imperial China* (Stanford, CA: Stanford University Press, 2001), pp. 122, 175–82, 246–55.

29. See below, p. 145.

30. Stephen R. Platt, *Provincial Patriots: The Hunanese and Modern China* (Cambridge, MA: Harvard University Press, 2007), pp. 8–33, 102–4.

31. Jonathan D. Spence, *Emperor of China: Self-portrait of K'ang-hsi* (Harmondsworth: Penguin, 1977), p. 43.

32. A late seventeenth-century writer quoted in Helen Dunstan, *Conflicting Counsels to Confuse the Age: A Documentary Study of Political Economy in Qing China, 1644–1840* (Ann Arbor: University of Michigan, Center for Chinese Studies, 1996), pp. 151–2.

33. Elliott, *The Manchu Way*, pp. 287, 296–7.

34. Jonathan Spence, *Treason by the Book* (London: Allen Lane, 2001).

35. Pei Huang, *Autocracy at Work: A Study of the Yung-cheng Period, 1723–1735* (Bloomington: Indiana University Press, 1974), p. 21.

36. Iona D. Man-Cheong, *The Class of 1761: Examinations, State and Elites in Eighteenth-Century China* (Stanford, CA: Stanford University Press, 2004), pp. 1–2, 17, 24.

37. Peter Perdue, *China Marches West: The Qing Conquest of Central Asia* (Cambridge, MA: The Belknap Press of Harvard University Press, 2005), pp. 256–89.

38. James A. Millward, Ruth W. Dunnell, Mark C. Elliott, and Philippe Forêt (eds), *New Qing Imperial History: The Making of Inner Asian Empire at Qing Chengde* (London: Routledge, 2004), pp. 3–4.

39. Albert Feuerwerker, *State and Society in Eighteenth-Century China: The Ch'ing Empire in its Glory* (Ann Arbor: University of Michigan Center for Chinese Studies, 1976), p. 84.

40. Mark Elvin, *The Pattern of the Chinese Past* (London: Eyre Methuen, 1973), pp. 285–315.

41. Kung-chuan Hsiao, *Rural China: Imperial Control in the Nineteenth Century,* (Seattle: University of Washington Press, 1967), p. 144.

42. Pierre-Etienne Will and R. Bin Wong, *Nourish the People: The State Civilian Granary System in China, 1650–1850* (Ann Arbor: University of Michigan, Center for Chinese Studies, 1991).

43. Dunstan, *Conflicting Counsels*, pp. 203–45, 293.

44. Kenneth Pomeranz, *The Great Divergence: China, Europe, and the Making of the Modern World Economy* (Princeton, NJ: Princeton University Press, 2000); Philip C.C. Huang, 'Development of involution in eighteenth-century Britain and China? A review of Kenneth Pomeranz's *The Great Divergence: China, Europe, and the Making of the Modern World Economy*', *Journal of Asian Studies*, 61.2 (May 2002), pp. 501–38. See also Kenneth Pomeranz's reply, pp. 539–90 in the same issue.

45. Waley-Cohen, *The Culture of War*, p. 21.

46. Elliott, *The Manchu Way*, pp. 21, 358–9.

47. On this dispute, see: Ping-ti Ho, 'The significance of the Ch'ing period in Chinese history', *Journal of Asian Studies*, 26.2 (1967), pp. 189–95; Mark Elliott, review of Herbert Franke and Denis Twitchett (eds.), *The Cambridge History of China, vol. 6. Alien Regimes and Border States, 907–1368* (Cambridge: Cambridge University Press, 1994) in *Journal of Asian Studies*, 55.1 (February 1996), pp. 146–9; Evelyn S. Rawski, 'Reenvisioning the Qing: The significance of the Qing period in Chinese history', *Journal of Asian Studies*, 55.4 (November 1996), pp. 829–50; and Ping-ti Ho, 'In defense of sinicization: A rebuttal of Evelyn Rawski's 'Reenvisioning the Qing',' *Journal of Asian Studies*, 57.1 (February 1998), pp. 123–55.

48. James A. Millward, *Beyond the Pass: Economy, Ethnicity, and Empire in Qing Central Asia, 1759–1864* (Stanford, CA: Stanford University Press, 1998).

49. Benjamin A. Elman, *From Philosophy to Philology: Intellectual and Social Aspects of Change in Late Imperial China* (Cambridge, MA: Harvard University Press, 1984).

50. Paul S. Ropp, *Dissent in Early Modern China: Ju-lin wai-shih and Ch'ing Social Criticism* (Ann Arbor: University of Michigan Press, 1981).

51. Cao Xueqin, trans. David Hawkes, *The Story of the Stone*, 5 vols (Harmondsworth: Penguin, 1973–86).

52. Susan Mann, 'Learned women in the eighteenth century', in Christina K. Gilmartin, Gail Hershatter, Lisa Rofel, and Tyrene White (eds), *Engendering China: Women, Culture, and the State* (Cambridge, MA: Harvard University Press, 1994), pp. 27–46.

53. Wu Cuncun, *Homoerotic Sensibilities in Late Imperial China* (London: RoutledgeCurzon, 2004), pp. 92–105.

54. Dorothy Ko, *Teachers of the Inner Chambers: Women and Culture in Seventeenth-Century China* (Stanford, CA: Stanford University Press, 1994).

55. Susan Mann, *Precious Records: Women in China's Long Eighteenth Century* (Stanford, CA: Stanford University Press, 1994).

56. Wilt Idema and Beata Grant (eds.), *The Red Brush: Writing Women of Imperial China* (Cambridge, MA: Harvard University Press, 2004), p. 7.

57. Kathryn Bernhardt, 'A Ming-Qing transition in Chinese women's history? The perspective from law', in Gail Hershatter, Emily Honig, Jonathan N. Lipman, and Randall Stross (eds), *Remapping China: Fissures in Historical Terrain* (Stanford, CA: Stanford University Press, 1996), pp. 42–58.

58. Madeleine Zelin, *The Magistrate's Tael: Rationalizing Fiscal Reform in Eighteenth-Century Ch'ing China* (Berkeley: University of California Press, 1984), pp. 265–6.

59. Feuerwerker, *State and Society*, pp. 74–5.

CHAPTER 5

1. J. Mason Gentzler (ed.), *Changing China: Readings in the History of China from the Opium War to the Present* (New York: Praeger, 1977), pp. 23–8.

2. James L. Hevia, 'The Macartney embassy in the history of Sino-Western relations', in Robert A. Bickers (ed.), *Ritual and Diplomacy: The Macartney Mission to China, 1792–1794* (London: British Association for Chinese Studies, and the Wellsweep Press, 1993), pp. 57–79.

3. Joseph W. Esherick, 'Cherishing sources from afar', *Modern China*, 24.2 (April 1998), pp. 135–61.

4. Joanna Waley-Cohen, *The Sextants of Beijing: Global Currents in Chinese History* (New York: W.W. Norton, 1999), pp. 124–8.

5. John King Fairbank, *Trade and Diplomacy on the China Coast: The Opening of the Treaty Ports, 1842–1854*, rev. edn (Stanford, CA: Stanford University Press, 1969), p. 74.

6. D. K. Fieldhouse, *Economics and Empire 1830–1914* (London: Weidenfeld and Nicolson, 1973), p. 212.

7. Carl A. Trocki, *Opium, Empire and the Global Political Economy: A Study of the Asian Opium Trade* (London: Routledge, 1999), p. 98.

8. Mao Zedong, 'The Chinese revolution and the Communist Party' (1940), quoted in Stuart Schram, *The Political Thought of Mao Tse-tung*, revised and enlarged edition (London: Frederick A. Praeger, 1969), p. 262.

9. Jane Kate Leonard, *Controlling from Afar: The Daoguang Emperor's Management of the Grand Canal Crisis, 1824–1826* (Ann Arbor: University of Michigan Center for Chinese Studies, 1996).

10. Randall A. Dodgen, *Controlling the Dragon: Confucian Engineers and the Yellow River in Late Imperial China* (Honolulu: University of Hawai'i Press, 2001), pp. 4–5, 106, 146.

11. Karl Marx, *New York Daily Tribune,* 14 June 1853, reprinted in Dona Torr (ed.), *Marx on China, 1853–1860: Articles from the New York Daily Tribune* (London: Lawrence & Wishart, 1968), pp. 1–2.

12. Jonathan Spence, *God's Chinese Son: The Taiping Heavenly Kingdom of Hong Xiuquan* (London: Harper Collins, 1996), p. 65.

13. Yu-wen Jen, *The Taiping Revolutionary Movement* (New Haven, CT: Yale University Press, 1973), p. 6.

14. Pamela Kyle Crossley, *A Translucent Mirror: History and Identity in Qing Imperial Ideology* (Berkeley: University of California Press, 1999), p. 342.

15. Elizabeth J. Perry, *Rebels and Revolutionaries in North China, 1845–1945* (Stanford, CA: Stanford University Press, 1980), p. 130.

16. David G. Atwill, *The Chinese Sultanate: Islam, Ethnicity, and the Panthay Rebellion in Southwest China, 1856–1873* (Stanford, CA: Stanford University Press, 2005), pp. 7–10.

17. James A. Millward, *Beyond the Pass: Economy, Ethnicity, and Empire in Qing Central Asia, 1759–1864* (Stanford, CA: Stanford University Press, 1998), p. 251.

18. James Reardon-Anderson, *Reluctant Pioneers: China's Expansion Northward, 1644–1937* (Stanford, CA: Stanford University Press, 2005), pp. 97–101.

19. Ping-ti Ho, *Studies on the Population of China, 1368–1953* (Cambridge, MA: Harvard University Press, 1959), pp. 236–48, 275–8.

20. Mary Clabaugh Wright, *The Last Stand of Chinese Conservatism: The T'ung-chih Restoration, 1862–1874,* 2nd edn (Stanford, CA: Stanford University Press, 1962), p. ix.

21. Barry C. Keenan, *Imperial China's Last Classical Academies: Social Change in the Lower Yangzi, 1864–1911* (Berkeley: University of California Press, 1994).

22. Ssu-yu Teng and John K. Fairbank, *China's Response to the West: A Documentary Survey, 1839–1923* (New York: Atheneum, 1963), pp. 30–35.

23. Ibid., pp. 50–54.

24. Ibid., p. 76. It was customary for a Mongol to refer to himself as a slave when addressing the emperor.

25. Albert Feuerwerker, *China's Early Industrialization: Sheng Hsüan-huai (1844–1916) and Mandarin Enterprise* (New York: Atheneum, 1970), p. 30.

26. Benjamin A. Elman, *A Cultural History of Modern Science in China* (Cambridge, MA: Harvard University Press, 2006), p. 196.

27. Albert Feuerwerker, 'Economic trends in the late Ch'ing empire, 1870–1911', *CHC*, 11, pp. 1–69.

28. Robert Gardella, *Harvesting Mountains: Fujian and the China Tea Trade, 1757–1937* (Berkeley: University of California Press, 1994), pp. 81–3, 110–11, 170–74.

29. Madeleine Zelin, *The Merchants of Zigong: Industial Entrepreneurship in Early Modern China* (New York: Columbia University Press, 2005), pp. xiii–xvi, 168–73.

30. Reardon-Anderson, *Reluctant Pioneers*, pp. 243–51.

31. Leang-li T'ang, *China in Revolt: How a Civilization Became a Nation* (London: Noel Douglas, 1927), reprinted in Jessie G. Lutz (ed.), *Christian Missions in China: Evangelists of What?* (Boston: D. C. Heath, 1965), pp. 51–9.

32. Hosea Ballou Morse, *International Relations of the Chinese Empire,* 3 vols (New York: Longmans, Green, 1910–18), vol. III, pp. 158–9.

33. Stephen R. Platt, *Provincial Patriots: The Hunanese and Modern China* (Cambridge, MA: Harvard University Press, 2007), pp. 66–93.
34. Jack Gray, *Rebellions and Revolutions: China from the 1800s to 2000*, 2nd edn (Oxford: Oxford University Press, 2002), pp. 132–3.
35. The argument put forward by Victor Purcell that the Boxers began as an anti-dynastic movement but later shifted to a pro-dynastic stance has been discredited. Recent evidence, some derived from oral histories, shows that the Boxers from the beginning were a loyalist movement and that there never was an anti-dynastic phase. See: Victor Purcell, *The Boxer Uprising: A Background Study* (Cambridge: Cambridge University Press, 1963); and Joseph W. Esherick, *The Origins of the Boxer Uprising* (Berkeley: University of California Press, 1987), p. xvi.
36. Paul A. Cohen, *History in Three Keys: The Boxers as Event, Experience, and Myth* (New York: Columbia University Press, 1997), pp. 251–60.
37. Frederic Wakeman, Jr., *The Fall of Imperial China* (New York: The Free Press, 1975), p. 236; Ryan Dunch, *Fuzhou Protestants and the Making of Modern China 1857–1927* (New Haven: Yale University Press, 2001), pp. 84–6; Joan Judge, *Print and Politics: 'Shibao' and the Culture of Reform in Late Qing China* (Stanford, CA: Stanford University Press, 1996), pp. 186–93.
38. Wakeman, *The Fall of Imperial China*, p. 228.
39. Edward J. M. Rhoads, *Manchus and Han: Ethnic Relations and Political Power in Late Qing and Early Imperial China, 1861–1928* (Seattle: University of Washington Press, 2000), pp. 286–8.

CHAPTER 6

1. Kristin Stapleton, *Civilizing Chengdu: Chinese Urban Reform, 1895–1937* (Cambridge, MA: Harvard University Press, 2000), pp. 1–10.
2. Man Bun Kwan, *The Salt Merchants of Tianjin: State-Making and Civil Society in Late Imperial China* (Honolulu: University of Hawai'i Press, 2001), pp. 10–11.
3. Marianne Bastid-Bruguière, 'Currents of social change', *CHC*, 11, pp. 535–602, at p. 561.
4. S. A. Smith, *Like Cattle and Horses: Nationalism and Labor in Shanghai, 1895–1927* (Durham, NC: Duke University Press, 2002), p. 55.
5. Joan Judge, *Print and Politics: 'Shibao' and the Culture of Reform in Late Qing China* (Stanford, CA: Stanford University Press, 1996), pp. 1–13, 33–5, 83, 123.
6. Ryan Dunch, *Fuzhou Protestants and the Making of Modern China 1857–1927* (New Haven, CT: Yale University Press, 2001), pp. xvii–xviii, 69–79, 117.
7. Dorothy Ko, *Cinderella's Sisters: A Revisionist History of Footbinding* (Berkeley: University of California Press, 2005), pp. 17–39.
8. Dunch, *Fuzhou Protestants*, pp. 49–55. See also Joyce A. Madancy, *The Troublesome Legacy of Commissioner Lin: The Opium Trade and Opium*

Suppression in Fujian Province (Cambridge, MA: Harvard University Press, 2003).

9. Mary Clabaugh Wright, 'Introduction: The rising tide of change', in Mary Clabaugh Wright (ed.), *China in Revolution: The First Phase, 1900–1913* (New Haven, CT: Yale University Press, 1973), pp. 1–63.

10. Joan Judge, *The Precious Raft of History: The Past, the West, and the Woman Question in China* (Stanford, CA: Stanford University Press, 2008), pp. 215–23.

11. Joseph W. Esherick, *Reform and Revolution in China: The 1911 Revolution in Hunan and Hubei* (Berkeley: University of California Press, 1976), p. 175.

12. Edward J. M. Rhoads, *Manchus and Han: Ethnic Relations and Political Power in Late Qing and Early Imperial China, 1861–1928* (Seattle: University of Washington Press, 2000), pp. 187–93.

13. Ernest P. Young, *The Presidency of Yuan Shih-k'ai: Liberalism and Dictatorship in Early Republican China* (Ann Arbor: University of Michigan Press, 1977), p. 243.

14. Franz Michael, 'Introduction', in Stanley Spector, *Li Hung-chang and the Huai Army: A Study in Nineteenth-Century Chinese Regionalism* (Seattle: University of Washington Press, 1964), pp. xxi–xliii.

15. Jerome Ch'en, *Yuan Shih-k'ai, 1859–1916: Brutus Assumes the Purple,* 2nd edn (London: George Allen & Unwin, 1972), p. 214.

16. Edward A. McCord, *The Power of the Gun: The Emergence of Modern Chinese Warlordism* (Berkeley: University of California Press, 1993), pp. 309–15.

17. James E. Sheridan, *China in Disintegration: The Republican Era in Chinese History, 1912–1949* (New York: Free Press, 1975), pp. 183–206.

18. Julia C. Lin, *Modern Chinese Poetry: An Introduction* (London: George Allen & Unwin, 1972), p. 85.

19. Smith, *Like Cattle and Horses*, pp. 92–7.

20. Hua R. Lan and Vanessa L. Fong (eds), *Women in Republican China: A Sourcebook* (Armonk, NY, M. E. Sharpe, 1999), pp. ix–xvi.

21. W. T. de Bary, W. Chan, and B. Watson (eds), *Sources of Chinese Tradition,* 2 vols (New York: Columbia University Press, 1964), vol. II, pp. 156–67.

22. S. Y. Teng and J. K. Fairbank (eds), *China's Response to the West: A Documentary Survey, 1839–1923* (New York: Atheneum, 1963), p. 239.

23. Ibid., pp. 252–5.

24. Jean Chesneaux, *The Chinese Labor Movement, 1919–1927* (Stanford, CA: Stanford University Press, 1968), pp. 177–210.

25. John Fitzgerald, *Awakening China: Politics, Culture, and Class in the Nationalist Revolution* (Stanford, CA: Stanford University Press, 1996), p. 348.

26. Harold R. Isaacs, *The Tragedy of the Chinese Revolution* (London: Secker & Warburg, 1938), p. 126.

27. Stuart R. Schram, *The Political Thought of Mao Tse-tung,* revised and enlarged edition (New York: Frederick A. Praeger, 1969), pp. 250–59.

28. C. Martin Wilbur, 'The Nationalist Revolution: From Canton to Nanking, 1923–28', *CHC,* 12, pp. 527–720, at p. 690.

29. Albert Feuerwerker, 'Economic trends, 1912–1949', *CHC,* 12, pp. 28–127.

30. Han-seng Chen, *Landlord and Peasant in China: A Study of the Agrarian Crisis in South China* (New York: International Publishers, 1973); Ramon

H. Myers, *The Chinese Peasant Economy: Agricultural Development in Hopei and Shantung, 1890–1949* (Cambridge, MA: Harvard University Press, 1970).

31. Zwia Lipkin, *Useless to the State: 'Social Problems' and Social Engineering in Nationalist Nanjing, 1927–1937* (Cambridge, MA: Harvard University Press, 2006), pp. 196–9.

32. Frederic Wakeman, Jr., 'A revisionist view of the Nanjing Decade: Confucian Fascism', in Frederic Wakeman, Jr. and Richard Louis Edmonds (eds), *Reappraising Republican China* (Oxford: Oxford University Press, 2000), pp. 141–78.

33. Douglas S. Paauw, 'The Kuomintang and economic stagnation 1928–1937', in Albert Feuerwerker (ed.), *Modern China* (Englewood Cliffs, NJ: Prentice-Hall, 1964), pp. 126–35.

34. Thomas G. Rawski, *Economic Growth in Prewar China* (Berkeley: University of California Press, 1989), pp. xxi–xxi, 332, 344.

35. Guoqi Xu, *Olympic Dreams: China and Sports 1895–2008* (Cambridge, MA: Harvard University Press, 2008), pp. 39–45.

36. Lloyd E. Eastman, *The Abortive Revolution: China under Nationalist Rule, 1927–1937* (Cambridge, MA: Harvard University Press, 1974); Robert E. Bedeski, 'China's wartime state', in James C. Hsiung and Steven I. Levine (eds), *China's Bitter Victory: The War with Japan 1937–1945* (New York: M. E. Sharpe, 1992), pp. 33–49; Julia C. Strauss, *Strong Institutions in Weak Polities: State Building in Republican China, 1927–1940* (Oxford: Clarendon Press, 1998), p. 8; Richard Louis Edmonds, 'The state of studies on Republican China', in Wakeman and Edmonds (eds), *Reappraising Republican China*, pp. 1–5.

37. Iris Chang, *The Rape of Nanking: The Forgotten Holocaust of World War II* (New York: Penguin, 1997); Joshua A. Fogel (ed.), *The Nanjing Massacre in History and Historiography* (Berkeley: University of California Press, 2000). For recent studies on this subject, see: Bob Tadashi Wakabayashi (ed.), *The Nanking Atrocity, 1937–38: Complicating the Picture* (New York: Berghahn Books, 2007).

38. Stephen R. MacKinnon, *Wuhan, 1938: War, Refugees and the Making of Modern China* (Berkeley: University of California Press, 2008), pp. 1–4.

39. Diana Lary and Stephen MacKinnon (eds), *The Scars of War: The Impact of Warfare on Modern China* (Vancouver, University of British Columbia Press, 2001), p. 112.

40. David P. Barrett, 'Introduction', and Peter J. Seybolt, 'The war within a war: A case study of a county on the North China Plain', in David P. Barrett and Larry N. Shyu (eds), *Chinese Collaboration with Japan: The Limits of Accommodation* (Stanford, CA: Stanford University Press, 2001), pp. 1–17; 201–25.

41. Lloyd E. Eastman, *Seeds of Destruction: Nationalist China in War and Revolution, 1937–1949* (Stanford, CA: Stanford University Press, 1984), p. 43.

42. Odd Arne Westad, *Decisive Encounters: The Chinese Civil War, 1946–1950* (Stanford, CA: Stanford University Press, 2003), p. 29.

43. John S. Service, *Lost Chance in China: The World War II Despatches of John S. Service* (New York: Random House, 1974), pp. 178–81.

44. Chalmers A. Johnson, *Peasant Nationalism and Communist Power: The Emergence of Revolutionary China, 1937–1945* (Stanford, CA: Stanford University Press, 1962), p. 59.
45. Donald G. Gillin, "Peasant nationalism" in the history of Chinese Communism', *Journal of Asian Studies*, 23.2 (February 1964), pp. 269–89; Mark Selden, *The Yenan Way in Revolutionary China* (Cambridge, MA: Harvard University Press, 1974).
46. Odoric Y. K. Wou, *Mobilizing the Masses: Building Revolution in Henan* (Stanford, CA: Stanford University Press, 1994), p. 379; Ralph A. Thaxton, Jr., *Salt of the Earth: The Political Origins of Peasant Protest and Communist Revolution in China* (Berkeley: University of California Press, 1997), p. 319; Pauline B. Keating, *Two Revolutions: Village Reconstruction and the Cooperative Movement in Northern Shaanxi, 1934–1945* (Stanford, CA: Stanford University Press, 1997); David S. G. Goodman, *Social and Political Change in Revolutionary China: The Taihang Base Area in the War of Resistance to Japan, 1937–1945* (Lanham, MD: Rowman & Littlefield, 2000), pp. 268–73; Feng Chongyi and David S. G. Goodman (eds), *North China at War: The Social Ecology of Revolution 1937–1945* (Lanham, MD: Rowman & Littlefield, 2000).
47. Thomas D. Lutze, *China's Inevitable Revolution: Rethinking America's Loss to the Communists* (Basingstoke: Palgrave Macmillan, 2008), pp. 1–10.
48. Christopher R. Lew, *The Third Chinese Revolutionary Civil War, 1945–49: An Analysis of Communist Strategy and Leadership* (London: Routledge, 2009).
49. Joseph W. Esherick, 'Collapse of the old order, germination of the new: Chinese society during the civil war, 1945–1949', in Werner Draguhn and David S. G. Goodman (eds), *China's Communist Revolutions: Fifty Years of the People's Republic of China* (London: Routledge, 2002), pp. 23–49.
50. Odd Arne Westad, *Decisive Encounters*, p. 7.
51. Joseph K. S. Yick, *Making Urban Revolution in China: The CCP-GMD Struggle for Beiping-Tianjin 1945–1949* (Armonk, NY: M. E. Sharpe, 1995), p. 10.

CHAPTER 7

1. Julia Strauss, 'Introduction: In search of PRC history', *The China Quarterly*, 188 (December 2006), pp. 855–69.
2. For a discussion of this issue, see: James Leibold, *Reconfiguring Chinese Nationalism: How the Qing Frontier and Its Indigenes Became Chinese* (Basingstoke: Palgrave Macmillan, 2007).
3. Xinxin Zhang and Ye Sang, *Chinese Lives: An Oral History of Contemporary China* (London: Penguin Books, 1989), p. 119.
4. Barry Naughton, 'The pattern and legacy of economic growth in the Mao era', in Kenneth Lieberthal, Joyce Kallgren, Roderick MacFarquhar, and Frederic Wakeman, Jr. (eds), *Perspectives on Modern China: Four Anniversaries* (New York: M. E. Sharpe, 1991), pp. 226–54.

5. Mark Selden, *The People's Republic of China: A Documentary History of Revolutionary Change* (New York: Monthly Review Press, 1979), p. 402.
6. Harry Wu and Carolyn Wakeman, *Bitter Winds: A Memoir of My Years in China's Gulag* (New York: John Wiley & Sons, 1994).
7. Merle Goldman, 'The Party and the intellectuals', *CHC*, 14, pp. 218–58.
8. Maurice Meisner, *Mao's China: A History of the People's Republic* (New York: Free Press, 1977), p. 205.
9. Alexander Eckstein, *China's Economic Revolution* (Cambridge: Cambridge University Press, 1977), pp. 58–9.
10. Nicholas R. Lardy, 'The Chinese economy under stress, 1958–1965', *CHC*, 14, pp. 360–97.
11. Ralph Thaxton, Jr., *Catastrophe and Contention in Rural China: Mao's Great Leap Forward and the Origins of Righteous Resistance in Da Fo Village* (Cambridge: Cambridge University Press, 2008).
12. Alan S. Whiting, 'The Sino-Soviet split', *CHC*, 14, pp. 478–538.
13. Benjamin Yang, *Deng: A Political Biography* (New York: M. E. Sharpe, 1998), p. 151. The quotation is usually rendered as 'Black cat or white cat...'
14. Judith Shapiro, *Mao's War Against Nature: Politics and the Environment in Revolutionary China* (Cambridge: Cambridge University Press, 2001), pp. 115–37.
15. Meisner, *Mao's China*, p. 285.
16. Shaun Breslin, *Mao* (London: Longman, 1998), pp. 125–6 and n. 6.
17. Jiaqi Yan and Gao Gao, *Turbulent Decade: A History of the Cultural Revolution* (Honolulu: University of Hawai'i Press, 1996), p. 32.
18. David Milton, Nancy Milton, and Franz Schurmann (eds), *People's China: Social Experimentation, Politics, Entry onto the World Scene, 1966–72* (Harmondsworth: Penguin, 1977), pp. 269–81.
19. Mark Lupher, 'Revolutionary Little Red Devils: The social psychology of rebel youth, 1966–1967', in Anne Behnke Kinney (ed.), *Chinese Views of Childhood* (Honolulu: University of Hawai'i Press, 1995), pp. 321–43; on the relationship between the iconoclasm of the Red Guards and that of the May Fourth radicals, see: Rana Mitter, *A Bitter Revolution: China's Struggle with the Modern World* (Oxford: Oxford University Press, 2004), pp. 200–207.
20. Yan and Gao, *Turbulent Decade*, p. 529.
21. Yang Su, 'Mass killings in the Cultural Revolution', in Joseph W. Esherick, Paul G. Pickowicz, and Andrew Walder, *The Chinese Cultural Revolution as History* (Stanford, CA: Stanford University Press, 2006), pp. 96–123.
22. Roderick MacFarquhar and Michael Schoenhals, *Mao's Last Revolution* (Cambridge, MA: Belknap Press of Harvard University Press, 2006), p. 3.
23. Dwight H. Perkins, 'China's economic policy and performance', *CHC*, 15, pp. 475–539, at pp. 482–3.
24. Suzanne Pepper, *Radicalism and Education Reform in 20th-Century China: The Search for an Ideal Development Model* (Cambridge: Cambridge University Press, 1996), pp. 381, 385.
25. Jung Chang and Jon Halliday, *Mao: The Unknown Story* (London: Jonathan Cape, 2005); John Gittings, *The Guardian*, 23 July 2005. For a detailed refutal of the claims made in *The Unknown Story*, see: Mobo Gao,

The Battle for China's Past: Mao and the Cultural Revolution (London: Pluto Press, 2008). For more balanced assessments of Mao's career, see: Jonathan Spence, *Mao* (London: Weidenfeld & Nicolson, 1999); and Philip Short, *Mao: A Life* (New York: Henry Holt, 2000).

26. Jack Gray, 'Mao in perspective', drafted shortly before his death in 2004 and published in *The China Quarterly*, 187 (September 2006), pp. 659–79.

CHAPTER 8

1. Joanna Z. Li and David C. Yang, 'Guangdong: China's economic powerhouse – The past, the present and the future', in Tung X. Bui, David C. Yang, Wayne D. Jones, and Joanna Z. Li (eds), *China's Economic Powerhouse: Reform in Guangdong Province* (Basingstoke, Palgrave Macmillan, 2003), pp. 208–30.
2. Roger Handberg and Zhen Li, *Chinese Space Policy: A Study in Domestic and International Politics* (London: Routledge, 2007), pp. 84–8.
3. Tyrene White, *China's Longest Campaign: Birth Planning in the People's Republic, 1949–2005* (Ithaca, NY: Cornell University Press, 2006), pp. 61–9.
4. Colin Mackerras, *China's Ethnic Minorities and Globalisation* (London: RoutledgeCurzon, 2003), p. 38.
5. Michael Dillon, *Xinjiang: China's Muslim Far Northwest* (London: RoutledgeCurzon, 2004), pp. 72–6; S. Frederick Starr (ed.), *Xinjiang: China's Muslim Borderland* (Armonk, NY: M. E. Sharpe, 2004); James A. Millward, *Eurasian Crossroads: A History of Xinjiang* (New York: Columbia University Press, 2006), pp. 357–61.
6. Jeffrey N. Wasserstrom, *Student Protests in Twentieth-Century China: The View from Shanghai* (Stanford, CA: Stanford University Press, 1991), p. 304.
7. John Gittings, obituary of Yang Shangkun, *The Guardian*, 15 September 1998.
8. Jonathan Fenby, *The Penguin History of Modern China: The Fall and Rise of a Great Power, 1850–2009* (London: Penguin, 2009), p. 633.
9. Hung-mao Tien and Yun-han Chu (eds), *China under Jiang Zemin* (Boulder, CO: Lynne Rienner, 2000), pp. 99–114.
10. David L. Shambaugh, *China's Communist Party: Atrophy and Adaptation* (Berkeley: University of California Press, 2008), pp. 111–15.
11. Wei-wei Zhang, *Transforming China: Economic Reform and Its Political Implications* (Basingstoke: Macmillan, 2000), pp. 132–40.
12. Qiusha Ma, *Non-Governmental Organizations in Contemporary China: Paving the Way to a Civil Society?* (London: Routledge, 2006), pp. 1–15, 98–100.
13. Tony Saich, *Governance and Politics of China* (Basingstoke: Palgrave Macmillan, 2004), pp. 329–37; June Grasso, Jay Corrin, and Michael Kort, *Modernization and Revolution in China: From the Opium Wars to the Olympics*, 4th edn (Armonk, NY: M. E. Sharpe, 2009), pp. 299–300.
14. *The Guardian*, 9 October 2010.

15. Paul J. Bolt and Albert S. Willner (eds), *China's Nuclear Future* (Boulder, CO: Lynne Rienner, 2005).

16. Handberg and Li, *Chinese Space Policy*, pp. 138–44.

17. Information Office of the State Council, 'Fifty Years of Democratic Reform in Tibet', *China Daily*, 3 March 2009; James Leibold, *Reconfiguring Chinese Nationalism: How the Qing Frontier and Its Indigenes Became Chinese* (Basingstoke: Palgrave Macmillan, 2007), pp. 182–3.

18. Robert E. Gamer, 'China beyond the heartland', in Robert E. Gamer (ed.), *Understanding Contemporary China*, 2nd edn (Boulder, CO: Lynne Rienner, 2003), pp. 155–94; Colin Mackerras, 'China's minorities and national integration', in Leong H. Liew and Shaoguang Wang (eds), *Nationalism, Democracy and National Integration in China* (London: RoutledgeCurzon, 2004), pp. 147–69.

19. James Leibold, 'The Xinjiang riots', http://thechinabeat.blogspot.com/2009/07/xinjiang; *The Guardian*, 11 July 2009.

20. Melissa J. Brown, *Is Taiwan Chinese? The Impact of Culture, Power, and Migration on Changing Identities* (Berkeley: University of California Press, 2004), pp. 1–3.

21. BBC 4, *When China Met Africa*, 21 June 2010.

22. *The Guardian*, 18 June 2005.

23. Yanrui Wu, *China's Economic Growth: A Miracle with Chinese Characteristics* (London: RoutledgeCurzon, 2003), pp. 1–6; Shi Cheng, *China's Rural Industrialization Policy: Growing under Orders Since 1949* (Basingstoke: Palgrave Macmillan, 2006), pp. 1–8.

24. Tamara Jacka, *Rural Women in Urban China: Gender, Migration, and Social Change* (London: M. E. Sharpe, 2006), pp. 4–8, 97–105; Ngai Pun, *Made in China: Women Factory Workers in a Global Workplace* (Durham, NC: Duke University Press, 2005), pp. 4–6; Feiling Wang, 'Renovating the great floodgate: The reform of China's *hukou* system', in Martin King Whyte (ed.), *One Country, Two Societies: Rural-Urban Inequality in Contemporary China* (Cambridge, MA: Harvard University Press, 2010), pp. 335–64.

25. Jonathan Watt and Huang Lisha, 'The big steal', *The Guardian*, 27 May 2006; Kevin J. O'Brien and Lianjiang Li, *Rightful Resistance in Rural China* (Cambridge: Cambridge University Press, 2006), pp. 1–24.

26. Terry Sicular, Yue Ximing, Björn Gustafsson, and Li Shi (eds), 'The urban–rural income gap and inequality in China', *Review of Income and Wealth*, 53.1 (March 2007), pp. 93–125.

27. *The Guardian*, 3 February and 15 March 2010.

28. Richard Louis Edmonds, 'China's environmental problems', in Gamer (ed.), *Understanding Contemporary China*, pp. 255–80; *The Guardian*, 20 May 2006.

29. In July 2010, China overtook the United States as the world's biggest energy user. *The Guardian*, 4 August 2010.

30. Yun-wing Sung, *The Emergence of Greater China: The Economic Integration of Mainland China, Taiwan and Hong Kong* (Basingstoke: Palgrave, 2005), pp. 210–11; Chris Bramall, *Chinese Economic Development* (Abingdon: Routledge, 2009), pp. 552–4.

31. Tyrene White, 'Domination, resistance and accommodation in China's one-child campaign', in Elizabeth J. Perry and Mark Selden (eds), *Chinese Society: Change, Conflict and Resistance,* 2nd edn (London: RoutledgeCurzon, 2003), pp. 183–203.

32. Ma Rong, 'Population growth and urbanization', in Gamer (ed.), *Understanding Contemporary China,* pp. 227–54; Qiusheng Liang and Che-Fu Lee, 'Fertility and population policy: An overview', in Dudley L. Poston, Che-Fu Lee, and Chiung-Fang Chang (eds), *Fertility, Family Planning, and Population Policy in China* (Abingdon: Routledge, 2006), pp. 8–19.

33. *The Guardian,* 29 February 2008; *China Daily,* 3 March 2009.

34. www.avert.org/aidsline.htm; *The Guardian,* 18 April 2008.

35. *The Guardian,* 20 June 2005; James A. Levine, 'Obesity in China: Causes and solutions', *Chinese Medical Journal,* 121.11 (2008), pp. 1043–50.

36. *The Guardian,* 17 May 2008.

37. http://article.wn.com/view/2010/03/02/Work_accidents_killed_more_than_83000_in_China_last_year/, accessed 18 February 2011.

38. *China Daily,* 2 May 2010.

39. *The Guardian,* 28 March 2007.

40. Christopher R. Hughes and Gudrun Wacker, *China and the Internet: Politics of the Digital Leap Forward* (London: RoutledgeCurzon, 2003), pp. 1–7.

41. Daniel L. Overmyer, 'Religion in China today: Introduction', *The China Quarterly,* 174 (June 2003), pp. 307–16; 'The new cybersects: Resistance and repression in the reform era', in Perry and Selden (eds), *Chinese Society,* pp. 247–70.

42. Heather Angel, *Wild China* (London: Stacey International, 2008), pp. vii–viii.

43. Guoqi Xu, *Olympic Dreams: China and Sports, 1895–2008* (Cambridge, MA: Harvard University Press, 2008), pp. 246–7.

44. *Amnesty Magazine,* 149 (May/June 2008).

45. *The Guardian,* 9 August 2008.

46. Kevin Latham, 'Media, the Olympics and the search for the 'Real China',' *The China Quarterly,* 197 (March 2009), pp. 25–43.

47. Shambaugh, *China's Communist Party,* pp. 161–81; *The Guardian,* 21 May 2009.

48. *The Guardian,* 22 April 2010.

Chronology

Dynasties and Rulers	Events and Personalities
Banpo occupied (4500 BCE–)	Rice cultivated
Culture Heroes (*c.* 2852 BCE–)	Fuxi (domesticated animals); Shen Nung (agriculture); Yellow Emperor (writing)
Sage Kings (*c.* 2697 BCE–)	Yao and Shun
Xia (2070–1600 BCE)	Erlitou site
Shang (1600–1046 BCE)	
Early Shang (1600–1300 BCE)	Erligang culture
Later Shang (1300–1046 BCE)	Anyang; oracle bones
Zhou (1122–256 BCE)	
Western Zhou (1122–771 BCE)	
Eastern Zhou (771–221 BCE)	
Spring and Autumn (771–481 BCE)	Confucius (*c.* 551–479 BCE)
Warring States (481–221 BCE)	Mencius (*c.* 372–289 BCE)
	Zhuangzi (*c.* 369–286 BCE)
Qin (221–206 BCE)	
Qin Shi Huangdi (*r.* 221–21 BCE)	Li Si and Legalism; Terracotta army
Former or Western Han (206 BCE–CE 9)	
Han Gaozu (*r.* 206–195 BCE)	Mawangdui tomb (*c.* 168 BCE)
Wudi (*r.* 141–87 BCE)	Sima Qian, Grand Historian (*c.* 145–85 BCE)
Xin (CE 9–23)	
Wang Mang (*r.* CE 9–23)	
Later or Eastern Han (CE 25–220)	First mention of a Buddhist community (CE 65)
Three Kingdoms (220–80)	Setting for *The Romance of the Three Kingdoms*

(continued)

345

Continued

Dynasties and Rulers	*Events and Personalities*
Sixteen Kingdoms (316–84)	
Northern Wei (386–534)	Capital transferred to Luoyang (493)
Southern dynasties (304–589)	
Sui (589–618) 　Sui Wendi (*r.* 581–604) 　Yangdi (*r.* 604–18)	China reunified New capital at Chang'an Grand Canal completed
Tang (618–907) 　Taizong (*r.* 626–49) 　Empress Wu (Zhou dynasty) (690–705) 　Xuanzong (*r.* 712–56)	Defeat of Eastern Turks, Issyk Kul (657) Li Bo (701–62) and Du Fu (712–70) Rebellion of An Lushan (755–63) Suppression of Buddhism (845)
Five Dynasties and Ten Kingdoms (907–60)	
Qidan Liao (907–1125)	
Song (Northern Song) (960–1127) 　Song Taizu (*r.* 960–76) 　Shenzong (*r.* 1068–85)	Examination system improved Reforms of Wang Anshi Jurchen invasion of north China (1125)
Jurchen Jin (1115–1234)	Yellow River shifts to southern course (1194)
Southern Song (1127–1279)	Hangzhou the world's greatest city Zhu Xi (1130–1200) Neo-Confucian synthesis
Yuan (Mongol) (1279–1368)	Marco Polo in China (1275–91)

(*continued*)

Continued

Dynasties and Rulers	*Events and Personalities*
Ming (1368–1644)	
Hongwu (*r.* 1368–98)	Yellow Books and 'fish-scale' charts
Yongle (*r.* 1403–24)	Zheng He's maritime expeditions (1405–21)
	Capital moved to Beijing (1421)
Zhengtong (1435–49; 1457–64)	Emperor captured by Oirat at Tumu (1449)
	Construction of Ming Great Wall (1474–)
	Portuguese reach China (1514)
	Li Shizhen, *Systematic Materia Medica* (1596)
Qing (1644–1912)	
Kangxi (*r.* 1661–1722)	Rebellion of Three Feudatories (1673–81)
Qianlong (*r.* 1736–95)	Chinese occupation of Tibet (1751)
	Maritime trade restricted to Guangzhou (1760)
	Macartney Mission (1793)
	White Lotus rebellion (1796–1804)
Daoguang (*r.* 1820–50)	First Opium War (1839–42)
	Taiping rebellion (1851–64)
	Arrow incident and Anglo-French war (1856–60)
Tongzhi (*r.* 1862–74)	Tongzhi restoration
	Anqing arsenal established (1862)
Guangxu (*r.* 1875–1908)	Sino-French war (1883–5)
	Sino-Japanese war (1894–5)
	The 100 Days' reforms (1898)
	Boxer Uprising (1898–1901)
Republic of China (1911–49)	
Yuan Shikai President (1912–16)	Guomindang (Nationalist) Party founded (1912)

(*continued*)

Continued

Dynasties and Rulers	Events and Personalities
Warlord Era (1916–28)	May Fourth incident (1919) Chinese Communist Party founded (1921)
Nanjing decade (1928–37)	Long March (1934–5) Sino-Japanese War (1937–45) Civil war and Communist victory, 1946–9
People's Republic of China (1949–)	Soviet Period (1953–8) Great Leap Forward (1958) Tibetan revolt suppressed (1959) Sino-Soviet split (1960) Cultural Revolution (1966–9) Death of Mao Zedong (1976) One-child family policy introduced (1979) Tiananmen Square massacre (1989) Death of Deng Xiaoping (1997) Beijing Olympics (2008)

Further Reading

The number of books on Chinese history available in English is already vast and is increasing rapidly. The following suggestions for further reading highlight a number of classic works and a selection from recent literature.

GENERAL THEMES

Recent general histories of China include: Patricia Buckley Ebrey, *The Cambridge Illustrated History of China* (Cambridge: Cambridge University Press, 1996); John K. Fairbank, *China: A New History* (Cambridge, MA: Harvard University Press, 1994); J. A. G. Roberts, *The Complete History of China: An Illustrated History* (Stroud: Sutton Publishing, 2003); John Keay, *China: A History* (London: Harper Press, 2008); and Harold M. Tanner, *China: A History* (Cambridge: Hackett, 2009).

Recent histories of modern China include: John S. Gregory, *The West and China since 1500* (Basingstoke: Palgrave, 2003); Immanuel C. Y. Hsü, *The Rise of Modern China,* 6th edn (Oxford: Oxford University Press, 2000); Jonathan D. Spence, *The Search for Modern China* (London: Hutchinson, 1990); Rana Mitter, *A Bitter Revolution: China's Struggle with the Modern World* (Oxford: Oxford University Press, 2004); Michael Dillon, *Contemporary China: An Introduction* (London: Routledge, 2008); and Jonathan Fenby, *The Penguin History of Modern China: The Fall and Rise of a Great Power, 1850–2008* (London: Penguin, 2009).

See also: W. T. de Bary, Wing-tsit Chan and Burton Watson (eds), *Sources of Chinese Tradition,* 2 vols (New York: Columbia University Press, 1960); Lloyd E. Eastman, *Family, Fields and Ancestors* (Oxford: Oxford University Press, 1988); Mark Elvin, *The Pattern of the Chinese Past* (London: Eyre, Methuen, 1973); J. K. Fairbank, *The Chinese World Order* (Cambridge, MA: Harvard University Press, 1968); Ping-ti Ho, *Studies on the Population of China, 1368–1953* (Cambridge, MA: Harvard University Press, 1959); Ramon H. Myers, *The Chinese Economy: Past and Present* (Belmont, CA: Wadsworth, 1980); Paul S. Ropp (ed.), *Heritage of China: Contemporary Perspectives on Chinese Civilization* (Berkeley: University of California Press, 1990); and John E. Wills, Jr., *Mountain of Fame: Portraits in Chinese History* (Princeton, NJ: Princeton University Press, 1994).

The following introduce some new themes: Thomas J. Barfield, *The Perilous Frontier: Nomadic Empires and China* (Oxford: Basil Blackwell, 1989);

Kathryn Bernhardt, *Women and Property in China, 960–1949* (Stanford, CA: Stanford University Press, 1999); Joan Judge, *The Precious Raft of History: The Past, the West, and the Woman Question in China* (Stanford, CA: Stanford University Press, 2008); Dorothy Ko, *Cinderella's Sisters: A Revisionist History of Footbinding* (Berkeley: University of California Press, 2005); and Ping-chen Hsiung, *A Tender Voyage: Children and Childhood in Late Imperial China* (Stanford, CA: Stanford University Press, 2005).

The Cambridge History of China, General Editors Denis Twitchett and John K. Fairbank (Cambridge: Cambridge University Press, 1978–) is not a continuous history of China but a collection of essays on periods of Chinese history. These volumes are referred to as *CHC*, 1, etc.

PREHISTORY AND EARLY HISTORY

Michael Loewe and Edward L. Shaughnessy (eds), *The Cambridge History of Ancient China: From the Origins of Civilization to 221 B.C.* (Cambridge: Cambridge University Press, 1999) covers the main themes in Chinese prehistory and the Shang and Zhou dynasties. Robin Dennell, *The Palaeolithic Settlement of Asia* (Cambridge: Cambridge University Press, 2009) and Robert L. Thorp, *China in the Early Bronze Age: Shang Civilization* (Philadelphia: University of Pennsylvania Press, 2006) bring together the results of recent archaeology. David N. Keightley, *The Ancestral Landscape: Time, Space, and Community in Late Shang China (ca. 1200–1045 B.C.)* (Berkeley: University of California Press, 2000) provides a fascinating insight into the mindset of the people of that time. A new field of China's prehistory was introduced in Steven F. Sage, *Ancient Sichuan and the Unification of China* (New York: State University of New York Press, 1992).

On the archaeology and history of the Zhou period, see also Cho-yun Hsü and Katheryn M. Linduff, *Western Chou Civilization* (New Haven, CT: Yale University Press, 1988); Lothar von Falkenhausen, *Chinese Society in the Age of Confucius (1000–250 BC): The Archaeological Evidence* (Los Angeles: Cotsen Institute of Archaeology, University of California Press, 2006); and Mark Edward Lewis, *Sanctioned Violence in Early China* (New York: State University of New York Press, 1990). On the literature of the period, see D. C. Lau (trans. and ed.), *Mencius* (Harmondsworth: Penguin, 1970); *Lao Tzu: Tao Te Ching* (Harmondsworth: Penguin, 1975); and *Confucius: The Analects* (Harmondsworth: Penguin, 1985). The best biography of Confucius is Raymond Dawson, *Confucius* (Oxford: Oxford University Press, 1981). On the Qin empire, see Derk Bodde, 'The state and empire of Ch'in', *CHC*, 1, pp. 20–102; Mark Edward Lewis, *The Early Chinese Empires: Qin and Han* (Cambridge, MA: Belknap Press of Harvard University Press, 2007); and Nicola di Cosmo, *Ancient China and Its Enemies: The Rise of Nomadic Power in East Asian History* (Cambridge: Cambridge University Press, 2002).

On the Han period, see several books by Michael Loewe, including *Early Imperial China during the Han Period, 202 BC–AD 220* (London: Carousel, 1973) and *Crisis and Conflict in Han China, 104 BC–AD 9* (London: George

Allen and Unwin, 1974); and Cho-yun Hsü, *Han Agriculture: The Formation of Early Chinese Agrarian Economy (206 BC–AD 220)* (Seattle: University of Washington Press, 1980). Recent works on social themes include Bret Hinsch, *Women in Early Imperial China* (Lanham, MD: Rowman and Littlefield, 2002); and Anna Behnke Kinney, *Representations of Childhood and Youth in Early China* (Stanford, CA: Stanford University Press, 2004).

THE PERIOD OF DIVISION AND THE SUI AND TANG DYNASTIES

On the Period of Division and the Sui dynasty, see Patricia Buckley Ebrey, *The Aristocratic Families of Early Imperial China: A Case Study of the Po-ling Ts'ui Family* (Cambridge: Cambridge University Press, 1978); W. J. F. Jenner, *Memories of Loyang: Yang Hsüan-chih and the Lost Capital (493–534)* (Oxford: Clarendon Press, 1981); Arthur F. Wright, 'The Sui dynasty (581–617)', *CHC*, 3, pp. 48–149; and Mark Edward Lewis, *China Between Empires: The Northern and Southern Dynasties* (Cambridge, MA: Belknap Press of Harvard University Press, 2009).

On the history and culture of the Tang period, see Mark Edward Lewis, *China's Cosmopolitan Empire: The Tang Dynasty* (Cambridge, MA: Belknap Press, Harvard University Press, 2009); John C. Perry and Bardwell L. Smith (eds), *Essays on T'ang Society: The Interplay of Social, Political and Economic Forces* (Leiden: E. J. Brill, 1976); Edwin G. Pulleyblank, *The Background of the Rebellion of An Lu-shan* (London: Oxford University Press, 1955); Denis C. Twitchett, *Financial Administration under the T'ang Dynasty*, 2nd edn (Cambridge: Cambridge University Press, 1970); Arthur F. Wright and Denis Twitchett (eds), *Perspectives on the T'ang* (New Haven, CT: Yale University Press, 1973); and Charles Benn, *Daily Life in Traditional China: The Tang Dynasty* (Westwood, CT: Greenwood Press, 2002).

For an introduction to Tang poetry, see Arthur Cooper (trans. and ed.), *Li Po and Tu Fu* (Harmondsworth: Penguin, 1973). Aspects of Tang religion are dealt with in Stanley Weinstein, *Buddhism under the T'ang* (Cambridge: Cambridge University Press, 1987). Tang expansion southwards is treated imaginatively in Edward H. Schafer, *The Vermilion Bird: T'ang Images of the South* (Berkeley: University of California Press, 1967) and in socio-economic terms in Hugh R. Clark, *Community, Trade, and Networks: Southern Fujian Province from the Third to the Thirteenth Century* (Cambridge: Cambridge University Press, 1991).

THE SONG AND YUAN DYNASTIES

James T. C. Liu has written a number of important studies on Song China, including *Reform in Sung China, Wang An-shih, 1021–1086 and His New Policies* (Cambridge, MA: Harvard University Press, 1959) and *China Turning Inward: Intellectual-Political Changes in the Early Twelfth Century* (Cambridge,

MA: Harvard University Press, 1988). His interpretation has been questioned by Edward L. Davis in *Society and the Supernatural in Song China* (Honolulu: University of Hawai'i Press, 2001). Several books have been written about the Song bureaucracy and examination system, including John C. Chaffee, *The Thorny Gates of Learning in Sung China* (Cambridge: Cambridge University Press, 1985); Richard L. Davis, *Court and Family in Sung China, 960–1279: Bureaucratic Success and Kinship Fortunes for the Shih of Ming-chou* (Durham, NC: Duke University Press, 1986); and Winston W. Lo, *An Introduction to the Civil Service of Sung China, with Emphasis on Its Personnel Administration* (Honolulu: University of Hawai'i Press, 1987). The emergence of the gentry is discussed in Brian E. McKnight, *Village and Bureaucracy in Southern Sung China* (Chicago: University of Chicago Press, 1971) and Robert P. Hymes, *Statesmen and Gentlemen: The Elite of Fu-chou, Chiang-si, in Northern and Southern Sung* (Cambridge: Cambridge University Press, 1986).

For an influential discussion of economic developments under the Song, see Yoshinobu Shiba, *Commerce and Society in Sung China* (Ann Arbor: University of Michigan Press, 1970). Song foreign relations are dealt with in Morris Rossabi, *China Among Equals: The Middle Kingdom and Its Neighbors* (Berkeley: University of California Press, 1983).

On the Mongol conquest and Yuan China, see John D. Langlois, Jr. (ed.), *China under Mongol Rule* (Princeton, NJ: Princeton University Press, 1981); Frederick W. Mote, 'Chinese society under Mongol rule, 1215–1368', *CHC*, 6, pp. 616–64; and Morris Rossabi, *Khubilai Khan: His Life and Times* (Berkeley: University of California Press, 1988).

THE MING AND EARLY QING PERIODS

On the founding of the Ming dynasty and its early history, see Edward Dreyer, *Early Ming China: A Political History, 1355–1435* (Stanford, CA: Stanford University Press, 1982). On the Ming voyages, see J. V. G. Mills (trans. and ed.), *Ma Huan, Ying-yai sheng-lan: 'The Overall Survey of the Ocean's Shores' [1433]* (Cambridge: Cambridge University Press, 1970); and Edward L. Dreyer, *Zheng He: China and the Oceans in the Early Ming Dynasty, 1405–1433* (London: Pearson Longman, 2007). Financial issues are dealt with in Ray Huang, *Taxation and Governmental Finance in Sixteenth-Century Ming China* (Cambridge: Cambridge University Press, 1974) and matters relating to gentry society are considered in Hilary J. Beattie, *Land and Lineage in China: A Study of T'ung-ch'eng County, Anhwei, in the Ming and Ch'ing Dynasties* (Cambridge: Cambridge University Press, 1979); Timothy Brook, *Praying for Power: Buddhism and the Formation of Gentry Society in Late-Ming China* (Cambridge, MA: Harvard University Press, 1993); and John W. Dardess, *A Ming Society: T'ai-ho County, Kiangsi, Fourteenth to Seventeenth Centuries* (Berkeley: University of California Press, 1996). Timothy Brook, *The Chinese State in Ming Society* (London, RoutledgeCurzon, 2005) and Sarah Schneewind, *Community Schools and the State in Ming China* (Stanford, CA: Stanford University Press, 2006) present new assessments of the relationship between state and society. Benjamin A. Elman, *On Their Own Terms: Science in China, 1550–1900* (Cambridge MA: Harvard University Press, 2005), examines the development of scientific thought under the Ming and later.

On the decline and fall of the Ming, see Ray Huang, *1587: A Year of No Significance – The Ming Dynasty in Decline* (New Haven, CT: Yale University Press, 1981); James W. Tong, *Disorder under Heaven: Collective Violence in the Ming Dynasty* (Stanford, CA: Stanford University Press, 1991); and James Bunyan Parsons, *The Peasant Rebellions of the Late Ming Dynasty* (Tucson: University of Arizona Press, 1970).

The rise of the Manchus and their conquest of China is dealt with at length in Frederic Wakeman, Jr., *The Great Enterprise: The Manchu Reconstruction of the Imperial Order in Seventeenth-Century China*, 2 vols (Berkeley: University of California Press, 1985). For vivid insights into that event, see Lynn A. Struve (trans. and ed.), *Voices from the Ming-Qing Cataclysm: China in Tigers' Jaws* (New Haven, CT: Yale University Press, 1993).

On the early years of Manchu rule, see Lawrence D. Kessler, *K'ang-hsi and the Consolidation of Ch'ing Rule, 1661–1684* (Chicago: University of Chicago Press, 1978); and Jonathan D. Spence, *Emperor of China: Self-Portrait of K'ang-hsi* (Harmondsworth: Penguin, 1973).

On the middle years of the Qing dynasty, see Beatrice S. Bartlett, *Monarchs and Ministers: The Grand Council in Mid-Ch'ing China (1723–1820)* (Berkeley: University of California Press, 1991); Pei Huang, *Autocracy at Work: A Study of the Yung-cheng Period, 1723–35* (Bloomington, IN: Indiana University Press, 1974); Harold L. Kahn, *Monarchy in the Emperor's Eyes: Image and Reality in the Ch'ien-lung Reign* (Cambridge, MA: Harvard University Press, 1971); Susan Naquin and E. S. Rawski, *Chinese Society in the Eighteenth Century* (New Haven, CT: Yale University Press, 1987); and Madeleine Zelin, *The Magistrate's Tael: Rationalizing Fiscal Reform in Eighteenth-Century Ch'ing China* (Berkeley: University of California Press, 1984). A lively reinterpretation of China's economic development may be found in Kenneth Pomeranz, *The Great Divergence: China, Europe, and the Making of the Modern World Economy* (Princeton, NJ: Princeton University Press, 2000).

Two books pick out signs of tension in the late eighteenth century: P. A. Kuhn, *Soulstealers: The Chinese Sorcery Scare of 1768* (Cambridge: Cambridge University Press, 1990); and Susan Naquin, *Shantung Rebellion: The Wang Lun Uprising of 1774* (New Haven, CT: Yale University Press, 1981).

The topic of the condition of women in the Qing period has produced some outstanding work, including Dorothy Ko, *Teachers of the Inner Chambers: Women and Culture in Seventeenth-Century China* (Stanford, CA: Stanford University Press, 1994); and Susan Mann, *Precious Records: Women in China's Long Eighteenth Century* (Stanford, CA: Stanford University Press, 1994).

Four books based on Manchu sources have greatly enhanced understanding of the achievement of the Manchus: Evelyn S. Rawski, *The Last Emperors: A Social History of Qing Imperial Institutions* (Berkeley: University of California Press, 1998); Pamela Kyle Crossley, *A Translucent Mirror: History and Identity in Qing Imperial Ideology* (Berkeley: University of California Press, 1999); Edward J. M. Rhoads, *Manchus and Han: Ethnic Relations and Political Power in Late Qing and Early Imperial China, 1861–1928* (Seattle: University of Washington Press,

2000); and Mark C. Elliott, *The Manchu Way: The Eight Banners and Ethnic Identity in Late Imperial China* (Stanford, CA: Stanford University Press, 2001). Recent contributions on this theme include Peter C. Perdue, *China Marches West: The Qing Conquest of Central Asia* (Cambridge, MA: Belknap Press of Harvard University Press, 2005); Joanna Waley-Cohen, *The Culture of War in China: Empire and the Military under the Qing Dynasty* (London: I. B. Tauris, 2006); and James Leibold, *Reconfiguring Chinese Nationalism: How the Qing Frontier and its Indigenes Became Chinese* (Basingstoke: Palgrave Macmillan, 2007).

CHINA IN THE LATE QING PERIOD

Of the extensive literature on the Opium Wars, John King Fairbank, *Trade and Diplomacy on the China Coast: The Opening of the Treaty Ports, 1842–1854,* revised edn (Stanford, CA: Stanford University Press, 1969), has become a classic. The Chinese perception of these events is presented in Frederic Wakeman, Jr., *Strangers at the Gate: Social Disorder in South China, 1839–1861* (Berkeley: University of California Press, 1966); and James M. Polachek, *The Inner Opium War* (Cambridge, MA: Harvard University Press, 1992).

On dynastic decline and the rise of rebellion, see: Jane Kate Leonard, *Controlling from Afar: The Daoguang Emperor's Management of the Grand Canal Crisis, 1824–1826* (Ann Arbor: University of Michigan Center for Chinese Studies, 1996); and Randall A. Dodgen, *Controlling the Dragon: Confucian Engineers and the Yellow River in Late Imperial China* (Honolulu: University of Hawai'i Press, 2001). The mid-nineteenth-century rebellions are dealt with in Philip A. Kuhn, *Rebellion and Its Enemies in Late Imperial China: Militarization and Social Structure, 1794–1864* (Cambridge, MA: Harvard University Press, 1970); Franz Michael and Chung-li Chang, *The Taiping Rebellion: History and Documents,* 3 vols (Seattle: University of Washington Press, 1966–71); Elizabeth J. Perry, *Rebels and Revolutionaries in North China, 1845–1945* (Stanford, CA: Stanford University Press, 1980); Stanley Spector, *Li Hung-chang and the Huai Army: A Study in Nineteenth-Century Chinese Regionalism* (Seattle: University of Washington Press, 1964); and Jonathan Spence, *God's Chinese Son: The Taiping Heavenly Kingdom of Hong Xiuquan* (London: HarperCollins, 1996).

A reassessment of the significance of Central Asia to the history of China may be found in two books by James A. Millward: *Beyond the Pass: Economy, Ethnicity, and Empire in Qing Central Asia, 1759–1864* (Stanford, CA: Stanford University Press, 1998) and *Eurasian Crossroads: A History of Xinjiang* (New York: Columbia University Press, 2009).

On China in the late nineteenth century, see: Mary Clabaugh Wright, *The Last Stand of Chinese Conservatism: The T'ung-chih Restoration, 1862–1874,* 2nd edn (Stanford, CA: Stanford University Press, 1962); and Jonathan Ocko, *Bureaucratic Reform in Provincial China: Tang Jih-ch'ang in Restoration Kiangsu, 1867–1870* (Cambridge, MA: Harvard University Press, 1983).

A classic study of economic history is Albert Feuerwerker, *China's Early Industrialization: Sheng Hsuan-huai (1844–1916) and Mandarin Enterprise*

(Cambridge, MA: Harvard University Press, 1958); on developments in science and technology see Benjamin A. Elman, *A Cultural History of Modern Science in China* (Cambridge, MA: Harvard University Press, 2006). The copious literature on economic imperialism includes Robert Y. Eng, *Economic Imperialism in China: Silk Production and Exports, 1861–1932* (Berkeley: University of California Press, 1986); Robert Gardella, *Harvesting Mountains: Fujian and the China Tea Trade, 1757–1937* (Berkeley: University of California Press, 1994); Robert Lee, *France and the Exploitation of China, 1885–1901* (Hong Kong: Oxford University Press, 1989); and Madeleine Zelin, *The Merchants of Zigong: Industial Entrepreneurship in Early Modern China* (New York: Columbia University Press, 2005).

On missionaries, see: Paul A. Cohen, *China and Christianity: The Missionary Movement and the Growth of Chinese Antiforeignism, 1860–1870* (Cambridge, MA: Harvard University Press, 1963). On the emergence of nationalism, see: John E. Schrecker, *Imperialism and Chinese Nationalism: Germany in Shantung* (Cambridge, MA: Harvard University Press, 1971).

For the 100 Days' reforms, the Boxer uprising and the late Qing reforms, see: Joseph W. Esherick, *The Origins of the Boxer Uprising* (Berkeley: University of California Press, 1987); Paul A. Cohen, *History in Three Keys: The Boxers as Event, Experience, and Myth* (New York: Columbia University Press, 1997); Marianne Bastid, *Educational Reform in Early Twentieth-Century China* (Ann Arbor: University of Michigan Press, 1988); Charlton M. Lewis, *Prologue to the Chinese Revolution: The Transformation of Ideas and Institutions in Hunan Province, 1891–1907* (Cambridge, MA: Harvard University Press, 1976); and Edward J. M. Rhoads, *Manchus and Han: Ethnic Relations and Political Power in Late Qing and Early Imperial China, 1861–1928* (Seattle: University of Washington Press, 2000).

REPUBLICAN CHINA

On the 1911 revolution, see Joseph W. Esherick, *Reform and Revolution in China: The 1911 Revolution in Hunan and Hubei* (Berkeley: University of California Press, 1976); Edward J. M. Rhoads, *China's Republican Revolution: The Case of Kwangtung, 1895–1913* (Cambridge, MA: Harvard University Press, 1975); and Mary Clabaugh Wright (ed.), *China in Revolution: The First Phase, 1900–1913* (New Haven, CT: Yale University Press, 1973). Two recent studies investigate aspects of 'Young China' before the revolution: Ryan Dunch, *Fuzhou Protestants and the Making of Modern China, 1857–1927* (New Haven, CT: Yale University Press, 2001); and Joan Judge, *Print and Politics: 'Shibao' and the Culture of Reform in Late Qing China* (Stanford, CA: Stanford University Press, 1996).

On Yuan Shikai, the May Fourth period and the warlord era, see: Ernest P. Young, *The Presidency of Yuan Shih-k'ai: Liberalism and Dictatorship in Early Republican China* (Ann Arbor: University of Michigan Press, 1977); Tse-tsung Chow, *The May Fourth Movement: Intellectual Revolution in Modern China* (Cambridge, MA: Harvard University Press, 1960); Edward A. McCord, *The Power of the Gun: The Emergence of Modern Chinese Warlordism*

(Berkeley: University of California Press, 1993); and Arthur Waldron, *From War to Nationalism: China's Turning Point, 1924–1925* (Cambridge: Cambridge University Press, 1995).

The rise of the Nationalist Party and the record of the Nanjing decade are discussed in: John Fitzgerald, *Awakening China: Politics, Culture, and Class in the Nationalist Revolution* (Stanford, CA: Stanford University Press, 1996); Donald A. Jordan, *The Northern Expedition: China's National Revolution of 1926–1928* (Honolulu: University of Hawai'i Press, 1976); Elizabeth J. Perry, *Shanghai on Strike: The Politics of Chinese Labor* (Cambridge: Cambridge University Press, 1995); Lloyd E. Eastman, *The Abortive Revolution: China under Nationalist Rule, 1927–1937* (Cambridge, MA: Harvard University Press, 1974); and Parks M. Coble, *The Shanghai Capitalists and the Nationalist Government, 1927–1937* (Cambridge, MA: Harvard University Press, 1986). For an assessment of the Nanjing decade, see: Frederic Wakeman, Jr. and Richard Louis Edmonds, *Reappraising Republican China* (Oxford: Oxford University Press, 2000).

On the early history of the Chinese Communist Party, see: Arif Dirlik, *The Origins of Chinese Communism* (Oxford: Oxford University Press, 1989); Fernando Galbiati, *P'eng P'ai and the Hai-lu-feng Soviet* (Stanford, CA: Stanford University Press, 1985); Roy Hofheinz, Jr., *The Broken Wave: The Chinese Communist Peasant Movement, 1922–1928* (Cambridge, MA: Harvard University Press, 1977); Zedong Mao, *Report from Xunwu* (Stanford, CA: Stanford University Press, 1990); and Benjamin Yang, *From Revolution to Politics: Chinese Communists on the Long March* (Boulder, CO: Westview Press, 1990).

For the Sino-Japanese War and the Civil War, see: Lloyd E. Eastman, *Seeds of Destruction: Nationalist China in War and Revolution, 1937–1949* (Stanford, CA: Stanford University Press, 1984); Bob Tadashi Wakabayashi (ed.), *The Nanking Atrocity, 1937–38: Complicating the Picture* (New York: Berghahn Books, 2007); Chalmers A. Johnson, *Peasant Nationalism and Communist Power: The Emergence of Revolutionary China, 1937–1945* (Stanford, CA: Stanford University Press, 1962); Mark Selden, *The Yenan Way in Revolutionary China* (Cambridge, MA: Harvard University Press, 1971); Steven I. Levine, *Anvil of Victory: The Communist Revolution in Manchuria, 1945–1948* (New York: Columbia University Press, 1987); James C. Hsiung and Steven I. Levine (eds), *China's Bitter Victory: The War with Japan 1937–1945* (New York: M. E. Sharpe, 1992); and Suzanne Pepper, *Civil War in China: The Political Struggle, 1945–1949*, 2nd edn (Berkeley: University of California Press, 1999). Studies on how the Communists gained support during the war with Japan include: Odoric Y. K. Wou, *Mobilizing the Masses: Building Revolution in Henan* (Stanford: Stanford University Press, 1994); Ralph A. Thaxton, Jr., *Salt of the Earth: The Political Origins of Peasant Protest and Communist Revolution in China* (Berkeley: University of California Press, 1997); Pauline B. Keating, *Two Revolutions: Village Reconstruction and the Cooperative Movement in Northern Shaanxi, 1934–1945* (Stanford, CA: Stanford University Press, 1997); and Feng Chongyi and David S. G. Goodman (eds), *North China at War: The Social Ecology of Revolution 1937–1945* (Lanham, MD: Rowman & Littlefield, 2000). On wartime collaboration, see: David P. Barrett and Larry N. Shyu (eds),

Chinese Collaboration with Japan: The Limits of Accommodation (Stanford, CA: Stanford University Press, 2001).

CHINA SINCE THE 1949 REVOLUTION

On the period of consolidation, the First Five-Year Plan and the Great Leap Forward, see: Lowell Dittmer, *China's Continuous Revolution: The Post-Liberation Epoch, 1949–1981* (Berkeley: University of California Press, 1987); Kenneth G. Lieberthal, *Revolution and Tradition in Tientsin, 1949–1952* (Stanford, CA: Stanford University Press, 1980); Vivienne Shue, *Peasant China in Transition: The Dynamics of Development toward Socialism, 1949–1956* (Berkeley: University of California Press, 1980); Ezra F. Vogel, *Canton under Communism: Programs and Politics in a Provincial Capital, 1949–1968* (Cambridge, MA: Harvard University Press, 1969); Jasper Becker, *Hungry Ghosts: China's Secret Famine* (London: John Murray, 1996); Ralph A. Thaxton, Jr., *Catastrophe and Contention in Rural China: Mao's Great Leap Forward and the Origins of Righteous Resistance in Da Fo Village* (Cambridge: Cambridge University Press, 2008); and Judith Shapiro, *Mao's War Against Nature: Politics and the Environment in Revolutionary China* (Cambridge: Cambridge University Press, 2001).

For the Cultural Revolution, see David Milton, Nancy Milton and Franz Schurmann (eds), *People's China: Social Experimentation, Politics, Entry on to the World Scene, 1966–72* (Harmondsworth: Penguin, 1977); Shaun Breslin, *Mao* (London: Longman, 1998); Joseph W. Esherick, Paul G. Pickowicz and Andrew G. Walder (eds), *The Chinese Cultural Revolution as History* (Stanford, CA: Stanford University Press, 2006); and Roderick MacFarquhar and Michael Schoenhals, *Mao's Last Revolution* (Cambridge, MA: Belknap Press of Harvard University Press, 2006).

On China in the 1980s and 1990s, see: Barry Naughton, *Growing out of the Plan: Chinese Economic Reform, 1978–1993* (Cambridge: Cambridge University Press, 1995); and Gregor Benton and Alan Hunter (eds), *Wild Lily, Prairie Fire: China's Road to Democracy, Yan'an to Tian'anmen, 1942–1989* (Princeton, NJ: Princeton University Press, 1995). Biographies of Deng Xiaoping include: Richard Evans, *Deng Xiaoping and the Making of Modern China,* revised edn (London: Penguin, 1997); and Benjamin Yang, *Deng: A Political Biography* (New York: M. E. Sharpe, 1998).

On social themes during the period, see: Suzanne Pepper, *Radicalism and Education Reform in 20th-Century China: The Search for an Ideal Development Model* (Cambridge: Cambridge University Press, 1996); Judith Banister, *China's Changing Population* (Stanford, CA: Stanford University Press, 1987); Colin Mackerras, *China's Minority Cultures: Identities and Integration since 1912* (New York: Longman, 1995); Margery Wolf, *Revolution Postponed: Women in Contemporary China* (Stanford, CA: Stanford University Press, 1985); and Guoqi Xu, *Olympic Dreams: China and Sports 1895–2008* (Cambridge, MA: Harvard University Press, 2008).

Studies of present-day China include: Wei-wei Zhang, *Transforming China: Economic Reform and Its Political Implications* (Basingstoke: Macmillan, 2000); Daniel B. Wright, *The Promise of Revolution: Stories of Fulfillment and Struggle in China's Hinterland* (Lanham, MD: Rowman & Littlefield, 2003); Robert E. Gamer (ed.), *Understanding Contemporary China*, 3rd edn (Boulder, CO: Lynne Rienner, 2008); Elizabeth J. Perry and Mark Selden (eds), *Chinese Society, Change Conflict and Resistance*, 2nd edn (London: RoutledgeCurzon, 2003); Leong H. Liew and Shaoguang Wang (eds), *Nationalism, Democracy and National Integration in China* (London: RoutledgeCurzon, 2004); Ngai Pun, *Made in China: Women Factory Workers in a Global Workplace* (Durham, NC: Duke University Press, 2005); Martin King Whyte (ed.), *One Country, Two Societies: Rural–Urban Inequality in Contemporary China* (Cambridge, MA: Harvard University Press, 2010); Kevin J. O'Brien and Lianjiang Li, *Rightful Resistance in Rural China* (Cambridge: Cambridge University Press, 2006); Chris Bramall, *Chinese Economic Development* (Abingdon: Routledge, 2009); and David L. Shambaugh, *China's Communist Party: Atrophy and Adaptation* (Washington, DC: Woodrow Wilson Press, 2008).

Index

Note: 'Early China' refers to the period before 221 BCE. 'Early empire' refers to 221 BCE to CE 1368.